THE INDIVIDUAL INVESTOR'S GUIDE TO

COMPUTERIZED
INVESTING

THE INDIVIDUAL INVESTOR'S GUIDE TO

COMPUTERIZED INVESTING

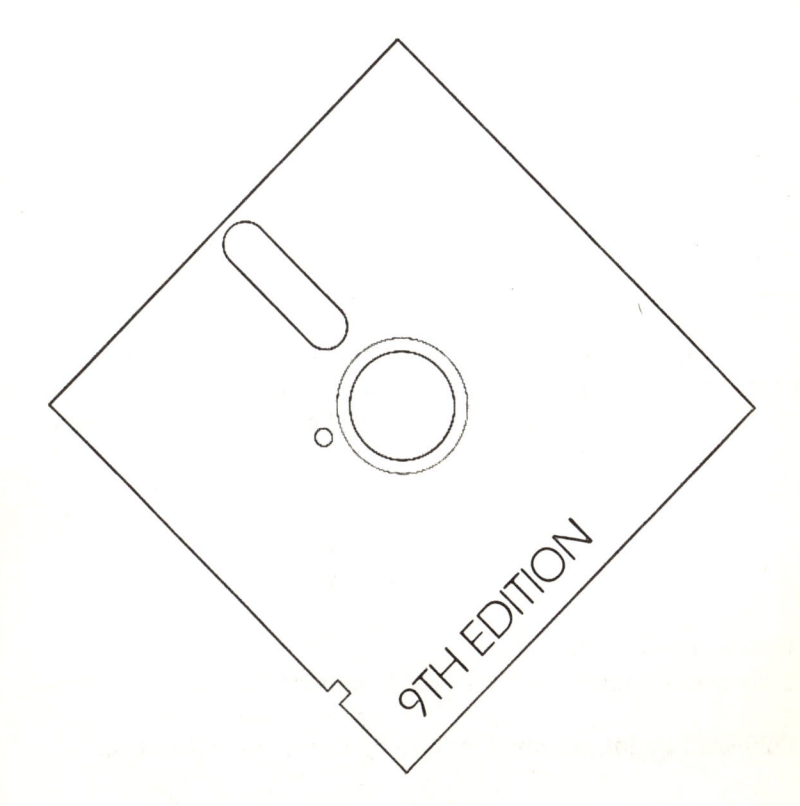

9TH EDITION

AMERICAN ASSOCIATION OF INDIVIDUAL INVESTORS

INTERNATIONAL PUBLISHING CORPORATION
CHICAGO

The American Association of Individual Investors is an independent, not-for-profit corporation formed in 1978 for the purpose of assisting individuals in becoming effective managers of their own assets through programs of education, information and research.

©1992 by The American Association of Individual Investors
All Rights Reserved. This publication may not be reproduced in whole or in part by any means without prior written consent from

American Association of Individual Investors
625 North Michigan Avenue, Department CI
Chicago, Illinois 60611
(312) 280-0170

ISBN 0-942641-39-6
Library of Congress Catalog Card Number: 91-76292

Published by International Publishing Corporation, Chicago.

Data in this *Guide* were gathered from company releases. Factual material is not guaranteed but has been obtained from sources believed to be reliable.

TABLE OF CONTENTS

PREFACE vii

Chapter 1   HOW TO USE THIS GUIDE 1
BOOK ORGANIZATION 1
USING THE BOOK 1
FINDING THE RIGHT PRODUCT FOR YOU 3
INVESTMENT SOFTWARE 4
FINANCIAL INFORMATION SERVICES 6

Chapter 2   COMPUTERIZED INVESTING
                 FOR INDIVIDUALS 11
SELECTING INVESTMENT SOFTWARE AND
    FINANCIAL DATABASES 12
TYPES OF INVESTMENT SOFTWARE AND SERVICES . 12
    Portfolio Management and Financial Planning Software 15
    Fundamental Analysis 17
    Fundamental Investment Screening 17
    Fundamental Valuation Techniques 18
    Technical Screening 19
    Financial Information Services 20
    On-Line Trading Services 23
    Disk and CD-ROM Based Information Services 23
    Specialized Investment Software 23
PCs FOR INVESTMENT RESEARCH 24

Chapter 3   PC HARDWARE 27
THE CURRENT STATE OF THE PC MARKETPLACE .. 27
SOME BASICS FOR NEW
    (OR SOON-TO-BE NEW) USERS 29
DIFFERENCES IN PC HARDWARE 31

INFORMATION STORAGE		32
Memory		32
Disk Storage		34
VIDEO STANDARDS		35
PRINTER CHOICES		38
COMMUNICATIONS HARDWARE		38
DIFFERENCES IN OPERATING SYSTEMS		41
PUTTING IT ALL TOGETHER		42
An Entry-Level System		44
Intermediate Systems		45
An Advanced System		46
Macintosh Systems		46
WHERE TO BUY IT		47
WHAT THE FUTURE MIGHT HOLD		50
Chapter 4	GUIDE TO INVESTMENT SOFTWARE	55
Chapter 5	GUIDE TO INFORMATION SERVICES	309
Chapter 6	INVESTMENT SOFTWARE GRID	386
Chapter 7	FINANCIAL INFORMATION SERVICES GRID	445
Appendix I	*THE COMPUTERIZED INVESTING* BBS	465
Appendix II	STOCK MARKET OR BUSINESS RELATED BBSs	473
Appendix III	COMPUTER SPECIAL INTEREST GROUPS (SIGs)	475
Appendix IV	GLOSSARY OF COMPUTER AND INVESTMENT TERMS	481
INDEX		491

PREFACE

This year we publish the ninth annual edition of *The Individual Investor's Guide to Computerized Investing*. Again, we have made several changes to improve the book. The basic purpose, however, remains that of helping you manage your investment program more efficiently by providing you with information about PCs and investment-related software, services, on-line databases and bulletin boards and PC special interest groups.

    This edition covers a broad array of investment software and services, some new and others well-seasoned. The software list changes from year to year as some vendors succeed and others fail. There are 98 new software products and 32 new information services that appear this year, while 108 software products and 10 information services available last year no longer appear. There are 445 software products and 135 databases in this edition; last year there were 451 software listings and 102 information services. We do not include products and services intended primarily for professionals rather than individual investors. In addition, some vendors did not respond to repeated requests for information and their products are not included.

    With this edition we have expanded the information about software. Included now are any special requirements necessary to run the software, return policy and cost for restocking and how technical support is provided, if any. You should still remember that new upgrades can appear on the market at any time. It would be wise to check with the vendor for the current version of the product since old inventory can remain on dealers' shelves.

    In the first Chapter we will tell you how to effectively use the *Guide* and offer suggestions on how to find the best investment software or service to meet your needs. Chapter 2 offers an overview of the types of investment programs and services available and what they can and cannot do for you. With this in mind you can evaluate the programs listed later in the *Guide*. Chapter 3 details the current state of PC hardware and operating systems, including Windows, DOS 5.0 and OS/2. It is followed with a short view of what the future might hold in light of these and other developments. Chapter 4 contains the investment software descriptions and Chapter 5 covers financial databases. Chapters 6 and 7 are the comparison grids for software and data services, respectively.

We again include several updated appendixes this year. Appendix I discusses how to use AAII's Computerized Investing Bulletin Board System. Appendix II lists bulletin board systems specializing in investments, and Appendix III is a listing of AAII and other computer users groups. The final appendix is a glossary of computing and financial terms.

The handy reference grid for investment software has changed. We have combined the three separate software grids into one comprehensive grid covering all systems. The grid's focus has changed from concentrating on hardware requirements to focus on software functions. The Financial Information Services Grid has been expanded. It now provides information on how the data is transmitted by the vendors. In addition, the categorization of functions and data type has been expanded.

In utilizing the grid and product descriptions, remember that these are based on data provided by the sellers of the products. Some vendors may have a broad definition of what constitutes a particular function. For example, some sellers may feel that their product performs portfolio management if it handles more than one kind of investment vehicle. We do not have the resources to verify all the vendors' claims, but we make every effort, on the basis of the information we are provided, to categorize products appropriately.

We have updated the appendices listing bulletin board systems and computer SIGs throughout the country. Finally, we have expanded the glossary of financial and computer terms as an aid for beginners. These terms are also generally defined in the text when they first appear.

Many people contributed to the completion of this book and made suggestions that have improved its presentation and style. My thanks to all of them. Particular thanks for this edition again go to John Bajkowski, Associate Editor of *Computerized Investing*, who oversaw the updating of product descriptions and grids, revised the section describing the *CI* bulletin board system and compiled the list of BBSs in Appendix II. Edwin Srutowski and Marie Swick gathered information from companies, updated the product descriptions and compiled the indexes and software comparison charts.

We have made every effort to provide a publication that meets your needs and answers the questions you have when you are planning a computer or software purchase. Nevertheless, we are always looking for ways to further improve the *Guide* and we welcome your suggestions. We hope this year's edition helps you in your investment program.

Fred Shipley, Ph.D.
Editor, *Computerized Investing*
Associate Professor of Finance, *DePaul University*
Chicago

HOW TO USE THIS GUIDE   1

The personal computer holds great potential as a tool for assisting investors in their investment program. Our goal, throughout this book, is to help people realize this potential. This chapter presents information on how to use the book in ways that make sense to you. You may be tempted to skip past this chapter and dive right into the product descriptions in Chapters 4 and 5. That is fine. This book is designed as a reference source; it is not meant to be read cover to cover. But if you want to get the most out of this book, you should read this chapter to understand how the book is organized, what it contains and how to select and develop a system that is right for you.

BOOK ORGANIZATION

The book is organized into four main sections. Chapters 2 and 3 provide an introductory examination of computerized investment software and information services, along with the proper computer hardware required to make use of these programs. Chapters 4 and 5 provide descriptions of software products and information services. Chapters 6 and 7 include reference grids to locate products that meet your needs. And finally, the appendixes provide information on the *Computerized Investing* BBS, other BBSs that have an investment focus, user groups that focus on computerized investing and a glossary of computer and investment terms. We have provided an index at the end of the book which lists the companies and products listed in Chapters 4 and 5.

USING THE BOOK

Chapter 2 examines the software and information services market as it relates to investing. When dealing with computers, common sense dictates that you first find the software and data services that meet your needs, and then obtain the necessary hardware to operate these systems. Good advice, but without knowledge of available software and its capabilities, it is difficult to make software decisions. Chapter 2 provides that information. It even includes a table that shows how much software is available for various hardware platforms. When you move on to Chapter 3 to examine the hardware field you will know which hardware to consider. Chapter 2 also takes the software market and breaks it into functional segments — from the universal personal finance programs to the more analytical programs such as fundamental analysis systems. In going over these categories, pointers are provided on what to look for when considering these applications and what things these programs do well and what they do poorly. Chapter 2 also explores the area of financial information services. Read this to get a feel for the types of data and services available to investors, the different ways you can obtain this data and the things to look out for when selecting an information service. The chapter's ideas are tied together in its final section: PCs for Investment Research. Even if you are familiar with investing and investing software, you should find this section a good reminder that PCs are tools that should assist investing and that they supplement but do not replace your judgement.

Chapter 3 explores the hardware arena as it supports the investment market. The chapter examines the current computer market, describes basic computer components and looks at how the components fit together in a complete system. It details various systems for users at different levels and explores where you can purchase this equipment. And finally, some of the changes on the horizon and how they might affect you are examined. Readers familiar with computers may want to skip the computer basics and concentrate on the first and last sections which explore current and future trends. Those who now are unfamiliar with computers may want to start out at the computer basics section. It presents information on the major system components such as processors, information storage systems, video systems, printers, communications hardware and operating systems. The discussion of these areas focuses on what each system does, the current options on the market and what can be gained or lost using different levels of equipment. The interdependence of these components becomes apparent as the process of putting together the system that is right for you is examined. Various systems are constructed for entry-level, intermediate and advanced users. Guidelines are provided for what to expect in performance at different levels of sophistication and cost.

The next section deals with the issue of what your options are when it comes to buying equipment, where you should make your purchases given your knowledge and what to expect in terms of warranties and service from different dealers. And finally, no chapter on hardware would be complete without a brief examination of the future direction of the market.

FINDING THE RIGHT PRODUCT FOR YOU

Computer programs really offer no new analysis techniques, only the ability to apply techniques more rapidly and perhaps more consistently. Anyone who has studied the markets even briefly will quickly realize that there are many techniques that can be applied to value the market and various securities. Before you can take the next step and select your system you must focus on what you want your system to accomplish. Chapter 2 provides a framework for categorizing programs, but if you are not familiar with the capabilities of computerized systems, it would be helpful to page through the listings and descriptions of software programs in Chapter 4 and financial information systems in Chapter 5. Doing so will familiarize you with the diversity of the market — here are products with capabilities and prices that cover a wide spectrum.

When analyzing your situation, you need to examine the tasks you are doing now and may consider doing in the future, the types of securities you plan to hold in your portfolio and whether you plan to enter your data by hand or rely on a data service.

If you want to see what other individuals are actually doing, there are two good avenues. There are groups that meet on a regular basis to discuss and present approaches to a computerized investment program. These computer special interest groups or SIGs are a valuable resource that can also be used to get opinions on the pros and cons of various systems when you get to the point of picking a package. The AAII operates a no-fee BBS based in Chicago. Details on how to access and use the system are presented in Appendix I. Appendix II presents a nationwide listing of other BBSs devoted to investing. Appendix III provides a list of computer SIGs from across the nation. Most are affiliated with the AAII local chapter network, but a listing of other groups or networks is also provided. If there is no group in your area, or you are just looking for further contacts on the subject, electronic bulletin board systems (BBS) provide a way for computer users with modems to exchange ideas and even program with each other.

Once you have a list of tasks that you want your computerized system to perform you are ready to approach the reference grids in Chapters 6 and 7. In structuring the book, we have provided separate reference grids for software programs and information services. These grids allow you to quickly narrow down your search to those products which match your needs.

INVESTMENT SOFTWARE

The software grid breaks down programs into five key areas — the system required to run the program, the types of securities or assets the program can handle, the types of analysis the program performs and the sources of electronic data the program can make use of. The grid then provides a page reference for the product description so you can get more detailed information.

Paging through the grid, you should be able to narrow down your search to a reasonable number of products that merit further investigation. In examining your list here are the things you should consider and look for:

- Talk to other users, see what they are using and what they think about your final candidates. A list of local computerized user groups and investment related BBSs can be found in the appendixes.

- Is the price within your budget? Do not make the mistake of thinking that the higher the price the better the program. There are excellent products at every price range.

- Does the program use a cost-effective data service? If you plan on using a data service to save time from data entry, you may quickly find out that initial program cost was just a small part of the overall cost of operating the system. Programs vary in data service support. Before you commit to a product, find out how much it will cost to obtain electronic data. Data service prices and information are listed in Chapter 5, but prices do change (up and down) so it is best to call the service directly. Also, services price data access in different ways—connect time, extra charges for certain data or a charge per character of information downloaded. Generating comparable costs from different services can take some time.

- Make sure that the program can export its data if needed. An indication is provided whether a program can import and export data and the type of file formats supported. This will allow you to share data among programs and allow you to continue to use the data you have collected should you want to switch programs in a few years.

- Contact the software vendor to request the most recent program information. Investment programs make up a narrow niche and are not readily available in software stores. You will generally need to deal with the vendors directly. Get a demo of the programs you are interested in, even if there is a small fee. Programs differ in their ease of use. Without working with a program you do not have a way of knowing whether you can or even want to learn how to use the package. And even more importantly the demo will help to ensure that the programs you are looking at actually do what you think they do.

- Look at the support policies of the company. Do they offer telephone support and, if so, when is it available. Some vendors charge for providing help. Some may operate a BBS that you can connect to, not only to solve problems but also to get operating tips. Some vendors produce product newsletters that can be a valuable resource for getting the most out of the product. New to the guide this year is an indication of the availability and type of support given by the company.

- Before you make your purchase, check on the company's return policy. Some software vendors offer full refunds but provide a time limit; others charge a restocking fee or do not refund the postage and handling, while others do not provide any refund. Understand the policy before you buy the product, not after. For this year's *Guide* we have asked the vendor to supply this information.

- It is best to purchase mail order items with a credit card. If you have problems either receiving the product or getting it to work then you have some recourse or even bargaining power. The Fair Credit Billing Act gives you some power to withhold payment on items purchased if you have made a good faith effort to return an item or have given a seller a reasonable opportunity to correct any problems. With a check, once it has been cashed, you have little recourse to get your money back.

FINANCIAL INFORMATION SERVICES

Financial information services supply the electronic data and services used by investors. Like software programs they vary greatly in scope and purpose. In selecting the services, you need to focus on how they provide data, what they provide, which systems can use the data, the service cost and even how they determine what to charge for the data. A glance through Chapter 5 should give you an understanding of what is available. In doing this you may notice that some are strictly raw data providers while others are complete system sources of software and data.

For this year's edition, we have moved some programs from the software section because the program relied totally on data sold only through the software vendor and were useless without this data. These were mainly database/screening programs for stocks and mutual funds that had self-contained data.

The quickest way to find the data service that fills your needs is to use the Financial Services grid in Chapter 7. Its purpose is to present the type of data each service provides, how it gets the data to you and the functions the service provides. The grid also contains a page reference so that you can easily read a detailed description of each service and examine the cost structure.

In selecting a data service you should take into account the following factors:

- Take a close look at the features the service is supplying. Obviously the service should supply the information you are searching for, but a quick look through the grids or product descriptions will show that services vary greatly in breadth and depth. If you are a technician, then you should probably seek a service that specializes only in providing historical data for the markets you analyze. You do not want to pay for features that you will never use.

- The data services can vary greatly in how much is charged for access and data. The best way to compare two services is to determine the type of data that you are going to need, and compute how much it is going to cost to obtain it. Pricing data is provided along with product descriptions in Chapter 5, but it makes sense to call when you are doing the comparison and request a price schedule directly from the service. They should be able to provide you with an up-to-date and complete pricing guide.

- If you are looking for real-time security data watch out for exchange fees. Exchanges charge individuals for access to real-time data. All real-time vendors must collect this fee but may not mention it in their pricing lists. When looking at real-time quote services make sure that you know if the exchange fee is included.

- Check to see if there is a monthly minimum. Some services require that you spend a certain amount every month or bill you the minimum. If you are an infrequent user, you may be paying for data that you never use.

- Examine how often you plan to use the service. This may dictate which product you select. If you desire a fundamental screening system and plan to run screens frequently, then a service that provides updates on a regular basis at a fixed cost may make sense. However, if you are going to run screens very infrequently, then you may wish to look for an on-line service that provides screening on an as-needed basis and charges you only when you access that feature.

- The information services vary greatly in how they get their product to you. An indication of which transmission methods are available is provided in both the grid and product description page.

- If it is a dial-up service, ask where the closest access number is. The cost balance between two services may change if you have to place a long-distance phone call.

- While demos are less frequent with information services, some do make demo disks available. Others sell subscription kits which include a few hours of on-line time to explore the system. Often this free time expires if you do not use it up within a short time, so take advantage of the time if it is available. A few services even provide free trials of their service to get you to try the system.

- If the service charges by the minute, see if there are any software programs available which allow you to construct your data request off-line and then automatically connect, retrieve data and log off, keeping time and expenses to a minimum.

- If the service supplies both software and data, check to see if the data can be exported for use in other programs. Some systems are closed.

- If you are looking for a data service to supply data for a specific program, it makes sense to call the program's vendor. They should be able to suggest the best source of data for that program. Some of the more popular programs have their own user groups. The program vendors may be able to put you in touch with these groups to get their opinion.

We hope this *Guide* answers your basic questions and eases the task of investment and portfolio management. Please let us know if you have any suggestions, comments, questions or problems using the book. We make every effort to improve the *Guide* each year.

COMPUTERIZED INVESTING FOR INDIVIDUALS

2

Personal computers (PCs) continue to drop in price while their power increases. Software is increasingly sophisticated yet easier-to-use. On-line databases and information services are more accessible and more reasonably priced. All these developments have brought the capabilities of professional investment analysis home to the individual investor. These powerful tools make it easier for an individual to keep investment records, track portfolio performance, gather investment data, evaluate and select securities and execute security transactions.

These advances in computer technology and the lower costs of hardware and software have pitfalls for which an individual investor should be on the watch. The thrill of using a computer should not obscure the real costs associated with its use. Not only are there the obvious costs of buying hardware and software, there are potentially significant costs of on-line access and connect charges for financial databases.

If you are considering buying a PC for investment analysis and management, you must recognize both the costs and the benefits of that decision. Only incremental costs and benefits are relevant — that is, only those costs or benefits that change as a result of buying the PC. For example, if you decide to do all of your investment research and analysis with your computer, you might decide to rely on the services of a discount broker to handle transactions for you, saving commission costs. Those savings would be incremental benefits to you, offsetting the costs of buying the computer and software. If you still need to rely on a full-service broker, you will not realize these savings. Evaluating whether to buy a computer for investment management should be judged by the same criteria as your investments themselves — does this purchase offer greater benefits than its cost? Of course, some of these costs and benefits will be difficult to measure, but you should at least attempt to identify them.

SELECTING INVESTMENT SOFTWARE AND FINANCIAL DATABASES

Good quality commercial investment software for some home computer systems is rare, while it exists in abundance for other systems. Owners of IBM and compatible PCs (which we will generally refer to as **DOS** computers) will find a wide selection — literally hundreds of packages are available. The problem here is one of sifting through the offerings to find a package that is useful rather than simply finding something that is available. Software for the Apple II line is slowly disappearing. Table 2-1 shows the trends in software availability for IBM and Macintosh systems. The product descriptions in Chapter 5 will allow you to determine whether or not the software does what you want it to do.

TYPES OF INVESTMENT SOFTWARE AND SERVICES

Investment software and services can be generally categorized as: portfolio management and financial planning, fundamental investment screening, fundamental techniques of valuation, technical screening or technical analysis and charting, on-line financial information services and on-line trading services (which may frequently be offered by the same vendor), disk-based database services and specialized investment programs.

Portfolio management refers to the recordkeeping necessary to determine returns realized by an investor, and financial planning refers to the establishing of objectives for allocating resources to different assets. These can range from a simple program to balance your checkbook to a detailed 20-year financial investment and saving plan to meet a number of long-term personal financial goals.

Fundamental screening evaluates basic economic, financial and accounting information in order to select securities that meet specific valuation or performance criteria. Fundamental valuation

EXHIBIT 2-1
Programs Available for IBM and Macintosh

	Edition 1991	Edition 1992
IBM and Compatible Systems—Totals	259	398
Fundamental Analysis	37	28
Technical Analysis	119	145
Portfolio Management	85	120
Databases and Screening	18	45
Macintosh Systems—Totals	44	64
Fundamental Analysis	8	6
Technical Analysis	16	19
Portfolio Management	27	17
Databases and Screening	3	7

programs apply concepts of security valuation to analyze the worth of a security in relation to its current market value.

Technical analysis involves analyzing stock price and volume patterns and using the results in forecasting performance. Frequently the information so generated is displayed in graphical form for ease of analysis.

Financial information services and on-line databases provide both historical financial, market and economic information plus current stock market prices and financial news. They may also provide, or another service may provide, the ability to make transactions on-line. Diskette-based data services offer the same current fundamental financial data as on-line services as well as historical financial data and price information.

More specialized programs include statistical and quantitative analysis software, and programs for options and futures valuation. Many of the programs that investment professionals, economists and investment consultants use on mainframe computers have now migrated down to personal computers and workstations. While many of these programs are designed primarily for the professional investor, a sophisticated individual with the requisite background and a substantial portfolio might find them useful. With a few general purpose exceptions, these more specialized programs are not described in this *Guide*.

In addition to these broad categories, there are many general purpose programs that can be used for investment analysis. For example, spreadsheet programs such as 1-2-3, Quattro and Excel are very suitable for users wishing to develop their own analytical models. Many of the on-line financial databases provide software that allows the user to download data directly into their spreadsheets or other analysis programs. For many investors such programs provide all the necessary flexibility and sophistication. *Computerized Investing*, our bimonthly newsletter, offers on a regular basis many investment analysis and portfolio management spreadsheet applications.

It is now possible to duplicate at home the in-depth research performed at financial institutions and brokerage houses. Programs that perform sophisticated statistical analysis, such as multi-variate regression, moving averages and time series modeling, are available for personal computers at a reasonable cost. Time series analysis is the academic's counterpart to technical analysis. It is used, for example, to forecast interest rate movements, stock market indexes or other economic variables. Regression analysis is used to estimate or study the relationship among economic or financial variables and might be used to forecast future stock performance. The processing of these more complex analyses can take considerable time without one of the more powerful computers, but it can be done — just plan on taking a break for awhile if you're working on a large problem.

Portfolio Management and Financial Planning Software

Among the simpler and more popular types of investment software programs are those that keep track of portfolio performance and account for cash flows into and out of a portfolio. However, some of these programs may not provide the information the investor needs to evaluate performance accurately. Many are simply bookkeeping systems whose benefits may be limited. For example, once you have entered the data initially needed to begin using the program, you may later realize substantial time-savings as future calculations are done by the program. In addition, some programs may allow access to on-line data services to update portfolio values with current price quotations.

The essence of a financial planning system should be an integrated set of program modules that allows the individual to perform basic home budgeting, to reconcile a personal check register, to examine the tax consequences of different purchase and investment decisions, to flag expenses for tax purposes, to prepare projections of net worth and income for retirement planning purposes, and perhaps to take care of insurance planning and real estate property management. Some investors may not want all these options and can find programs that meet their more specific needs. Others will want a package that can put everything together.

What you must remember is that the computer does not make you a better recordkeeper, nor will it solve financial problems. If you never save any money, using a computer will not provide for your retirement. If you hate writing down all your expenses for tax purposes, you will like it even less if you have to enter all this data into the computer.

The process of portfolio management should be more than mere recordkeeping; it should permit the analysis of total portfolio wealth allocation. Investors should also be interested in determining insurance needs, cash and security holdings that are appropriate for their lifestyle, financial needs, income and overall wealth. The focus should be prescriptive programs that can be used for investment analysis.

Even in describing an investor's current situation, there are subtleties that must be dealt with. For instance, most investors' portfolio transactions do not occur at regular, equally spaced intervals. The accurate determination of portfolio performance requires that they be able to deal with transactions as they occur, even if at irregularly spaced intervals. Moreover, withdrawals must be accounted for properly to determine portfolio returns.

Internal rate of return is the appropriate time-weighted measure of portfolio return. This is the rate of return, when earned each period, that makes the starting value of your portfolio equal its ending value, with full accounting for cash withdrawals and deposits. This measure can be compared to market returns to determine whether you are earning a sufficient return.

Implicit in the use of the portfolio internal rate of return is the assumption that all investment cash flows are reinvested in the portfolio and earn that rate of return. If you withdraw a cash dividend, it reduces your realized portfolio return since it is not reinvested. Even if you reinvest the dividends, as your realized investment returns change over time, so will your portfolio realized rate of return. Portfolio management software should be able to deal with this and also have the capability of handling not only all your current investments but also any of the investment vehicles you might consider in the future.

If the program does not actually prepare a tax return, it should be able to group information so that you can do so yourself, or with another program. A final feature that is very useful, especially for investors with large portfolios or for active traders, is the ability to link with an on-line database to obtain current price information for portfolio updating. When used in conjunction with information on the market itself, such as the Standard and Poor's 500 Stock Index, this can provide the basis for making fundamental portfolio allocation decisions.

Fundamental Analysis

Fundamental analysis is the name given to methods of analyzing basic financial, accounting and economic information and using that information to assess the value of a particular security. This general term covers specific valuation models such as the present value of dividends or price-earnings ratio approaches and screening of databases on some financial variables.

Fundamental Investment Screening

Indeed most (but not all) of the commercially available fundamental investment software is designed to screen data rather than judge a security's worth on the basis of fundamental valuation principles. There are now a number of programs on the market that will screen a data set of 1,000 to 6,000 companies on any number of fundamental variables. Typically, these programs come with their own data, with the scope of the coverage depending on the database the software uses.

As an illustration of the process, consider an investor who is aware of the published research showing that in the past, smaller market-value companies have outperformed the market as a whole — even allowing for the risks these companies might pose. The investor could decide to screen the database for companies with a market value of, say, between $20 and $100 million. In addition, the investor might look for those stocks in this group whose price-earnings ratios are low, say below 10. The screening program could go through the data rapidly and select those companies meeting these criteria. Of course, once these stocks are selected, the investor must always look further before making any investment. There are many important judgmental factors that the computer cannot analyze.

One problem with this technique is that it is possible to establish seemingly reasonable screening criteria that none of the companies in the database satisfy. Without a basic theory that determines the relative importance of your criteria, you cannot adjust your screens to create a list of securities for further analysis.

Some of the databases allow users to set the relative importance of different criteria.

In summary, a fundamental screening program should give the investor access to a large database and the flexibility to create different criteria for screening — the investor should not be locked into preset criteria. The program should allow the user to transfer these data to other uses, such as a spreadsheet program. Without this latter capability the user cannot do the further analysis essential for effective security selection. Similar screening features are offered by on-line data services.

Fundamental Valuation Techniques

Valuation techniques use fundamental data to assess the worth of a security and judge its desirability as an investment. The basic premise is that investors are generally rational in making investment decisions and value the cash flows the investment can be expected to provide over some future period. By determining the risk of the investment relative to some market standard, an investor can estimate the return the security should offer over time. The return compensates for this market risk and is the benchmark for comparison with expected or promised future returns.

One such approach looks at future dividends and their projected growth as the primary determinant of value. All future value, including an estimate of future selling price, is related to these cash flows. Earnings are important not in themselves but because they generate the cash that can be used for future capital investment and dividend payments. For companies that currently pay no dividends, their future dividend potential is estimated from current earnings and capital investment policies. This approach is valuable for an investor with a long-term time horizon. It emphasizes the cash flows the investor will actually be able to spend or reinvest and focuses on the security's risk and the return that is compensation for taking that risk.

Earnings valuation techniques are similar to the dividends approach but focus on the interrelationship between reinvested earnings and potential future growth, the profitability of the company relative to sales and other accounting information. This valuation approach is related to the dividend valuation model but essentially moves the process one step back.

Until recently the cost of a detailed program of fundamental stock analysis was beyond the means of most individuals. The high cost was not the result of a difficult process but because collecting the data necessary to perform the analysis was expensive and time-consuming.

Technical Screening

The term technical analysis covers a variety of techniques that study relationships between securities' current price movements and past price and volume information. The relationships generated are then used to forecast individual stock and market price changes. This analysis is generally best interpreted with the use of graphs, and in many cases the analysis is entirely graphically based.

One such approach is to compute a moving average price. This is just an average over several time periods — days, weeks or whatever time period the analyst feels is appropriate. The interval remains constant, but the beginning and ending points move through time and so reflect new information and market conditions. The analyst is not concerned with the reason prices move but simply with the pattern of movements. If the stock crosses the moving average line on an upswing, it is generally regarded as a buy signal.

The problem with technical analysis is that it is only concerned with price patterns, and the user must rely on these patterns repeating themselves. Since the analysis ignores the economic, financial or other factors that have caused the price trends, the investor has no way to predict whether similar circumstances will occur in the future. There have been many studies of the performance of various technical trading rules. While they have not exhausted all the possibilities for evaluating the technical approach to stock selection and market timing, most of the studies have shown that it is impossible to outperform the market with any technical trading rule, especially when trading costs are considered.

Technical analysis might provide some insights as an aid when an investor has funds available and is trying to make a fundamental decision on asset allocation. With access to a good fundamental database and some insight into the current economic climate, an investor might be able to locate sectors of the market that have not participated in the current market trend. In combination with fundamental analysis, a technical view of the market may provide some insights into the timing aspects of investment decisions. For example, those investors who had the misfortune of getting into the market in the middle 1970s had to wait for a long time to see their rewards reach historical averages. With the inflation rate experienced then, financial assets were simply not a good investment vehicle. Real assets profited most from the inflation, so real estate, some art works and precious metals did very well, while stocks and bonds did poorly.

Since the essence of technical analysis is price trends, it is essential that these programs provide access to current price and volume information. In addition, if a program accesses an on-line database, it should allow the investor to capture information for later analysis while off-line in order to minimize connect charges. Ideally the program should also link with a database of fundamental financial variables so the investor can analyze that information in conjunction with the technical data.

There are a number of programs and data services available that will not only compute the price and/or volume graphs that you want, but they also can log onto an information service, automatically obtain the latest information and update the graphs with that information.

Financial Information Services

These products provide the information investors use in carrying out their investment analyses. This information may be provided via diskette or CD-ROM or on-line. Data can also be accessed through direct satellite transmission or FM carrier (usually restricted to major metropolitan areas). Though the on-line services are perhaps better known, several of the largest financial information services are now making available directly to investors some of their data along with programs to screen the data.

From the very earliest days of financial markets, the gathering and processing of information has been crucial, and the stock exchanges have used state-of-the-art communications networks. Most of this communication has involved transmitting the latest price quotes to investors, and this remains the focus today. Nevertheless, investors can now obtain detailed and comprehensive information on securities. This includes current and historical financial and market data to aid in their analyses. On-line databases provide the necessary information for fundamental and technical analysis and for portfolio management and performance evaluation. These databases are available by modem, FM sideband, cable TV and direct satellite transmission.

Information services may be broadly based networks such as CompuServe, Dow Jones News/Retrieval (DJN/R) and Prodigy, which can provide information on a variety of topics extending far beyond the investment field. In contrast, some systems may limit themselves to providing information on a specific type of asset, such as futures or options.

The investor must ensure that it is possible to access the database with a local phone call. Since some of these services provide many databases that are not of interest to investors, to save connect charges it should be possible to get directly to the relevant database without accessing several layers of command menus. Finally, investors should carefully analyze all the charges that apply to the information they need. Some on-line services have special fees to access certain databases, and there may be additional charges for special reports. The service should detail all these charges. Ideally, the service will offer a demonstration package so the potential user can examine at first hand the available information.

A few on-line services and some of the larger commercial banks offer "home banking" services. This allows the individual to pay some bills (those from firms which have an agreement with the bank), transfer funds, get account information and perform other banking services.

In addition, there are some areas of the country where computers can receive information from Videotext systems. Videotext systems are broadly based information services which might include real estate listings, local retail store offerings, home shopping and other locally useful information. The kinds of services offered are limited only by their imagination and your willingness to pay. So far, this local videotext service has not been widely used and accepted by consumers.

Some of the on-line databases offer information in graphics form, so that you can actually receive stock and commodity price charts. You might also receive weather charts. Unless you are a farmer or commodity speculator, whose trades depend on prediction of droughts in the Midwest or freezes in Florida or Brazil, this service is not likely to be worth your while.

On-line databases generally provide access to information similar to that on the disk-based screening programs. In addition, they provide access to current financial and economic news that may affect a security's value. These databases may also provide price quotes on a delayed basis — or real-time quotes for an extra charge.

For the infrequent trader, there are several less costly ways to acquire this kind of financial information. Many of the financial information services offer current market quotes on a 15- to 20-minute delay at considerably lower cost than real-time quotes. Quotes are available for options, bond and futures markets, as well as the stock markets. Some companies are providing price information on disk that is already formatted for immediate use in a spreadsheet program. If they provide more information than you reasonably need or can use, you can simply pick up your *Wall Street Journal* or *Barron's* and enter the current price data yourself. For long-term investors with moderate portfolios, the latter course is not only the cheapest but also probably the easiest.

On-Line Trading Services

Finally, several of these services are linked to a brokerage, allowing you to trade securities with your computer while at home. Remember, though, that your order goes to the market through the brokerage's normal channels, so there may be no great time saving over simply calling your broker. These services do not offer access to the exchanges' direct order systems, rather they offer on-line access to a brokerage, which then executes the transactions in the normal fashion.

Some of these services offer discounts to investors using them for trading and, of course, offer access to account information so you can check account positions, cash balances and other relevant data.

Disk and CD-ROM Based Information Services

Financial information services that are distributed on disk — either floppy disk or on CD-ROM — generally contain historical information and a program to screen that data. The information is typically updated periodically by sending out a new data disk. In evaluating such services it is critical to know how many companies are covered and from what exchange they are drawn. You want to ensure that the companies you will be evaluating are represented in the database. If you are interested in smaller companies, for example, the database should extend beyond those securities listed on the New York Stock Exchange.

Specialized Investment Software

As might be expected, there is also a wide variety of software designed for very specific analyses. For almost every type of asset, there are programs used to evaluate its worth. Investors dealing in specialized markets can find programs for the analysis of options, financial futures, commodities, bond trading strategies, mutual fund tracking, interest rate arbitrage, real estate investment analysis and more.

For example, there is a generally accepted model, the Black-Scholes model, used to evaluate the worth of options, especially call options. As a consequence, there are a number of programs that can apply that model to evaluate whether option premiums are in line with their theoretical value. Many of these programs also provide the kind of graphs that we associate with technical analysis and can examine a variety of strategies to take advantage of any discrepancy that is found. With the exception of programs that cover broad categories of investment vehicles, such as bonds or mutual funds, these programs will be of use to only a limited number of investors.

PCs FOR INVESTMENT RESEARCH

PCs are excellent tools for investment analysis and financial research and planning. What the computer *should* allow you to do is spend your time evaluating the results of your research, rather than spending your time on repetitious tasks. The computer can process a lot of information rapidly, it can do numerous iterations testing sensitivity to changes in your fundamental assumptions, and it can display that information in an easily understandable format with graphics.

You should remember, though, that you are relying on the financial expertise of the authors of any software package or service you are using, so carefully check the documentation they provide. If the manual does not explain what the program does and why it does it, you should view the product with some skepticism. The program should tell you more than simply what to do. The advice of the computer is no more relevant than the advice of a human being — after all, it was a human who told the computer what to do in the first place. Remember that almost all investment analysis software is based on observation of past market trends and relationships and some grounding in the theory of valuation. If the past is not a guide to the future, using a computer will make you no better an investor than you were before. If you do not understand these valuation principles, you cannot be an effective investor with or without a computer.

Perhaps the best strategy is to view your computer as a tool, a little more sophisticated than your pencil and a tablet of scratch paper but the same kind of tool. With this tool and a basic understanding of financial markets, of investment analysis techniques and of your personal financial objectives, you can be a better investor. With an understanding of the past performance of different investments and of your own needs, you can formulate reasonable financial goals. Then the computer will be a valuable aid in reaching those goals.

PC HARDWARE   3

THE CURRENT STATE OF THE PC MARKETPLACE

The PC marketplace seems to be entering a brave, new world. Hardware development, for many years more advanced than software development, is entering a dormant phase as manufacturers try to lengthen the product cycle and generate more cash flow from current designs. Some of this relaxation simply reflects the sophistication of current microprocessors. With the Intel 80386 and 80486 chips (used in IBM and compatible computers) and the Motorola 68030 and 68040 chips (used in the Macintosh), there is sufficient power for most current and soon-to-come applications. Current developments in chip technology are oriented toward making the computing capacity less power-consuming and therefore suitable for laptop computers. Of course, just as with mainframe computers, there is always a demand for more power. At the moment, though, this demand is not as incessant as it has been.

What is occurring now are arguments over the computer's control system, or operating system, and how users interact with it. These arguments, or strategic disagreements, if you prefer, could not even have occurred three or four years ago — the processing power of PCs was insufficient to support the range of options being discussed. In order to understand these issues and their impact on your buying decisions, you need to know a little about how the market is divided and what role processors and operating systems play in the overall performance of a PC.

The market segmentation is based on both computer hardware (the processor that handles calculations and the "architecture" or "bus" that determines how data is transferred internally) and operating systems (the program that determines how the computer works). Either of these hardware or operating system factors could be the predominant force in splitting the market, but originally they worked in tandem. One processor family, the Intel 8088 used in the original IBM PC had one operating system, DOS, and another processor family, the Motorola 68000 used in the Apple Macintosh had another operating system, Mac OS.

Applications software development had to proceed along different lines for each machine, and there was no expectation that the two would ever cross. Neither, however, was there much expectation that different operating systems would be used for any one processor. While some companies tried to insulate users from remembering arcane DOS commands with a "shell" that offered a menu of choices, no one thought that there would be many ways of using the same operating system through different interfaces — directly via DOS commands, or indirectly through a graphical interface like Windows, or even through input with a "pen-based" system, rather than a keyboard or mouse.

Users face, then, several distinctions in dealing with personal computers. First, there is the fundamental difference between IBM and compatible computers and everything else. We will refer to these machines as DOS machines. They all use one of the Intel family of microprocessors, from the 8088 through the 80486, and use the operating system developed by Microsoft and IBM, MS- or PC-DOS.

The everything else side of the market includes a wide variety of hardware and operating systems, but for investors the most important part currently is the Apple Macintosh, which uses one of the Motorola 68000 series of processors and Mac OS. Other machines, including the Apple II family, the Ataris, Commodores and even the older CP/M-based microcomputers are no longer relevant for investors. It is true that there is investment software for this equipment, and that they can indeed perform useful investment analysis, but they do not make sense currently as computer choices for investors. As a consequence, we will discuss only the Mac relative to DOS machines.

Once you get beyond hardware and software differences, you have price differences to consider. Machines costing under

$2,000 are typically thought of as "home" computers, while more expensive machines are regarded as "office" or "business" computers. Originally, this distinction put both DOS and Mac PCs into the "business" class. Price declines have made available machines in this price range for the home market.

As the price you pay gets higher, so does the usefulness. The more powerful and expensive "home" computers, ranging in price from $1,500 to $2,500, offer the opportunity to completely outfit an investor for detailed investment analysis, including access to on-line databases. You can spend more if you insist on better-known brand-name equipment.

A PC system costing $1,500 to $2,500 will satisfy most individuals. For that price you can get a PC with a hard disk, graphics display, modem and printer. You can expect to pay an additional several hundred dollars for software. This may include communications software, a spreadsheet, a word processor and investment software. At the high end of the price spectrum, $3,000 to $7,000, you can buy the most sophisticated hardware, complete with superior graphics and printing capabilities, communications and a large hard disk for data storage.

SOME BASICS FOR NEW (OR SOON-TO-BE NEW) USERS

For most individuals the process of buying a computer starts with questions about hardware. What is the latest machine available? Who makes the fastest processor I can buy? Which machine will give me the jazziest graphics? Yet even the most sophisticated computer does you little good if there is no software that will run on your machine or take advantage of its capabilities. In fact, you should first evaluate what you want your computer to do, then see what software will do that, and only then should you select the computer system itself.

Another problem for users is that hardware changes have typically outpaced software development. It is quite fair to say that most of today's software was written for machines that have been available for several years. As a consequence, much software does not exploit fully the capabilities of today's hardware. At the current rate of development, it will still be some years before we have software that really utilizes the power of today's most powerful microprocessors. This forces potential buyers to think ahead. You must guess what software might become available later to utilize the capabilities of the newer technology.

Obsolescence will always be a fact of life in the PC market. For an individual investor, however, it should not be a constant concern. Rather you should concentrate on finding a system that will serve your current needs, has some potential for future expansion and has a large base of available software. You may not have the fastest computer on your block, but if you can do the analysis you want, you should not care. The standard-setting companies in the market — Apple and IBM — have encouraged outside software development. This should ensure a base for the future, even if your hardware is "obsolete." Given the much slower pace of software development, relative to hardware changes, a mid-range PC probably will be technically sufficient for years into the future.

In addition, most DOS systems can be upgraded with hardware that takes advantage of more advanced technology. For example, you can add the newer graphics boards to older PCs, realizing the benefits of improved display and readability. Newer software that requires more memory may be used by adding memory to the system. Adding a hard disk allows the storage of much more data and may be necessary for some software. And a number of DOS computer manufacturers are explicitly offering PCs in which you can upgrade the actual processor.

This is not to say that you will always be able to run the latest software. As microprocessors become more powerful, more powerful software requiring these processors will become available. To some extent this has already occurred. For example, Lotus 1-2-3 comes in four versions. Release 3.1 is a more powerful spreadsheet and can be used only by those with the most powerful hardware. Release 2.3 has less features for the rest of the world. In addition, there is a version for the Mac and one for Windows. Microsoft Excel for Windows will not run on anything less than an 80286, and even that does not make much sense — an 80386SX is realistically a minimum requirement.

DIFFERENCES IN PC HARDWARE

Microcomputer systems vary greatly. To understand the differences, it is helpful to know a bit (sorry for the pun) about how a computer processes information. For further reference, check the glossary at the end of this book.

Computers process information in bits — an on-off (or 0-1) condition indicated by the absence or presence of an electrical charge. These bits are generally processed in chunks known as bytes, each of which is 8 bits. Information is built up from these tiny pieces of data, and the computer processes these bytes of information very rapidly. We usually speak of large multiples of bytes — a kilobyte is 1,024 bytes (abbreviated KB or just K) and a megabyte (abbreviated MB or just M) is 1,000 kilobytes. The part of the computer that processes information is the central processing unit or CPU.

The speed at which a PC operates is determined by three factors: the number of bits processed simultaneously by the CPU, the number that are transferred in a group from the memory to the processor and the CPU's clock speed.

Early microcomputers processed and transferred information in 8 bit (or 1 byte) chunks. The latest PCs process and transfer 32 bits of information at once, the same as large minicomputers. The amount of data processed and transferred at once is not the only factor in processing capability. The other significant factor is the clock speed — or how fast the computer's processor deals with instructions. Clock speed is measured in megahertz (MHz) or millions of cycles per second. The faster the cycle time between instructions, the more information the computer can deal with. Early PCs operated at a clock speed of less than 5 MHz; current machines operate at up to 50 MHz; and the next generation of PCs will operate at 50 to 100 MHz. The faster the clock speed and the more information that is transferred at once, the greater the power of the computer. You should not assume, however, that more advanced processors always operate at the fastest clock speed. One of the tradeoffs manufacturers make to lower costs is to offer more advanced processors operating at slower clock speeds.

Nor should you fall into the trap of thinking that a faster CPU will always result in noticeably faster work. For much of the time it is being used, the brains of the computer are in fact idle waiting instructions from the user or reading data from or writing it to a disk file. A very significant improvement in processing power will not usually result in the same increase in productivity, unless the supporting hardware is also upgraded. Beyond the choice of processors and clock speed, the most important choices a user will make is to determine information storage capacity and video display capability.

INFORMATION STORAGE

Information is stored in a computer in two ways. First is the memory which stores programs and data currently in use. This memory depends on continued power and is lost when the computer is turned off or the system is restarted. Second is disk storage which holds data and programs that are not currently used.

Memory

The memory a computer has and can use is a key consideration and depends, in part, on the CPU. CPUs are physically limited in the amount of memory they can recognize. An 8-bit CPU, such as in older PCs, can only access 64K of memory; a 16-bit CPU, such as the 8088 in the original IBM PCs, can only access 1 MB of memory using DOS. 32-bit CPUs such as the 80386 and 80486 can access 32 MB of memory, but to remain "compatible" with older DOS systems they act as if 1 MB is the limit. Some of this memory is occupied by the operating system, which instructs the computer how to perform, so the memory available for programs and data is even less. On the IBM PCs, for example, no more than 640K of the available 1 MB can be used for the operating system, programs and data; the remainder is reserved for other tasks, such as the video display and system information.

Originally this 640K, more than 10 times the memory available on the first PCs, seemed larger than anyone could conceivably need. We know now that memory can be a constraint, but for many investment programs 1 MB is sufficient. Only if you are dealing with a very large spreadsheet or trying to run more than one program will memory be a real barrier. The constraint now is not so much with data requiring more than 1 MB, rather it is with programs and operating systems that really need more than 1 MB for effective operation.

There are a number of ways of dealing with this memory constraint, but none currently offers a complete solution. Microsoft's Windows and Quarterdeck's Desqview are two programs that allow some swapping of programs and data, effectively allowing access to more than 640K of memory on a DOS PC. While Windows and Desqview will work on the 8088, albeit slowly, using Windows on anything less than a '286 does not make sense. The newer computer systems will require more memory, but they generally will also be equipped with it. Most of the more advanced PCs are equipped with from 2 MB to 8 MB standard. The Macintosh has the ability to address more memory directly.

When a program says that it requires 256K of memory, that means 256K of the memory your computer has installed and is available *after* the operating system and any resident utilities are loaded. Usually, the minimum requirement is exactly that. Many programs can and will make effective use of all available memory. Dealing with the minimum usually means that the program will be frequently transferring program information to and from disk — a time-wasting operation in comparison to the speed with which the CPU works. (Typically, a hard disk will transfer data 1,000 times or more slower than can memory.)

While memory is a relatively cheap addition to your computer, its costs can vary considerably. Nevertheless, the requirements of today's software strongly suggest that investors should install as much memory as their computer can access and use.

Interestingly enough, the ability of the processor to deal with information in memory can exceed the ability of the memory chips to deliver it. The CPU may then insert a pause or "wait state" into its operation. This wait state allows the memory time to retrieve the data before the processor tries to do something with it. Unfortunately, this is wasted time for the processor; it is idle and there is nothing else it can do. The more powerful systems come with a memory cache, a special storage place for recently accessed data that speeds up the processing of information.

Disk Storage

The second type of storage is non-volatile, or permanent, storage, generally on either floppy or hard disk drives. (Permanent storage may be something of a misnomer to which anyone who has experienced disk problems can attest. Nevertheless, it accurately describes what we try to do with these media.) These disks store programs and data for transfer to other systems, for sale to consumers and for a user's permanent files. A floppy disk can store varying amounts of information, depending on the disk itself and the computer with which it is used. The floppy disk on the original IBM PC held 160K, while the newer 3.5" disk can store up to 2.88 MB, though 1.44 MB is more typical. The newest Macs can store 1.44 MB and can read and write data in a format that can be recognized by a PC with a 3.5" disk drive. The 3.5" disk is no longer the smallest disk available. Some new Zenith laptops use a 2" disk with a capacity of 720K, but the 3.5" disk is the common standard. Unfortunately, disks of the same size are not always interchangeable, though this is less a problem with the 3.5" disks than the 5.25" disks.

The storage capacity of the disk depends on how information is written onto the disk. Data are recorded onto the disk in much the same fashion as music is recorded on an audio cassette tape — with magnetic read and write heads that move mechanically over the disk. The disk, unlike the audio cassette tape, must be formatted, or initialized, in order for your computer to read and write data. Formatting simply sets the disk up in the pattern your computer expects to find data. When you write to the disk, the write head realigns the magnetic particles on the disk into a pattern that your computer recognizes as data. The newer disks allow the read/write heads to pack that data more densely. A hard disk works in the same way as a floppy but stores much information more densely and is usually not removable or transportable. A typical hard disk that stores 20 MB is a common minimum size on low-end equipment and 200 MB or more typical on high-end machines.

VIDEO STANDARDS

The array of video standards in use today is extensive and can be quite confusing. (Table 3-1 provides a detailed summary.) There are different basic configurations, each with different costs. For most individuals, however, there are only two basic choices you must make as a user. First, you must decide whether or not you want color. Second, you must determine the resolution you want and how much resolution your programs can display. The interaction of these two factors will determine how much you will have to spend. The most significant in terms of cost is whether you want a monochrome or color display.

One of the more obvious changes in PCs over the past several years has been the common acceptance of color displays and the improved resolution those displays can offer. Even the

TABLE 3-1
Video Adapter Standards for IBM and Compatibles

Standard	Maximum Resolution	Displays Graphics	Max. Colors/ Out of Total
MDA	720 × 348	No	1
Hercules	720 × 348	Yes	1
EGA	640 × 350	Yes	16/64
VGA	640 × 480	Yes	16/262,144
Super VGA	800 × 600	Yes	256/262,144
	1024 × 768	Yes	256/262,144

Mac now supports an array of color displays and resolutions. Along with these improved displays has come a decrease in costs. But resolution in itself is not the whole story. The programs you use must be able to take advantage of the capabilities of your hardware. Spending $700 to $1,000 or more on a new graphics adapter and color display does not make much sense if all the programs you use will still appear exactly the same. Even programs that are only a few years old may not be able to take advantage of what the new hardware can show. While most of the better-known commercial programs will be able to utilize the best currently available resolution, investment programs from smaller companies are less likely to do so. In addition, the higher resolution means that screen characters are smaller. This can present difficulties for those people with less than perfect eyesight. Unfortunately, the cost of larger color monitors is very high, easily running to $2,000.

Because of memory requirements with graphics adapters, there is a tradeoff between the number of colors displayed, the maximum resolution possible and the speed with which the display is updated. This is a function of memory, since each screen dot occupies a piece of memory and so does each color. The maximum resolution may also depend on whether the display is text (character-based) or graphics. Most display adapters offer different video modes, with the ability to trade off resolution and colors. Each mode specifies the number of colors that can be shown, whether graphics or text can be displayed and the resolution available. When discussing resolution, we will refer to the maximum available from each adapter standard in graphics mode. Color adapters show maximum resolution in color and text modes; it may be possible to obtain higher resolution with only two colors.

The original IBM PC offered a monochrome display adapter (MDA) with good resolution but no ability to display graphs. Graphs could only be displayed in four colors with the color graphics adapter (CGA), but only at a lower resolution. When IBM introduced the PC/AT, it offered a new video standard, the EGA (Enhanced Graphics Adapter) — capable of displaying 640×350 lines of resolution and 16 colors from a possible 64.

The EGA adapter changed the technical aspects of the display and so required a different class of monitor to convey the greater resolution and color information. The change made CGA monitors incompatible with monitors for the EGA and later standards; but the EGA adapter could display graphics in CGA mode. To deal with this change, NEC introduced the first multi-scanning monitor, which had the ability to work not only with the new EGA standard but also was compatible with earlier video standards.

The EGA did not remain the standard for long. First, manufacturers found they could provide extra resolution beyond the EGA with these multisync monitors. Suddenly people were offering enhanced EGA cards (often identified as EGA+ or some variant thereof) and the software necessary to make popular programs like 1-2-3 or Windows operate in this enhanced mode. Second, when IBM introduced the PS/2 series of computers, they added yet another video standard, the VGA (Video Graphics Array). In addition to offering all EGA (including the older CGA) resolution modes, the VGA is capable of displaying 16 colors (from a possible 262,144 colors).

As with the EGA, companies are also offering Super VGA resolutions, with the possibility of 1024×768 lines, about the best currently supported. To get this resolution, the manufacturers must make available special software, called drivers, for your programs. Only the best-selling programs have such Super VGA drivers. However, the spreadsheet programs all take advantage of the VGA, and the difference in graphical display is significant. Excel is notable in this regard. The current versions of 1-2-3 and Quattro Pro offer enhanced graphics capability. Most technical analysis programs require a graphics adapter. Almost any program that can display graphs will require some graphics adapter. Remember, though, that what you can see is not necessarily what you can print. Your printer must also be able to take advantage of the new features these programs offer. Most technical analysis programs offer the means to print what is displayed, and the more sophisticated ones will support a vast array of printers.

PRINTER CHOICES

A printer is an essential part of any PC system. Most software can use a wide variety of printers, and many printers can be set up to emulate a standard printer, such as the IBM graphics printer, by setting a switch or sending a software code. This means there is a wide range of printer choices.

It is no longer possible to make a simple distinction between "letter quality" and "dot matrix printers." A dot matrix printer operates by striking a series of pins (typically 9 or 24) to print dots in a pattern that creates the impression of a character. The dot matrix printer offers the ability to create graphics output by striking these dots in different patterns.

With the introduction of 24-pin printers, or by over-printing, dot matrix printers can now provide output that is virtually as good as a letter-quality printer. For the least cost, a 9-pin printer will handle most jobs. If you want the ability to generate decent looking business correspondence and higher quality printed graphics, then a 24-pin printer is appropriate.

The latest printer technology uses a laser beam to create letters and graphics in much the same way as a xerographic copier. These laser printers produce letter output that is as good as a daisy wheel printer and can print high quality graphics. The initial cost and continuing costs of operation make this an expense that can be easily put off.

For a lower initial cost, some manufacturers are offering print quality equivalent to that of a laser printer with a printer that works by spraying a tiny jet of ink onto the page. These inkjet printers can also produce graphics. Inkjet printers are available for both IBM and Macintosh computers.

COMMUNICATIONS HARDWARE

A last piece of equipment that users should consider is a modem. A modem is a device that transforms computer information so that it can be sent over telephone lines. There have been slow, but steady, changes in the capabilities of communications hardware and programs over the past several years. While the communication process is not necessarily any easier to use or understand, it is faster and less error-prone. In addition, some of the changes have made for faster transmission by using data compression techniques. This increased speed can be misrepresented in advertisements and is a factor for which investors should be on the watch. The faster speed is only possible if the modems on both ends of the link operate the same way. Data compression also makes error detection more critical, and error-checking will offset some of the speed increase from compression.

The basic purpose of a modem is to communicate with the outside world — in this case with other computer users. This part of the world is not only quite large but also potentially quite helpful. You can communicate person-to-person by typing messages to one another; but this is not, and should not be, the major use of a modem. (If you type as fast as I do, talking is much faster.)

There are a number of important reasons for having (and using) a modem: connecting with a financial information service for current price quotes on your investment holdings, tapping into a local bulletin board system (BBS) to get programs or games, logging onto the *Computerized Investing* BBS to download current programs or to get help in the use of a program from the vendor.

Modems can be installed internally or connected externally through a serial port. The speed at which a modem transmits data is measured by its baud rate (bits of data per second). Modems offer a variety of transmission speeds, generally from 300 baud to 9600 baud. 300 baud modems are not only obsolete, but cost-ineffective now, unless you have an older computer system that requires that transmission speed.

Today, a 1200 baud modem should be regarded as the low-end for cost-conscious consumers. A 2400 baud modem is the logical choice, and most on-line services and BBSs support this speed. Manufacturers are offering 9600 and 19200 baud modems, with 9600 baud the next standard beyond 2400 baud. These high-speed modems will also operate at the more prevalent slower speeds. There are some factors you should consider before purchasing a higher-speed modem. First, the number of services and BBSs that support 9600 baud transmission is somewhat limited, though many are offering, or will offer soon, this support. Second, the speed figures quoted in advertising copy could reflect optimum conditions that might not prevail in practice.

Since modems use telephone lines for communication, they are subject to the same noise problems faced when talking. When talking, noise can be compensated for by repeating a phrase or sentence. Not only must a modem be prepared to do the same thing, it must also be able to detect when an error has occurred. Transmission of digital data like computer programs are even more sensitive to such problems. The difference between saying "I'll meet you on the course tomorrow at 10:00" and receiving "I'll see you on the course tomorrow at 10:00" presents little difficulty. The difference between a program that sends a 0001 and receives a 000F can be disastrous — and that can represent a difference in only one digit out of millions transmitted.

Error correction itself is something users do not generally have to worry about, since communications software takes care of it. Manufacturers, however, have combined error correction with data compression techniques and use this to bolster data transmission speed claims. The important fact to remember is that these transmission protocols work only if both the sending and receiving modems and software support them. Not all BBSs currently support these compression techniques.

You should also remember that one way modems compensate for telephone line noise is by reducing transmission speed. This difficulty is more likely with long distance calls and when weather conditions are bad. Improvements in local and long distance networks are reducing the potential for this kind of problem. Finally, you must remember the level of usage on the system to which you are connected will affect how rapidly the system can transmit data. The greater the usage, the more time the system must work on other people's requests rather than your own. If you are using the modem for teleconferencing (talking to others on-line), then the modem will transmit only as fast as you can type. In this case, the advantages of a high-speed modem are limited. For most users, the 2400 baud modem offers the best price-performance tradeoff.

To use a modem you will need a communications program. Many modems come bundled with such a program. This program not only tells the computer how to interpret incoming data and to format outgoing data, it also usually provides a number of options to make communications easier. For example, you may be able to automatically dial an on-line database, log in with your assigned password, obtain and display the data you want and log off without having to enter any of these commands yourself. You may also be able to program the software to redial if it detects a busy signal, and you may instruct it to call automatically at night when rates may be lower. Financial databases often provide specialized communications software to automatically retrieve and download price and other investment information.

In addition to the commercial communications software, there are many freeware and shareware programs. Freeware (or public domain) programs are those that an author has provided free for use by others. Shareware programs are those that an author has provided for others to use on a trial basis. You are requested to register and pay a modest fee if you use these programs regularly and wish technical support. The charge for registering shareware programs is usually small — $25 to $50 is common. You may obtain these programs from a bulletin board system, such as the *Computerized Investing* BBS. (See Appendix I for more information.) Among the best communications shareware programs is Procomm. This program has been so successful as shareware that an improved version, Procomm Plus, is now commercially available.

DIFFERENCES IN OPERATING SYSTEMS

The software that runs the computer is the operating system. Essentially, the operating system is a "traffic cop." It directs how and when the computer responds to different commands and also handles basic manipulations such as copying and naming files or directing files to the printer. While all operating systems perform the same kinds of functions, they are usually incompatible with each other. As a consequence, programs that are written for one kind of system, like the Apple, will not run on an IBM PC, and vice versa. This means that you must take care in selecting a computer and determining whether it will operate the programs you want it to run. For the most part, this now means making a choice between DOS and Macintoshes. These decisions could become less a concern in the future, if software companies actually succeed in making a generic operating system. Of course, the other extreme is also possible, with UNIX being yet another standard that could intrude into the process.

Originally, the difference between operating systems for the Mac and DOS machines was chiefly distinguished by the "user interface" — that is, the way in which users entered commands. On DOS computers, users typed in commands to be executed; on Macs users moved a mouse pointer to an icon representing a file or program to be executed. With Windows 3.0 and OS/2 Presentation Manager, DOS users now can execute commands in much the same way as Mac users. This process is not always easy though. The Mac operating system was designed from the beginning as a graphical environment. Consequently, programs that run on the Mac take advantage of this. The DOS operating system was not designed this way; rather Windows and OS/2 act as an intermediary between the user and DOS. In turn, this means that only programs written explicitly to work under one of these graphical interfaces will take advantage of these features.

PUTTING IT ALL TOGETHER

What, then, is an appropriate computer system for an individual investor? How do you, as a potential user, decide what an appropriate investment in computer equipment and software should be? The first, and most important, step is to realistically decide what you want to do. While "professionals" always tell users that this is the logical first step, they seldom offer a means of completing this step. The problem here is not that it is so difficult to determine what you want to do now; rather the problem is determining whether you will be doing anything more complex in the future.

As a guideline, sit down and draw up a list of tasks you want the computer to help you with. You should limit yourself to no more than ten specific objectives. Trying a greater number can easily require more time than most beginners are willing to spend, and then you can get frustrated because you are not accomplishing all the tasks you wanted to. In designing these objectives, consider which are the most important and which are the most time-consuming. While doing so, decide whether you are going to rely solely on the computer to perform the task, or whether you are going to replicate what the computer is doing with paper and pencil.

For example, many users start with the idea of using a PC to track their investment portfolios. This means getting current market prices on some regular basis, using those prices to update portfolio values and to determine their portfolio rate of return. This is in fact something a computer can do quite readily and automatically. Many investors start by picking up a newspaper, tracking down their holdings and then writing down the security name or symbol and the price on a piece of paper. This paper record then becomes the source of information to be entered into the portfolio tracking program. This process introduces a second recordkeeping function that may become a source of error but which can also be used to audit the results of the program. More importantly, it means that users are performing manually much of what the computer can do. Doing a job twice can also breed frustration.

For beginners, this redundancy provides a backup should they inadvertently lose data. Nevertheless, the process can be completely automated, and most users quickly get to that point — having their PC dial an on-line service, obtain the relevant price information, download it and update security and portfolio values.

Once you've decided what you want to do with the computer, determine whether you are going to design and program your own analysis or purchase software. For most tasks, purchased software will perform the analysis perfectly well, if not better than you could yourself. In addition, commercial software saves you the necessity of having to reinvent the wheel. Our software listings in Chapter 4 are designed to help you in this process. In particular, you can quickly see what is required to run the software you might purchase. You should also consider buying some program of general use such as a simple word processor and a spreadsheet. As you get more advanced and more comfortable using the computer, you may want to explore additional software packages.

An Entry-Level System

With the advances in computing power and the decline in prices that seem to be an inevitable part of the PC market, the hardware for a beginning system is significantly different than that of only a year ago. While DOS systems based on the Intel 8088 (PC/XT and clones) could have been considered a starting point last year, these systems are not attractive choices in today's market. This is not to say that users cannot perform investment analysis and portfolio management with such machines. Rather the cost savings from this equipment do not justify the limited performance they offer and the even more limited potential for upgrading in the future. Individuals on a limited budget, and unsure of their interest in using a PC for their investment program, can consider this level of equipment. We do not recommend it, however.

With this in mind, an investor looking for a basic DOS system should plan on one that uses, at least, an 80286 processor (sometimes referred to as an AT or AT-clone). The basic configuration would include 1 MB of memory with the possibility of expanding to 2-4 MB, a single floppy (with the 3.5" preferred) and a hard drive of at least 20 MB capacity. The size of most current programs, however, makes 20 MB a bare minimum; with 40 MB being a more reasonable alternative. In addition, a printer is essential, with a 9-pin version offering the cheapest alternative.

Optional upgrades that go beyond the basic system include a modem for communication with on-line services and BBSs. A 2400 baud modem is the appropriate choice here and should not cost more than $100-$150. If you think you will need additional disk capacity, many '286 systems are offered with, or can be configured with, a larger hard drive. 40 MB would be a minimal upgrade with 60 MB being reasonable for a user planning on using Windows or more than one or two major software packages. (Many of the major word processing, spreadsheet or database programs will use 3-5 MB of hard disk storage each. It is surprisingly easy to use up large amounts of disk space before you even realize it!)

Intermediate Systems

While the '286 can be considered a very basic entry-level system, it does not offer as much potential for future enhancements or operating ease as does the 80386SX. Because of internal differences between the two chips, the '386 is a much better alternative than the '286. Of course, this better alternative carries a higher price, but the difference is eroding. The added cost of the SX system may be as low as $100 or as much as $500, but the '386SX system will also typically have some enhancements over the '286 system. Given a $100 price differential, anyone considering a '286 would be well advised to purchase a '386SX. With a $500 differential, the 80286-based machine is a little more attractive for budget-conscious buyers, but has limited future potential.

Probably the most important reason for using the 80386SX system is that it offers a very low-cost way of getting into the operating environment that seems to be taking hold of the DOS market — the graphical user interface (GUI, or "gooey", as it is commonly known). Given the sales success of Windows (although the program is certainly not fault-free) and the introduction of 1-2-3 and WordPerfect for Windows, it seems likely that there will be more investment-oriented software explicitly written for this environment. Do not expect this to occur immediately, though.

An intermediate-level machine would be based on the 80386 (or 80386DX, to distinguish it from the SX). Such a computer would be used by someone operating under Windows, rather than DOS, who expects to do a considerable amount of spreadsheet and data manipulation, database screening or graphical analysis. The basic configuration would include 2-4 MB of memory, VGA (or Super VGA) graphics, a 2400 baud modem and a hard drive of at least 60 MB capacity. If you are planning to use Desqview or Windows for multi-tasking, then 4 MB of memory should be considered a minimum. For ease of transferring data, a user could add a second (5.25") floppy drive. If you are planning on using a number of newer, larger programs, upgrading the hard disk to more than 100 MB makes sense. In addition, users planning to do a lot of graphical analysis or use Windows and Windows-based programs will find a color monitor a reasonable addition.

An Advanced System

The advanced user, or someone planning to become advanced, will opt for an 80486 computer. Such a system will have at least 4 MB, and more reasonably 8 MB, of memory, both 3.5" and 5.25" floppies, a 9600 baud modem and a hard disk with 120 to 200 MB capacity. At the time of this writing, such computers are available through direct mail sources for under $3,500; other alternatives can raise the cost as high as $7,500. Additions to this high-end system would include a fax/modem combination board, a larger hard disk drive (though 200 MB will probably serve most individuals quite well) or more memory. Users could save about $300 with a 2400 baud, rather than the 9600 baud modem choice. More than 8 MB of memory will be useful only to people expecting to load and run several programs at once.

Macintosh Systems

For the user who prefers a Macintosh system, the entry level configuration would be a Mac Classic with 1 MB of memory, a 40 MB hard drive and a 2400 baud modem. Optional upgrades would include moving up to the Classic II, which has the more powerful 16 MHz 68030 processor and 2 MB of RAM. Buyers of the Classic II can also upgrade the hard disk to an 80 MB capacity disk.

The intermediate user would go with a Mac IIsi with 3 MB of memory, a 2400 baud modem and an 80 MB hard drive. This system could be configured with additional memory; but users who wanted a little more power would probably want to buy the Mac IIci. This system has a more powerful processor and includes the memory management chip that allows the Mac to use virtual memory, which is the ability to use hard disk storage as if it were memory.

The advanced user would get a Mac IIfx with 4 to 8 MB of memory, a 160 MB hard drive and a 2400 baud modem. The upper end of this price spectrum would be one of the new Quadra models, either the 700 or 900. These machines are based on the 68040 processor but operate at a slower clock speed than the fx. Nevertheless, performance is rated at about 40 percent greater than that of the fx.

Tables 3-2 and 3-3 summarize the basic computing configurations for both DOS and Mac machines. In addition, we have a table summarizing the system components we have described.

WHERE TO BUY IT

The final and one of the most difficult decisions a user must make is whether to purchase direct through a mail-order vendor or through a local retail outlet. While many DOS machines are available only from mail order sources, several large and reliable manufacturers, such as Dell, Tandy/Radio Shack and Compaq, make machines which are available at retail. In addition, there are a growing number of computer "superstores," such as CompUSA that market PCs. These stores offer convenience as well as discounted prices. They carry a wide range of software as well as hardware, though users should not expect to find many of the specialized investment software packages there.

The tradeoffs are basic, though substantial. Most mail order sources are reputable, but just as with a retailer you must consider

TABLE 3-2
Intel/DOS Systems Summary

Computer	Processor (Intel)	Clock Speed (MHz) Minimum	Clock Speed (MHz) Maximum	Maximum Memory DOS	Maximum Memory Windows, OS/2 Protected Mode	Minimum	Operating Systems Configuration Recommended	Operating Systems Configuration Maximum
XT	8088	4.77	8	640 K	1 MB	DOS	DOS 5.0 or Desqview	DOS 5.0 or Desqview
AT and Compatibles	80286	8	20	640 K	16 MB	DOS	DOS 5.0 or Desqview	DOS 5.0 or Windows 3.0
	80386SX	12	20	640 K	32 MB	DOS	DOS 5.0, Windows 3.0 or OS/2 1.3 or 2.0	DOS 5.0, Windows 3.0 or OS/2 1.3 or 2.0
	80386	16	40	640 K	32 MB	DOS		
	80486	25	33	640 K	32 MB	DOS		

TABLE 3-3
Macintosh Systems Summary

Computer	Processor (Motorola)	Clock Speed (MHz) Minimum	Clock Speed (MHz) Maximum	Memory Minimum	Memory Maximum	Operating System Minimum	Operating System Recommended
Classic	68000	8	8	1 MB	1 GB	System 6	System 7
LC	68020	16	16	2 MB	4 GB	System 6	System 7
Classic II, IIsi	68030	16	40	2 MB	4 GB	System 7	System 7
IIci, IIfx	68030 & 68882	25	40	4 MB	4 GB	System 6	System 7
Quadra	68040	25	25	4 MB	4 GB	System 6	System 7
Powerbook 100	68000	16	16	2 MB	4 GB	System 7	System 7
Powerbook 140	68030	16	25	2 MB	4 GB	System 7	System 7
Powerbook 170	68030 & 68882	25	25	4 MB	4 GB	System 7	System 7

the possibility that everything will not work as smoothly as you would like. Firms like 47th Street Computers, Dell Computers, Gateway 2000 and Northgate all have a good reputation for delivering what they promise and when they promise it. A typical mail order source will charge from 30% to 35% below the manufacturer's suggested list price. Direct mail vendors such as Gateway will offer equipment that may be 20% to 25% less than a comparable machine through other sources. You must also add shipping and handling charges, but generally you will save the sales tax, if applicable.

The tradeoff is that you do not have the retailer to offer direct assistance should something go wrong. You may have little direct technical support, but most of the direct-mail vendors offer telephone technical support as well as on-site service for a limited period. This should take care of simple problems and installation. Beyond that, however, maintenance is the responsibility of the owner. Many vendors are offering on-site service for a year after purchase, and this should cover most potential problems. Again, many of the larger mail order companies have signed agreements with third party concerns to provide continuing maintenance, but these contracts can be quite expensive for the purchaser. You should probably view them in the same light as a maintenance contract for any other major appliance. There are plenty of people in the business, so it must be profitable; but for most of us, it is an option that we will hopefully seldom use. If your computer does not fail within 90 days (the usual warranty period), it is not too likely to do so later. Another factor to consider with direct mail shopping is that most credit card companies offer "buyer protection plans" when you use their cards for a purchase. This offers an additional level of protection for the shopper.

For these reasons, a mail-order source is most appropriate for someone who is comfortable dealing with the details of setting up a machine. These details are really not that difficult — you may have to simply push a switch from one side to the other — but you have to be able to determine which switch must be set and where that switch is located. If the manual provided by the manufacturer is not clear, that may be difficult.

Buying from a retailer may not necessarily mean paying list price. Many retailers will offer a discount on hardware or a package deal with a system purchase that can provide a savings to the consumer. On the other hand, it may be difficult to get a retailer to provide free consultation once you buy the machine. Once again, reputation is the chief concern. The important factor is that you have a local vendor who can (and should) be able to help with any problems.

Talking to people in your area who have purchased from a specific retailer is the best way to gather information. Attend a meeting of the local AAII chapter computer interest group if there is one in your area. (See Appendix III for a listing.) You can also try the Better Business Bureau or state Department of Consumer Affairs for further details.

WHAT THE FUTURE MIGHT HOLD

This *Guide* would be remiss without at least a peek into the future. The rapid technological changes and the frequent additions to software make it imperative. The focus in computer processor development is not on the next evolution of current chips (an Intel 80586 or a Motorola 68050) but rather on the next big step, which for investors is several years away — the development of so-called RISC (reduced instruction set computing) computers and the software necessary for their use. While RISC computers have been available for a few years, they are not a serious component of the PC market; they probably will be by 1993 or 1994. These chips have been a factor, albeit currently a small one, in workstations and desktop "mini-computers" and so-called "mini-super-computers" used mostly for computationally intensive graphics, design and simulation.

Recently, Apple and IBM forged an alliance to create operating system software that will run on a variety of computer systems. For the most part, the possible short-term effects of this alliance should be minimal. Except to fuel Bill Gates' and others' paranoia at Microsoft, Apple and IBM are not looking to achieve

TABLE 3-4
Comparative Power of Microprocessors

Intel Processor	Year of Introduction	Speed When First Introduced (MHz)	Speed 2 Years Later (MHz)	MIPS (Millions Instructions/Second)
8086	1981	4.77	8	0.5 to 1.5
80286	1984	6	12	1.5 to 3.0
80386	1986	16	33	4.0 to 8.0
80486	1989	25	50	12.0 to 24.0
Next Generation 80586 (?)	1992(?)	50	100	35.0 to 70

any goals in the near future. Rather this alliance is about longer term shifts in the PC marketplace, especially at the corporate level. In the short run, most of the concerns about DOS versus OS/2 are irrelevant. Rather, there are DOS limitations that must still be addressed.

The limitations of DOS are related to memory management. Dealing with the gap in memory between 640K and 1 MB is difficult at best and downright debilitating at worst. Because so many programs actually expect this gap, operating systems' programmers cannot just pretend the gap doesn't exist. Nor can they just design an operating system that deals with memory starting at 0K and going as far as you would want. Thus Windows and other enhancements become unstable because of the need to try to anticipate whether any particular program wants, needs or expects this memory gap to occur. (Allegedly, a forthcoming version of Windows will operate similarly to OS/2 and the Mac OS and have "flat" memory management; that is, all memory will be treated the same. Only time will tell if that feature is actually delivered as anticipated.)

The Macintosh operating system, and to some extent Windows and OS/2, have changed the way users enter commands. These shifts in how PCs operate are not really expected to show up in machines that will be used on corporate and home desktops for several years. Yet the changes are potentially profound.

Most current microprocessors are based on CISC (complex instruction set computing) chips, which means that the processor is capable of dealing directly with a complete array of basic instructions. While many of these instructions are used infrequently, the processor must be able to access them. In fact, this can slow the processor down with excess overhead. Newer designs, currently used mostly in "workstation" computers, have processors that are directly capable of executing a more limited number of instructions. These are called RISC (reduced instruction set computing) chips. Because these processors can execute fewer instructions, the operating system must be more complex. But the faster speed of the processing is more than enough to offset the slower and more complex operating system.

One of the main efforts of the alliance between Apple and IBM is the development of a RISC based personal computer and operating system. These processors are designed to improve overall processing speed by trying not to do everything. RISC processors work by reducing instruction overhead but of course must have other ways of dealing with the missing instructions when a program calls for them.

RISC-based computing is moving into the PC mainstream, albeit at a slow pace. Part of the reason for this can be detected by observing the types of computers RISC chips are used for. These workstations are primarily used for engineering and design applications, which are graphically intensive. The PC is also moving toward a user interface that is graphically based. Of course, the Macintosh has been so for some time, but only the acceptance of Windows on DOS PCs has caused much excitement in the DOS camp (and much of that enthusiasm seems to be marketing hype from Microsoft). These graphical interfaces use a significant amount of the microprocessor's power. Thus any development that helps speed up graphics is welcome. Enter the RISC processor.

If the direction of change in how we, as users, deal with the PC is towards an icon-based, graphical interface, then both IBM and Apple have something significant to gain by linking up with each other. At the moment, Microsoft has a virtual monopoly on the graphical interface for DOS machines. Apple, of course, is in the same position with the Macintosh, but this has little significance since the Mac is still only a small part of the PC market. IBM has been selling a graphical interface, OS/2 Presentation Manager, but it has met with little market success. Part of the reason is the limited acceptance of PS/2s and the confusion that OS/2 is for PS/2s only. Part of the reason for the slow acceptance of OS/2 is it's substantial memory and processor requirements and the limited advantages the operating system offers over DOS. (Some might say the same about Windows, and not be far off, but Microsoft seems to have convinced people that this is not a concern. It is!)

To succeed, Apple and IBM have to deliver an operating system that will not only work on this new generation of processors, but which can also be used on the Intel processors that dominate the market currently. Like Windows, it will not be able to run on the less powerful 8088 processor; it is likely that at least an 80386 will be required. By the time such a product appears, however, the 80386 will probably be the low-end processor.

In addition, the companies must ensure that the way users deal with applications through this operating system is nearly the same no matter what the application. That is, users will have to learn to deal with the system more so than learning applications. There is some hope that the companies will be able to achieve this, given Apple's success with the Macintosh operating system. But IBM and its management will probably have to let the Apple software engineers run the show. And that is not guaranteed.

For most users, these machines remain a distant vision; while there may be light at the end of this development tunnel, it is a faint and wavering one. One of the realities of the microcomputer world is the leapfrogging of operating systems, hardware and software applications. For the last several years, the hardware and its capabilities have progressed significantly beyond what the operating system can support. This is particularly true in the DOS arena.

What seems likely to develop, probably over several years, is a new standard that will eventually make obsolete the operating system and software currently in use. On the other hand, with the evidence we have about the promises of what the hardware and software can deliver and the reality of what they *do* deliver, it will be some time before we have to give up our current state-of-the-art computers.

GUIDE TO INVESTMENT SOFTWARE 4

This Chapter is our latest guide to investment software, covering over 445 programs, including 98 new software listings and 4 which were classified as financial services last year. These descriptions are based on information provided by the software publishers and do *not* represent first-hand knowledge by *Computerized Investing* staff members. We have worked hard to get current information, but the market for investment software is in constant flux. There are frequent modifications to existing software and many price changes. These programs are often produced by small companies — they may not survive; those that do may decide that a new name is more indicative of their current products or may find new distribution channels. When a product name has changed, and/or a product is being distributed by a new vendor, we have indicated the former name and/or vendor. New software listings are identified with an asterisk after their names. We have recategorized some products which appeared in the financial information services chapter in previous editions. These are identified with a diamond following their names.

In compiling this Chapter we have concentrated on financial investment software, but a number of spreadsheet programs, as well as programs for tax planning, real estate analysis, statistical analysis and charting are included. Also included, as Chapter 6, are the product grids which list each software package alphabetically. It is designed to quickly give you the information necessary to determine what the software does and whether it will work on your computer system.

The product descriptions in this Chapter are listed alphabetically by publisher, as many companies publish several programs. Each software listing includes the name of the product, the types of securities the program handles, its function, systems, special software or hardware requirements, price, discounts (for AAII members), the vendors return policy, the availability of a demonstration version and its cost, if any, the technical support provided by the vendors and any cost for these services, and a brief description.

To get the most effective use of the *Guide* we suggest that you search through the grid in Chapter 6 to identify those products which meet your needs and will operate on your system. After you have a list of products, contact the software manufacturers directly, mentioning that you saw their product(s) listed here, to get their most recent information. Then compare those programs that seem to offer the features you need. Once you have screened the programs for those that provide the functions you need and that fit within your budget, try to see the software work. The manufacturer may offer a demo disk, or investors at the local AAII Chapter (listed in Appendix III) may be familiar with the program. You may also try contacting a BBS (listed in Appendix II) and leave a message. Such firsthand information will give you the best evaluation of how you can use the software. Compare the technical support offered by the competing vendors. The support times are Monday through Friday unless otherwise noted.

Finally, many software firms offer discounts to AAII members. These discounts typically apply to purchases direct from the software publisher and may not be available at retail stores. Those companies offering a member discount are so indicated in the product descriptions and grids. Prices do not include shipping and handling or sales tax where applicable. Before you purchase the product make sure that you understand the vendors return policy. Many vendors will not refund your money.

Abacus Software
5370 52nd Street S.E.
Grand Rapids, MI 49512

(800) 451-4319
(616) 698-0330
fax: (616) 698-0325

Product: PERSONAL PORTFOLIO MANAGER
Securities: Stock, Bond, Index, Mutual Fund, Option, Futures
Function(s): Communications, Portfolio Management
System(s): IBM
Special Requirements: None
Price: $150   **AAII Discount:** None
Return Policy: NA
Demo: Yes
Technical Support: Phone

Description: Keeps track of stocks, bonds, options, etc. Information updating can be done manually or automatically via the Dow Jones News/Retrieval or Warner on-line services. User can customize reports according to preferences and analysis requirements or use the ready-to-run reports for tracking gains/losses, tax liabilities, buy/sell alarms, year-to-date transactions and others.

ADS Associates, Inc.
23586 Calabasas Road
Suite 200
Calabasas, CA 91302

(800) 852-3888
(818) 347-9100
fax: (818) 347-5908

Product: GLOBAL TRADER (formerly Global Trader Calculator)
Securities: Bond
Function(s): Bond Analysis
System(s): IBM
Special Requirements: None
Price: $150   **AAII Discount:** 10%
Return Policy: 30 Days
Demo: Yes ($19.95)
Technical Support: Phone (7 a.m. - 6 p.m. PST)

Description: A software calculator for all fixed-income securities, domestic and foreign. Calculates yield to maturity, yield to call, average life, yield to average life, duration, accrued interest, principal amount, total cost/proceeds, next interest amount, simple margin and discount margin in a single key-stroke. Defaults to the standard conventions for over 60 security types. User can change variables such as pricing, interest day count, interest payment frequency, sinking fund schedule and face amount. Handles odd coupons. Has a yield pickup swap analysis function comparing the sale of one security and purchase of another displaying the variances of principal amount, yield, accrued interest, total proceeds/cost and annual income. Can save and recall over 200 swaps and individual security calculations.

Advanced Analysis, Inc. (313) 981-0681
6370 Pickwick Drive fax: (313) 981-4680
Canton, MI 48187

Product: PROSPER-II PLUS
Securities: Stock, Bond, Index, Mutual Fund, Option, Futures
Function(s): Communications, Portfolio Management, Security Screening, Technical Analysis
System(s): IBM
Special Requirements: MarketWatch, Radio Exchange, Signal or X*Press
Price: $395   **AAII Discount:** 20%
Return Policy: NA
Demo: Yes ($5)
Technical Support: $100/year, includes: Phone (9 a.m.- 5 p.m. EST)

Description: A technical analysis program for trading stocks, futures, options and indexes. User can analyze daily and weekly quote data for up to 4,620 issues. Has more than 40 indicators and tools for presenting signals of price reversals, trends, volume accumulation or distribution. Indicators include percentage movement of investment, spread, value, Bollinger Bands, commodity channel index, K%D, RSI, ROC, directional movement, stops, MACD, MAOSC, moving average, AAI Index, compare, group, volume, EquiVolume, on-balance volume, volume accumulation, Crocker's Method, Carpino's Method, etc. Tools include cycle finding, channel charting and bar chart zooming. Performs automatic search for stocks that meet user's criteria. Autosave updates quote data automatically without intervention. Other utility functions allow for efficient data management. Program performs on-line analysis with Radio Exchange or Signal; access to a variety of data services—MarketWatch, TeleScan, Dow Jones News/Retrieval, MetaStock Data Files and all other ASCII files.

Product: PROSPER-II POWERONLINE (formerly Prosper-II OnLine)
Securities: Stock, Bond, Index, Mutual Fund, Option, Futures
Function(s): Communications, Technical Analysis
System(s): IBM
Special Requirements: Hard drive, 80286 or higher processor, Radio Exchange or Signal
Price: $495   **AAII Discount:** 20%
Return Policy: NA
Demo: Yes ($5)
Technical Support: $100/year, includes: Phone (9 a.m. - 5 p.m. EST)

Description: An on-line intra-day technical analysis program that works with Radio Exchange or Signal analyzing quote data at cycles less than 20 seconds. Designed to deal with the volatility of the market. Program helps identify the market reversal points. Analyzes up to 30 tickers for 3 day's data for futures, indexes, options and stocks. Program has 3 modes: Quote Listing Mode lists quotes as they are gathered. Value Mode lists value of holdings as a function of the latest quote. Analysis Mode presents the instantaneous analysis results for various indicators including price, volume, RSI, K%D, m-K%D, MACD, price channels, percentage of movement, spread between any 2 tickers, etc. Using these market indicators, price reversal points are identified.

Advanced Financial Planning   (714) 855-1578
20922 Paseo Olma
El Toro, CA 92630

Product: PLAN AHEAD
Securities: Not Applicable
Function(s): Financial Planning
System(s): IBM
Special Requirements: None
Price: One module, $29.95;   **AAII Discount:** 15%
    two modules, $49.94;
    three modules, $59.95
Return Policy: NA
Demo: Yes
Technical Support: None

Description: Three-module package includes retirement planning, life insurance planning and college funding. Modules share a common database, are menu-driven and offer inflation adjustment capabilities. Specific features include budget and net worth statements and plans for each of the module topics.

Advanced Investment Software (303) 750-5535
7535 E. Hampden Avenue fax: (303) 750-8801
Suite 101
Denver, CO 80231

Product: RAMCAP—THE INTELLIGENT ASSET ALLOCATOR
Securities: Stock, Bond, Index, Mutual Fund, Futures, Real Estate
Function(s): Financial Planning, Portfolio Management
System(s): IBM
Special Requirements: DOS 3.0+, graphics card
Price: $595, program; $234/year for updates   **AAII Discount:** 17%
Return Policy: NA
Demo: Yes ($30)
Technical Support: Phone (8:30 a.m. - 5 p.m. MST), Newsletter

Description: An optimizing tool that finds the best mix of asset classes for an investment portfolio. Considers 59 asset classes in its optimization routine including real estate, leasing and foreign stocks and bonds. The optimizing routine is set by the user. Pull-down menus help minimize training time. Finds the portfolio mix with the least amount of risk at any level of expected return or the best returns available at any level of risk using the asset classes selected by the user. Uses historical data for risk, return and co-variance that provides the basis for building optimal portfolios. Includes graphics.

Advanced Investment Systems (800) 942-9555
7031 E. Camelback Road (602) 483-9095
Suite 569 fax: (602) 943-4259
Scottsdale, AZ 85251

Product: AIS MARKET ANALYST (formerly T-Bill Analyst ETC)
Securities: Futures
Function(s): Communications, Technical Analysis
System(s): IBM
Special Requirements: Modem for data downloading

Price: $1,395   **AAII Discount:** 35%
Return Policy: NA
Demo: Yes
Technical Support: $200/year, includes: Phone (off-hours), Newsletter

Description: System works with the Technical Tools database to develop buy, sell and hold recommendations for approximately 37 markets. Program downloads the day's data, calculates positions for the next opening and presents charts and statistics for all the markets. Can be customized to follow only some of the markets and do back-testing of past recommendations. Can be used as a stand-alone trade generator or as an adjunct to existing trade strategies.

Advent Software, Inc.   (800) 678-7005
512 Second Street   (415) 543-7696
San Francisco, CA 94107   fax: (415) 543-5070

Product: PROFESSIONAL PORTFOLIO
Securities: Stock, Bond, Index, Mutual Fund, Option, Futures, Real Estate
Function(s): Communications, Financial Planning, Portfolio Management
System(s): IBM
Special Requirements: Modem for data downloading
Price: Varies with size of instal-   **AAII Discount:** None
lation, $2,700+, call vendor
Return Policy: 60 Days
Demo: Yes
Technical Support: Varies, $500+/year, includes: Phone (6 a.m. - 5 p.m. PST), Newsletter

Description: Menu-driven portfolio package tracks all trades, splits, interest, dividends and gains and losses. Stocks, bonds, options, mutual funds, CDs, cash and equivalents, convertible securities and Treasury bills are tracked. User defines asset classes, security types and industry groups. User can enter transactions through each individual transaction file or through the Trade Blotter which simplifies block trading and reinvestment of dividends for mutual fund investors. Additional features include networking and a link to the Depository Trust Company.

AIQ Systems, Inc.
916 Southwood Boulevard
Suite 2C, P.O. Drawer 7530
Incline Village, NV 89450

(800) 332-2999
(702) 831-2999
fax: (702) 831-6784

Product: INDEXEXPERT
Securities: Index, Option
Function(s): Communications, Options Analysis, Portfolio Management, Security Screening, Simulations/Games, Technical Analysis
System(s): IBM
Special Requirements: DOS 3.0+, hard drive, 640K RAM; modem for downloading
Price: $1,588   **AAII Discount:** Occasional special discounts
Return Policy: NA
Demo: Yes ($44)
Technical Support: 90 days free, annual support fee varies, includes: Phone (7:30 a.m. - 4 p.m. PST), Newsletter

Description: Helps buy, sell and write stock-based index options. Inference procedure combines AIQ's Market Timing system with a Black-Scholes analytical model. Outcome is an Expert Rating on market direction and a specific option strategy generated by the option analysis section. Graphically displays 24 different technical indicators, many adjustable. Built-in communication interface allows downloading of daily pricing data from DIAL/DATA Services.

Product: MARKETEXPERT
Securities: Index, Mutual Fund, Option, Futures
Function(s): Communications, Security Screening, Technical Analysis
System(s): IBM
Special Requirements: DOS 3.0+, hard drive, 640K RAM; modem for downloading
Price: $488   **AAII Discount:** Occasional special discounts
Return Policy: 45 Days, Restocking Fee: None
Demo: Yes ($44)
Technical Support: See IndexExpert

Description: Helps determine direction stock market will move. Combines 17 pieces of daily market data and 32 technical analysis indicators to form a fact base. Inference procedure then combines fact base with a rule base (85 decision rules derived by technical analysis experts) to an expert rating which tells the user when and in which direction the stock market will move in the short- to intermediate-term. Program graphically displays the pricing activity of the DJIA, NYSE and the SPX; 24 technical indicators display a comprehensive technical study of the market. Built-in communication interface to update from DIAL/DATA Services.

Product: OPTIONEXPERT
Securities: Stock, Option
Function(s): Communications, Options Analysis, Portfolio Management, Security Screening, Simulations/Games, Technical Analysis
System(s): IBM
Special Requirements: DOS 3.0+, hard drive, 640K RAM; modem for data downloading
Price: $1,588   **AAII Discount:** Occasional special discounts
Return Policy: NA
Demo: Yes ($44)
Technical Support: See IndexExpert

Description: Uses artificial intelligence to interpret technical indicators to generate optimum short-term buy and sell signals. An indicated value (forecast) is then calculated. Black-Scholes analytics and strategy selection models are applied to equity options suggesting which strategy, position and number of contracts to buy or sell. Profit manager provides mechanical stop levels for closing positions based on defined risk tolerance level. The knowledge base allows user to see why the buy or sell was developed; 24 technical indicators are graphically displayed and may be adjusted for detailed analysis. Communications built-in for automatic data retrieval from DIAL/DATA.

Product: STOCKEXPERT
Securities: Stock
Function(s): Communications, Portfolio Management, Security Screening, Simulations/Games, Technical Analysis
System(s): IBM
Special Requirements: DOS 3.0+, hard drive, 640K RAM; modem for data downloading
Price: $988   **AAII Discount:** Occasional special discounts

Return Policy: NA
Demo: Yes ($44)
Technical Support: See IndexExpert

Description: Uses dozens of technical indicators and computes an expert rating for every stock in its database, then prints reports listing those stocks with the day's highest expert ratings both upside and downside. Next, Profit Manager can protect both principal and profits by setting personal stop-loss parameters. Stock Plots displays a 7-month period of market action for every stock allowing a graphic study of price, performance and the concurrent behavior of technical indicators. Prints price activity and technical indicators for up to 1 year. Expert rating can be displayed for any stock on any market date allowing "what if" simulations.

American River Software (916) 483-1600
1523 Kingsford Drive
Carmichael, CA 95608

Product: MUTUAL FUND INVESTOR
Securities: Stock, Bond, Index, Mutual Fund, Real Estate
Function(s): Communications, Financial Planning, Portfolio Management, Security Screening, Tax Planning, Technical Analysis
System(s): IBM
Special Requirements: Modem for data downloading
Price: $69.95   **AAII Discount:** None
Return Policy: NA
Demo: Yes ($10)
Technical Support: Phone (8:30 a.m. - 5 p.m. PST)

Description: Enables close performance monitoring of up to 104 funds and other securities as well as complete client portfolio tracking. Several thousand client portfolios may be tracked (32,000 transactions per client) with reporting of current portfolio value, share balance, internal rate of return, FIFO and average cost basis, profit/loss reports, as well as cross referencing of open accounts to portfolios. Reports may be generated for one or any "family" of portfolios. Program charts daily and weekly adjusted prices over time, displays moving averages and relative strength and computes total return performance, volatility, momentum and buy/sell signals. Allows comparisons between buy and hold versus switching strategies. Graphs and reports can be printed on laser or dot matrix printers and may be exported to other graphics programs. Data may be entered manually or automatically via a modem from CompuServe or Investment Company Data. Example portfolios and free data are supplied for 30 funds and indexes. Program performs sorting and screening criteria on over 2,000 mutual funds on a data disk updated monthly from Investment Company Data.

Analytic Associates (213) 541-0418
4817 Browndeer Lane
Rolling Hills Estates, CA 90274

Product: PLANEASE
Securities: Real Estate
Function(s): Real Estate Analysis
System(s): IBM
Special Requirements: None
Price: $595; $995 with Partnership Models   **AAII Discount:** None
Return Policy: 30 Days, Restocking Fee: None
Demo: Yes ($50)
Technical Support: $95/year, includes: Updates, Phone (9 a.m.- 5 p.m. PST), Newsletter

Description: Performs financial analysis and cash flow projections for income-producing property. Handles calendaring for user-specified holding periods and provides internal rate of return, net present value, financial management rate of return and sensitivity and Monte Carlo risk analysis. Reflects the 1986 Tax Reform Act.

Product: PLANEASE PARTNERSHIP MODELS
Securities: Real Estate
Function(s): Real Estate Analysis
System(s): IBM
Special Requirements: None
Price: $495   **AAII Discount:** None
Return Policy: 30 Days, Restocking Fee: None
Demo: Yes ($50)
Technical Support: $95/year, includes: Updates, Phone (9 a.m. - 5 p.m. PST), Newsletter

Description: An addition to PlanEASe. Converts any property projection into a limited partnership forecast with final reports and graphs. Handles partnership fees, separate tax and cash benefits, preferred return and staged investments. Reflects the 1986 Tax Reform Act.

Analytical Service Associates (617) 593-2404
21 Hollis Road
Lynn, MA 01904

Product: BOND MANAGER
Securities: Bond
Function(s): Bond Analysis, Portfolio Management
System(s): IBM
Special Requirements: 5.25" disk drive
Price: $79.95   **AAII Discount:** None
Return Policy: NA
Demo: No
Technical Support: None

Description: Provides 8 bond management programs on a single disk including convertible bond analysis, bond yield-to-maturity, price, return, internal rate of return over time and create and update a portfolio. Taxes are considered with provisions to prevent obsolescence.

Product: CONVERTIBLE BOND ANALYST
Securities: Bond
Function(s): Bond Analysis
System(s): IBM
Special Requirements: 5.25" disk drive
Price: $99.95   **AAII Discount:** None
Return Policy: NA
Demo: No
Technical Support: None

Description: Created to find undervalued convertibles. Evaluates convertible bonds, calculating the premium over investment value in points and percent, conversion parity price, premium over conversion in percent, current yield, payback in years, break-even time in years and yield-to-maturity.

Product: STOCK MANAGER
Securities: Stock, Option
Function(s): Financial Planning, Portfolio Management, Tax Planning
System(s): IBM
Special Requirements: 5.25" disk drive
Price: $79.95   **AAII Discount:** None
Return Policy: NA
Demo: No
Technical Support: None

Description: Consists of 9 programs: stock evaluation model, dual graphics, graphics, selling price of stock, stock and option data, make and update a portfolio, internal rate of return, compound interest and annuity and tax percentages. Taxes are considered; provision is made to change the holding period as well as long- and short-term rates to prevent obsolescence.

Applied Decision Systems   (617) 861-7580
99 Hayden Avenue   fax: (617) 861-8294
Lexington, MA 02173

Product: MULTBJ MULTIVARIABLE BOX-JENKINS
Securities: Stock, Bond, Index, Mutual Fund, Option, Futures, Real Estate
Function(s): Financial Planning, Statistical Analysis
System(s): IBM
Special Requirements: None
Price: $250   **AAII Discount:** 15%
Return Policy: NA
Demo: No
Technical Support: None

Description: Has cross-autocorrelation computations and graphics between the whitened dependent variable and each of the whitened independent variables. Aids in identifying type of terms in the MARMA model. MARMA model forecasts (with 95% confidence bounds) are produced for the dependent variables based on the past values or ARMA model forecasts of each of the independent variables. User can supply estimates of one or all of the independent variables, which can override program-generated estimates. New dependent-variable forecasts are computed and printed.

Product: SIBYL/RUNNER INTERACTIVE FORECASTING
Securities: Stock, Bond, Index, Mutual Fund, Option, Futures, Real Estate
Function(s): Financial Planning, Statistical Analysis
System(s): IBM
Special Requirements: None
Price: $495   **AAII Discount:** 15%
Return Policy: NA
Demo: Yes
Technical Support: None

Description: SIBYL advises methods suitable for user's data, selecting from 18 recognized time-series methods. RUNNER summarizes statistics for each selection. Complete statistics: 10 aggregate error measures displayed, actual/forecast graphics ex-post and ex-ante forecast statistics. Sends forecasts to Lotus software for spreadsheet and graphics; reads data from dBase files, Lotus 1-2-3 or Symphony; links to PC/dBase for large forecasting tasks.

Arms Equivolume Corp.   (800) 223-2767
1650 University Boulevard   (505) 247-8118
Suite 300
Albuquerque, NM 87102

Product: EQUIVOLUME CHARTING SOFTWARE
Securities: Stock, Bond, Index, Mutual Fund, Option, Futures
Function(s): Communications, Technical Analysis, Screening
System(s): IBM
Special Requirements: Modem for data downloading
Price: $365-$565   **AAII Discount:** None
Return Policy: NA
Demo: Yes ($15)
Technical Support: None

Description: Consists of 2 parts: charting and search methods. The charting routine draws Equivolume charts on the computer screen or printer, allowing user to vary the time frames and moving averages. Entering the stock symbol delivers a complex chart in accordance with predefined variables. Each routine may be conducted using pre-established parameters; or, the user may vary the parameters, to search for different time frames or volume requirements which suit individual needs. Each search produces a series of chart displays for those stocks which qualify.

Asset Backed Securities Group   (800) 322-0047
477 Madison Avenue   (212) 754-1010
18th Floor   fax: (212) 832-6738
New York, NY 10022

Product: POOL*
Securities: Bond
Function(s): Bond Analysis, Communications, Financial Planning, Fundamental Analysis, Portfolio Management, Security Screening
System(s): IBM
Special Requirements: 2,400+ baud modem, 80286+ processor
Price: $150/month license fee, variable   **AAII Discount:** None
usage charges based upon activity
Return Policy: 30 Days, Restocking Fee: None
Demo: Yes
Technical Support: Phone (8 a.m. - 6 p.m. EST), Newsletter

Description: An analytical system which provides access to mortgage backed, collateralized mortgage, asset backed and market related fixed income securities. User can view current and historical disclosure data, factors, market prices and cash flow valuations on all MBS pools, CMO/REMIC Tranches and ABS deals; Analyze price/yield, prepayment scenarios, cash flows, geographic distribution, quartile data and transaction settlement; report principal and interest calculations and market valuations for custom portfolio on the screen or printed; download disclosure data, factors and market prices. Includes disclosure data direct from U.S. Government and government sponsored agencies, private agencies and security underwriters. Provides information on: GNMA I, GNMA II, FHLMC, FNMA, CMO/REMIC and ABS, SBA, CNMA (Canadian) and U.S. Treasury fixed income instruments.

A-T Financial Information, Inc.   (312) 939-5594
327 S. LaSalle Street   fax: (312) 939-3265
Suite 1232
Chicago, IL 60604

Product: OPENING BELL*
Securities: Stock, Bond, Index, Mutual Fund, Option, Futures
Function(s): Communications, Financial Planning, Options Analysis, Portfolio Management, Security Screening, Spreadsheet, Technical Analysis
System(s): IBM
Special Requirements: DOS 5.0+, Windows 3.0, communications processor board for stand-alone application, S&P ComStock
Price: $400/unit installation charge, monthly data and software license fee: $400 1st unit, $325 2nd unit, $250 3rd unit, $200/additional unit   **AAII Discount:** None
Return Policy: NA
Demo: None
Technical Support: Phone (9 a.m. - 5 p.m. CST)

Description: Provides real-time market data access to quotes, analysis and news on a wide range of financial instruments. Offers securities monitoring capabilities—multiples pages with up to 540 instruments per page, 5 presentation formats, various sorting methods, color trend indicator, page-specific tickers and baskets, audible and visual limit alerts; option analytics; charting, including moving average envelope, RSI and oscillator studies with user-defined parameters and a 1-year database on NYSE, AMEX and NASDAQ NMS stocks and on U.S. futures and indexes; fundamental data; news—Dow Jones scrolling headlines, news and news retrieval with keyword search and news alert capabilities; symbol guide; a 5-day, real-time and sales feature covering all U.S. and European equities and U.S. futures and indexes; programmable screen formats and hot keys.

Atlantic Systems, Inc.   (212) 757-6600
45 Rockefeller Center   fax: (212) 765-6788
Suite 520
New York, NY 10111

Product: VALUATION RESEARCH STATION
Securities: Stock, Index
Function(s): Communications, Fundamental Analysis, Security Screening, Spreadsheet, Technical Analysis
System(s): IBM
Special Requirements: Javelin Plus, modem

Price: $12,000　　　　　　　　　　　　　　AAII Discount: 15%
Return Policy: NA
Demo: Yes
Technical Support: NA

Description: Links on-line sources of U.S. and Japanese financial data (e.g., Compustat, Nikkei and I/B/E/S) with fundamental research and classic discounted cash flow valuation analytics. Allows analysts with limited PC skills to make full use of advanced financial modeling tools. Data can be downloaded from several on-line or CD-ROM distributors (e.g., Warner Computer, Nikkei Telecom, IDD's Tradeline Plus, Compustat's PC Plus and Salomon's StockFacts). Has 4 components: On-Line Cash Flow Forecaster (OCFF), On-Line Ratios, On-Line Financials and On-Line Stocks, which offer traditional financial statement, ratio and stock chart analysis tools. By combining reports and charts, user can dissect the financial and market performance of any public company. User can compare the complete financial histories and forecast cash flows of dozens of companies simultaneously and to customize the valuation formulas to fit internal methodology or to meet needs of a particular project.

AVCO Financial Corp.　　　　　　　　　　(203) 661-7381
8 Grigg Street　　　　　　　　　　　　　fax: (203) 869-0253
Suite 3
Greenwich, CT 06830

Product: RECURRENCE: REAL-TIME CURRENCY TRADER*
Securities: Bond, Index, Futures
Function(s): Technical Analysis
System(s): IBM
Special Requirements: Real-time quotes and charting package
Price: $3,000　　　　　　　　　　　　　　AAII Discount: None
Return Policy: NA
Demo: No
Technical Support: Phone (8 a.m. - 5 p.m. EST)

Description: Includes 12 recurrence patterns: recurrence and reverse recurrence, T.G.T.B.T., 60% hook, A.D.F., OscD., A.D.P., S.A.V.E., scalp, 8:30 big report, 90-minute breakout, market-on-open. Menu-driven and written in high-speed assembly format (cuts calculation time down to less than 5 seconds per market). Calculates buy, sell, stop points in advance of the market.

Berge Software (formerly Palmer Berge Co.)   (800) 426-2135
1200 Westlake Avenue N.   (206) 284-7610
Suite 612   fax: (206) 286-3554
Seattle, WA 98109

Product: ACQUISITION & DISPOSITION ANALYSIS
Securities: Real Estate
Function(s): Real Estate Analysis
System(s): IBM
Special Requirements: None
Price: $195   **AAII Discount:** 10%
Return Policy: 30 Days, Restocking Fee: $50
Demo: No
Technical Support: Phone (8 a.m. - 4 p.m. PST), Newsletter

Description: Comprised of several programs: Exchange Recap; Installment Sale/Alternative Offers; IRR; FMRR and NPV Analysis, and Alternative Investments/FMRR Analysis. Addresses various methods of acquiring and disposing of real properties, including tax-deferred exchange and installment sale; computes yield on cash flows and compares alternative series of cash flows.

Product: COMMERCIAL FINANCE
Securities: Real Estate
Function(s): Real Estate Analysis
System(s): IBM
Special Requirements: None
Price: $95   **AAII Discount:** 10%
Return Policy: 30 Days, Restocking Fee: $50
Demo: No
Technical Support: Phone (8 a.m. - 4 p.m. PST), Newsletter

Description: Programs address the financing of commercial real estate. The 6 programs are: Wraparound Financing, Variable Payment Financing, Accrued Interest Financing, Participation Financing, Constant Principal Financing and Amortized Loan.

Product: INVESTMENT ANALYSIS
Securities: Real Estate
Function(s): Real Estate Analysis
System(s): IBM
Special Requirements: None
Price: $295　　　　　　　　　　　**AAII Discount:** 10%
Return Policy: 30 Days, Restocking Fee: $50
Demo: No
Technical Support: Phone (8 a.m. - 4 p.m. PST), Newsletter

Description: Includes 2 programs. Income/Expense Analysis is designed to analyze the income, vacancy and credit loss and expenses attributable to the operations of an income-producing property. Cash Flow Analysis analyzes the acquisition, holding and eventual disposition of an income-producing property.

Product: LAND & LEASE ANALYSIS
Securities: Real Estate
Function(s): Real Estate Analysis
System(s): IBM
Special Requirements: None
Price: $195　　　　　　　　　　　**AAII Discount:** 10%
Return Policy: 30 Days, Restocking Fee: $50
Demo: No
Technical Support: Phone (8 a.m. - 4 p.m. PST), Newsletter

Description: Includes 4 programs: Raw Land Analysis analyzes the acquisition, holding and eventual disposition of an unimproved property; Sub-Lease Analysis provides a method by which a leasehold interest may be determined via the differential and discounted cash flow methods; Lease/Own Analysis offers 2 methods of comparing, owning and leasing a property—present value (net cost) and differential cash flow; IRR, FMRR and NPV performs different types of discounted cash flow analysis.

Product: PROPERTY INCOME ANALYSIS
Securities: Real Estate
Function(s): Real Estate Analysis
System(s): IBM

Special Requirements: None
Price: $195   **AAII Discount:** 10%
Return Policy: 30 Days, Restocking Fee: $50
Demo: No
Technical Support: Phone (8 a.m. - 4 p.m. PST), Newsletter

Description: Includes 2 programs: Base Period Income/Expense Analysis computes vacancy and credit loss, effective rental income, gross operation income, total operating expenses, and net operating income for a base period; Multi-Period Income/Expense Analysis performs detailed analysis of lease income and operating expenses. Enter data on any number of leases including percentage rent and expense passthrough information including any number of expense items. The program allows analysis on an annual or monthly basis.

Product: RESIDENTIAL FINANCE
Securities: Real Estate
Function(s): Real Estate Analysis
System(s): IBM
Special Requirements: None
Price: $95   **AAII Discount:** 10%
Return Policy: 30 Days, Restocking Fee: $50
Demo: No
Technical Support: Phone (8 a.m. - 4 p.m. PST), Newsletter

Description: A creative financing program. The package includes 6 programs: Wraparound (Blended Rate) Financing, Graduated Payment Mortgage, Pledged Account Mortgage, Growing Equity Mortgage, Adjustable Rate Mortgage and Amortized Loan.

Black River Systems Corp.   (800) 841-5398
4680 Brownsboro Road   (919) 759-0600
Building C   fax: (919) 759-0632
Winston-Salem, NC 27106

Product: MACRO*WORLD INVESTOR
Securities: Stock, Bond, Index, Mutual Fund, Futures
Function(s): Fundamental Analysis, Portfolio Management, Security Screening, Simulations/Games, Technical Analysis
System(s): IBM

Special Requirements: None
Price: $899.95   **AAII Discount:** 22.2%
Return Policy: 30 Days, Restocking Fee: None
Demo: No
Technical Support: $399.95/year, includes: Monthly Data Updates, Phone (9 a.m. - 5 p.m. EST)

Description: Forecasting and investment analysis provides projected rates of return, degree of risk, buy/hold/sell signals for user-specified portfolios, optimal risk/return mix for buy recommendations, simulations of past results, forecasts of fundamental performance (earnings, book value, dividends, economic values and ratios) and the best leading indicators. Features summary reports covering short-term outlook, turning points and exceptions; forecast ranges, confidence levels and recession periods; and custom portfolio optimizations. Equipped with 5-10 years of stock price data on the 100 highest ROE companies on the NYSE with 10-25 years of data for over 120 U.S. and international business and financial indicators including Canada, Japan, Germany and the U.K. Exchanges history and forecasts with other systems to allow users to include additional data. Monthly update service provides new data, historical revisions, bulletins and telephone support.

Blue Chip Software   (800) 572-2272
c/o Britannica Software   (415) 597-5555
345 Fourth Street   fax: (415) 546-1887
San Francisco, CA 94107

Product: AMERICAN INVESTOR
Securities: Stock
Function(s): Simulations/Games
System(s): IBM
Special Requirements: None
Price: $149.95   **AAII Discount:** None
Return Policy: NA
Demo: No
Technical Support: None

Description: An investment simulation of the American Stock Exchange. Developed jointly with the AMEX, the program teaches a professional approach to portfolio management, fundamental research, technical analysis and trading strategies. Using actual historical data from 48 companies listed on the AMEX and the AMEX's Major Market Index option, the user can simulate trading options and equities over a 9-month period.

Product: MANAGING FOR SUCCESS
Securities: Not Applicable
Function(s): Simulations/Games
System(s): IBM
Special Requirements: None
Price: $49.95 **AAII Discount:** None
Return Policy: NA
Demo: No
Technical Support: None

Description: A business management simulation that allows user to be the CEO of a major corporation with 8 different departments: finance, research and development, engineering, materials control, manufacturing, production, quality control and marketing. The challenge is to keep the company running at a profit. Monthly financial statements, sales reports and departmental memos are used to make decisions. Mimicking real corporate life, many of these reports and memos come in simultaneously further complicating the decision-making process. Built-in editor allows user to customize the program to take on the characteristics of a particular business.

Product: MILLIONAIRE
Securities: Stock
Function(s): Simulations/Games
System(s): Commodore, Macintosh
Special Requirements: None
Price: Commodore, $29.95; Macintosh, $49.95 **AAII Discount:** None
Return Policy: NA
Demo: No
Technical Support: None

Description: A stock market simulation in which user starts out with $10,000 and tries to work up to $1 million. In 77 simulated weeks, user trades stocks from blue chip companies such as IBM, GM and others.

Similar to real life, stock prices are affected by market conditions and world events. User learns about puts, calls, margins and net worth.

Product: MILLIONAIRE II
Securities: Stock
Function(s): Simulations/Games
System(s): Apple II, IBM, Macintosh
Special Requirements: None
Price: Apple II, $39.95; **AAII Discount:** None
  IBM PC, Macintosh $49.95
Return Policy: NA
Demo: No
Technical Support: None

Description: An updated version of Millionaire. User starts with $10,000 and tries to make $1 million. Decisions are based on weekly news events, price fluctuations and market trends. As more money is earned, status rises from novice to investor, speculator, professional and, finally, broker. The farther the advance, the more options available: buying on margin, using puts and calls and borrowing from the bank. There are 90 weeks of play, new company information, more graphing, color, pull down menus, and a 2-player option. User can change interest rates and commissions, calculate interest on cash and sell short. Built-in program generator guarantees the same game will never be played twice. Unfinished games can be saved.

BNA Software (800) 424-2938
1231 25th Street, N.W.
Suite 3-200
Washington, DC 20037

Product: BNA ESTATE TAX SPREADSHEET
Securities: Not Applicable
Function(s): Financial Planning, Tax Planning
System(s): IBM
Special Requirements: None
Price: $1,295 **AAII Discount:** None
Return Policy: NA
Demo: Yes (NC)
Technical Support: Phone (9 a.m. - 5 p.m. EST)

Description: An estate planning system allowing users to manipulate data to determine the effect different "what if" scenarios will have on the net value of an estate. Simultaneously calculates 3 family estate plans or 6 plans for a single decedent. Computes federal estate taxes and state death taxes for all 50 states and D.C. Performs interrelated residue calculations to evaluate both marital and charitable deduction options. Custom worksheets can be created to itemize individual estate assets, expense details, etc. Future value computations are available on every data entry row giving functional and tax information. Program generates an estate tax summary with supporting worksheets.

Product: BNA FIXED ASSET MANAGEMENT SYSTEM
Securities: Bonds
Function(s): Bond Analysis, Financial Planning, Tax Planning
System(s): IBM
Special Requirements: None
Price: $995　　　　　　　　　　　　　　**AAII Discount:** None
Return Policy: NA
Demo: Yes
Technical Support: Phone (9 a.m. - 5 p.m. EST)

Description: A stand-alone package used to maintain information about fixed assets, compute depreciation and generate reports. Calculates federal, state and book depreciation for up to 20,000 assets for a given reporting period or tax year. Offers 32 standard methods of depreciation including straight line, declining balance, ACRS, MACRS and a manual override. Automatically calculates AMT, ACE and earnings and profits depreciation; determines and applies mid-quarter convention; applies Sec. 179 company limitations. User chooses from 40 predefined reports providing summary, tax and asset management information. Customized reports can be created. Program reflects the AMT accelerated depreciation options outlined in the Technical and Miscellaneous Revenue Act of 1988.

Product: BNA INCOME TAX SPREADSHEET WITH FIFTY STATE
　　　　　　PLANNER
Securities: Not Applicable
Function(s): Financial Planning, Tax Planning
System(s): IBM

Special Requirements: None
Price: $890; Federal only $495   **AAII Discount:** None
Return Policy: NA
Demo: Yes
Technical Support: Phone (9 a.m. - 5 p.m. EST)

Description: A stand-alone individual tax planning program that computes federal and state income taxes for all 50 states, NYC and D.C. for any period between 1984 and 1999. All calculations, schedules, phase-ins and limitations of the Tax Reform Act of 1986, the Revenue Act of 1987 and the Technical and Miscellaneous Revenue Act of 1988 are built in. Simultaneously calculates 7 side-by-side cases for any tax year or projects taxes over 7 years. Can check tax returns, calculate estimated tax payments and file extensions. Automatic calculation of Alternative Minimum Tax, individual passive activity worksheets with automatic calculation of limitations and carryovers and calculation of investment interest expense. Worksheets can be created to list such items as interest, dividends and deductions. Help is on every data entry row, giving functional and tax information.

Product: BNA REAL ESTATE INVESTMENT SPREADSHEET
Securities: Real Estate
Function(s): Financial Planning, Real Estate Analysis, Tax Planning
System(s): IBM
Special Requirements: None
Price: $595   **AAII Discount:** None
Return Policy: NA
Demo: Yes
Technical Support: Phone (9 a.m. - 5 p.m. EST)

Description: Enables users to analyze new and existing real estate investments. Shows tax and cash flow consequences of financing, purchasing, holding and selling assets held for investment. Projects cash flow for up to 40 years, both before and after taxes. As many as 10 assets, 10 loans, 10 other passive activities and 225 income and expense items can be included in a single analysis. Custom worksheets can be created to list additional income or expense items. Projection includes calculation of IRR, MIRR, NPV, cumulative cash and cash-on-cash return. Utilizes operating data, depreciation and amortization schedules, and sale data to produce 16 detailed summary reports.

Federal and state marginal tax rates can be entered for each year to calculate regular, capital gains and the alternative minimum tax on the investment.

Bond-Tech, Inc. (513) 836-3991
P.O. Box 192 fax: (513) 836-3991
Englewood, OH 45322

Product: FISTS
Securities: Bond, Option, Futures
Function(s): Bond Analysis, Options Analysis, Portfolio Management
System(s): IBM
Special Requirements: None
Price: $1,250 **AAII Discount:** 10%
Return Policy: NA
Demo: No
Technical Support: Phone (9 a.m. - 5 p.m. EST)

Description: Oriented to all fixed income security markets. Combines analytical power with a database management system capable of storing an unlimited number of securities and producing reports to assist user. Features a range of computations, including the calculation of odd first coupon security yields using both the Securities Industry Association and U.S. Treasury methods, the batch processing mode which permits several reports to be generated while the computer is unattended, and the incorporation of financial futures and options with the traditional fixed income securities markets. Includes both Black-Scholes and Cox-Ross-Rubinstein option valuation methods. Includes the capability to perform bond swap analysis and comparative breakeven analysis.

Bristol Financial Services, Inc. (203) 834-0040
15 River Road fax: (203) 762-0525
Suite 251
Wilton, CT 06897

Product: INSIGHT
Securities: Stock, Index, Mutual Fund, Option, Futures
Function(s): Options Analysis, Portfolio Management, Security Screening, Technical Analysis
System(s): IBM

Special Requirements: DOS 5.0, 4 MB RAM, Signal or ComStock
Price: $150/month; permanent license, $2,500 **AAII Discount:** 10%
Return Policy: 30 Days, Restocking Fee: None
Demo: Yes
Technical Support: Based on hourly use, Phone (9 a.m. - 5 p.m. EST)

Description: Continually organizes Signal or ComStock data into real-time lists of trading ideas that can be reviewed through charting, statistical pages and real-time ticker filters. User can view trading lists as customized screens or send to printer. The trading ideas (symbols) list can then be scrolled and reviewed one at a time in both daily and interval bar, point and figure or Market Profile chart formats. Features include Hot-Key menu commands, compound and cloned symbols, real-time alert screening and printed reports, sorted and ranked by the trader using over 90 technical parameters per symbol.

Business Forecast Systems (617) 484-5050
68 Leonard Street fax: (617) 484-9219
Belmont, MA 02178

Product: FORECAST PRO
Securities: Communications, Spreadsheet, Statistical Analysis
System(s): IBM
Special Requirements: None
Price: $495 **AAII Discount:** None
Return Policy: 30 Days, Restocking Fee: None
Demo: Yes
Technical Support: Phone (9 a.m. - 5 p.m. EST), BBS

Description: A stand-alone forecasting system for the business person. Uses artificial intelligence and methodology for forecasting accuracy. Contains methods found most effective for business data (Exponential Smoothing Models, Box-Jenkins and Dynamic Regression). A built-in expert system analyzes user's data and recommends the appropriate technique. Provides automatic fitting routines and guidance making the need for a background in statistics unnecessary.

BV Engineering (714) 781-0252
2023 Chicago Avenue
Suite B13
Riverside, CA 92507

Product: GRAFMAKER (formerly PCPlot and PDP)
Securities: Stock, Bond, Index, Option, Futures
Function(s): Technical Analysis
System(s): IBM
Special Requirements: Graphics card
Price: $195   **AAII Discount:** None
Return Policy: 30 Days (if unopened), Restocking Fee: $10
Demo: No
Technical Support: Phone (8 a.m. - 5 p.m. PST)

Description: PCPlot and PDP combined in a stand-alone, high-resolution graphics program makes multicolor screen, printer and pen plotter graphs. For CGA, EGA, VGA and Hercules mono graphics, 34 pen plotters, 9- and 24-pin Epson dot matrix and HP LaserJet compatible printers. Graphics language output files such as HPGL, DM/PL and many others are supported. Creates line graphs, polar plots, graphs with error bars, bar charts, stacked bar charts and stock market type charts with no limit to the number of data points or data files plotted.

Product: TEKCALC
Securities: Stock, Bond, Index, Mutual Fund, Option, Futures
Function(s): Statistical Analysis, Technical Analysis
System(s): IBM
Special Requirements: None
Price: $150   **AAII Discount:** None
Return Policy: NA
Demo: No
Technical Support: Phone (8 a.m. - 5 p.m. PST)

Description: Programmable scientific calculator solves real, complex mathematical problems. Has built-in graphics, statistics, user extendible functions, a data table window, 11 different types of curve fittings and compatibility with other BVE software. Solve trigonometric, logarithmic, exponential, hyperbolic, complex, special and user-definable functions. Save formulas, computations and data on disk to create a customized math environment. Plot mathematical functions, data files and data tables on the screen in bit-mapped or character graphics with full labeling. Plots may be dumped to any graphics printer that currently supports graphics screen dump. Make linear regression and standard deviation calculations using simple keyboard commands. Has 30 user-defined functions with up to 6 variables and unlimited nesting or arithmetic expressions.

Byte Research & Trading   (800) 367-4670
7 Pierson Street   (516) 724-7299
Nesconset, NY 11707

Product: IT'S ALIVE*
Securities: Stock, Bond, Index, Mutual Fund, Option, Futures
Function(s): Communications, Technical Analysis
System(s): IBM
Special Requirements: 640K RAM, Signal
Price: $195   **AAII Discount:** 10%
Return Policy: 7 Days, Restocking Fee: Shipping
Demo: No
Technical Support: Phone (11 a.m. - 6 p.m. EST)

Description: Allows use of existing, daily-based charting software for real-time, on-line, intra-day charting and technical analysis. Captures data coming from Signal receiver. Automatically stores all the securities from Signal portfolio in 5-, 15-, 30- and 60-minute files. Capture occurs in background, leaving computer free to run most other software in the foreground. Run technical analysis programs such as Compu Trac, MetaStock or Byte Research's Professional Breakout System for intra-day charting.

Product: PROFESSIONAL BREAKOUT SYSTEM*
Securities: Stock, Bond, Index, Mutual Fund, Option, Futures
Function(s): Communications, Security Screening, Simulations/
    Games, Technical Analysis
System(s): IBM
Special Requirements: EGA graphics or better, hard drive, modem
    for data downloading
Price: $385 version 2.02; $595 version 3.00   **AAII Discount:** 10%
Return Policy: 30 Days, Restocking Fee: Shipping
Demo: Yes
Technical Support: Phone (11 a.m. - 6 p.m. EST), Newsletter

Description: Gives entry and exit signals for stocks, futures, options and indexes. Provides full graphic charting, as well as a proven mechanical trading method. Uses volatility breakout system with charting and technical analysis features to filter and confirm the trades indicated by the mechanical portion of the system. Directly reads any data in CSI, Compu Trac, MetaStock or ASCII formats. Free downloading software is supplied. Features: historical profitability testing of the built-in volatility system, plus testing of user defined trading systems or ideas. No programming is required to test any system. Walking-forward testing for real-time results. Seventeen technical indicators and 4 trading reports. High resolution color charting. 3D graphics to spot best parameters. Optimizable stops.

CableSoft, Inc. (913) 888-4449
8207 Melrose Drive fax: (913) 888-4475
Suite 111
Lenexa, KS 66214

Product: LIVEWIRE PERSONAL INVESTOR (formerly LiveWire)
Securities: Stock, Bond, Index, Mutual Fund, Option, Futures
Function(s): Communications, Portfolio Management, Tax Planning, Technical Analysis
System(s): IBM
Special Requirements: Hard drive, Hercules, CGA or EGA graphics, Signal, DTN or X*Press
Price: $345 for X*Press, Signal, **AAII Discount:** call
DTN Wall Street
Return Policy: NA
Demo: Yes ($45, 30 day trial)
Technical Support: $150, includes: Phone (9 a.m. - 5 p.m. CST), Newsletter

Description: An integrated software system. Operates with both real-time and delayed data services. Integrates live quotes with portfolio management, price and volume alarms, historical graphs, technical analysis and real-time accounting. Automatically updates position and builds live graphs on screen, including hourly, daily, weekly and intra-day charts. Technical analysis includes: moving averages, channels difference oscillators, trendlines and comparison charts. Can have multiple portfolios and track over 500 instruments. The Portfolio Manager gives continuous updates on position in the market showing dollar gain, percent gain and annualized rate of return. Gives complete transaction accounting and reporting including tax reports. Can collect quotes while user works in other programs. Data services supported: Signal, X*Press, and Data Transmission Network (DTN Wall Street).

Product: LIVEWIRE PROFESSIONAL*
Securities: Stock, Bond, Index, Mutual Fund, Option, Futures
Function(s): Communications, Portfolio Management, Tax Planning, Technical Analysis
System(s): IBM
Special Requirements: Hard drive, Hercules, CGA, EGA or VGA, ComStock, DTN, Signal or X*Press
Price: $695   **AAII Discount:** call
Return Policy: NA
Demo: Yes ($45, 30 day trial)
Technical Support: $150, includes: Phone (9 a.m. - 5 p.m. CST), Newsletter

Description: Tracks and collects historical data on up to 1,000 symbols. Users can view quote windows and set price and volume alarms. Historical data can be viewed as tick data or intra-day (1-60 minute intervals), hourly, daily and weekly bar charts. Twenty-eight technical studies are available. Provides multiple portfolio management with cash accounting. Users can view dollar gain, percentage gain and rate of return for symbols and portfolios. Works with ComStock, DTN Wall Street, Signal and X*Press.

California Scientific Software   (800) 284-8112
10141 Evening Star Drive #6   (916) 477-7481
Grass Valley, CA 95945   fax: (916) 477-8656

Product: BRAINMAKER NEURAL NETWORK SIMULATOR
Securities: Stock, Bond, Index, Mutual Fund, Option, Futures, Real Estate
Function(s): Technical Analysis—neural network time series forecasting
System(s): IBM, Macintosh
Special Requirements: None
Price: $195   **AAII Discount:** None

Return Policy: NA
Demo: No
Technical Support: Phone (8:30 a.m. - 5 p.m. PST), BBS

Description: A complete software system for designing, building, training, testing and running neural networks which parallel computers modeled after the human brain, combine the brain's ability to analyze and learn with the computer's ability to process data quickly and accurately. Includes NetMaker, a network generation and data manipulation program with spreadsheet style display which has the ability to perform complex arithmetic operations on user's data and build network description and training files automatically. Data may be read from Lotus, dBase, ASCII and Excel files. Support for graphics post-processing of network results is provided. Fact files may be connected together to create very large databases.

Caribou Codeworks (218) 663-7118
HLC 3-Box 71
Lutsen, MN 55612

Product: QTRADER*
Securities: Stock, Index, Mutual Fund, Futures
Function(s): Technical Analysis
System(s): IBM
Special Requirements: EGA color monitor, 1 MB RAM, hard drive, 80286 processor
Price: $269   **AAII Discount:** 20%
Return Policy: 30 Days, Restocking Fee: $20
Demo: Yes ($20)
Technical Support: Phone (10 a.m. - 3 p.m. CST)

Description: Produces high-resolution, full-color charts for the graphic analysis of futures and stocks. Over 20 indicators plus precision line drawing tools. The current trend and reversal price, current position, projected highs and lows, high/low breakout points and stops are all displayed on screen with the bar chart and indicators. Supports virtually all printers and will save charts to disk as .PCX files. Optional modules available for trade accounting and the construction of personal system to generate trading signals. CSI and Compu Trac compatible.

CDA, Investment Technologies, Inc.　　　　　(800) 232-2285
1355 Piccard Drive　　　　　　　　　　　　　(301) 975-9600
Rockville, MD 20850　　　　　　　　　　fax: (301) 590-1350

Product: ASSET MIX OPTIMIZER
Securities: Stock, Bond, Mutual Fund, Real Estate
Function(s): Portfolio Management
System(s): IBM
Special Requirements: None
Price: $700/year for semi-annual updates　　**AAII Discount:** None
Return Policy: NA
Demo: Yes
Technical Support: Phone (8:30 a.m. - 5:30 p.m. EST)

Description: Determines how much of a portfolio should be invested in various asset classes. Users can choose up to 10 of the 32 asset classes per portfolio mix; estimate risk tolerance; incorporate rate of return forecasts for each asset class or use their own and include or exclude transaction costs and set upper/lower limits for the holdings of any asset class. Program determines the ideal percentage of a portfolio that should be in aggressive growth, metals, high yield and more, and compares current versus optimum portfolios, determining how each will perform under best and worst circumstances.

Product: MUTUAL FUND HYPOTHETICALS
Securities: Mutual Fund
Function(s): Portfolio Management
System(s): IBM
Special Requirements: None
Price: $600/year　　　　　　　　　　　　**AAII Discount:** None
Return Policy: NA
Demo: Yes
Technical Support: Phone (8:30 a.m. - 5:30 p.m. EST)

Description: Provides 10 years of historical data for over 1,400 mutual funds. By arrangement with The Donoghue Organization, Inc., established a pseudo money-market fund called the "Donoghue Money Market Average," a no-load fund with a constant net asset value of $10 per share and monthly distribution of income. In a hypothetical illustration, users may specify the following: name of the client for whom the report is being prepared, mutual fund of choice, time period covered (up to 10 years), front-end load, whether income or capital gains distributions are to be reinvested, tax rate on income and on capital gains, redemption fee and any pattern of investments and withdrawals by date and amount. Generates a complete cash flow statement showing investments, withdrawals, dividends, taxes, market value of the position and annual internal rate of return. Output can be monthly, quarterly or by fiscal year. System also can produce color graphs (with color plotter) portraying the market value of the investment over time. User can create a single-fund hypothetical and a multi-fund composite and compare funds against one another and a fund versus 1 index. Also creates "mountain" charts that show principal, capital gains and income over a 10-year period. A new option, Multi-Fund Composite With Reallocations, allows user to reallocate capital between the funds chosen for a multi-fund composite as often as monthly and shows a detailed schedule of investments and withdrawals for each of the components. Updated quarterly, diskettes are mailed within 5 days of each quarter end.

Charles L. Pack (415) 949-0887
25303 La Loma Drive
Los Altos Hills, CA 94022

Product: PERSONAL PORTFOLIO ANALYZER
Securities: Stock, Bond, Mutual Fund, Option, Futures
Function(s): Portfolio Management
System(s): IBM
Special Requirements: None
Price: $39.95   **AAII Discount:** None
Return Policy: NA
Demo: No
Technical Support: None

Description: Performs recordkeeping, numerical analysis and reporting on an existing portfolio of stocks, bonds, mutual funds, cash and other security types. Calculates market values, gains and losses, holding periods, annual appreciation (IRR), total return and expected annual income, yield before and after taxes, portfolio beta and annual return. Security prices can be entered manually or imported from an external ASCII file. Reports include: income and taxability analysis, gain/loss since purchase by security and by tax lot and realized gain/loss (schedule D). Income can be broken down by month and quarter and by security type and taxability (Federal and State). Total market value can be broken down by security type and industry category. Up to 5 portfolios may be combined in all reports, which may be displayed or printed. Security sales may be applied on a FIFO or LIFO basis or applied to a particular purchase lot; when necessary, a purchase lot is automatically split into 2 parts. Program handles stock splits and fund distributions, and dividend reinvestments are treated as new purchases. Is menu-driven with context-sensitive on-line screens and is compatible with the Stock Charting System.

Product: STOCK CHARTING SYSTEM
Securities: Stock, Bond, Index, Mutual Fund, Option, Futures
Function(s): Portfolio Management, Technical Analysis
System(s): IBM
Special Requirements: None
Price: $49.95   **AAII Discount:** None
Return Policy: NA
Demo: No
Technical Support: None

Description: An integrated system which performs both technical analysis and portfolio management. Graphics features include high/low/close chart (or line graph for funds) with up to 3 moving averages and optional trading band. A volume histogram, on-balance volume or 1 of 6 different oscillators are optional. Also available is a full-screen relative strength chart on which the price action of any security may be compared to any other security and used as a base. Current or historical data may be entered manually or imported from external ASCII files, allowing the user to obtain information from almost any database service (using an external spreadsheet or communications program). Portfolio manager handles any number of portfolios consisting of bonds, stocks, funds or other security types. Individual tax lots are segregated and up to 5 portfolios may be combined in reports designed to monitor portfolio performance and include gain/loss, holding period, beta, annual appreciation (IRR), total return and asset allocation. Security prices are from the stock charts. Is menu-driven with context-sensitive on-line screens and is compatible with the Personal Portfolio Analyzer.

Charles Schwab & Company, Inc.   (800) 334-4455
101 Montgomery Street   fax: (415) 403-5503
Department S
San Francisco, CA 94104

Product: EQUALIZER
Securities: Stock, Bond, Mutual Fund, Option
Function(s): Communications, Portfolio Management
System(s): IBM
Special Requirements: None
Price: $99; on-line fees additional   **AAII Discount:** None
Return Policy: NA
Demo: No
Technical Support: Phone (24 hours/day)

Description: Users can trade a wide variety of securities from their personal computers for speed, privacy, control, convenience; get real-time quotes when needed; access Dow Jones News/Retrieval and S&P's MarketScope to get investment advice and to see what many of Wall Street's leading independent analysts are saying; read current and historical investment news about companies; keep in touch with stories that affect the market; evaluate market trends and review technical and fundamental data; screen for and monitor stocks; manage portfolio with automatic updating; and track hypothetical portfolios. Also, users have instant access to Schwab account information and can export data for use by other programs.

ChipSoft, Inc.   (800) 755-1040
6330 Nancy Ridge Road   (619) 453-8722
Suite 103   fax: (619) 453-1367
San Diego, CA 92121

Product: MACINTAX 1040 1991 PERSONAL EDITION*
Securities: Not Applicable
Function(s): Financial Planning, Tax Planning
System(s): Macintosh
Special Requirements: Macintosh Plus or greater, hard drive or second 800K floppy
Price: $99.95; annual update $54.95   **AAII Discount:** None
Return Policy: NA

Demo: No
Technical Support: Phone (6 a.m. - 9 p.m. PST during tax season), BBS, Newsletter

Description: Displays over 74 forms and schedules in their exact form on screen. Tax calculations are performed automatically, and since all forms, schedules and worksheets are linked, they are updated every time a change is made. User double-clicks the mouse on any line to get complete IRS instructions. All printouts are exact replicas and can be filed with the IRS. Text files from spreadsheets, databases and accounting programs, such as Quicken, MacMoney and if:X Personal Tax Analyst, can be directly imported into MacInTax. Fourteen state programs can be purchased separately.

Product: TURBOTAX PERSONAL 1040
Securities: Not Applicable
Function(s): Financial Planning, Tax Planning
System(s): IBM
Special Requirements: None
Price: $75; annual update $37.50   **AAII Discount:** None
Return Policy: NA
Demo: Yes
Technical Support: Phone (6 a.m. - 9 p.m. PST), BBS, Newsletter

Description: Provides tax preparation, planning and recordkeeping. Inputs are similar to a spreadsheet with full-screen IRS forms. Menu-driven commands and on-line help are available. Computations are done for over 60 forms, schedules and worksheets. The package provides on-line IRS instructions, a quick-link forms finder for the user, tax forms printed to IRS specifications and a data examiner to check for omissions in the tax return. Companion programs for preparing state taxes are available for 44 states.

Coast Investment Software   (904) 654-5999
86 Cobia Street   fax: (904) 654-5828
Destin, FL 32541

Product: FIBNODES
Securities: Stock, Mutual Fund, Option, Futures

Function(s): Options Analysis, Technical Analysis
System(s): IBM
Special Requirements: None
Price: $795   **AAII Discount:** 20%
Return Policy: All sales final
Demo: No
Technical Support: Phone (8 a.m. - 5 p.m. CST)

Description: A computerized Fibonacci retracement and objective calculator specially designed for hectic, high-pressure, intra-day trading and position trading where high accuracy stop placement and targeted profit objectives are needed. Calculates the 2 major nodes or up to 58 combined nodes per market swing; recalculates up to 58 nodes within 10 seconds of a new market high or low; analyzes market moves, like those in the S&P, into bite-size, recognizable, tradable pieces; calculates high accuracy profit objectives; highlights user selected nodes for instant recognition and indicates areas for proper stop placement. Manual includes many specific examples. Contains automatic 32nd conversion for T-Bonds.

Product: TRADING PACKAGE
Securities: Stock, Bond, Index, Mutual Fund, Option, Futures
Function(s): Communications, Options Analysis, Technical Analysis
System(s): IBM
Special Requirements: Modem for data downloading
Price: $495   **AAII Discount:** 20%
Return Policy: All sales final
Demo: Yes
Technical Support: Phone (8 a.m. - 5 p.m. CST)

Description: A trading and market research tool that allows user to speculate as CIS does or to select an alternative method that reflects individual objectives and needs. Provides end-of-day intra-day signals. Includes: bar chart capability of high, low and close with manual or automatic scale selection; RSI, stochastics, MACD, trendlines and Hurst cycle projection capability. A variety of moving average studies including time displaced MAs can graphically display the "key of the day" alone or in combination with the CIS proprietary, intermediate- and long-term trend indicators. Variable detrended oscillator study filters high-risk trades; proprietary CIS Oscillator Predictor Study indicates which price changes will produce overbought and oversold conditions in the market place. Comprehensive database manager.

Coherent Software Systems   (401) 683-5886
771 Antony Road
Portsmouth, RI 02871

Product: RORY TYCOON OPTIONS TRADER
Securities: Option, Futures
Function(s): Communications, Options Analysis, Spreadsheet
System(s): IBM
Special Requirements: Spreadsheet program, modem
Price: $49.95   **AAII Discount:** None
Return Policy: NA
Demo: No
Technical Support: Phone (12 p.m. - 5 p.m. EST)

Description: Spreadsheet template retrieves quotations and analyzes over 50 possible option trades. User enters a stock symbol and up to 3 contract months; system automatically retrieves the current stock price from an electronic quote service, constructs appropriate option symbols and retrieves quotations for a variety of trading strategies suited to the current stock price. Quotes are displayed in a table that may be used for manual data entry if no electronic service is available. The table of quotes is merged into risk/reward formulas that evaluate the trading strategies. One-page reports are printed by menu. Includes interface to Dow Jones News/Retrieval, CompuServe and Signal.

Product: RORY TYCOON PORTFOLIO ANALYST
Securities: Stock, Bond, Mutual Fund, Option, Futures
Function(s): Communications, Portfolio Management, Spreadsheet, Technical Analysis
System(s): IBM
Special Requirements: Spreadsheet program, modem
Price: $150   **AAII Discount:** None
Return Policy: NA
Demo: No
Technical Support: Phone (12 p.m. - 5 p.m. EST)

Description: Real-time and historical charting with portfolio management spreadsheet template. Historical charts include price, volume, momentum and moving averages of any duration. Charts may be viewed on screen or as high-resolution printouts. Dimensions of printed charts are variable up to full-page size for inclusion in reports. Signal users may chart price, volume, momentum and block trading in real time. Program will continuously display market price and volume for up to 90 securities on a text display while cycling through a list of constantly updated charts on a graphics monitor. Includes interfaces to DJN/R and CompuServe for quote retrieval.

Product: RORY TYCOON PORTFOLIO MANAGER
Securities: Stock, Bond, Mutual Fund, Option, Futures
Function(s): Communications, Portfolio Management, Spreadsheet
System(s): IBM
Special Requirements: Spreadsheet program, Signal optional
Price: Basic $49.95; advanced $99.95   **AAII Discount:** None
Return Policy: NA
Demo: No
Technical Support: None

Description: Spreadsheet template that organizes, tracks and reports on up to 2,500 investments in stocks, bonds, options, cash accounts, CDs, precious metals, mutual funds, futures contracts and IRA, Keogh and employee profit sharing plans. Calculates net worth, profit/loss, yield-to-maturity, asset distribution, margin value, margin requirement, brokerage commissions, imputed interest, bond amortization and book value and annual income projections for covered call and naked put options. Calculations are displayed for individual investments, investment categories or the whole portfolio. Will generate 19 printed reports, including short- and long-term Schedule D reports. Quotations may be imported from Signal.

Commodity Exchange, Inc.   (800) 333-2900
Four World Trade Center   (212) 938-7921
Room 7451   fax: (212) 938-2660
New York, NY 10048

Product: COMEX COMCALC
Securities: Option, Futures

Function(s): Options Analysis
System(s): IBM
Special Requirements: None
Price: $49.95   **AAII Discount:** None
Return Policy: NA
Demo: No
Technical Support: Phone (9 a.m. - 5 p.m. EST)

Description: Program aids in determining fair value, implied volatility and delta of a futures option.

Product: COMEX, THE GAME
Securities: Option, Futures
Function(s): Simulations/Games
System(s): IBM
Special Requirements: None
Price: $69.95   **AAII Discount:** 30%
Return Policy: NA
Demo: No
Technical Support: Phone (9 a.m. - 5 p.m. EST)

Description: A realistic simulation of the gold and silver marketplace that teaches the basics of options and futures trading. User enters several opening parameters, then tests trading acumen in a computer-generated, 180-day market environment. Includes extensive options and futures price data; price history charts; automatic calculation of margin requirements, net debit/credit and downside/upside break-even points; profit and loss graphs; and a news ticker relating next day price movements.

Product: HEDGEMASTER
Securities: Option, Futures
Function(s): Simulations/Games
System(s): IBM
Special Requirements: None
Price: $99.95   **AAII Discount:** None
Return Policy: NA
Demo: No
Technical Support: Phone (9 a.m. - 5 p.m. EST)

Description: Simulates the trading and hedging environment of a professional trader using the physical, forward, futures and options markets. Allows user to enter positions and trades for the different forms of metals owned, namely bullion inventories, forward commitments, futures, options and consignments. Through use of historical data, user can try different strategies and simulate the profit and loss outcome ("what if" situations).

Commodity Systems, Inc. (CSI)　　　　　　　(800) 327-0175
200 W. Palmetto Park Road　　　　　　　　　　(407) 392-8663
Boca Raton, FL 33432　　　　　　　　　fax: (407) 392-1379

Product: QUICKPLOT/QUICKSTUDY
Securities: Stock, Index, Futures
Function(s): Technical Analysis
System(s): Apple II, IBM
Special Requirements: None
Price: $60 plus $39 account initiation fee　　　**AAII Discount:** None
Return Policy: NA
Demo: Yes
Technical Support: Phone (8 a.m. - 11 p.m. EST), Newsletter

Description: Designed for use with Commodity Systems, Inc. Data Retrieval Service. Creates graphic displays and numeric output of daily prices, volume and open interest activity in the futures and stock markets. Provides wide variety of technical studies including: stochastics, moving averages with data shifts and bands, commodity channel index, momentum, spreads, ratios, on-balance and non-seasonal volume, trendlines, William's %R and moving average convergence/divergence. Provides 3 proprietary studies: Probable Direction Index (PDI) to determine the probable market direction; CSI-Trend to determine if market is in trending or trading (scalping) position and CSI Stop to project tomorrow's high, low and close as well as provide protective stops. User must purchase CSI format data or manually input through CSI's Quicktrieve software system.

Product: QUICKTRIEVE/QUICKMANAGER
Securities: Stock, Index, Mutual Fund, Option, Futures
Function(s): Communications, Technical Analysis
System(s): Apple II, IBM

Special Requirements: Modem
Price: $39 **AAII Discount:** 10%
Return Policy: NA
Demo: No
Technical Support: Phone (8 a.m. - 11 p.m. EST), Newsletter

Description: Takes users from data collection and file management to graphing and analysis of market information. There are 3 modules: Quicktrieve, the communications link with CSI, provides access to current and historical data on commodities, stocks, options and mutual funds and includes a check-sum feature for accurate data delivery. Quickmanager creates, edits, moves and condenses data files allowing for manual input and database management. Quickplot, a graphics program, produces a bar chart with daily volume and open interest or P/E ratio. Includes: 3 moving averages, RSI, trendlines, difference oscillators, split screen, color annotated charts and screen dump.

Product: TRADE$K*
Securities: Stock, Index, Futures
Function(s): Communications, Portfolio Management
System(s): IBM
Special Requirements: 640K RAM, hard drive, VM 386, Deskview and Windows 3.0 supported, graphics card, 80286 or better processor recommended
Price: $299+ depending on number of accounts tracked **AAII Discount:** 10%
Return Policy: 30 Days, Restocking Fee: $49
Demo: No
Technical Support: Phone (8 a.m. - 11 p.m. EST), Newsletter

Description: Keeps an unlimited number of trading accounts in balance, keeps track of all open orders, takes daily notes on both accounts and individual contracts and lets user review all interrelated data in a variety of report formats. Acts as a Personal Information Manager optimized for a commodity trader. Program is configured in separate modules: Manages open and closed trades for an unlimited number of trading accounts, maintains contract specifications for an unlimited number of contracts or issues, employs a text editor to keep daily notes for each trading account and contract.

Product: TRADING SYSTEM PERFORMANCE EVALUATOR (T.S.P.E)*
Securities: Stock, Bond, Index, Mutual Fund, Option, Futures
Function(s): Technical Analysis
System(s): IBM
Special Requirements: 640K RAM, hard drive, co-processor recommended
Price: $199   **AAII Discount:** 20%
Return Policy: NA
Demo: No
Technical Support: Phone (8 a.m. - 11 p.m. EST), Newsletter

Description: Objective is to find the probability that a proposed dollar goal can reasonably be achieved with a given capital stake and to compute the expected level of goal satisfaction. Also assigns a merit level to trading systems for comparative purposes. Attempts to uncover the more promising trading systems and warn users against committing funds to improperly conceived methods. Draws upon forecasting theory and random simulation to assess performance; takes any profit/loss input record and determines whether a similar result can be repeated by chance with randomly drawn samples from the original profit/loss set.

Compu-Cast Corporation   (213) 476-4682
1015 Gayley Avenue
Suite 506
Los Angeles, CA 90024

Product: STOCK MARKET SECURITIES PROGRAM
Securities: Stock, Bond, Index, Mutual Fund, Option
Function(s): Communications, Technical Analysis
System(s): IBM
Special Requirements: Modem for downloading
Price: $260   **AAII Discount:** 10%
Return Policy: NA
Demo: Yes ($25)
Technical Support: First year free, Phone (9 a.m. - 5 p.m. PST)

Description: Produces accumulation/distribution charts that include closing prices. Charts indicate changes of price direction ahead of moving averages. Includes an advance/decline chart that shows market turning points and direction. Information can be entered manually or retrieved from DJN/R and CompuServe. Reviews securities daily and points out which securities have unusual action. Announces, on screen, approaching top/bottom in securities and the market, buy/sell alert and serious accumulation/distribution.

Computer Investing Consultants (512) 681-0491
9002 Swinburne Court
San Antonio, TX 78240

Product: DBC/LINK1
Securities: Option
Function(s): Communications
System(s): IBM
Special Requirements: MarketWatch account
Price: $149   **AAII Discount:** 20%
Return Policy: NA
Demo: Yes ($20)
Technical Support: Phone (9:30 a.m. - 3:30 p.m. CST)

Description: Permits MarketWatch subscribers to read, test and update up to 500 stock/option prices from a MarketWatch Monitor file to the OptionVue IV options analysis program. Multiple Monitor files can be coupled together so that an unlimited number of stocks and related options can be saved for technical analysis on a daily basis. Used on an intra-day basis, the program can selectively transfer one or several stock prices and the related options to OptionVue for immediate analysis. Automatically updates the volatility studies in OptionVue as a part of the data transfer process.

Product: DBC/LINK2
Securities: Stock, Index, Mutual Fund, Option
Function(s): Communications
System(s): IBM
Special Requirements: MarketWatch account
Price: $98   **AAII Discount:** 20%
Return Policy: NA
Demo: No
Technical Support: Phone (9:30 a.m. - 3:30 p.m.CST)

Description: Permits MarketWatch subscribers to transfer data on 10 to 2,000 stocks to MetaStock, Compu Trac and N-Squared charting database. A single command reads, tests and updates any number of stock and index prices to the database. Also, an optional output formatted as a .PRN file for spreadsheet use can be generated. The program will identify: missing stock symbols, closing price moves beyond a preset percent change; current day relative volume above any preset level and questionable or erroneous price data. Will also automatically add new symbols to the database. Alarms are provided and a complete transaction record is stored to disk. An optional name-date coding of the daily data files permits saving these files for historical purposes. Can append, insert or overwrite MarketWatch data to the appropriate charting data file.

Product: DBC/LINK6
Securities: Bond, Futures
Function(s): Communications
System(s): IBM
Special Requirements: MarketWatch account
Price: $98; $69 if purchased with DBC/Link 2   **AAII Discount:** 20%
Return Policy: NA
Demo: No
Technical Support: Phone (9:30 a.m. - 3:30 p.m. CST)

Description: Similar to DBC/Link2. However, the program handles commodity prices and settlement issues. All data is stored in a standard 7 field data format.

Product: LINK/UTILITY*
Securities: Stock, Bond, Index, Mutual Fund, Option, Futures
Function(s): Communications
System(s): IBM
Special Requirements: MarketWatch account
Price: $49   **AAII Discount:** 20%
Return Policy: NA
Demo: No
Technical Support: Phone (9:30 a.m. - 3:30 p.m. CST)

Description: Link/Utility is a collection of utility programs for use with MetaStock/Compu Trac databases. Programs include: a sort routine that permits individual stocks to be coded by industry group, multiple data directory sorts by equity name, industry group and directory location; selective deletion of old history; convert volume from raw shares to round lots and reverse; build MarketWatch monitor files from MetaStock/Compu Trac database; read and insert ASCII file into center of existing database and other features.

Compu Trac Software, Inc. (800) 535-7990
1017 Pleasant Street (504) 895-1474
New Orleans, LA 70115 fax: (504) 895-3416

Product: COMPU TRAC
Securities: Stock, Bond, Index, Mutual Fund, Option, Futures
Function(s): Options Analysis, Security Screening, Spreadsheet, Statistical Analysis, Technical Analysis
System(s): IBM, Macintosh
Special Requirements: None
Price: IBM $695-$1,900; Macintosh $695   **AAII Discount:** None
Return Policy: NA
Demo: Yes
Technical Support: $300/year, includes: Phone (8 a.m. - 5 p.m. CST), Newsletter, Software Updates

Description: Complete set of technical analysis tools and studies. Features analytical routines from bar charts and moving averages to oscillators and stochastics. Precision charts, trendlines and user programming capabilities are supported. Can be automated to run unattended. Regularly updated with program revisions sent automatically to users.

Compu-Vest Software (708) 469-4437
545 Fairview Avenue
Glen Ellyn, IL 60137

Product: STOCK OPTION CALCULATIONS AND STRATEGIES
Securities: Mutual Fund, Option
Function(s): Options Analysis

System(s): IBM
Special Requirements: None
Price: $40 postpaid, $50 outside N. America   **AAII Discount:** 10%
Return Policy: NA
Demo: Yes
Technical Support: None

Description: Nine menu-driven programs. Identifies over 90 different put and/or call strategies with or without stock positions and projects P/L and break-even points. User can calculate fair market prices of options and hedge ratios (Black-Scholes); calculate days to option expiration and volatility by recent price history or implied volatility; project option prices and reward/risk ratio at the end of a specified holding period; calculate the probability a stock will be above or below a range of future prices; establish and maintain files of prices and other market action data; keep record of mutual fund investments; calculate simple, exponential and weighted moving averages of file data; choose discount or full-service broker's commissions. All buy and sell calculations include commissions.

Cyber-Scan, Inc.   (612) 682-4150
Route 4, P.O. Box 247
Buffalo, MN 55313

Product: DISCOVERY
Securities: Stock, Index, Option, Futures
Function(s): Communications, Technical Analysis
System(s): IBM
Special Requirements: DTN account for automatic data updating
Price: $350   **AAII Discount:** 15%
Return Policy: NA
Demo: Yes
Technical Support: None

Description: Charts futures, stocks and options; consists of technical tools to fully analyze trades. Contains more than 40 technical studies including bar charts, moving averages, RSI, stochastics, MACD, point and figure charts, CCI, spreads and stop systems. Can update each day and accumulate historical price data with no limit to size and number of files. Features data update using DTN Monitor, step-by-step tutoring on audio tapes, detailed written documentation, complete auto-run capability and on-line help screens.

Product: QUOTE COMMANDER*
Securities: Stock, Bond
Function(s): Communications, Portfolio Management
System(s): IBM
Special Requirement(s): 1 MB EMS memory, DTN account
Price: $99.95   **AAII Discount:** None
Return Policy: NA
Demo: Yes
Technical Support: None

Description: Collects and displays unlimited stock and bond prices. Features include: listed quotes by symbols up to 2,500 each and 36 lists; random quote—any of 19,000 quotes by symbol; alarms to notify if instrument trades at specific level for up to 20 issues; automatic export of data in ASCII format at specified time for use with other analysis programs. Program makes available all quotes on DTN which can be accessed by randomly entering the ticker symbol.

Dantes' Financial, Inc.   (801) 752-1821
911 N. 1400 E.
Logan, UT 84321

Product: DANTES' RETIREMENT PLANNER
Securities: Not Applicable
Function(s): Financial Planning
System(s): IBM
Special Requirements: None
Price: $30   **AAII Discount:** 16.5%
Return Policy: 30 Days, Restocking Fee: None
Demo: Yes ($6)
Technical Support: Phone (6 p.m. - 9 p.m. MST)

Description: Designed for individuals 10 to 50 years away from retirement. Illustrates how to accumulate an adequate retirement fund. Employs a pull-down menu to allow easy entry and modification of over 40 variables including desired retirement income, desired remaining estate, current investment resources, investment returns, payment growth rates, retirement income from other sources, tax assumptions and inflation estimates. Reports display generated summary and detailed schedules of required payments and balances in 5 investment categories. Help messages for assumptions can be accessed by pressing the F1 key. Can also be used to plan education, life insurance and lump-sum payment and balance requirements.

Data Base Associates (808) 926-5854
P.O. Box 1838 fax: (808) 926-5851
Honolulu, HI 96805

Product: SPLOT!
Securities: Stock, Bond, Index, Mutual Fund, Option, Futures
Function(s): Communications, Financial Planning, Portfolio Management, Tax Planning, Technical Analysis
System(s): IBM
Special Requirements: EGA or better, modem for data downloading
Price: $135   **AAII Discount:** 20%
Return Policy: 30 Days, Restocking Fee: $25
Demo: Yes ($10)
Technical Support: Phone (8:30 a.m. - 4:30 p.m. IPT)

Description: A data collection and charting program that tracks individual stocks, mutual funds, options, bonds, indexes, commodities and portfolios. Graphics help users spot short- and long-term trends not apparent in tabular data. System imports daily and historical data from a number of sources including X*Press, CompuServe, Signal, DJN/R and Stock Data. Features: up to 12 years of data handling for 200 individual listings and 100 portfolios; logarithmic scales; moving helpline which operates like a tickertape; automatic stock split calculation and portfolio adjustments; printouts of plots, stock and portfolio value files; portfolio summary tables. Generates 3 types of plots: individual issues, portfolios and comparisons. Users can toggle between weekly/daily plots, zoom/unzoom for closer inspection of data, overlay plots with growth/loss percentage lines, move starting/ending days one day/week or 10 days/weeks at a time, skip from beginning to end of available data, change plot parameters—including all colors and scale adjustments—directly from plot screens. Creates ASCII files for use with other programs.

Data Transmission Network Corp.
9110 W. Dodge Road
Suite 200
Omaha, NE 68114

(800) 779-5000
(402) 390-2328
fax: (402) 390-7188

Product: DTN QUOTE CATCHER
Securities: Stock, Bond, Index, Mutual Fund, Futures
Function(s): Communications
System(s): IBM
Special Requirements: DTN account
Price: $50 plus $15/month for datafeed   **AAII Discount:** None
Return Policy: NA
Demo: Yes
Technical Support: None

Description: Allows all the electronically-updated quotes from DTN Wall Street to be passed through the serial communications port on the DTN receiver. Provides approximately 15,000 NYSE, AMEX and NASDAQ quotes. DTN Wall Street subscribers can store, view or translate quote data which is passed through the DTN serial port interface. Designed to capture, manage and store quote information using background data capture. View the status of either a single quote or custom-format screen of multiple quotes simply by entering the trading symbol. The only limitation to the number of quotes users can "capture" is the available memory of their computers. Also stores quotes on hard-disk for a permanent record or for import into other compatible programs.

Product: WALL STREET PORTFOLIO MANAGER
Securities: Stock, Bond, Mutual Fund
Function(s): Communications, Portfolio Management
System(s): IBM
Special Requirements: DTN account for data downloading
Price: $49.95   **AAII Discount:** None
Return Policy: NA
Demo: Yes
Technical Support: None

Description: User can automatically download information from DTN Wall Street; update and manage stocks, bonds, mutual funds, treasuries, etc.; create multiple portfolios for virtually unlimited securities; automatically calculate gains and losses; record standard buy and sell transactions, short sales, dividend and interest payments and stock splits; track both hypothetical and actual portfolios; generate detailed tax reports; print reports of all transactions and changes and more.

David Bruce & Co. (312) 641-2207
211 W. Wacker Drive (312) 641-7219
Suite 440
Chicago, IL 60606

Product: RISK ANALYSIS SYSTEM*
Securities: Stock, Bond, Index, Option, Futures
Function(s): Communications, Options Analysis, Portfolio Management, Simulations/Games
System(s): IBM
Special Requirements: None
Price: Purchase global license **AAII Discount:** None
$185,000/license; lease $2,000/month
Return Policy: NA
Demo: No
Technical Support: Lease NA, purchase 18%, includes: Phone (7:30 a.m. - 7:30 p.m. CST)

Description: Systems measure portfolio exposure to various market scenarios (e.g., change in price, volatility, spread, basis, interest rates and time to expiration). Risk is defined in terms of profit/loss, account equity at risk, market exposure (delta), gap exposure (gamma), volatility exposure (omega), time exposure (theta) and interest rate exposure (rho). Profit/loss is measured 2 ways: theoretical marks using a combination of market/estimated prices for active/inactive instruments and accounting marks based on the latest market prices. Systems summarize risk in 2 or 3 dimensions, in report or graphic format.

Decisioneering, Inc. (303) 447-6464
1727 Conestrogg Street fax: (303) 441-2487
Boulder, CO 80301

Product: CRYSTAL BALL*
Securities: Not Applicable
Function(s): Spreadsheet, Statistical Analysis
System(s): Macintosh
Special Requirements: Excel, WingZ, Foil Impact
Price: $395   **AAII Discount:** None
Return Policy: NA
Demo: Yes
Technical Support: Phone (8 a.m. - 5 p.m. MST)

Description: A forecasting and risk analysis program. Features include Monte Carlo simulation, automates the "what if" process and determines the probability of all possible results; confidence levels, provides likelihood of any target outcome; intuitive graphic interface; trend charts; correlated assumptions, lets user understand relationships between factors affecting situation; reporting and exporting lets user document work or move results to other programs; documentation and help.

Decision Programming Corp.   (301) 585-7121
8701 Georgia Avenue
Suite 607
Silver Spring, MD 20910

Product: MASTER BRAIN BOND PORTFOLIO MANAGEMENT*
Securities: Bond
Function(s): Bond Analysis, Portfolio Management, Spreadsheet
System(s): IBM, Macintosh
Special Requirements: Lotus 1-2-3, Symphony or compatible spreadsheet
Price: $379   **AAII Discount:** 10%
Return Policy: NA
Demo: Yes ($14.95, 5.25" disk)
Technical Support: 1 hour free

Description: Fixed income portfolio management program. Weighted averages and totals for bond portfolios including weighted average duration. Features portfolio repricing, portfolio projections for any interest rate scenario and a built-in, full-featured bond calculator program. Ideal for management of small to large portfolios and those needing the ability to quickly compare alternate portfolio positions (swaps) under current or changing interest rate environments.

Product: MASTER BRAIN POP-UP BOND CALCULATOR*
Securities: Bond
Function(s): Bond Analysis
System(s): Apple II, IBM, Macintosh
Special Requirements: None
Price: $149   **AAII Discount:** 20%
Return Policy: 30 Days, Restocking Fee: $45
Demo: Yes ($4.95, 5.25"; $6.95, 3.5")
Technical Support: Optional

Description: Fixed income analysis program. Bond prices, yields to maturity and/or call, after-tax yields, accrued interest. Industry-standard results for munis, zeros, corporate bonds, U.S. Treasuries, short-term notes, money market instruments, U.S. bills and Eurobonds. "What if" horizon analysis lets user vary interest rates, prices or yields for a projected date. Analytical features include 4 durations, convexity, value of an 01/05 for price/yield sensitivity indicator. Includes a labeled print-out for bond comparison. Memory-resident option.

Delphi Economics, Inc.   (800) 873-3574
8 Bonn Place   (201) 867-4303
Weshawken, NJ 07087   fax: (201) 867-4666

Product: VIKING
Securities: Stock, Bond, Index, Mutual Fund, Option, Futures
Function(s): Communications, Fundamental Analysis, Options Analysis, Portfolio Management, Security Screening, Technical Analysis
System(s): IBM
Special Requirements: None
Price: $500   **AAII Discount:** 10%
Return Policy: 30 Days, Restocking Fee: None
Demo: Yes
Technical Support: Phone (9 a.m. - 6 p.m. EST)

Description: Technical analysis section includes 40 technical models including all the standard models used today as well as some models proprietary to Delphi Economics. Models can be presented in limitless formats. Uses a special feature for exceptionally quick analysis. Fundamental analysis section allows storage of balance sheet P/L data. Users can define ratios or use standard ones such as P/E. Companies can then be ranked according to user-defined criteria, assisting in the location of the most secure investments. Allows user to design, test and optimize trading models. Models can be tested for annual percent gain versus a buy and hold strategy. Models can also be used together simultaneously to create multi-signal rankings (e.g., number of buy/sell signals, etc.). Proprietary indexes can also be created, including Hausse indexes.

Denver Data, Inc.   (303) 790-7327
9785 Maroon Circle
Meridian One Suite G-126
Englewood, CO 80112

Product: MUTUAL FUND MANAGER
Securities: Mutual Funds, Money Market Funds
Function(s): Technical Analysis
System(s): IBM
Special Requirements: None
Price: $49 (version 1.5 without graphs   **AAII Discount:** None
    available for $35)
Return Policy: 90 Days, Restocking Fee: None
Demo: Yes ($5)
Technical Support: Phone (9 a.m. - 4:30 p.m. MST)

Description: User can monitor the status and performance of any size mutual fund or money market portfolio. Maintains an annual record of fund transactions including all purchases, redemptions and distributions. Produces 3 performance reports including a Weekly Report offering weekly gain or loss, current net asset values and percentage of change for each fund and the total portfolio comparing the performance with leading market indexes. Fund Track and Performance Summary permits user to examine moving averages over any time period, from 1 to 52 weeks. Report also generates an exclusive "beta-predicted performance" feature that compares current and historical fund performance. Portfolio Distribution Analysis Report displays the percent of net asset value by each fund and fund type in a portfolio and calculates composite beta for the portfolio. Records money market accounts and calculates, displays and prints weekly interest earnings. Generates bar graph or line graph performance charts. Line graph feature may be adjusted to show moving averages.

Diamond Head Software (602) 939-5520
4536 W. Maryland
Glendale, AZ 85301

Product: STOCK CHARTING
Securities: Stock
Function(s): Communications, Technical Analysis
System(s): IBM
Special Requirements: Modem for data downloading
Price: $69.95   **AAII Discount:** 20%
Return Policy: NA
Demo: Yes ($15)
Technical Support: None

Description: Provides user with a price-bar and volume-bar chart: 290 data points can be stored—if daily data is stored this equates to some 14 months and with weekly data this equates to 5 years. A moving average of the user's choice is computed and plotted on each chart. Will access the Warner Computer System database and automatically retrieve the necessary data to construct these charts. Manual operation possible for economy. Charts can be printed without additional software and include advance/decline, on-balance volume, trading band and 2 moving average charts. Source code (BASICA) included.

Disk-Count Software, Inc. (800) 333-8776
1751 W. Country Road B (612) 633-0730
Suite 107 fax: (612) 633-8678
St. Paul MN 55113

Product: FINANCIAL PLANNING ORGANIZER
Securities: Not Applicable
Function(s): Financial Planning
System(s): IBM
Special Requirements: None

Price: $34.95   **AAII Discount:** None
Return Policy: 30 Days, Restocking Fee: None
Demo: No
Technical Support: Phone (8 a.m. - 5 p.m. CST)

Description: Helps user to organize financial perceptions as well as financial paper. Process begins with questions that guide user through tables and forms. A personalized report produced by the computer is designed to assist user and user's advisors in developing financial plans. Framework allows users to state their financial goals, assess tolerance for financial risk and organize facts, data and documentation.

Product: PORTFOLIO MANAGER PLUS
Securities: Stock, Index, Mutual Fund, Option
Function(s): Communications, Portfolio Management
System(s): IBM
Special Requirements: Modem for data downloading
Price: $49.95   **AAII Discount:** 10%
Return Policy: 30 Days, Restocking Fee: None
Demo: Yes
Technical Support: Phone (8 a.m. - 5 p.m. CST)

Description: Manage mutual funds, stocks, bonds and other securities in an unlimited number of portfolios. Track buying and selling of securities, stock splits, short sales, dividends and interest payments. Program automatically updates prices of user's securities via modem. Choose from DJN/R, CompuServe, DTN and Prodigy.

DollarLink Software   (415) 641-0721
1407 Douglas Street   fax: (415) 282-8486
San Francisco, CA 94107

Product: DOLLARLINK
Securities: Stock, Index, Mutual Fund, Option, Futures
Function(s): Communications, Options Analysis, Portfolio Management,   Technical Analysis
System(s): IBM
Special Requirements: Real-time Quote Service

Price: $1,300 or $100/month rental AAII Discount: 10%
Return Policy: NA
Demo: Yes ($50)
Technical Support: $300/year after 1st year, includes: Phone (9 a.m. - 4 p.m. PST), Newsletter

Description: Real-time technical analysis program for stocks, indexes, options and commodities. Uses Bonneville, Signal or PC Quote data, feeds and tracks up to 1,000 symbols. Chart and do over 60 intra-day and historic studies in up to 144 windows on any portfolio symbol at any time. Zoom, draw trendlines, bands and channels, Fibonacci and Gann levels, etc. Data can be imported and exported. Built-in programmable keyboard macros eliminate repetitive keystroking. User-created custom indexes update automatically and can be charted. Auto-pilot modes automate start-ups, shutdowns, data management and keyboard macros. Studies can be customized and generate alerts based on user's logic. Dual monitors supported. Offers a theoretical real-time option pricing model and strategies. Automatically keeps track of 20,000 active options and computes accurate market-implied volatilities.

Donald H. Kraft & Associates (708) 673-0597
9325 Kenneth Avenue
Skokie, IL 60076

Product: PORTFOLIO SPREADSHEETS 3
Securities: Stock, Bond, Mutual Fund
Function(s): Communications, Financial Planning, Portfolio Management, Simulations/Games, Spreadsheet
System(s): IBM
Special Requirements: Lotus 1-2-3 release 2.3, 3.1, 1-2-3 for Windows
Price: $195 AAII Discount: None
Return Policy: NA
Demo: Yes ($10)
Technical Support: Phone (9 a.m. - 5 p.m. CST)

Description: Enables users to manage an unlimited number of portfolios of stocks, bonds and options, mutual funds; calculate net worth and distribution of assets. Tracks stocks not owned, calculates bond yield to maturity and evaluates covered call writes. Spreadsheets controlled by menus with over 100 choices. Select from 30 pre-designed printed reports and 8 charts to help manage portfolios. Theoretical portfolios are also tracked. Features include: arrange portfolios of stocks and bonds into desired sequence (e.g., gain/loss, maturity date, early call date, current yield) before printing reports; calculates diversification by stock and industry, anticipates monthly income from dividends and interest, posts dividends and interest as received; records location of each security, how dividends or interest are paid (coupon or check), owner of the security, displays charts depicting portfolio performance, alerts for price objectives, compares performance with market indicators, Plan bond purchases with ladder of maturities report; schedule D information, displays in color with proportionally spaced type fonts. Users can modify spreadsheets. Current prices are typed or downloaded from DJN/R or Signal.

Dow Jones & Company, Inc. (800) 522-3567
P.O. Box 300 (609) 520-4641
Princeton, NJ 08543 fax: (609) 520-4660

Product: MARKET ANALYZER
Securities: Stock, Bond, Index, Mutual Fund, Option
Function(s): Communications, Technical Analysis
System(s): IBM
Special Requirements: Hayes Smartmodem or compatible, graphics card
Price: $349   **AAII Discount:** 30%
Return Policy: 30 Days, Restocking Fee: $20
Demo: Yes ($7.75)
Technical Support: Phone (9 a.m. - 9 p.m. EST), Newsletter

Description: Collects historical price and volume data for stocks, bonds, Treasury issues, options, mutual funds and market indexes from DJN/R. Off-line constructs charts that reveal underlying trends for individual stocks and the market as a whole. Charts include bar, comparison and relative strength. Analysis features include moving averages, support/resistance lines and volume indicators. The auto run capability allows users to program and save for subsequent use a sequence of charting and analysis commands that can be automatically applied to user-selected stocks.

Product: MARKET ANALYZER PLUS
Securities: Stock, Bond, Index, Mutual Fund, Option, Futures
Function(s): Communications, Portfolio Management, Security Screening, Technical Analysis
System(s): IBM, Macintosh
Special Requirements: Hayes Smartmodem or compatible, graphics card
Price: $499   **AAII Discount:** 30%
Return Policy: 30 Days, Restocking Fee: $20
Demo: Yes ($7.75)
Technical Support: Phone (9 a.m. - 9 p.m. EST), Newsletter

Description: Collects from DJN/R historical quotes for stocks, bonds, Treasury issues, options, mutual funds, market indexes and commodities. Creates bar, comparison, relative strength, and point and figure charts. The Macintosh version creates candlestick charts. Analysis tools include moving average convergence-divergence, commodity channel index, William's %R, directional movement, Wilder Relative Strength, scale changes, trendlines, moving averages, support/resistance lines and stochastics which can be used as is or modified for personalized analysis. The technical screening reports compare current price volume to past activity and point out stocks with the greatest profit potential. The IBM version manages up to 800 portfolios.

Product: MARKET MANAGER PLUS
Securities: Stock, Bond, Mutual Fund, Option, Futures, Real Estate
Function(s): Communications, Portfolio Management
System(s): IBM, Macintosh
Special Requirements: Hayes Smartmodem or compatible
Price: $299   **AAII Discount:** 30%
Return Policy: 30 Days, Restocking Fee: $20
Demo: Yes ($7.75)
Technical Support: Phone (9 a.m. - 9 p.m. EST), Newsletter

Description: A portfolio management program that values holdings with current prices for stocks, bonds, options, mutual funds and Treasury issues from DJN/R. Monitors dividends, tracks broker commissions and generates a variety of reports including holdings, realized gain/loss and security and cash transactions. Alert reports include option expirations and bond maturity. Also allows for hypothetical portfolios, contains a calendar for tracking of daily financial activity, updates selected portfolios and saves security data in a format for subsequent analysis in user's spreadsheet.

Product: MARKET MANAGER PLUS PROFESSIONAL VERSION
Securities: Stock, Bond, Mutual Fund, Option
Function(s): Communications, Portfolio Management
System(s): IBM
Special Requirements: Hayes Smartmodem or compatible
Price: $499   **AAII Discount:** 30%
Return Policy: 30 Days, Restocking Fee: $20
Demo: Yes ($7.75)
Technical Support: Phone (9 a.m. - 9 p.m. EST), Newsletter

Description: A portfolio management program. Updates portfolios with current security prices from DJN/R. Handles buy and sell, short sell and buy-to-cover plus receive and deliver transactions; keeps track of cash balances; and provides a calendar of financial activity. Client-support features include the creation of client profiles to define goal, activity and risk and the merging of this data with word processor files for mass mailings. Includes standard reports such as holdings and gain/loss, which can be modified to meet individual preferences or company specifications.

Dynacomp, Inc.   (800) 828-6772
The Dynacomp Office Building   (716) 671-6160
178 Phillips Road
Webster, NY 14580

Product: BUYSEL
Securities: Stock, Option, Futures
Function(s): Options Analysis, Technical Analysis
System(s): IBM, CP/M
Special Requirements: None
Price: $99.95   **AAII Discount:** 20%
Return Policy: 30 Days, Restocking Fee: 25%
Demo: No
Technical Support: Phone (9 a.m. - 5 p.m. EST)

Description: Analyzes stocks, commodities and options. Contains 4 distinct trading methods and money management systems which produce explicit buy/sell transaction signals; Black-Scholes call option model over any time period for a common stock; statistical correlation computation between several stocks or commodities; automatically scaled closing price charts; price data entry and validation on a daily basis or quick approximation of long periods of real price data.

Product: CALCUGRAM STOCK OPTIONS SYSTEM
Securities: Option, Futures
Function(s): Options Analysis
System(s): IBM, TRS-80
Special Requirements: None
Price: $169.95 for IBM, $169.95 for CP/M   **AAII Discount:** 20%
Return Policy: 30 Days, Restocking Fee: 25%
Demo: No
Technical Support: Phone (9 a.m. - 5 p.m. EST)

Description: Guides in the selection of options and the best combination. The daily follow-up program lets the user know when to close out at best advantage. The pricing model used is based on Modern Portfolio Theory. The first program in the software package computes normal (theoretical) values, differences from actual prices and implied volatilities for the options on a stock. The main program, Options Hedging, examines the prospects of spreads and combinations. Because option prices fluctuate around the normal values, the profit in any hedge position varies from day to day. A third program lets the investor follow the progress on a daily basis.

Product: COMPUSEC PORTFOLIO MANAGER
Securities: Stock, Mutual Fund, Option, Futures
Function(s): Communications, Portfolio Management
System(s): Apple II
Special Requirements: Modem for data downloading
Price: $79.95   **AAII Discount:** 20%
Return Policy: 30 Days, Restocking Fee: 25%
Demo: No
Technical Support: Phone (9 a.m. - 5 p.m. EST)

Description: Has all essential portfolio accounting features. Ranks each stock in any portfolio showing which stocks should be reduced or eliminated and which should be increased. Calculates for any stock the compound growth rate between the earnings-per-share for an earlier time period and earnings-per-share for a later time period. Calculates the payback period. Shows daily volume, records date and time when quotes were fetched, shows unrealized gains and losses with subtotals and an analogous breakdown for realized capital gains and losses. Shows the number of securities held, the total number of shares held, and the average cost per share for total holdings of each security as well as average cost per share for each separate holding. Program can also download quotes by telephone when using a modem and Dow Jones News/Retrieval Services.

Product: COVERED OPTIONS
Securities: Option, Futures
Function(s): Options Analysis
System(s): IBM
Special Requirements: CGA optional
Price: $99.95   **AAII Discount:** 20%
Return Policy: 30 Days, Restocking Fee: 25%
Demo: No
Technical Support: Phone (9 a.m. - 5 p.m. EST)

Description: Emphasizes options "covered" by owned securities. Includes use of uncovered or long positions. Allows users to evaluate the options on a stock so they can select the highest value for sale or cheapest value for purchase. The annualized option gain is computed to show how effective a position is. Program gives both graphic and tabular representations of what will happen to the gain as the stock price changes for any future date. Computes probability that the stock will remain within a profitable range. Provides a printed report of the gains or losses in the stock (bond) and the options and the present annualized option yield.

Product: CREDIT RATING BOOSTER
Securities: Not Applicable
Function(s): Financial Planning, Credit History Log

System(s): IBM, TRS-80
Special Requirements: None
Price: $29.95   **AAII Discount:** 20%
Return Policy: 30 Days, Restocking Fee: 25%
Demo: No
Technical Support: Phone (9 a.m. - 5 p.m. EST)

Description: Provides a printout or full screen display of user's up-to-date credit history in a way designed to satisfy a loan officer.

Product: FAMILY BUDGET
Securities: Not Applicable
Function(s): Financial Planning, Tax Planning
System(s): Apple II, Atari, TRS-80
Special Requirements: None
Price: $34.95   **AAII Discount:** 20%
Return Policy: 30 Days, Restocking Fee: 25%
Demo: No
Technical Support: Phone (9 a.m. - 5 p.m. EST)

Description: A 2-part electronic home data recordkeeping program. Part 1, budget, is used to record expenditures, both cash and credit, and income on a daily basis for the period of 1 calendar year. Three categories are used to record tax deductible items, namely interest and taxes, medical expenses and charitable donations. Part 2, charge accounts, provides a continuous record of all credit transactions. Each program provides options for hardcopy printout.

Product: FINANCIAL MANAGEMENT SYSTEM
Securities: Stock, Bond, Index, Mutual Fund, Option, Futures, Real Estate
Function(s): Fundamental Analysis
System(s): CP/M, IBM
Special Requirements: None
Price: $149.95   **AAII Discount:** 20%
Return Policy: 30 Days, Restocking Fee: 25%
Demo: No
Technical Support: Phone (9 a.m. - 5 p.m. EST)

Description: Menu-driven set of coordinated sub-programs. Topics include: financial ratios (liquidity, leverage, activity, profitability), DuPont Analysis, break-even analysis, lease-buy decision, net present value, rates of return, profitability index, inventory model, capital budgeting under uncertainty and refunding a bond and stock valuation.

Product: FUNDWATCH
Securities: Stock, Bond, Mutual Fund
Function(s): Portfolio Management, Security Screening
System(s): IBM
Special Requirements: None
Price: $39.95   **AAII Discount:** 20%
Return Policy: 30 Days, Restocking Fee: 25%
Demo: No
Technical Support: Phone (9 a.m. - 5 p.m. EST)

Description: Simplifies evaluation and comparison of various common investments, including mutual funds, stocks, bonds and many commodities. Calculates yields, evaluates trends with moving averages, creates comparative graphs, provides direct comparisons with interest-earning investments and maintains basic portfolio information.

Product: HOME APPRAISER
Securities: Real Estate
Function(s): Real Estate Analysis
System(s): CP/M, IBM
Special Requirements: None
Price: $39.95   **AAII Discount:** 20%
Return Policy: 30 Days, Restocking Fee: 25%
Demo: No
Technical Support: Phone (9 a.m. - 5 p.m. EST)

Description: Estimates potential market value of real property. Allows user to approximate effects of various physical, economic and territorial factors with impact on the overall value of the property. User supplies selected information about the house (or condo), and the computer provides a depreciated value and a bottom-line estimate of projected market value.

Product: INVESTING ADVISOR
Securities: Stock, Index, Mutual Fund, Real Estate
Function(s): Technical Analysis
System(s): IBM, TRS-80
Special Requirements: None
Price: $39.95   **AAII Discount:** 20%
Return Policy: 30 Days, Restocking Fee: 25%
Demo: No
Technical Support: Phone (9 a.m. - 5 p.m. EST)

Description: Helps user make unemotional decisions about buying and selling investments. Incorporates a means of timing the purchase and sale of investments based on a price-trend analysis and on buy/sell rules. Includes the ability to track both long- and short-term trends to pick best strategy. User can initialize database, add or delete investments and calculate the action to take and adjust the database for splits of the investment.

Product: IRMA
Securities: Stock, Bond, Index, Mutual Fund, Option, Real Estate
Function(s): Financial Planning, Portfolio Management, Tax Planning
System(s): Atari, IBM
Special Requirements: None
Price: $49.95   **AAII Discount:** 20%
Return Policy: 30 Days, Restocking Fee: 25%
Demo: No
Technical Support: Phone (9 a.m.-5 p.m. EST)

Description: Records and tracks investment information. Pertinent data for a diversified portfolio of up to 90 different investments are entered. Handles common and preferred stocks, bonds, deposit accounts, funds, partnerships, options and taxable and non-taxable investments. Varied presentations of user's data support decision-making in 3 areas: financial, tax and investment planning.

Product: LOAN ARRANGER
Securities: Not Applicable
Function(s): Financial Planning, Tax Planning
System(s): Atari, IBM

Special Requirements: None
Price: $29.95   **AAII Discount:** 20%
Return Policy: 30 Days, Restocking Fee: 25%
Demo: No
Technical Support: Phone (9 a.m. - 5 p.m. EST)

Description: Helps user keep track of up to 25 personal loans, such as a home mortgage, automobile, education and home improvement. User can monitor the remaining balance of each loan, the number of payments left and the date of the final payment; see and print reports on the current status of all obligations and on year-to-date payments for each; print complete or partial amortization tables for each loan; combine various terms (principal, interest rates and number of payments) to compare monthly payments and the total interest paid.

Product: MARKET FORECASTER
Securities: Stock, Mutual Fund
Function(s): Technical Analysis
System(s): Apple II, IBM, Macintosh
Special Requirements: None
Price: IBM, $299.95;   **AAII Discount:** 20%
   Apple and Macintosh, $269.95
Return Policy: 30 Days, Restocking Fee: 25%
Demo: No
Technical Support: Phone (9 a.m. - 5 p.m. EST)

Description: Attempts to predict the magnitude and direction of stock market movements over the next 2 to 4 months. Suggests when to buy stocks, mutual funds or options or when to retreat. Features include: the ability to play "what if" games; an audio signal warning when it is time to take action; self-checker to assure the right forecast; an encrypted forecast and other recorded information available by phone.

Product: MARKET TIMER
Securities: Mutual Fund
Function(s): Technical Analysis
System(s): IBM
Special Requirements: CGA graphics for charts
Price: $119.95   **AAII Discount:** 20%

Return Policy: 30 Days, Restocking Fee: 25%
Demo: No
Technical Support: Phone (9 a.m. - 5 p.m. EST)

Description: Provides the necessary buy and sell signals based on a trend analysis of the Value Line Composite Index. Generates buy and sell equity market switch signals; allows performance testing of different market trend sensitivities on past data; includes a daily 10-year history of the Value Line Composite Index; maintains a list of the mutual funds user is invested in; can be updated from daily newspapers; displays charts with trendlines for any selected time period.

Product: MICROCOMPUTER BOND PROGRAM
Securities: Bond
Function(s): Bond Analysis, Security Screening
System(s): Apple II, Atari, Commodore, CP/M, IBM, Macintosh, TRS-80
Special Requirements: None
Price: $59.95 **AAII Discount:** 20%
Return Policy: 30 Days, Restocking Fee: 25%
Demo: No
Technical Support: Phone (9 a.m. - 5 p.m. EST)

Description: Estimates prices and yields of fixed-income securities under a range of assumptions and makes estimates about the future.

Product: MICROCOMPUTER CHART PROGRAM
Securities: Stock, Index, Mutual Fund
Function(s): Technical Analysis
System(s): CP/M, IBM, TRS-80
Special Requirements: None
Price: $59.95 **AAII Discount:** 20%
Return Policy: 30 Days, Restocking Fee: 25%
Demo: No
Technical Support: Phone (9 a.m. - 5 p.m. EST)

Description: Features price charts, volume bar charts, smoothed volume lines, up to 3 overlays, smoothed velocity (price change) line and on balance volume using percent price change.

Product: MICROCOMPUTER STOCK PROGRAM
Securities: Stock
Function(s): Technical Analysis
System(s): Apple II, Atari, Commodore, CP/M, IBM, Macintosh, TRS-80
Special Requirements: None
Price: $59.95 **AAII Discount:** 20%
Return Policy: 30 Days, Restocking Fee: 25%
Demo: No
Technical Support: Phone (9 a.m. - 5 p.m. EST)

Description: Gives buy and sell timing signals based on auto-regressive price trend analysis. The only data required are weekly high, low and closing prices and volume.

Product: MONEY
Securities: Real Estate
Function(s): Financial Planning, Real Estate Analysis, Tax Planning
System(s): CP/M, IBM
Special Requirements: None
Price: $39.95 **AAII Discount:** 20%
Return Policy: 30 Days, Restocking Fee: 25%
Demo: No
Technical Support: Phone (9 a.m. - 5 p.m. EST)

Description: Features interest and depreciation calculation as well as analysis of real estate sales and short-term loans.

Product: MONEY DECISIONS
Securities: Stock, Bond, Index, Mutual Fund, Real Estate
Function(s): Communications, Bond Analysis, Financial Planning, Real Estate Analysis, Tax Planning, Technical Analysis
System(s): IBM
Special Requirements: Modem for data downloading
Price: $149.95 **AAII Discount:** 20%
Return Policy: 30 Days, Restocking Fee: 25%
Demo: No
Technical Support: Phone (9 a.m. - 5 p.m. EST)

Description: Consists of 70 interactive problem-solving programs for investments, loans, business management, forecasting and graphics. A communications interface is provided along with 1 free hour of connect time to CompuServe.

Product: OPTIONS ANALYSIS
Securities: Option, Futures
Function(s): Options Analysis
System(s): Apple II, CP/M, IBM, Macintosh, TRS-80
Special Requirements: None
Price: $99.95 **AAII Discount:** 20%
Return Policy: 30 Days, Restocking Fee: 25%
Demo: No
Technical Support: Phone (9 a.m. - 5 p.m. EST)

Description: Using the Black-Scholes formula, program determines the value of put and call options as a function of both stock price and time to expiration.

Product: PERSONAL BALANCE SHEET
Securities: Not Applicable
Function(s): Financial Planning
System(s): CP/M, IBM
Special Requirements: None
Price: $29.95 **AAII Discount:** 20%
Return Policy: 30 Days, Restocking Fee: 25%
Demo: No
Technical Support: Phone (9 a.m. - 5 p.m. EST)

Description: User creates a statement of financial position. Calculates total assets (cash, accounts receivable, stocks, bonds, real property, etc.) and liabilities; includes debt/worth, current and acid test ratios. User can forecast changes in net worth based on changes in investments and liabilities.

Product: PERSONAL COMPUTER—AUTOMATIC INVESTMENT MANAGEMENT
Securities: Stock

Function(s): Portfolio Management, Technical Analysis
System(s): CP/M, IBM
Special Requirements: None
Price: $149.95　　　　　　　　　　　　　　**AAII Discount:** 20%
Return Policy: 30 Days, Restocking Fee: 25%
Demo: No
Technical Support: Phone (9 a.m. - 5 p.m. EST)

Description: Based on a concept developed by Robert Lichello in his book, *How to Make $1,000,000 Automatically*. Enables user to create and maintain data files containing company/corporation name, number of shares, cash and interest earned. Calculates stock value, portfolio value, buy/sell, market orders and return on investment (ROI). Maintains current and historical records of all transactions for evaluation of investment performance.

Product: PERSONAL FINANCE MANAGER
Securities: Not Applicable
Function(s): Financial Planning
System(s): Apple II, CP/M, IBM, Macintosh
Special: BASIC
Price: $49.95　　　　　　　　　　　　　　**AAII Discount:** 20%
Return Policy: 30 Days, Restocking Fee: 25%
Demo: No
Technical Support: Phone (9 a.m. - 5 p.m. EST)

Description: Includes all of the features of Dynacomp's Personal Finance System plus several more for users with more complicated and extensive financial records. Up to 4 savings accounts and 4 checking accounts can be simultaneously maintained with the balance in each account automatically displayed in the menu mode. A "cash" account is included. Program can sort, search and merge.

Product: PERSONAL FINANCE PLANNER
Securities: Stock, Bond, Mutual Fund, Real Estate
Function(s): Financial Planning
System(s): Apple II, IBM
Special Requirements: BASIC
Price: $29.95　　　　　　　　　　　　　　**AAII Discount:** 20%

Return Policy: 30 Days, Restocking Fee: 25%
Demo: No
Technical Support: Phone (9 a.m. - 5 p.m. EST)

Description: Prepares personal balance sheets, income statements and detailed financial analyses. Provides insurance, real estate, stocks, bonds, mutual funds and IRA analyses and projections. Facilitates the performance of complex "what if" projections to depict the long-term effects of changes in saving and spending patterns. Helps pinpoint problem areas and opportunities. Projections can be made for retirement or for any other time period.

Product: PERSONAL FINANCE SYSTEM
Securities: Not Applicable
Function(s): Financial Planning
System(s): Apple II, Atari, Commodore, CP/M, IBM, Macintosh, TRS-80
Special Requirements: None
Price: $39.95   **AAII Discount:** 20%
Return Policy: 30 Days, Restocking Fee: 25%
Demo: No
Technical Support: Phone (9 a.m. - 5 p.m. EST)

Description: Keeps track of all tax deductible items, bank deposits, monthly charges, cash payments, etc. Will automatically deduct any check fees if desired. Does financial summaries for any category on a per item, monthly or yearly basis. Prints results in detail or summary form, accesses the printer and plots results on a monthly bar graph.

Product: PORTFOLIO DECISIONS
Securities: Stock, Bond, Index, Mutual Fund, Option, Futures, Real Estate
Function(s): Communications, Portfolio Management
System(s): IBM
Special Requirements: Modem for data downloading
Price: $149.95   **AAII Discount:** 20%
Return Policy: 30 Days, Restocking Fee: 25%
Demo: No
Technical Support: Phone (9 a.m. - 5 p.m. EST)

Description: Helps organize, record and evaluate investments. Program can communicate with the Dow Jones or CompuServe services allowing immediate updates of market prices as well as access to other CompuServe facilities, and automatic daily updating of user's portfolio. Reports include: tax return interest report, dividend, capital gains/losses report, portfolio activity detail summary, ticker reports and monthly income forecast.

Product: PORTFOLIO STATUS
Securities: Stock, Bond, Index, Mutual Fund, Option, Futures
Function(s): Portfolio Management
System(s): IBM
Special Requirements: None
Price: $29.95   **AAII Discount:** 20%
Return Policy: 30 Days, Restocking Fee: 25%
Demo: No
Technical Support: Phone (9 a.m. - 5 p.m. EST)

Description: Generates timely analysis of security portfolios. User enters the name of each security, ticker symbol, number of shares, purchase date and cost. To generate an analysis of the portfolio, the user enters the price of each security, and the program proceeds to compute the current market value, profit or loss, percent profit and days since purchase for each security and then computes totals.

Product: PORTVIEW 2020
Securities: Stock, Bond, Index, Mutual Fund, Option, Futures, Real Estate
Function(s): Portfolio Management, Real Estate Analysis, Tax Planning
System(s): IBM
Special Requirements: None
Price: $79.95   **AAII Discount:** 20%
Return Policy: 30 Days, Restocking Fee: 25%
Demo: Yes ($24.95)
Technical Support: Phone (9 a.m. - 5 p.m. EST)

Description: Combines recordkeeping, tax planning and investment analysis. Computes ROI for any investment—stocks, bonds, mutual funds, real estate, commodities, partnerships, options, etc.—with optional adjustments for taxes and inflation. Reports for any list of holdings include investment history, price history, net worth on any date and performance between any 2 dates.

Product: RATIOS
Securities: Stock
Function(s): Fundamental Analysis
System(s): IBM
Special Requirements: GW-BASIC
Price: $29.95 **AAII Discount:** 20%
Return Policy: 30 Days, Restocking Fee: 25%
Demo: No
Technical Support: Phone (9 a.m. - 5 p.m. EST)

Description: Computes various financial ratios given certain financial data. Includes: net operating margin, ROA, ROE, current ratio, quick ratio, debt ratio, inventory turnover, times interest earned, fixed charges, coverage, funded debt to working capital, net working capital turnover and earnings per share.

Product: REAL ESTATE RESIDENT EXPERT
Securities: Real Estate
Function(s): Real Estate Analysis
System(s): IBM
Special Requirements: None
Price: $99.95 **AAII Discount:** 20%
Return Policy: 30 Days, Restocking Fee: 25%
Demo: No
Technical Support: Phone (9 a.m. - 5 p.m. EST)

Description: Analyzes single family homes and fully estimates the factors that affect their value. Guides users through the decision-making process carefully asking questions regarding the type and condition of specifics such as the foundation, faucets, sewer lines, electrical service, siding, insulation, heating systems, etc. Grades conditions on a scale of 1 to 10 and records and analyzes input.

Product: STOCKAID 4.0
Securities: Stock
Function(s): Communications, Technical Analysis
System(s): IBM
Special Requirements: CGA graphics, modem for data downloading
Price: $69.95   **AAII Discount:** 20%
Return Policy: 30 Days, Restocking Fee: 25%
Demo: No
Technical Support: Phone (9 a.m. - 5 p.m. EST)

Description: Has enhanced graphics and the ability to automatically retrieve data from the Dow Jones News/Retrieval. Lets user maintain, view and study the history and performance of up to 64 NYSE stocks on the same disk. Graphic displays illustrate stock actions, trends and indicators.

Product: STOCK MARKET BARGAINS
Securities: Stock
Function(s): Fundamental Analysis
System(s): IBM
Special Requirements: None
Price: $69.95   **AAII Discount:** 20%
Return Policy: 30 Days, Restocking Fee: 25%
Demo: No
Technical Support: Phone (9 a.m. - 5 p.m. EST)

Description: Provides 2 tests for finding undervalued stocks: The Graham approach and a parameter test of price/earnings ratio, ratio of assets to liabilities, change in earnings per share, number of institutional investors and current earnings per share. Allows user to display and/or print all stocks satisfying tests 1 and 2, display complete data on file about any given stock, add new stocks for analysis at any time and update data for stocks already in data files.

Product: WALL STREET TRAINER
Securities: Stock, Option, Futures
Function(s): Simulations/Games

System(s): IBM
Special Requirements: None
Price: $29.95   AAII Discount: 20%
Return Policy: 30 Days, Restocking Fee: 25%
Demo: No
Technical Support: Phone (9 a.m. - 5 p.m. EST)

Description: Simulates fast action, long or short trading in the stock and futures markets; 8 different types of put and call options may be traded on low margins. One or 2 users may compete. Buy on price dips and sell on rallies or follow an extended bullish or bearish move that could get bigger or melt away. Learn how to use optional real world automatic stop-loss orders to prevent large losses in a market move downturn and how to use optional automatic take profit orders.

Product: ZENTERPRISE REAL ESTATE INVESTOR
Securities: Real Estate
Function(s): Real Estate Analysis
System(s): IBM
Special Requirements: None
Price: $69.95   AAII Discount: 20%
Return Policy: 30 Days, Restocking Fee: 25%
Demo: No
Technical Support: Phone (9 a.m. - 5 p.m. EST)

Description: User can calculate profitability of investment real estate; compare the potential gains from different properties under various scenarios; change assumptions such as appreciation rate, depreciation term, rental income, maintenance expenses, etc; compute the monthly before- and after-tax cash flows and the after-tax rate of return; calculate the price in order to meet a chosen profitability goal. Each screen shows the financial projections for any 5-year period.

ECON   (213) 437-2036
800 E. Ocean Boulevard   fax: (213) 435-6843
Suite 1101
Long Beach, CA 90802

Product: ECONOMIC INVESTOR
Securities: Stock, Index

Function(s): Fundamental Analysis, Portfolio Management, Security Screening
System(s): IBM
Special Requirements: None
Price: $399   **AAII Discount:** None
Return Policy: NA
Demo: Yes
Technical Support: None

Description: Based on a separate econometric examination of over 1,200 companies and asset groups. In 1 mode, user inputs values for 7 key macroeconomic variables. The system then uses the difference between current and forecasted (or past and present) values to calculate the expected return on each stock along with the probability that the sign of the expected return is correct. In another mode, the program selects stocks to buy or sell from any portfolio to minimize risk. Estimates the portfolio's standard deviation and beta.

Ecosoft, Inc.   (800) 952-0472
8295 Indy Court   (317) 271-5551
Indianapolis, IN 46214   fax: (317) 271-5561

Product: MICROSTAT-II
Securities: Not Applicable
Function(s): Statistical Analysis
System(s): IBM
Special Requirements: None
Price: $395   **AAII Discount:** 25%
Return Policy: NA
Demo: Yes
Technical Support: None

Description: An advanced package. Includes descriptive statistics; canonical correlation, principal components analysis, orthogonal factor analysis, cluster analysis, ANOVA, hypothesis testing, chi-square and crosstabs, time series, non-parametric tests, frequency and probability distributions, combinations, permutations, factorials, plus a file administration system for data entry, transformations, sorting, ordering. Can read and write external files (ASCII, DIF, dBase, etc.). Is menu-driven in the interactive mode using a keyboard or mouse, plus command file processing. Includes interface routines to graphics packages. No need to learn a complex command language.

Electrosonics, Inc.   (800) 858-8448
36380 Garfield   (313) 791-0770
Suite 1   fax: (313) 791-3010
Fraser, MI 48026

Product: EXEC-AMORT LOAN AMORTIZER PLUS
Securities: Real Estate
Function(s): Financial Planning, Real Estate Analysis, Tax Planning
System(s): IBM
Special Requirements: None
Price: $149.95   **AAII Discount:** 10%
Return Policy: 60 Days, Restocking Fee: None
Demo: Yes ($5)
Technical Support: $79.95/year, includes: Phone (9 a.m. - 5 p.m. EST)

Description: Has loan amortization schedules with APRs. Includes fixed rate and ARMs. APRs with points and fees per U.S. regulation Z, balloon payments, prepaid interest calculations, solve for unknown, yields/IRR, PV, FV. Has 11 ways to schedule payments including bi-weekly; 6 ways to calculate payments; 360, 365, or 365/360 day interest calculations; 5 ways to schedule extra payments and credit and odd period interest calculations. User can operate the in-context help screens; calendar or fiscal year reporting and optional report titles and comment section, store and retrieve. Schedules loans to $100 trillion.

Emerging Market Technologies, Inc.   (404) 457-2110
P.O. Box 420507   fax: (404) 457-8438
Atlanta, GA 30342

Product: INVESTNOW!—PERSONAL
Securities: Stock, Index, Mutual Fund, Option
Function(s): Options Analysis
System(s): IBM
Special Requirements: None
Price: $79   **AAII Discount:** 10%
Return Policy: NA
Demo: No
Technical Support: None

Description: Personal version of InvestNow!-Professional geared toward the investor. Includes all of the windows related to stock investing found in the Professional version. However, the only option analysis window included is one for covered calls. A built-in typical brokerage commission schedule can automatically compute commissions. User can do "what if" analysis.

Product: INVESTNOW!—PROFESSIONAL
Securities: Stock, Mutual Fund, Option, Futures
Function(s): Financial Planning, Options Analysis
System(s): IBM
Special Requirements: None
Price: $129   **AAII Discount:** 10%
Return Policy: NA
Demo: Yes
Technical Support: None

Description: A memory resident program. Able to analyze the buying of calls and puts, writing naked and covered calls and writing naked puts. Determines a stock's return from dividends and its realized/unrealized profit or loss. Users can input actual brokerage fees or have the program provide "typical" commission rates on trades. Computes simple and annual returns on investments and applies applicable necessary margin requirements.

Energetex Engineering   (519) 886-2672
P.O. Box 744   fax: (519) 885-2738
Waterloo, ON N2J 4C2
Canada

Product: GRAND MASTER*
Securities: Futures
Function(s): Technical Analysis
System(s): IBM
Special Requirements: None
Price: $3,000   **AAII Discount:** 5%
Return Policy: 30 Days, Restocking Fee: $150
Demo: NA
Technical Support: Phone

Description: A commodity trading system that provides pre-programmed buy and sell indicators. Also provides back-testing to verify performance. Four years of data is provided on 9 commodities. Data may be entered manually. Supports CSI and Future Source data formats. A help menu is provided on-screen along with help windows.

EPIC Systems Group (818) 564-0383
3814 E. Colorado Boulevard fax: (818) 564-0322
Suite 101
Pasadena, CA 91107

Product: NEURALYST FOR EXCEL*
Securities: Stock, Bond, Index, Mutual Fund, Option, Futures, Real Estate
Function(s): Spreadsheet, Technical Analysis, Neural network analysis of any numeric data
System(s): IBM, Macintosh
Special Requirements: Windows and Excel version 2.0+
Price: $165 **AAII Discount:** 10%
Return Policy: 30 Days, Restocking Fee: Shipping/handling
Demo: NA
Technical Support: Phone (9 a.m. - 5 p.m. PST), BBS

Description: Provides neural network analysis capability for any numeric data series. Data can be stock prices, indexes, option prices, futures, valuation data, macro economic data, etc., in any combination. Program will learn from historical examples and identify patterns and relationships that may lead to successful predictions for future data. All Excel functions, macros and charts remain accessible for data pre- and post-processing. Includes a supplemental Traders Macro Library that facilitates the inclusion of a number of popular technical analysis indicators (moving averages, oscillators, momentum, RSI, stochastics, etc.) for the user's analysis.

EQUIS International (800) 882-3040
3950 South 700 East (801) 265-9996
Suite 100
Salt Lake City, UT 84107

Product: DOWNLOADER
Securities: Stock, Index, Mutual Fund, Option, Futures

Function(s): Communications
System(s): IBM
Special Requirements: Modem
Price: $195; Warner specific version, $69   **AAII Discount:** None
Return Policy: NA
Demo: No
Technical Support: Phone (8 a.m. - 5 p.m. MST), BBS, Newsletter

Description: Collects historical and end-of-day price quotes for use with MetaStock and compatible programs. Access 7 different data vendors to collect stock, bond, commodity, index, option and mutual fund information. Collect only the data needed from CompuServe, Dial/Data, Dow Jones, Marketscan, Warner Computer, Signal and X*Press Information Services. Features include pull-down menus, auto-dialing and unattended operation to access data vendors at predetermined times.

Product: METASTOCK—PROFESSIONAL
Securities: Stock, Bond, Index, Mutual Fund, Option, Futures
Function(s): Technical Analysis
System(s): IBM
Special Requirements: Hard drive, CGA or better
Price: $349   **AAII Discount:** 10%
Return Policy: NA
Demo: Yes ($6)
Technical Support: Phone (8 a.m. - 5 p.m. MST), BBS, Newsletter

Description: Studies the relationships between securities' price movement, past price and volume. More than 60 pre-programmed technical indicators to analyze stocks, bonds, commodities, futures, indexes, mutual funds or options. Contains over 75 math and statistic functions for creating custom indicators and formulas. Can display 36 charts simultaneously for comparison of securities, indexes and studies with up to 1,000 days, weeks or months of data. Candlestick charts give users a fresh view of commodity prices. Smart Charts remembers trendlines, moving averages, formulas, buy/sell arrows and grids. Binary Waves develops user's own expert system by combining custom formulas. Unique learn-as-you-plot mode allows user to study the data, make trading decisions and then advance that chart one day at a time to simulate real trading. Compatible with more than 25 national and international data services of charting historical and end-of-day prices. When paired with additional software, such as EQUIS International's DownLoader, users can automatically collect daily, weekly and monthly price quotes in minutes. Current price data can be updated manually.

Product: PULSE PORTFOLIO MANAGEMENT SYSTEM
Securities: Stock, Bond, Mutual Fund, Option, Futures, Real Estate
Function(s): Communications, Portfolio Management, Simulations/Games
System(s): IBM
Special Requirements: Hard drive, modem for data downloading
Price: $349   **AAII Discount:** 10%
Return Policy: NA
Demo: Yes ($5, trial version $49)
Technical Support: Phone (8 a.m. - 5 p.m. MST), BBS, Newsletter

Description: Can track stocks, options, bonds, futures, mutual funds, money market accounts, CDs, mortgages, collectibles, Treasury bills, real estate, zeros and precious metals. Offers accounting for cash and cash equivalent accounts, automatic reinvestment of dividends and distributions, splits, margin, short sales and tax lots. Has more than 80 pre-programmed calculations including accrued interest, annualized return, beta, yield, yield-to-call, yield-to-maturity, cost tax basis, liquidation value and estimated income. Monthly Events Calendar lets user see important investment activities at a glance with a pop-up detailed report of day's events including dividends expected, maturities, expirations, future income and transactions. Reports include holdings, diversification, fixed income, realized gains/losses, income received, expenses paid, portfolios summary, price alerts. All can be customized in spreadsheet-like fashion into hundreds of combinations. User can update portfolios manually or automatically retrieve current price data from Signal. Will also update price data from CompuServe, DJN/R, DIAL/DATA, Market Scan, Warner Computer Systems, ASCII files or MetaStock. Supports international date/ numeric formats and securities quoted in foreign currencies.

Product: TECHNICIAN
Securities: Index

Function(s): Communications, Technical Analysis
System(s): IBM
Special Requirements: Hard drive, CGA or better; modem for updating
Price: $395; modem updating service, $120/year   **AAII Discount:** 15%
Return Policy: NA
Demo: Yes ($5)
Technical Support: Phone (8 a.m. - 5 p.m. MST), BBS, Newsletter

Description: Graphics-oriented program that analyzes the stock market to anticipate price changes. Offers more than 100 specialized indicators and studies that chart momentum, sentiment, monetary and relative strength conditions of the market. Offers composite indicators and formulas to enable users to custom design their own indicators. Comes with more than 12 years of daily historical data. Includes daily stock and index averages, STIX, TRIN, short- and long-term interest rates, precious metals and foreign currencies. Users can manually update data or use an on-line database. Each chart can display up to 1,000 days of data, and as many as 36 high-resolution charts can be displayed on the screen simultaneously. Users can test their trading systems and define conditions that generate buy/sell signals. The program then displays buy/sell arrows on the chart and shows the amount of money that would be made or lost. The user's manual discusses indicator interpretation in fully indexed format with more than 100 examples, charts and illustrations.

Ergo, Inc.   (800) 772-6637
1419 Wyant Road   (805) 969-9366
Santa Barbara, CA 93108

Product: BONDSEYE
Securities: Bond
Function(s): Bond Analysis, Portfolio Management
System(s): IBM
Special Requirements: None
Price: $65   **AAII Discount:** None
Return Policy: NA
Demo: No
Technical Support: Phone (9 a.m. - 5 p.m. PST)

Description: A bond and money market instrument calculator. Functions provided are yield-to-maturity/call, price from yield, yield with external reinvestment rates, swap analysis, duration, accrued interest, dollar extensions, T-bill discount rate/pricing, equivalent bond yield, net present value, future value, sum of coupons, interest on interest, accretion schedules, convertible bond analysis, effective par rates, crossover yield/price and calendar functions. Analyzes odd first/second coupons, long/short accrued interest periods, redemption of principal after last coupon, premium amortization and unusual pay frequencies. Issue types include corporate, municipal and T-bonds, T-bills, CDs, repos, banker's acceptances, commercial paper and money market funds.

Essex Trading Company, Ltd.♦ (800) 726-2140
300 W. Adams Street (708) 416-3530
Chicago, IL 60606 fax: (708) 416-3558

Product: ADVANCED CHANNEL ENTRY (ACE)♦
Securities: Futures
Function(s): Technical Analysis
System(s): IBM
Special Requirements: Hard drive
Price: $995-$1,995
Return Policy: NA   **AAII Discount:** None
Demo: No
Technical Support: Phone

Description: A series of 7 programs focusing on specific groups of active trading markets (Treasury bonds, stock-index futures, foreign currency futures, grains, energies, metals and international stock indexes). Gives precise trading signals daily for each market. Each program also includes an historical testing routine, graphics displays and up to 14 years of historical data for each market.

Product: EUROTRADER*
Securities: Futures
Function(s): Technical Analysis
System(s): IBM
Special Requirements: None
Price: $995

Return Policy: NA **AAII Discount:** None
Demo: No
Technical Support: Phone

Description: Designed to capture profits from longer-term moves in today's active financial futures markets. The 7 markets covered include foreign currencies, T-bonds, Eurodollars and the S&P 500. Gives user clear, precise trading signals daily for all 7 markets and takes less than 5 minutes per day to use. Also included is an historical testing routine and 14 years of historical data for each market.

Product: TRADEX 21♦
Securities: Futures
Function(s): Technical Analysis
System(s): IBM
Special Requirements: Hard drive
Price: $3,000 **AAII Discount:** None
Return Policy: NA
Demo: No
Technical Support: Phone

Description: Gives trading signals daily on 21 of today's most liquid futures markets. Designed to capture profits from intermediate-term moves using proprietary trading techniques. Markets covered include currencies, stock-index futures, grains, metals, meats, foods and energies. Also includes an historical testing routine, graphical displays and up to 14 years of historical data for each market.

FBS Systems, Inc. (309) 582-5628
P.O. Box 248
Aledo, IL 61231

Product: MARKET WINDOW
Securities: Option, Futures
Function(s): Communications, Portfolio Management, Technical Analysis
System(s): IBM
Special Requirements: None
Price: $595-$1,695 **AAII Discount:** None
Return Policy: 30 Days, Restocking Fee: None

Demo: Yes ($50)
Technical Support: $39-$199/year, includes: Phone (8 a.m. - 5 p.m. CST)

Description: Commodity charting program that also handles options and cash. Available in 4 versions that build upon each other. Version 2.0 handles up to 48 commodities with unlimited historical capability. Provides daily, weekly, monthly and yearly bar charts; trendlines, Andrews median lines; 5 moving average lines; volume and open interest charts. Version 2.1 adds relative strength, stochastics, William's %R, spread, point and figure, moving average, crossover and user-defined charts and/or studies. Version 2.2 adds the ability to track cash prices on 48 markets per commodity, basis and cash charts, projected and actual profit/loss, open positions and account balances. Version 2.3 adds the ability to update options data from DTN and provides overlays for future charts.

Ferox Microsystems (703) 684-1660
901 N. Washington Street fax: (703) 684-1666
Suite 204
Alexandria, VA 22314

Product: ENCORE! PLUS
Securities: Not Applicable
Function(s): Financial Planning, Real Estate Analysis, Simulations/ Games, Spreadsheet, Technical Analysis
System(s): IBM
Special Requirements: None
Price: $895
Return Policy: NA   **AAII Discount:** 10%
Demo: Yes
Technical Support: Annual maintenance and updates $295 after 1st year, includes: Phone (9 a.m. - 6 p.m. EST), BBS, Newsletter

Description: A system for financial and investment analysis, decision support, planning and budgeting. Uses English language modeling commands. Functions include built-in U.S. corporate and personal tax tables, currency conversion, ACRS depreciation tables and regression. Includes all functions found in a financial modeling system, such as internal rate of return and net present value. Offers Monte Carlo Simulation for risk analysis. Graphics abilities include pie, line, bar charts and more advanced charts, such as Gant and stacked bar charts.

Has capabilities for generating reports. Has Executive Information System and mouse support.

Financial Navigator International (800) 468-3636
(formerly Money Care, Inc.) (415) 962-0300
254 Dolaris Avenue fax: (415) 962-0730
Mountain View, CA 94043

Product: FINANCIAL NAVIGATOR
Securities: Stock, Bond, Mutual Fund, Option, Real Estate
Function(s): Financial Planning, Options Analysis, Portfolio Management, Real Estate Analysis
System(s): IBM
Special Requirements: 400K RAM, DOS 3.0+
Price: $495 **AAII Discount:** 10%
Return Policy: 60 Days, Restocking Fee: Varies
Demo: Yes ($5)
Technical Support: $250/year, includes: Phone (8 a.m. - 5 p.m. PST), BBS, Newsletter

Description: Provides financial management for users with complex financial situations—investors with marketable securities, owners of real estate or oil and gas interests, trusts, non-profits, estates and business owners filing Schedule C. Combines the accuracy of double-entry bookkeeping with a simple, straightforward method of data entry. Handles multiple businesses, cash flow planning and multiple equity accounts. Provides a full audit trail, summarizes information for income tax preparation and tracks investments. Produces over 50 different reports, including balance sheets, income statements and tax summaries. Handles 2,500 accounts, 10,000 payees/payors and account balances up to $2 billion. Tracks executive stock options and working interest. Includes a cost-basis balance sheet and securities portfolio analysis. Version 5.0 features a graphical user interface with full mouse support, pull down menus, pop up lists and dialog boxes.

Product: NAVIGATOR ACCESS
Securities: Stock, Bond, Index, Futures, Options
Function(s): Communications
System(s): IBM
Special Requirements: Modem

Price: $99 **AAII Discount:** None
Return Policy: 60 Days, Restocking Fee: Varies
Demo: No
Technical Support: $250/year, includes: Phone (8 a.m. - 5 p.m. PST), BBS, Newsletter

Description: A securities information retrieval program. Can be used with Financial Navigator or as a stand-alone program. Uses a modem to give quick access to securities database supplied by Warner Computer Systems. Database covers over 30,000 securities including common and preferred stocks, mutual funds, corporate bonds, municipal bonds, traded options and stock market indexes. As a stand-alone, program can retrieve over 40 key data items for each security including dividend rate per share, year-to-date high and low prices, number of shares traded, earnings per share and stock split information. This information can be retrieved and printed or loaded into any popular spreadsheet program, such as Lotus 1-2-3, for further analysis.

Finger Tip Systems Corp. (304) 472-7890
P.O. Box L
Buckhannon, WV 26201

Product: STOCK PORTFOLIO EVALUATOR
Securities: Stock, Index, Mutual Fund
Function(s): Portfolio Management, Technical Analysis
System(s): IBM
Special Requirements: None
Price: $155 **AAII Discount:** 10%
Return Policy: 30 Days, Restocking Fee: None
Demo: Yes ($15)
Technical Support: Phone (8 a.m. - 4 p.m. EST)

Description: Analyzes a stock portfolio on both a risk and reward basis, allowing user to examine portfolio on stock-by-stock, market-sector-by-market-sector and total portfolio bases. Reports purchase price and the last posted price for comparison. Calculates risk of loss according to the program rules and reports it as high, medium, low and actual—taking into account the purchase price, the current market price and the stock's volatility as measured by its beta. The stock's breakeven price can be calculated, giving the price for each security necessary to get an inflation-adjusted cost back after commissions and taxes. A risk premium is calculated for each security, security group and the portfolio as a whole. Total return is calculated for individual stocks, sectors and a portfolio.

Fossware (713) 467-3195
1000 Campbell Road
Suite 208-626
Houston, TX 77055

Product: QUOTE EXPORTER
Securities: Stock, Index, Mutual Fund, Option, Futures
Function(s): Communications
System(s): IBM
Special Requirements: Quote Monitor
Price: $99   **AAII Discount:** None
Return Policy: NA
Demo: No
Technical Support: None

Description: Program transfers daily or intra-day price data from Quote Monitor directly to the formats of specific technical analysis programs. Formats include AIQ, Compu Trac, Investograph Plus, MetaStock, OptionVue, Savant, SCTA, FCTA, Systems Writer and The Right Time. Features multi-day updates, unattended operation, batch update of all securities, prompts for selective updates.

Product: QUOTE MONITOR
Securities: Stock, Index, Mutual Fund, Option, Futures
Function(s): Communications
System(s): IBM
Special Requirements: Telemet account
Price: $295   **AAII Discount:** None
Return Policy: NA
Demo: No
Technical Support: None

Description: Displays and saves real-time or delayed prices of stocks, options, futures, futures options and indexes. Features: bar charts with any selected time interval, unattended operation, price and volume limits and news headlines. User can monitor securities by value, combine securities into portfolios or indexes, monitor spreads and ratios. With Quote Exporter, user can export daily or intra-day data directly to specific technical analysis programs in required format.

Foundation for the Study of Cycles (800) 477-0741
2600 Michelson Drive (714) 261-7261
Suite 1570 fax: (714) 261-1708
Irvine, CA 92715

Product: BASIC CYCLE ANALYSIS*
Securities: Stock, Bond, Index, Mutual Fund, Option, Futures, Real Estate
Function(s): Technical Analysis
System(s): IBM
Special Requirements: EGA
Price: $350 for Foundation members,   **AAII Discount:** 20%
  $450 for non-members
Return Policy: 30 Days, Restocking Fee: None
Demo: Yes ($5)
Technical Support: Phone (10 a.m. - 4 p.m. PST)

Description: Designed to do a complete cycle analysis of a time series. Consists of sophisticated routines to find and statistically test cycles. Requires no technical skill or statistical expertise. All internal parameters can be customized by advanced users.

Product: MCCLELLAN OSCILLATOR PROGRAM*
Securities: Stock
Function(s): Technical Analysis
System(s): IBM
Special Requirements: EGA+
Price: $350 for Foundation members,   **AAII Discount:** 20%
  $450 for non-members
Return Policy: 30 Days, Restocking Fee: None
Demo: Yes ($5)
Technical Support: Phone (10 a.m. - 4 p.m. PST)

Description: Consists of timing tools for the stock market. Program graphically presents both the oscillator and summation index in issues and volume. Comes with integrated graphics and has a complete data entry routine. Four years or as little as one month of data can be viewed on the screen at one time. User can easily scroll through the entire database without reloading. Includes more than 30 years of stock market and issues data and nearly 20 years of volume data.

Futures Truth, Co.   (704) 697-0273
(formerly Futures Truth USA)   fax: (704) 692-7375
815 Hillside Road
Hendersonville, NC 28739

Product: EXCALIBUR
Securities: Stock, Index, Futures
Function(s): Technical Analysis
System(s): Macintosh
Special Requirements: None
Price: $2,900   **AAII Discount:** None
Return Policy: 30 Days, Restocking Fee: $200
Demo: Yes
Technical Support: 1st year free, $100/hour after first year. Includes: Phone (8 a.m. - 5 p.m. EST)

Description: User can test stock or commodity trading system in 3 steps: 1) modify Fortran code, usually no more than 20 lines using the bundled QUED/M text editor by Paragon Concepts, Inc.; 2) compile and execute code using the included MacFortran/020 compiler by Absoft; 3) review the reports and analysis of the completed run by scanning the color charts to verify buy and sell points. Test how any system would have performed over the last 20 years. Reports are generated automatically and detail statistical information, trade by trade reports, time of trade analysis, entry and exit filter analysis, daily equity curve, user-defined money management schemes, worst trades analysis, pyramid schemes and more. All popular technical indicators are given and can be reprogrammed with the included source code. No knowledge of Fortran required. Advanced programmers can add code indefinitely to customize all features. Included is daily data on 23 major commodities and 10 stocks, most starting before 1970, and over 6 years of 5-minute bar data for S&Ps, bonds and Swiss Francs.

Gannsoft Publishing Co.   (509) 548-5990
11670 Riverbend Drive   fax: (509) 548-4679
Leavenworth, WA 98826-9305

Product: GANNTRADER 2
Securities: Stock, Bond, Index, Mutual Fund, Option, Futures
Function(s): Technical Analysis
System(s): IBM
Special Requirements: Hercules, EGA+, graphics, mouse recommended
Price: $1,295 **AAII Discount:** 10%
Return Policy: 30 Days, Restocking Fee: None
Demo: Yes ($15)
Technical Support: Phone (8 a.m. - 5 p.m. PST)

Description: Program plots price charts with angles, squares and planets, and plots angles from highs, lows, 360 angles, or user selected. Analyze up to 5 Gann squares at a time from any price and time point; plot planets, aspects, averages, MOF, CE Average, etc., and calculate support and resistance points, Square of 9 as well as Hexagon chart positions.

G.C.P.I. (906) 226-7600
P.O. Box 790
Marquette, MI 49855

Product: FINANCIAL PAK
Securities: Mutual Fund
Function(s): Portfolio Management, Tax Planning
System(s): IBM
Special Requirements: None
Price: $149.95 **AAII Discount:** 20%
Return Policy: Restocking Fee: 15%
Demo: No
Technical Support: None

Description: Three separate menu-driven programs deal with stock investments, amortization schedules and lump-sum and annuity investments. The stock market investment aid reports stock and mutual fund buy and sell information based on an average-cost basis with an emphasis on obtaining consistent returns. The loan program provides amortization schedules and loan summaries for all types of loans including zero-interest and balloon loans. The third program provides information about lump sum and annuity investments. Handles periodic savings plans, mutual funds and IRA accounts.

Product: INVESTMENT MASTER
Securities: Mutual Fund
Function(s): Financial Planning, Tax Planning
System(s): IBM
Special Requirements: None
Price: $49.95   **AAII Discount:** 20%
Return Policy: Restocking Fee: 15%
Demo: No
Technical Support: None

Description: Provides an investment summary that lists all the input and calculated parameters for investments. Investment summaries can be output to display screen, printer or disk file. Solve for any unknown investment parameters. Can handle a deposit or withdrawal type of annuity or a lump-sum investment. Useful in obtaining answers about periodic savings deposit plans, mutual funds and IRA accounts.

Product: LOAN MASTER
Securities: Bond
Function(s): Financial Planning, Tax Planning
System(s): IBM
Special Requirements: None
Price: $49.95   **AAII Discount:** 20%
Return Policy: Restocking Fee: 15%
Demo: No
Technical Support: None

Description: Provides loan amortization schedules and loan summaries for all types of loan situations including zero-interest and balloon contracts. Users can obtain results based on each payment or summarized on an annual basis. Annual amortization schedule is useful for tax purposes and for analyzing home and auto loans.

Product: STOCK MASTER
Securities: Stock, Mutual Fund
Function(s): Portfolio Management, Technical Analysis
System(s): IBM
Special Requirements: None

Price: $49.95 AAII Discount: 20%
Return Policy: Restocking Fee: 15%
Demo: No
Technical Support: None

Description: Designed for user who needs buy/sell advice with an emphasis on consistent returns. Can be used on a periodic basis to obtain timely buy/sell instructions on stocks and mutual funds. Completely menu-driven with options for adding a transaction, listing the transaction log and checking any account status.

Genesis Financial Data Services (800) 642-8860
P.O. Box 49578 (719) 260-6111
Colorado Springs, CO 80949 fax: (719) 260-6113

Product: NAVIGATOR
Securities: Stock, Index, Mutual Fund, Option, Futures
Function(s): Communications, Technical Analysis
System(s): IBM, Macintosh
Special Requirements: None
Price: $150 AAII Discount: 50%
Return Policy: NA
Demo: Yes
Technical Support: Phone (8 a.m. - 8 p.m. MST), BBS, Newsletter

Description: Performs the following on stocks, commodity futures and options: cataloging, creating, deleting, printing and viewing contracts; editing data files; sorting the order of contracts by commodity/stock name, delivery year, delivery month, or by daily, weekly, monthly or quarterly type files; building Gann, Spot Month and Spread Difference continuous files; converting daily files to weekly, monthly and quarterly files; moving data files without pre-creating the file; scanning of the day's results using bar charts; converting files to or from CSI, Compu Trac, MetaStock, ASCII and Lotus formats; and daily updating for CSI, Compu Trac, MetaStock, AIQ, Lotus and ASCII formats.

Good Software Corp. (800) 925-5700
13601 Preston Road (214) 239-6085
Suite 500W fax: (214) 239-4643
Dallas, TX 75240

Product: AMORTIZER PLUS*
Securities: Not Applicable
Function(s): Financial Planning, Tax Planning
System(s): IBM
Special Requirements: None
Price: $99.95				**AAII Discount:** 10%
Return Policy: 30 Days, Restocking Fee: None
Demo: No
Technical Support: Phone (8:30 a.m. - 5:30 p.m.CST)

Description: Menu-driven loan amortization tool. User enters any 3 of 4 variables (original amount, interest rate, number of periods or payment amount), program then calculates the 4th. Override feature allows all 4 variables to be entered when information is known. User can print detailed or summary amortization schedules with three lines for comments or change the variables to perform "what if" scenarios. Accommodates variable phase loans—adjustable rate, graduated payments, negative amortization, interest only and multiple balloons—and calculates APR and wrap notes. Includes annual, semi-annual, quarterly, monthly, bi-weekly and exact-day interest compounding periods; accommodates Rule of 78s, fixed-principal and principal-only loans, payments in advance (leases) and other loan conditions.

Product: REMS INVESTOR 3000
Securities: Real Estate
Function(s): Real Estate Analysis
System(s): IBM
Special Requirements: None
Price: $595				**AAII Discount:** 10%
Return Policy: 30 Days, Restocking Fee: None
Demo: Yes
Technical Support: Phone (8:30 a.m. - 5:30 p.m. CST)

Description: Real estate financial analysis and reporting program for existing or proposed projects. Forecasts the cash flows from the acquisition, financing, development, operation and sale up to 25 years in the future. Accepts and reports up to 10 of 11 financing vehicles or groundleases; uses APOD (Annual Property Operating Data) format to detail operating income and expenses to project cash flows including NOI; provides for 10 individual or group partnerships allowing for active and passive income, losses allowed and ordinary and capital gains tax rates; handles extensive depreciation and amortized expenses; provides multiple methods of specifying the property sale amount (CAP rate, appreciation, specified price); evaluate lease versus buy, exchanges and installment sales; reports key financial ratios (IRR, FMRR, ROI, ROE, NPV and wealth accumulation). Reports can be exported to a file and imported into a word processor or spreadsheet for further analysis or customization. Accepts data from Lotus 1-2-3 and similar spreadsheets.

Granite Mountain Systems (800) 368-0340
P.O. Box 430 (916) 944-2670
Fair Oaks, CA 95628 fax: (916) 944-2670

Product: FINAL JUDGEMENT
Securities: Stock, Mutual Fund
Function(s): Fundamental Analysis, Portfolio Management, Tax Planning
System(s): IBM
Special Requirements: DOS 2.1+, 256K RAM
Price: $600 **AAII Discount:** 33%
Return Policy: 45 Days, Restocking Fee: None
Demo: No
Technical Support: Phone (7 a.m. - 7 p.m. PST), Newsletter

Description: Calculates instant buy, sell or hold rating for an unlimited number of stocks listed on the NYSE, NASDAQ or AMEX. User enters data from the *Wall Street Journal*. Required are: 52-week high, 52-week low, stock symbol, P/E ratio, yield and closing price. A letter category (e.g., A for autos, B for banks, C for chemicals, etc.) is entered. Unknown categories are included in a supplementary program. If a data item is updated, program automatically recalculates all dependent items. Combines user data with Granite Mountain Systems data to provide sorted reports including rating and payout ratio. Calculates buy and sell strike prices and potential result of replacing 1 stock with another, considering taxes, fees and yields.

Greenstone Software (416) 459-8242
20 Roehampton Circle
Brampton, Ontario, L6Y 2R4
Canada

Product: RAPID
Securities: Stock, Index, Mutual Fund, Option, Futures
Function(s): Technical Analysis
System(s): IBM
Special Requirements: None
Price: $277   **AAII Discount:** 15%
Return Policy: NA
Demo: Yes ($7)
Technical Support: Phone (8 a.m. - 9 p.m. EST)

Description: A graphing program for traders and investors to make decisions to buy and sell stocks and commodities using dozens of technical tools: RSI, stochastics, MACD, candlesticks, Bollinger Bands and moving averages. Three tools give absolute buy/sell signals and report total profit results. User can experiment with the parameters of each indicator to find the best predictive signals. Price data can be entered directly from the keyboard or can be purchased from dial-up data sources.

Guard Band Investment Software, Inc.   (213) 931-4247
138 N. Edinburgh Avenue   fax: (213) 933-9637
Los Angeles, CA 90048

Product: FUND PROFIT
Securities: Bond, Index, Mutual Fund
Function(s): Communications, Technical Analysis
System(s): IBM
Special Requirements: Modem for FP modem link
Price: $295, $75 for FP Modem Link   **AAII Discount:** 15%
Return Policy: 60 Days, Restocking Fee: $17.50
Demo: No
Technical Support: Phone (8 a.m. - 5 p.m. PST)

Description: Trend-following program needing only weekly updates. Utilizes an exponential moving average, stop curve and an emergency sell alert to arrive at profitable buy and sell signals. Ranks all funds in a directory from 1st to last at 3-week intervals, from 3 months to current. Excellent for sector funds. One key fully automatic update through DJN/R with optional program (FP Modem Link). Includes free family of funds data and free sign-up with DJN/R.

Guru Systems Ltd. (604) 299-1010
314 E. Holly fax: (604) 299-7722
Suite 106
Bellingham, WA 98225

Product: PC CHART PLUS
Securities: Stock, Bond, Index, Mutual Fund, Option, Futures
Function(s): Communications, Technical Analysis
System(s): IBM
Special Requirements: Hard drive, 640K RAM, CGA, EGA, HGC or VGA graphics, modem
Price: $160 **AAII Discount:** 10%
Return Policy: NA
Demo: Yes ($8)
Technical Support: First year free, Phone (9 a.m. - 5 p.m. EST)

Description: A set of technical analysis tools to help user decide when to buy and sell stocks and commodities. Generates stock charts and standard technical indicators such as moving averages, relative strength and RSI. Can use built-in telecommunications features to download historical, end of day, intra-day and real-time prices from All-Quotes, DIAL/DATA and GEnie. Supports PC Chart, ASCII, CSI and MetaStock and up to 800 files in one subdirectory. Adjustable technical indicators: OI, volume, candlesticks, RSI, moving averages, parabolic system, directional movement index, logarithmic plot, point and figure, stochastics, daily, weekly and monthly charts, money flow index, relative strength, volatility, alpha-beta, trend lines, speed lines, Fibonacci Retracements, Guru, Market Guru and A/D indicators.

Halvorson Research Associates (813) 261-4110
2900 14th Street
Naples, FL 33940

Product: HRA SELL/BUY EDUCATOR
Securities: Stock
Function(s): Fundamental Analysis
System(s): IBM
Special Requirements: None
Price: Program and 1st month, $79.95; **AAII Discount:** 30%
next 11 months, $20/month
Return Policy: NA

Demo: Yes
Technical Support: Phone (9 a.m. - 5 p.m. EST)

Description: Provides graphic displays of a stock's earnings growth rate history and shows how past prices have compared to HRA's Theoretical Market Price. Gives a specific buy/sell recommendation on the stock's price potential, a reading of current market sentiment and its direction and the degree that HRA considers the market to be over- or under-priced. Provides information on 30 stocks to buy including sales, book value, current ratio and capitalization. Follows 800 securities.

Hamilton Software, Inc.   (800) 733-9607
6432 E. Mineral Place   (303) 770-9607
Englewood, CO 80112

Product: INVESTOR'S ACCOUNTANT*
Securities: Stock, Bond, Index, Mutual Fund, Option, Futures, Real Estate
Function(s): Communications, Portfolio Management, Technical Analysis
System(s): IBM
Special Requirements: Modem for data downloading
Price: $395   **AAII Discount:** 25%
Return Policy: 30 Days if defective
Demo: Yes ($20)
Technical Support: Phone (9 a.m. - 6 p.m. MST)

Description: Investment portfolio accounting and analysis system. Provides maintenance, analysis, and reporting for an unlimited number of separate portfolios containing any type of investment or asset (over 32,000 per portfolio). Tracks performance of investments individually and by type, automatically adjusting basis and incorporating proceeds from dividends, option writing, return of capital, stock splits, mergers, etc. Calculates portfolio-specific rate of return, ROI, YTD tax liability and prints IRS schedules B and D. Provides automatic "sweep" transferring, foreign currency conversions, global updating of securities, price range and other market event alerts and portfolio merging. Allows both manual and automatic price updating (allowing numerous on-line sources), retains an unlimited number of transactions for as long as desired and holds personal information for each account. Includes fully integrated version of Hamilton's MARKETWATCH for tracking, evaluating and graphing securities.

Product: MARKETWATCH*
Securities: Stock, Bond, Index, Mutual Fund, Option, Futures
Function(s): Communications, Technical Analysis
System(s): IBM
Special Requirements: Modem for data downloading
Price: $59 **AAII Discount:** None
Return Policy: 30 Days if defective
Demo: No
Technical Support: Phone (9 a.m. - 6 p.m. MST)

Description: Evaluates and compares investments including mutual funds, stocks, options, commodities, money markets and market indexes. Either manual or automatic data entry. Annualizes yields including proceeds from dividends and distributions, evaluates price movement trends, graphs normalized performances of multiple funds along with moving averages and/or volumes, projects total returns on individual portfolios and provides comprehensive investment comparisons. Accommodates an unlimited number of securities for which share prices (and optional volumes) are updated according to user-specified time intervals and are combined with dividends, distributions and transactions to reveal total investment performance.

Product: PORTFOLIO ANALYZER*
Securities: Stock, Bond, Index, Mutual Fund, Option, Futures, Real Estate
Function(s): Communications, Financial Planning, Options Analysis, Portfolio Management, Tax Planning
System(s): IBM
Special Requirements: Modem for data downloading
Price: $99 **AAII Discount:** None
Return Policy: 30 Days if defective
Demo: Yes ($5)
Technical Support: Phone (9 a.m. - 6 p.m. MST)

Description: Investment portfolio management and analysis system for home, business and professional use. Integrated, menu-driven system provides analysis of investment portfolios containing stocks, bonds, options, cash, annuities, hard assets and others. Accommodates over 1,000 separate portfolios and produces numerous performance and financial reports. Tracks performance of investments individually and in groups including all proceeds from dividends, option writing, etc. Provides YTD tax liability and prints IRS schedules B and D. Allows both manual and automatic price updating, retains an unlimited number of transactions for as long as desired and holds descriptive information for each account.

H & H Scientific (301) 292-2958
13507 Pendleton Street
Fort Washington, MD 20744

Product: STOCK OPTION ANALYSIS PROGRAM
Securities: Option
Function(s): Communications, Options Analysis
System(s): IBM
Special Requirements: Modem or Signal for data downloading
Price: $150 **AAII Discount:** 10%
Return Policy: NA
Demo: Yes ($35)
Technical Support: Phone (9 a.m. - 5 p.m. EST)

Description: Uses Black-Scholes model to calculate the fair price of options. Expected profit (or loss) on transactions can be calculated and graphed for any time until the options expire. Can perform "what if" calculations for complicated stock option positions and for analyzing stock options such as debt options and commodity options. Includes 3 commission schedules, an option volatility file and a full Dow Jones News/Retrieval, Signal and Warner interface. Data may also be entered manually.

Product: STOCK OPTION SCANNER
Securities: Option
Function(s): Communications, Options Analysis, Security Screening
System(s): IBM
Special Requirements: Modem or Signal for data downloading
Price: $150 **AAII Discount:** 10%
Return Policy: NA

Demo: Yes ($35)
Technical Support: Phone (9 a.m. - 5 p.m. EST)

Description: Designed for stock option analysis. Can scan a list of 3,000 stock options (automatically downloaded from Dow Jones News/Retrieval, Signal or Warner or entered manually) and rank order the top 50 and bottom 50 options by any of 5 selection criteria based on the annual rate of return (such as the ratio of theoretical option price to actual current option price). Can convert data from the scan file (3,000 options) to a daily file (25 options) for use with the Stock Options Analysis Program.

Harloff, Inc. (216) 734-7271
26106 Tallwood Drive
North Olmsted, OH 44070

Product: CALL/PUT OPTIONS
Securities: Option
Function(s): Options Analysis
System(s): Apple II, IBM
Special Requirements: None
Price: $199   **AAII Discount:** None
Return Policy: NA
Demo: No
Technical Support: None

Description: Uses a proprietary model to predict current and future expected call and put prices, expected option price change for a given stock price change and time change and break-even prices for hedge positions. Evaluates "what if" scenarios and hedge positions and determines optimum call and put positions. Model evaluates option prices at non-expiration times, has an accurate put model and can determine optimum positions.

Heizer Software (800) 888-7667
P.O. Box 232019 (510) 943-7667
Pleasant Hill, CA 94523 fax: (510) 943-6882

Product: BOND PORTFOLIO
Securities: Bond

Function(s): Bond Analysis, Portfolio Management, Spreadsheet
System(s): IBM, Macintosh
Special Requirements: Excel
Price: $25   **AAII Discount:** None
Return Policy: NA
Demo: No
Technical Support: Phone (9 a.m. - 5 p.m. PST)

Description: Calculates duration, modified duration, duration based on periods, volatility and yields including current yield, yield to maturity and yield to first call. An entire bond portfolio may be tracked. Provides a summary that calculates the totals and averages based on the whole portfolio.

Product: BOND PRICING
Securities: Bond
Function(s): Bond Analysis, Portfolio Management, Spreadsheet
System(s): IBM, Macintosh
Special Requirements: Excel or Works
Price: $8   **AAII Discount:** None
Return Policy: NA
Demo: No
Technical Support: Phone (9 a.m. - 5 p.m. PST)

Description: Calculates current yield and yield to maturity from standard bond price, coupon and maturity data. Calculates the price required to meet user-defined yield criteria to the call date and to maturity.

Product: INVESTMENT PERFORMANCE CHART
Securities: Stock, Bond, Mutual Fund
Function(s): Financial Planning, Portfolio Management, Spreadsheet
System(s): IBM, Macintosh
Special Requirements: Excel
Price: $15   **AAII Discount:** None
Return Policy: NA
Demo: No
Technical Support: Phone (9 a.m. - 5 p.m. PST)

Description: Produces a graphical chart that displays the performance of long-term investment plans, i.e., an IRA or a company investment plan. Plots amount invested and value of the investment and provides guidelines to judge the equivalent annual interest rate at any time during the investment. Allows "what-if" analysis.

Product: MUTUAL FUND REINVESTMENT
Securities: Mutual Fund
Function(s): Portfolio Management, Spreadsheet
System(s): IBM, Macintosh
Special Requirements: Excel or Works
Price: $15   **AAII Discount:** None
Return Policy: NA
Demo: No
Technical Support: Phone (9 a.m. - 5 p.m. PST)

Description: Handles mutual fund recordkeeping when earnings are reinvested. Tracks number of shares, capital gains, total investment, average share price, growth rate and more.

Product: NAIC STOCK SELECTION GUIDE
Securities: Stock
Function(s): Fundamental Analysis, Security Screening, Spreadsheet
System(s): IBM, Macintosh
Special Requirements: Excel or Works
Price: $30   **AAII Discount:** None
Return Policy: NA
Demo: No
Technical Support: Phone (9 a.m. - 5 p.m. PST)

Description: Duplicates standard NAIC's Stock Selection Guide and performs all the calculations required to arrive at a buy/hold/sell recommendation.

Product: OPTION—WARRANT COMBO
Securities: Option, Futures
Function(s): Options Analysis, Spreadsheet

System(s): IBM, Macintosh
Special Requirements: Excel or Works
Price: $49　　　　　　　　　　**AAII Discount:** None
Return Policy: NA
Demo: No
Technical Support: Phone (9 a.m. - 5 p.m. PST)

Description: Has 2 programs: Option-Warrant Analyzer calculates theoretical values of up to 6 options and warrants based on the Thorp and Kassouf analysis. Can be used to find the most under- or overvalued option of any stock. Option-Warrant Analyzer calculates theoretical values of up to 6 options and warrants based on the Black-Scholes method.

Product: STOCK PORTFOLIO
Securities: Stock
Function(s): Portfolio Management, Spreadsheet
System(s): IBM, Macintosh
Special Requirements: Excel or Works
Price: $15　　　　　　　　　　**AAII Discount:** None
Return Policy: NA
Demo: No
Technical Support: Phone (9 a.m. - 5 p.m. PST)

Description: Fulfills routine trading record needs in common and preferred stocks. Records buy/sell dates and prices, commissions, dividends, overall portfolio performance statistics, etc. Handles partial sales, short sales and long- and short-term holding periods.

Product: STOCK VALUATION
Securities: Stock
Function(s): Fundamental Analysis, Portfolio Management, Spreadsheet
System(s): IBM, Macintosh
Special Requirements: Excel
Price: $25　　　　　　　　　　**AAII Discount:** None
Return Policy: NA
Demo: No
Technical Support: Phone (9 a.m. - 5 p.m. PST)

Description: Uses 5 methods to compute a stock's theoretical price to determine whether the stock is over- or under-valued. Includes a stock split/stock dividend adjusting template. Growth rate and expected return are also calculated.

Hinson Products   (515) 224-4467
Equitable Building   fax: (515) 288-0932
Suite 320
P.O. Box 10384
Des Moines, IA 50306

Product: PORTEVAL PORTFOLIO EVALUATOR
Securities: Stock, Bond, Index, Mutual Fund, Option, Futures, Real Estate
Function(s): Financial Planning, Portfolio Management
System(s): IBM
Special Requirements: None
Price: $99 version 4.01, $159 version 5.0   **AAII Discount:** 20%
Return Policy: NA
Demo: No
Technical Support: Phone (9 a.m. - 3 p.m. CST)

Description: Helps keep track of stocks, bonds, partnerships and other asset/liability type investments. Categories are user supplied and are basically unlimited. Printout is available in either screen, 80- or 132-column dot matrix printers and 132 daisy wheel printer and the 132-column compressed mode for 80-column dot matrix printers. Printout includes symbol, quantity, description, purchase date, costs, market values, unrealized gain/loss, dividends-income, percent yield and percent of portfolio. Sorts by category, then maturity date, then alphabetically. Market value is user-supplied.

HowardSoft   (800) 822-4829
1224 Prospect Street   (619) 454-0121
Suite 150   fax: (800) 248-2937
La Jolla, CA 92037

Product: REAL ESTATE ANALYZER*
Securities: Real Estate

Function(s): Financial Planning, Real Estate Analysis
System(s): Apple II, IBM
Special Requirements: IBM version requires GW-BASIC or BASICA
Price: Apple $350; IBM $395 **AAII Discount:** None
Return Policy: NA
Demo: Yes ($15)
Technical Support: Phone (8:30 a.m. - 4:30 p.m. PST), Newsletter

Description: Analyzes real estate investment opportunities. Compares properties, creative financing, tax consequences, depreciation, cash flow and more. Projects investment results with 30-year tables of pre- and after-tax cash flow and 7 measures of return on investment. Features 10 loans and 50 leases, built-in tax laws, menu-driven control, monthly precision, flexible inflation modeling and "what if" planning. Provides an investment guide, examples and on-screen help keys.

Product: TAX PREPARER
Securities: Not Applicable
Function(s): Financial Planning, Tax Planning
System(s): Apple II, IBM
Special Requirements: IBM version requires GW-BASIC or BASICA
Price: Apple $250 (annual updates, $79); **AAII Discount:** None
   IBM $295 (annual updates, $99)
Return Policy: NA
Demo: No
Technical Support: Phone (8:30 a.m. - 4:30 p.m. PST), Newsletter

Description: Automates preparation of tax returns for individuals by looking up numbers in tables, performing the arithmetic and then automatically completes and computes numerous IRS worksheets. Performs the math for the simple and complex returns. Transfers hundreds of numbers back and forth among forms and recalculates the entire return as often as necessary. Handles unlimited record-keeping and unlimited number of stocks, bonds, rentals, accounts and depreciated assets. Gives "what if" capabilities with tax laws built-in past the current year and hundreds of pages of line-by-line detail so that users see what the software is doing and can handle exceptions. Has built-in passive loss rules, automated handling of passive loss rules, IRS-accepted dot-matrix or laser printouts.

Product: TAX PREPARER: PARTNERSHIP EDITION
Securities: Not Applicable
Function(s): Financial Planning, Tax Planning
System(s): IBM
Special Requirements: GW-BASIC or BASICA
Price: $395, annual update $165   **AAII Discount:** None
Return Policy: NA
Demo: No
Technical Support: Phone (8:30 a.m. - 4:30 p.m. PST), Newsletter

Description: Has all the features of Tax Preparer: Federal Edition, plus helps plan tax strategies, keep tax records and prepare IRS-accepted partnership returns. Includes a distribution worksheet which handles complex partnership arrangements and automatically creates all the partners' K-1s. All of the A.C.R.S. tables and depreciation calculations are built-in and automatic.

Inmark Development Corporation   (415) 961-9000
2065 Landings Drive
Mountainview, CA 94043

Product: MARKET MAKER FOR WINDOWS
Securities: Stock, Bond, Index, Mutual Fund, Option, Futures
Function(s): Communications, Technical Analysis
System(s): IBM
Special Requirements: Microsoft Windows, modem
Price: $295   **AAII Discount:** 25%
Return Policy: 60 Days, Restocking Fee: None
Demo: Yes
Technical Support: Phone (9 a.m. - 5 p.m. PST)

Description: Integrates 3 primary programs. The Charts and Analysis program allows the user to chart securities and perform a wide variety of technical analysis studies. Using more than 35 functions, user can draw trendlines, trend channels, least squares and Gann angles, and calculate moving averages. Charts market studies such as relative strength, spreads directional movements, oscillators and cycle analysis. Screen and window management functions allow user to change graphs, zoom in on specific windows and selected time periods, change line type and line color, etc. The Data Manager performs various housekeeping functions on the actual files such as copying, deleting, modifying and adding data. Can adjust data for stock splits and stock dividends and can export and import Market Maker data files with Lotus 1-2-3 and Microsoft Excel. Spreadsheet interface allows users to implement and test different trading and investment strategies. The Communications Manager will automatically dial the database, log on, retrieve the price information, log off, and update the user's data files. If the user accesses 2 databases, the Communications Manager will automatically repeat the process for the other database. To update a portfolio, user presses only 1 key.

Institute for Options Research, Inc.   (800) 334-0854
P.O. Box 6586   (702) 588-3590
Lake Tahoe, NV 89449

Product: OPTION MASTER
Securities: Option
Function(s): Options Analysis
System(s): Apple II, IBM, Macintosh
Special Requirements: None
Price: $89 plus $8 handling fee   **AAII Discount:** 20%
Return Policy: 30 Days, Restocking Fee: $8 handling
Demo: No
Technical Support: Phone (8 a.m. - 5 p.m. PST)

Description: Measures the theoretical value of an option. Will also give the probability of profit when buying, writing or entering an option strategy. By making a few computer-prompted entries, user can determine the fair value of options on any stock or index or commodity. Does not require access to database or information service. All information can be obtained from the options listings in any major newspaper.

International Advanced Models, Inc.   (708) 369-8461
P.O. Box 1019
Oak Brook, IL 60522

Product: OPTIONEXPERT—THE STRATEGIST
Securities: Option
Function(s): Options Analysis
System(s): IBM
Special Requirements: None

Price: $124.50 AAII Discount: 20%
Return Policy: NA
Demo: No
Technical Support: None

Description: Decision support program allows the user to determine the expected return of any option strategy (up to 10 simultaneously) and select the best strategy consistent with stock price expectations. Both stock and index options can be analyzed. Calculates and displays the return; defines the risk; estimates the gain probability. Delta is also calculated. Individual option values are estimated using Black-Scholes model. Accounts for commissions and dividends and determines the volatility. Each strategy can combine different numbers of call and put options with various expiration times and strike prices, long or short. Ranks strategies using a weighted measure of the expected return, risk and gain probability, and the optimum strategy is determined. User can define stock-price probabilities for each date analyzed or use normal probability distributions generated by the program. Lists all possible answers to program prompts on the screen.

Intex Solutions, Inc. (617) 449-6222
35 Highland Circle fax: (617) 444-2318
Needham, MA 02194

Product: FINANCIAL TOOLKIT*
Securities: Not Applicable
Function(s): Financial Planning, Portfolio Management, Spreadsheet
System(s): IBM
Special Requirements: Lotus 1-2-3 or Symphony
Price: $199.95 AAII Discount: None
Return Policy: 30 Days, Restocking Fee: None
Demo: No
Technical Support: Phone (8 a.m. - 6 p.m. EST), Newsletter

Description: Program expands Lotus' basic PV, FV, i, n and PMT @functions with up to 7 optional arguments. Solves more complex loans that have variable interest rates, variable payment streams, blended rates, balloon payments or partial interim periods. New @functions include annual percentage rates, effective yields, depreciation rates and amortization schedules.

Product: FIXED INCOME DATA OBTAINER (FIDO)*
Securities: Bond
Function(s): Communications, Spreadsheet
System(s): IBM
Special Requirements: Lotus 1-2-3 or Excel, account with Interactive Data Corporation
Price: $95   **AAII Discount:** None
Return Policy: 30 Days, Restocking Fee: None
Demo: No
Technical Support: Phone (8 a.m. - 6 p.m. EST), Newsletter

Description: A real-time link to Interactive Data Corporation's (IDC) "end of day" database of fixed-income information. Automatically retrieves updated bond and MBS prices and other descriptive data. Menu selections bring data into Lotus 1-2-3 or Excel spreadsheet for further analysis.

Product: INTEX BOND AMORTIZATION*
Securities: Bond
Function(s): Bond Analysis, Portfolio Management
System(s): IBM
Special Requirements: None
Price: $295   **AAII Discount:** None
Return Policy: 30 Days, Restocking Fee: None
Demo: Yes
Technical Support: Phone (8 a.m. - 6 p.m. EST), Newsletter

Description: User generates bond amortization schedules with a few inputs. Enter bond's current price, par value, coupon rate, coupon frequency and settlement and maturity dates; the amortization schedules are then generated automatically. Optional arguments allow user to specify how interest is prorated, the amortization method (scientific or straight line) and the bond type (Treasury, agency, corporate or municipal). User can output to Lotus 1-2-3 for further analysis.

Product: INTEX BOND CALCULATIONS
Securities: Bond

Function(s): Bond Analysis, Portfolio Management, Spreadsheet
System(s): IBM
Special Requirements: Lotus 1-2-3, Symphony, Excel, Paradox
Price: $395 and up **AAII Discount:** None
Return Policy: 30 Days, Restocking Fee: None
Demo: Yes
Technical Support: Phone (8 a.m. - 6 p.m. EST), Newsletter

Description: An add-in program that lets user compute yield, price, duration, more within Lotus 1-2-3, Symphony or Paradox. Provides SIA-compliant calculations for bills, notes and bonds. Functions can be added to spreadsheet or database with a single keystroke.

Product: INTEX CMO/REMIC MODELING TOOLKIT*
Securities: Bond
Function(s): Bond Analysis, Portfolio Management
System(s): IBM
Special Requirements: None
Price: Varies **AAII Discount:** None
Return Policy: 30 Days, Restocking Fee: None
Demo: Yes
Technical Support: Phone (8 a.m. - 6 p.m. EST)

Description: Allows user to "reverse engineer" new or existing agency CMO models using the same technology as used for the CMO Modeling Service. Enables user to respond to CMO deals as needs dictate. A full range of static calculations and reports are provided, such as PAC collars, duration, cashflow, factors, weighted average life and yield to maturity.

Product: INTEX FIXED-INCOME SUBROUTINES*
Securities: Stock, Bond, Option, Futures
Function(s): Bond Analysis, Portfolio Management, Technical Analysis
System(s): IBM
Special Requirements: None
Price: Varies **AAII Discount:** None
Return Policy: 30 Days, Restocking Fee: None
Demo: No
Technical Support: Phone (8 a.m. - 6 p.m. EST)

Description: Program provides all key calculations for every type of bond instrument. Provides over 3 dozen different calculations including yield, duration, convexity and accrued interest. Ongoing development process assures compatibility with the industry's newest instruments. Subroutines are written in "C"—user can select subroutines for the PC, workstation or mainframe environments.

Product: INTEX MORTGAGE-BACKED CALCULATIONS
(formerly Mortgage-Backed Portfolio Calculations)
Securities: Bond
Functions: Bond Analysis, Portfolio Management, Spreadsheet
System(s): IBM
Special Requirements: Lotus 1-2-3, Symphony, Excel, Paradox
Price: $395 and up   **AAII Discount:** None
Return Policy: 30 Days, Restocking Fee: None
Demo: Yes
Technical Support: Phone (8 a.m. - 6 p.m. EST)

Description: A mortgage-backed security analysis program that computes all key MBS calculations, factoring in considerations such as prepayment rates, delay days and service costs. Functions are entered into spreadsheet or database with just a few commands. Three different versions: basic version offers a CPR prepayment model; advanced version provides CPR, PSA and FHA models and support for ARMs; excess servicing version provides added calculations for institutions which issue MBS instruments.

Product: INTEX OPTION-ADJUSTED SPREAD MODELS*
Securities: Bond
Function(s): Financial Planning, Options Analysis, Portfolio Management
System(s): IBM
Special Requirements: 80386 or better processor or DOS/Windows/RISC workstations
Price: Varies   **AAII Discount:** None
Return Policy: 30 Days, Restocking Fee: None
Demo: Yes
Technical Support: Phone (8 a.m. - 6 p.m. EST)

Description: Program allows user to deal with factors of uncertainty in the financial markets such as fluctuating interest rates, call provisions and prepayment rates. Can run from a PC to a workstation. Program employs two-factor Monte Carlo simulation for modeling of future scenarios, capturing the volatility of both long and short forward rates. Fully supports ARMs, CMOs and callable bonds.

Product: INTEX OPTION PRICE CALCULATIONS
Securities: Option
Function(s): Options Analysis, Portfolio Management, Spreadsheet
System(s): IBM
Special Requirements: Lotus 1-2-3, Symphony, Excel, Paradox
Price: $395 and up   **AAII Discount:** None
Return Policy: 30 Days, Restocking Fee: None
Demo: Yes
Technical Support: Phone (8 a.m. - 6 p.m. EST), Newsletter

Description: Three common pricing models are provided, appropriate for computing options on bonds as well as equities (stocks, commodities, futures and currencies). These models include Black-Scholes, Binomial and "Down and Out." Both puts and calls are supported as well as American and European methods. All the "Greek" sensitivity ratios (delta, gamma, theta, vega, rho and psi) are included for additional analysis along with essential volatility and implied volatility functions. Runs as an add-in with Lotus 1-2-3, Symphony, Excel and Paradox.

Investability Corporation   (312) 822-0237
P.O. Box 11162
Chicago, IL 60611

Product: INVESTABILITY MONEYMAP*
Securities: Not Applicable
Function(s): Financial Planning
System(s): IBM
Special Requirements: None
Price: $20   **AAII Discount:** 10%
Return Policy: 30 Days, Restocking Fee: $3
Demo: No
Technical Support: None

Description: Permits user to specify inflation rates, projected investment returns, portfolio sizes or income/contribution streams, frequency of cash flows and time periods. The output, on-screen or printed hard copy with the ability to produce personalized headings will show projected contribution/income amounts and portfolio balances for each cash flow date, providing an investment/retirement schedule that can act as a benchmark for actual investment or retirement programs. Format lets user specify target goals in present-day dollars, then produces the resulting schedule incorporating inflation adjustments. Also calculates present value, future value and payment amounts on a time-value-of-money basis. Use as an investment planning tool for a college fund or any other major investment program as well as pre- and post-retirement planning.

Investment Software (303) 563-9543
543 CR 312
Ignacio, CO 81137

Product: PERSONAL MARKET ANALYSIS (PMA)
Securities: Stock, Index, Mutual Fund, Futures
Function(s): Technical Analysis
System(s): IBM
Special Requirements: Graphics card
Price: $149   **AAII Discount:** 10%
Return Policy: 30 Days, Restocking Fee: None
Demo: No
Technical Support: Phone (8 a.m. - 5 p.m. MST)

Description: Calculates, charts, stores values of technical indicators. Indicators are predefined and an unlimited number of other indicators may be defined to user specifications. The manual discusses the predefined indicators and furnishes descriptions and set-up instructions for a variety of other indicators including: moving average convergence-divergence, relative strength index, momentum or rate-of-change indicators, stochastic oscillators, volume indicators (NVI, OBV, PVT and DVT), parabolic time/price system and directional movement indicator. Features: can combine and manipulate simple indicators to produce derivative indicators; input data can be charted to the same time scale and on the same chart as personal indicators; expanded charting capabilities—up to 3 curves per chart, charts any 12 consecutive month period, automatic chart scaling, insertion of flags to indicate significant points, addition of lines to indicate trends, bounds, etc., automatic printing of pre-selected chart groups, menu-driven, charts to highest standard resolution provided by computer system.

INVESTment TECHnology (903) 455-3255
5104 Utah Street
Greenville, TX 75401

Product: INVESTIGATOR+
Securities: Stock, Index, Mutual Fund, Option, Futures
Function(s): Communications, Portfolio Management, Technical Analysis
System(s): IBM
Special Requirements: None
Price: $99, access download software $29; **AAII Discount:** None
GRAFPlus printer control software $29
Return Policy: 30 Days
Demo: Yes ($10)
Technical Support: Phone (24 hours/day)

Description: A charting, technical analysis and data management program for stocks, options, indexes, mutual funds or commodities. Uses over 30 technical indicators such as moving averages, MACD, momentum, Williams %R, stochastics, RSI, OBV, TRIN and others.

Investment Tools Phone not available
P.O. Box 8254
Emeryville, CA 94662

Product: FUTURES MARKETS ANALYZER
Securities: Futures
Function(s): Technical Analysis
System(s): IBM
Special Requirements: Hard drive
Price: $995 **AAII Discount:** None
Return Policy: NA
Demo: Yes ($9)
Technical Support: None

Description: Monitors 36 futures contracts including stock index futures, currencies, meats, grains, metals, CRB index, crude oil, heating oil, cotton, sugar, coffee and cocoa. User inputs daily high, low and closing prices; generates a report giving buy/sell signal, entry price, exit price and stop for 36 futures contracts. Optimizes parameters automatically at the time of change of contract month. Will accept manual data input or ASCII file. File conversion program is included to convert daily quote file from Technical Tools, CSI and Genesis Data Services.

Jerome Technology, Inc. (908) 369-7503
P.O. Box 403 fax: (908) 369-5993
Raritan, NJ 08869

Product: WAVE WISE SPREADSHEET (formerly Wave Wise)
Securities: Stock, Bond, Index, Mutual Fund, Futures
Function(s): Spreadsheet, Technical Analysis
System(s): IBM
Special Requirements: 640K RAM, EGA or VGA graphics
Price: $495   **AAII Discount:** 20%
Return Policy: NA
Demo: Yes ($20)
Technical Support: Phone (8:30 a.m. - 6 p.m. EST)

Description: Spreadsheet combining a traditional spreadsheet with the graphics capabilities of stock market charting packages. Provides user with formula construction capabilities to make custom indicators and studies. Formulas can be automatically applied to the entire column for fast computations. Perform Elliott Wave analysis, cycle analysis, Fibonacci Retracements, "what if" analysis using built-in technical analysis and statistics functions. Has over 40,000 data cell capacity. Includes line and bar charts, full zoom capability and chart overlay/split screen capability.

John Pluth's Systems and Solutions, Inc. (602) 744-2202
(formerly Systems and Solutions, Inc.)
10011 N. Orange Ranch Road
Tucson, AZ 85741

Product: ENTRY/EXIT/EQUITY (E*E*E) SYSTEM
Securities: Stock, Index, Futures
Function(s): Portfolio Management, Technical Analysis
System(s): IBM

Special Requirements: Hard drive, 640K RAM
Price: $595-$695 for complete systems; **AAII Discount:** 10%
individual programs, $95-$395
Return Policy: 10 Days, Restocking Fee: 10%
Demo: Yes ($50)
Technical Support: 1 month free, cost varies, includes: Phone (8 a.m. - 12 a.m. MST)

Description: Consists of 3 separate but integrated programs: Entry, Exit and Equity analysis. Standard or advanced version price/time/oscillator pattern finder searches for entry and exit market formations and determines probabilities of market events. Capable of designing and analyzing entire mixed market trading portfolios by combining different trades created by the Entry and Exit components into the Equity program. Features include statistical verification of trades/models, calculation of confidence intervals, log-normal percents, and risk of ruin, optimization, cross validation techniques, interactive or batch mode processing and a data management utility program.

Koltys, Inc. (800) 633-4641
P.O. Box 862215 (404) 594-7860
Marietta, GA 30062

Product: BOLLINGER BANDS*
Securities: Stock, Index
Function(s): Technical Analysis
System(s): IBM
Special Requirements: None
Price: $185 **AAII Discount:** 10%
Return Policy: NA
Demo: Yes
Technical Support: $100, includes: Phone (9 a.m. - 5 p.m. EST)

Description: Automatically calculates a 20-day moving average of the S&P 500 and S&P 100 cash index along with an upper and lower volatility band and 2 standard deviations from the moving average using the last 100 days of data.

Larry Rosen Co. (502) 228-4343
7008 Springdale Road fax: (502) 228-4782
Louisville, KY 40241

Product: BOND PORTFOLIO MANAGER
Securities: Bond
Function(s): Bond Analysis, Financial Planning, Portfolio Management, Spreadsheet, Tax Planning
System(s): Apple II, IBM, Macintosh
Special Requirements: Spreadsheet (Lotus 1-2-3, Excel or AppleWorks)
Price: $89   **AAII Discount:** 20%
Return Policy: NA
Demo: No
Technical Support: Phone (9 a.m. - 5 p.m. EST)

Description: Keeps track of the market value of each bond and the entire portfolio (priced to the lesser value of call or maturity); the month and day that each interest payment is due (as interest is received or coupons are clipped receipts can merely be checked off the list for that month of receivables expected; also interest receipts can be balanced by month throughout the year); unrealized gain or loss for each bond, ranked in order of magnitude from the largest loss to largest gain. Calculations are made using taxable basis adjusted for amortization to determine which bonds to consider selling or swapping to create a tax loss. Evaluates and reports portfolios by credit worthiness of the bond issuer (e.g., 25% of portfolio is rated AAA, etc.) and date of maturity, call or put, (e.g., 18% of the portfolio matures or is expected to be called in 1998). Features housekeeping information such as bond location, serial number, whether registered or coupon, purchasing broker, call and put dates in chronological order. User enter fewer than 10 numbers and current date and the software then makes all the calculations. Calculated duration and convexity for both individual bonds and entire portfolio.

Product: COMPLETE BOND ANALYZER
Securities: Bond
Function(s): Bond Analysis, Financial Planning, Tax Planning
System(s): Apple II, IBM, Macintosh
Special Requirements: None
Price: $89   **AAII Discount:** 20%
Return Policy: NA
Demo: No
Technical Support: Phone (9 a.m. - 5 p.m. EST)

Description: Calculates bond yield-to-maturity, price, given yield-to-maturity, yield-to-call, accrued interest at purchase or sale, duration and revised duration, theoretical spot rates, etc. Results are computed for taxables or tax-exempts, for 360- or 365-day years, and for government, agency, conventional or zero-coupon bonds.

Product: FINANCIAL & INTEREST CALCULATOR
Securities: Stock, Bond, Index, Mutual Fund, Option, Futures, Real Estate
Function(s): Financial Planning, Portfolio Management
System(s): Apple II, IBM, Macintosh
Special Requirements: None
Price: $89   **AAII Discount:** 20%
Return Policy: NA
Demo: No
Technical Support: Phone (9 a.m. - 5 p.m. EST)

Description: User can perform studies including: IRR for retirement plans—with 1 or more cash flows per year, including multiple cash flows within the same year; loan amortization schedules; variable rate mortgage loan amortization schedules; mortgage points—how they effect the true cost of a loan; future value of a single or a series of investments—how much an investment today or a series of equal investments are worth in the future with growth at a stated interest rate; present value of a single future payment—the discounted value today of money due in the future; present value of an annuity—the discounted value today of a series of future equal periodic payments; internal rate of return (IRR) given a series of cash flows; super compounding—finds either the amount to invest to accumulate a stated sum in the future or the future value, assuming the 1st year investment is a stated amount. Contains documentation.

Product: INVESTMENT IRR ANALYSIS FOR STOCKS, BONDS & REAL ESTATE
Securities: Stock, Bond, Real Estate
Function(s): Financial Planning, Fundamental Analysis, Portfolio Management, Real Estate Analysis, Spreadsheet, Tax Planning
System(s): Apple II, IBM, Macintosh
Special Requirements: Spreadsheet

Price: $89   AAII Discount: 20%
Return Policy: NA
Demo: No
Technical Support: Phone (9 a.m. - 5 p.m. EST)

Description: Calculates internal rate of return (after taxes) for existing or proposed investments at any desired interest rate for reinvestment of cash flows, as well as with zero reinvestment. User can compute and display a complete year-by-year (up to 40 years) cash flow analysis.

Product: MORTGAGE LOANS—TO REFINANCE OR NOT
Securities: Real Estate
Function(s): Financial Planning, Real Estate Analysis, Spreadsheet
System(s): Apple II, IBM, Macintosh
Special Requirements: Spreadsheet
Price: $89   AAII Discount: 20%
Return Policy: NA
Demo: No
Technical Support: Phone (9 a.m. - 5 p.m. EST)

Description: Determines whether or not to refinance a loan by considering the interplay between the old and new interest rate; the costs to obtain the new loan appraisal; up-front fees to the lender—points; origination fees; number of years remaining on the old loan compared to the number of years over which the new loan is repayable; the length of time the borrower is likely to keep the new loan (before selling); the amount of the new loan; pay-off penalties, if any on both the old and new loans, etc. Applies time value of money concepts to help the borrower select the best path. Works with Lotus 1-2-3, Excel, Works and AppleWorks.

LINDO Systems, Inc.   (800) 441-2378
(formerly General Optimization)   (312) 871-2524
1415 N. Dayton   fax: (312) 871-1777
Chicago, IL 60622

Product: WHAT'SBEST!
Securities: Not Applicable
Function(s): Linear Programming, Spreadsheet

System(s): IBM, Macintosh
Special Requirements: Lotus 1-2-3, Symphony and Quatro Pro
Price: 400 variables $149; 1,500 variables $695; 4,000 variables $995; 16,000 variables $2,995; 32,000 variables $4,995   **AAII Discount:** None
Return Policy: 30 Days, Restocking Fee: None
Demo: Yes
Technical Support: Phone (9 a.m. - 5 p.m. CST), Newsletter

Description: Linear programming add-in for spreadsheets. Find answers that maximize profit and minimize cost on a variety of applications such as portfolio allocation and debt defeasance. Personal version, up to 400 variables; Commercial version, up to 1,500 variables; Professional version, up to 4,000 variables; Industrial version, up to 16,000 variables; and the Extended version, up to 32,000 variables.

Lotus Development Corporation (800) 343-5414
55 Cambridge Parkway (617) 577-8500
Cambridge, MA 02142

Product: LOTUS IMPROV 1.0*
Securities: Not Applicable
Function(s): Spreadsheet
System(s): NeXT
Special Requirements: NeXTstation running NeXTstep 2.0
Price: $695   **AAII Discount:** None
Return Policy: 90 Days, Restocking Fee: None
Demo: No
Technical Support: Phone (12 hours/day), Newsletter

Description: A spreadsheet program that allows users to view information dynamically at the click of a mouse, use English formulas instead of numerical syntax and create presentations using data, text, graphics, images and sound. Allows users to view and compare data in different ways without manually rebuilding the spreadsheet. Data can be viewed or arranged to compare data relationships, summarized data can be expanded to show detail or information can be hidden for clarity. Automatically and immediately displays the worksheet to reflect the new arrangement without recalculation or re-entry of formulas or data.

Product: LOTUS 1-2-3 for OS/2
Securities: Not Applicable
Function(s): Spreadsheet
System(s): IBM
Special Requirements: IBM OS/2
Price: $695   **AAII Discount:** None
Return Policy: NA
Demo: Yes
Technical Support: 3 months free, $99/year, includes: Phone (24 hours/day)

Description: A graphical version of Lotus 1-2-3 designed for OS/2. The Presentation Manager provides full user interface, including WYSIWYG display, full mouse support, windowing, pull-down menus and dialog boxes, enhanced graphing and presentation-quality output. Has previews and palettes in dialog boxes plus Graph Gallery for previewing and selecting graphs and charts. Includes advanced spreadsheet features such as 3D worksheets, file linking, direct access to external data sources through DataLens and network support. Also has Solver and advanced goal-seeking technology for answering sophisticated "what if" problems.

Product: LOTUS 1-2-3 RELEASE 2.3
Securities: Not Applicable
Function(s): Spreadsheet
System(s): IBM
Special Requirements: Hard disk
Price: $495 Standard Edition;   **AAII Discount:** None
     $595 Network Server Edition;
     $495 Network Node Edition
Return Policy: NA
Demo: Yes
Technical Support: 3 months free, $99/year, includes: Phone (24 hours/day)

Description: Unites DOS spreadsheet with an interactive, graphical work environment. Has WYSIWYG screen display and presentation-quality output, dialog boxes and mouse support, spreadsheet auditing tools for documenting and tracking formulas and computations, improved and expanded graphics and a file viewer, based on Lotus Magellan technology, for browsing, retrieving or linking to 1-2-3 files located on disk. Offers 8,192 rows and 256 columns of worksheet space and other features such as minimal recalculation, undo—an error correction mechanism, named ranges and cells, ability to copy ranges of data and insert or delete rows and columns, statistical, calendar, mathematical, logical, database and financial functions, macro programming language for repetitive tasks and for creating custom applications. Compatible with Windows 3.0.

Product: LOTUS 1-2-3 RELEASE 3.1
Securities: Not Applicable
Function(s): Spreadsheet
System(s): IBM
Special Requirements: 80286+, 1 MB RAM, hard disk
Price: $495 Standard Edition;   **AAII Discount:** None
   $695 Network Server Edition;
   $595 Network Node Edition
Return Policy: NA
Demo: Yes
Technical Support: 3 months free, $99/year, includes: Phone (24 hours/day)

Description: A 3D multi-page worksheet to organize, consolidate and compare information, WYSIWYG display and presentation-quality output. Has spreadsheet auditing tools for documenting and tracking formulas and computations, and a file viewer, based on Lotus Magellan technology, for browsing, retrieving or linking to 1-2-3 files located on disk. Supports multi-files in memory. Solver, a goal-seeking tool, solves problems defined in the spreadsheet environment, access to external data via DataLens, and extended, expanded and virtual memory support for building larger spreadsheets. Has graphic and drawing enhancements including wrapping text around graphics and placing and displaying an unlimited number of "live" graphs anywhere in the worksheet. Has 8,192 rows, 256 columns and 256 pages of worksheet space and other features (background recalculation and undo).

Product: LOTUS SPREADSHEET FOR DESKMATE
Securities: Not Applicable

Function(s): Spreadsheet
System(s): IBM
Special Requirements: None
Price: $219.95   **AAII Discount:** None
Return Policy: NA
Demo: Yes
Technical Support: 3 months free, $99/year, includes: Phone (8 a.m. - 8:30 pm)

Description: Combines 1-2-3 with Tandy DeskMate Graphical User Interface. Based on Lotus 1-2-3 Release 2.01, the program integrates spreadsheet, database and graphic capabilities to help users plan, analyze and better understand their businesses. Can produce professional-looking reports and store large amounts of information such as customer files, mailing lists and inventory information in its database. Uses the .WK1 file format, which is compatible with all products in the Lotus 1-2-3 spreadsheet product line, including 1-2-3 Release 2.0, 2.01, 2.2, 3.0 and Symphony. Supports a mouse, pull-down menus, dialog boxes and works with a range of DeskMate applications, from word processing to appointment calendars and all DeskMate accessories.

Product: LOTUSWORKS
Securities: Not Applicable
Function(s): Communications, Spreadsheet
System(s): IBM
Special Requirements: Modem for communications
Price: $149   **AAII Discount:** None
Return Policy: NA
Demo: Yes
Technical Support: $99/year, includes: Phone (8 a.m. - 8:30 p.m. EST)

Description: Integrates spreadsheet, database management, word processing, graphics and communications capabilities. Spreadsheet module uses the same file structure and contains similar graphing facilities as Lotus 1-2-3 Release 2.01. Spreadsheet features: automatic, manual or background recalculation, 8,192 rows by 255 columns matrix, named ranges, math co-processor support and reads and writes ASCII, DIF, .WK1 and .WKS files. Relational database module uses the same file structure as dBase III and III+. Charting module provides pie, exploding pie, line, x-y, bar and stacked bar charts. Communications module supports X modem, X modem/CRC, Y modem and Kermit protocols at up to 115,200 baud transmission.

Product: SYMPHONY
Securities: Not Applicable
Function(s): Communications, Spreadsheet
System(s): IBM
Special Requirements: Modem for communications
Price: $695   **AAII Discount:** None
Return Policy: NA
Demo: Yes
Technical Support: $99/year, Phone (8 a.m. - 8:30 p.m.)

Description: Combines word processing, spreadsheet analysis, communications, graphics, database management and other functions. Uses plain English commands and single keystroke entries within a window format; allows work on a letter, graph and spreadsheet simultaneously. Spreadsheet handles 8,192 rows by 256 columns and provides common statistical and financial functions. Communications facility captures information directly into the worksheet and features auto-dialing and auto-log on with error detection. Database handles 8,000 records; graphics program offers many charts to display spreadsheet data. Open-ended for addition of specialized Lotus programs.

Market Master   (614) 436-3269
P.O. Box 14111
Columbus, OH 43214

Product: AUTOPRICE
Securities: Futures
Function(s): Communications
System(s): IBM
Special Requirements: Data source via modem or cable
Price: $79   **AAII Discount:** 10%
Return Policy: 30 Days, Restocking Fee: 15%
Demo: Yes ($23.50 refundable on purchase)
Technical Support: None

Description: Program for commodity price and market news retrieval from the Data Transmission Network (DTN), Farm Bureau ACRES computer network and affiliated services such as ACRES/Satellite and AgriQuote. All data may be downloaded to a PC, captured to RAM memory, disk or printer. User can transfer futures price data from these services into the price chart files used by PCMarket. Retrieval of daily price data may be made entirely unattended (with the exception of DTN) through use of the AUTO command and a suitable clock board or timer.

Product: OPTMASTER (formerly Option Master)
Securities: Option, Futures
Function(s): Options Analysis
System(s): IBM
Special Requirements: None
Price: $89   **AAII Discount:** 10%
Return Policy: 30 Days, Restocking Fee: 15%
Demo: Yes ($23.50 refundable upon purchase)
Technical Support: None

Description: Measures historical and implied price volatility, calculates fair market value of any option and prints tables of put and call values for a mixture of strike and market prices. Output includes deltas, gammas, theta and vega. Features automatic lookup of strike price intervals for 29 optionable commodities. Includes built-in Days Until Expiration calculator. On-line help facility. May be used with the manual entry of data, or can read a PCMARKET data file and perform calculations based on real market performance. Gives volatility, delta and options derivative number.

Product: PCMARKET
Securities: Futures
Function(s): Technical Analysis
System(s): IBM
Special Requirements: None
Price: $189   **AAII Discount:** 10%
Return Policy: 30 Days, Restocking Fee: 15%
Demo: Yes ($23.50 refundable upon purchase)
Technical Support: Phone (6 p.m. - 9 p.m. EST)

Description: Bar charting program for stocks and commodities that has a weighted moving average trading system. Calculates and displays spread and basic charts. Percentage retracements, speedlines, stochastics, moving averages, volume and open interest, MAH/MAL, 5/5, %R and RSI may be overlaid on the bar chart display. Moving averages, RSI and percentage retracements are user selectable. Includes a Cycle Finder utility that projects the next market high or low (time and price). Weekly and monthly charts are supported. No limit on the number of commodities and options tracked. Automatically adjusts to the graphics hardware installed in machine.

Market Software (800) 736-6353
P.O. Box 394 (603) 772-6353
Stratham, NH 03885 fax: (603) 778-3126

Product: WHOLE MARKET MONITOR
Securities: Stock, Option, Futures
Function(s): Communications
System(s): IBM
Special Requirements: Hard drive, Telemet America quote service
Price: $295 **AAII Discount:** 10%
Return Policy: 30 Days, Restocking Fee: None
Demo: Yes
Technical Support: Phone (9 a.m. - 4 p.m. EST)

Description: Using Telemet America's quotation service, program collects and stores up to 5,000 end-of-day stocks/options/futures quotations nightly from NYSE, AMEX and OTC markets to a compressed database. Includes 1,500+ NYSE active issue list; an OTC/AMEX list available separately. Allows unlimited custom lists for tracking portfolios, industries, etc. Up to 3 lists may be collected unattended each night. Quotes viewer shows daily prices plus volatility statistics by entering issues' symbol and month desired. An on-line symbol/company name cross-reference with search capability is included. ASCII export allows entire daily database to be used in other analysis programs.

Markex (800) 888-6088 x111
6192 Oxon Hill Road (301) 839-0817
Suite 401 fax: (301) 839-0182
Oxon Hill, MD 20745

Product: MARKEX
Securities: Mutual Fund
Function(s): Technical Analysis
System(s): IBM
Special Requirements: None
Price: $89.95   **AAII Discount:** 10%
Return Policy: NA
Demo: No
Technical Support: Phone

Description: Answers 4 questions: what and when to buy, when to sell and what to do next. User buys recommended mutual funds and enters 7 numbers from the newspaper weekly. No analysis is required—the system contains the necessary decision rules and data to advise when to switch from equity funds to money funds and vice versa with a toll-free call.

Math Corp.   (414) 748-3422
545 E. Fond du Lac   fax: (414) 748-3456
P.O. Box 361
Ripon, WI 54971

Product: BEST BID
Securities: Bond
Function(s): Bond Analysis, Spreadsheet
System(s): IBM
Special Requirements: Lotus 1-2-3
Price: $499.95   **AAII Discount:** 15%
Return Policy: 15 Days, Restocking Fee: None
Demo: No
Technical Support: $100/year, includes: Phone (8 a.m. - 5:30 p.m. CST)

Description: Menu-driven bond bidding, analysis and reporting system. Figures net interest cost (NIC), true interest cost (TIC), average life years and, at the user's choice, TRUERATE%, Math Corp.'s index of the true rate of return. Can analyze serial bonds, term bonds and zero coupon bonds. All data entry is automated, and a debt service schedule is automatically produced. Principal or interest installments can occur annually, semi-annually, quarterly or monthly. Also used as a reporting system for analysis, final proposals, etc. All calculations are performed using standard SIA conventions.

Product: TRUERATE%
Securities: Stock, Bond, Index, Mutual Fund, Option, Futures, Real Estate
Function(s): Portfolio Management, Spreadsheet
System(s): IBM
Special Requirements: Lotus 1-2-3
Price: $499.95   **AAII Discount:** 15%
Return Policy: 15 Days, Restocking Fee: None
Demo: No
Technical Support: Phone (8 a.m. - 5:30 p.m. CST)

Description: Calculates the true rate of return by using Math Corp.'s proprietary internal rate of return calculation. User can calculate the Truerate%, the original cash flow or one of the other cash flows by entering other data. Enter as many cash flows as needed. Once a Truerate% has been calculated user may verify the figure by using verification facility. Includes 6 months of technical support and free upgrades.

Product: ZMATH
Securities: Not Applicable
Function(s): Spreadsheet
System(s): IBM
Special Requirements: Lotus 1-2-3
Price: $499.95   **AAII Discount:** 15%
Return Policy: 15 Days, Restocking Fee: None
Demo: No
Technical Support: Phone (8 a.m. - 5:30 p.m. CST)

Description: Collection of application templates dealing with all the time value of money calculations. Sections include original loan terms, events during the life of the loan, creative financing, savings (present and future values), creative saving, 12 annual percentage rate calculators and utilities. APRs are calculated on loans including single, irregular and graduated payment, adjustable/variable rate, graduated payment adjustable rate, wrap-around, compensating balance and 30 different payment stream loans. Each calculation includes a calendar that shows unit periods and days between the advance and first payment, allowing odd first payments. All calculations are based upon the equations documented in Appendix J of Regulation Z (Truth in

Lending) and include verifications (proofs) of the APR. Produces schedules with a single keystroke. Figure reimbursements are provided when the disclosed rate differs from the actual APR. User can customize debt modeling with modeling schedule.

MECA Software, Inc. (800) 288-6322
55 Wall Drive
Fairfield, CT 06430

Product: ANDREW TOBIAS' CHECKWRITE PLUS
Securities: Not Applicable
Function(s): Financial Planning
System(s): IBM
Special Requirements: None
Price: $49.95   **AAII Discount:** None
Return Policy: NA
Demo: No
Technical Support: 1 year free phone support; PLUS Plan is $54.45/year, includes: Phone, Newsletter, Annual Program Upgrade

Description: A budget and checkbook program for business or personal use. Handles multiple bank accounts and is able to consolidate transactions from multiple accounts for profit and loss statement, transaction analysis, payables and receivables, cash forecasting, etc. Handles money accounts and tracks several accounts, including checking and savings, CMA and non-cash accounts. Prints any size check with check editing option. Financial functions include loan management, invoicing and variable fiscal years. Records transactions by tax category. Includes an on-line calculator. Information can be exported to Andrew Tobias' Managing Your Money.

Product: ANDREW TOBIAS' FINANCIAL CALCULATOR
Securities: Stock, Bond, Real Estate
Function(s): Financial Planning, Real Estate Analysis, Tax Planning
System(s): IBM
Special Requirements: None
Price: $44.95   **AAII Discount:** None
Return Policy: NA
Demo: No

Technical Support: 1 year free phone support; PLUS Plan is $54.45/
year, includes: Phone, Newsletter, Annual Program Upgrade

Description: Developed from Andrew Tobias' Managing Your Money. Incorporates new features and applications within powerful subsections on tax planning, retirement planning, college planning, rental property analysis, investment analysis, cash flow analysis, mortgage refinancing, buy/rent/lease analysis, inflation/deflation calculator, internal rate of return calculations, bond yield analysis and compound interest calculations. Also offers a depreciation calculator and on-line calculator.

Product: ANDREW TOBIAS' MANAGING THE MARKET
Securities: Stock, Bond, Mutual Fund, Option
Function(s): Communications
System(s): IBM
Special Requirements: Modem
Price: $149.95   AAII Discount: None
Return Policy: NA
Demo: No
Technical Support: 1 year free phone support; PLUS Plan is $54.45/
year, includes: Phone, Newsletter, Annual Program Upgrade

Description: Communications package. Accesses DJN/R and acts with Andrew Tobias' Managing Your Money by automatically updating stock, bonds, options, treasuries and mutual funds in Chapter 7's Portfolio Manager. Works as a stand-alone package that downloads prices to most spreadsheets and word processors and offers the user the full range of DJN/R.

Product: ANDREW TOBIAS' MANAGING YOUR MONEY
Securities: Stock, Bond, Index, Mutual Fund, Option, Futures, Real
    Estate
Function(s): Financial Planning, Portfolio Management, Real Estate
    Analysis, Tax Planning
System(s): Apple II, IBM, Macintosh
Special Requirements: None
Price: Apple II $149.95; IBM,   AAII Discount: None
    Macintosh $219.98

Return Policy: NA
Demo: Yes
Technical Support: 1 year free phone support; PLUS Plan, $54.45/year, includes: Phone, Newsletter, Annual Program Upgrade

Description: Nine integrated programs in 1. Includes: budget and checkbook manager, investment counselor, tax estimator, financial calculator reminder pad, and for small businesses: accounts payable/receivable with aging and invoice printing capabilities. Gives analysis of tax shelters and investment portfolios and money-saving advice on insurance needs. Check-Free electronic bill paying option is a built-in feature. Fully integrated so user only need enter data once.

Product: ANDREW TOBIAS' TAX CUT
Securities: Stock, Bond, Mutual Fund, Option, Futures, Real Estate
Function(s): Tax Planning
System(s): IBM
Special Requirements: None
Price: $89.95   **AAII Discount:** None
Return Policy: NA
Demo: No
Technical Support: Phone

Description: Allows the user to experiment with "what if" scenarios showing the taxable consequences of important financial decisions before they are made. When decisions are made and forms are ready for printing, it is possible to view the information and make any changes. Instantly recalculates the entire return based on the changes. Prints 23 IRS-ready forms and schedules. Built-in auditor flags entries that might trigger an IRS audit. Compatible with Andrew Tobias' Checkwrite Plus and Andrew Tobias' Managing Your Money.

Memory Systems, Inc.   (708) 674-4833
P.O. Box 886
Skokie, IL 60076

Product: TECHNICAL TRADER
Securities: Stock, Index, Option, Futures
Function(s): Communications, Technical Analysis
System(s): Apple II, IBM

Special Requirements: Modem for data downloading
Price: Apple $450; IBM $675   **AAII Discount:** 10%
Return Policy: 30 Days, Restocking Fee: None
Demo: No
Technical Support: Phone (9 a.m. - 5 p.m. CST)

Description: Studies include: demand index, stochastics, relative strength index, moving averages, oscillators, directional movement index, MACD trading and Welles Wilder's methods and more. Supports advanced charting, optimization routines, historical testing, an automatic execution feature and customization routines. Price database routines allow user to create daily, weekly or monthly files. Price updating is manual or automatic over the telephone. Operates with price files in either the CSI or Compu Trac price file format.

Mendelsohn Enterprises, Inc.   (800) 732-5407
50 Meadow Lane   (813) 973-0496
Zephyrhills, FL 33544   fax: (813) 973-2700

Product: PROFITTAKER 2000
Securities: Bond, Index, Futures
Function(s): Technical Analysis
System(s): IBM
Special Requirements: None
Price: $1,995 ($1,500 discount with VantagePoint)   **AAII Discount:** 15%
Return Policy: NA
Demo: Yes
Technical Support: Phone (9 a.m. - 5 p.m. EST)

Description: User can create and test personalized trading models for all futures markets (including stock indexes, financials and currencies) prior to actually risking capital in the markets. User then applies the most profitable trading models in real-time and generates a daily trading report that gives exact entry/exit signals and stops in easy-to-understand language. All trading rules and logic are fully disclosed.

Product: VANTAGEPOINT*
Securities: Stock, Bond, Index, Futures

Function(s): Technical Analysis
System(s): IBM
Special Requirements: None
Price: $1,950 **AAII Discount:** 15%
Return Policy: NA
Demo: No
Technical Support: Phone (9 a.m. - 5 p.m. EST)

Description: Utilizes predictive artificial intelligence-based neural computing technology to scientifically forecast the next day's prices and trading signals. Combines "pretrained" neural trading systems with technical and fundamental analysis. Can be used alone or as a "filter" to an existing trading system. Predicts tops and bottoms 1 day before or on the day of the turning points. Includes a System Guide and a handbook entitled "Applying Neural Computing Technology to Futures Trading."

MESA (800) 633-6372
P.O. Box 1801 (805) 969-6478
Goleta, CA 93116 fax: (805) 969-1358

Product: EPOCH PRO
Securities: Stock, Bond, Index, Futures
Function(s): Technical Analysis
System(s): IBM
Special Requirements: Math co-processor; EGA or better desirable
Price: $995 **AAII Discount:** None
Return Policy: NA
Demo: Yes ($1)
Technical Support: Phone (6 p.m. - 10 p.m. PST)

Description: Program for mechanical trading based on short-term cycles. Unique feature is a 3D chart of profitability versus 2 trading parameters, allowing the parameters to be positioned in the most robust region with minimum sensitivity to market variations. Approach is different from conventional optimization. Buy/sell signals are derived from a leading indicator. Explicit stop/loss values are given to protect profits and to signal a position reversal. Trading record can be back-tested over any selected span of time.

Product: MESA
Securities: Stock, Bond, Index, Futures
Function(s): Technical Analysis
System(s): IBM
Special Requirements: Math co-processor; EGA or better desirable
Price: $350   **AAII Discount:** None
Return Policy: NA
Demo: Yes ($1)
Technical Support: Phone (6 p.m. - 10 p.m. PST)

Description: Measures short-term market cycles; uses the same maximum entropy technique used in seismic exploration and in missile defense systems. Measured cycles are recombined to form a prediction based on their continuation. The dominant cycle is plotted as a time graph below a conventional bar chart. Cycles are also displayed as a spectrograph for a complete picture of cycle activity. Trend modes and cycle modes are identified by the price action relative to an instantaneous trendline computed using a cycle filter. RSI, MACD and stochastic indicators are optimized for measured cycles.

Product: 3D*
Securities: Stock, Bond, Index, Futures
Function(s): Technical Analysis
System(s): IBM
Special Requirements: Math co-processor; EGA or better desirable
Price: $199   **AAII Discount:** None
Return Policy: NA
Demo: Yes ($1)
Technical Support: Phone (6 p.m. - 10 p.m. PST)

Description: Plots the profitability of 5 indicators as a 3-dimensional service. Allows selection of the best indicator to use because market conditions are constantly changing. User can select the combination of indicator parameters by locating the parameter intersection at the smoothest part of the 3D surface. The smooth surface means that the profitability has the least sensitivity to market variations. Trades resulting from the selected parameters can be viewed on a bar chart display. The 5 indicators are: stochastics, RSI, MACD, double moving average and parabolic stop and reverse.

MicroApplications, Inc.   (516) 821-9355
P.O. Box 43   fax: (516) 744-1225
71 Oakland Avenue
Miller Place, NY 11764

Product: A-PACK: AN ANALYTICAL PACKAGE FOR BUSINESS
Securities: Stock, Bond, Option, Futures, Real Estate
Function(s): Financial Planning, Fundamental Analysis, Statistical Analysis
System(s): IBM
Special Requirements: None
Price: $199   **AAII Discount:** 35%
Return Policy: NA
Demo: No
Technical Support: None

Description: A "toolbox" of frequently used formulas falling into 6 disciplines: financial, investment, mathematical and statistical analysis, operations research and file management.

Microcalc   (800) 755-7252
318 Mendocino Avenue   (707) 575-1459
Suite 22   fax: (707) 829-7203
Santa Rosa, CA 95404

Product: MICROCALC FINANCIAL CALCULATOR LIBRARY*
Securities: Real Estate
Function(s): Financial Planning, Real Estate Analysis
System(s): IBM, Macintosh
Special Requirements: None
Price: $189   **AAII Discount:** 53%
Return Policy: 30 Days, Restocking Fee: None
Demo: No
Technical Support: Phone (9 a.m. - 5 p.m. PST)

Description: Over 80 calculators. Solves formulas in personal finance—real estate, financial/business analysis, business/personal loans/leasing.

Microsoft Corp.   (800) 426-9400
One Microsoft Way   (206) 882-8080
Redmond, WA 98052

Product: MICROSOFT EXCEL
Securities: Not Applicable
Function(s): Spreadsheet
System(s): IBM, Macintosh
Special Requirements: IBM—Windows or OS/2
Price: $495   **AAII Discount:** None
Return Policy: NA
Demo: Yes
Technical Support: Phone (24 hours/day), BBS, Newsletter

Description: Full-featured, integrated spreadsheet, database and charting program based on a graphical interface. Macintosh version operates under system 6.0.2 or later, while the IBM version runs under Microsoft Windows or OS/2. Spreadsheet features include linking multiple spreadsheets, minimal recalculation that recalculates only spreadsheet formulas affected by a change, background recalculation that recalculates only when the user is not entering data, 131 built-in functions, the ability to create new functions and an extensive macro language. Includes 6 basic chart types: area, bar, column, line, pie and scatter, which can be combined to produce over 100 charts including 3-D charts and a high, low, close bar chart. Other features include a logarithmic scale, arrows and free floating text. Can read or write a variety of file formats including comma-separated value, SYLK, Lotus 1-2-3 release 1, 2 and 3 DIF and dBase.

MicroTempo, Inc.   (703) 243-9603
122B N. Bedford Street
Arlington, VA 22201

Product: BMW
Securities: Bond
Function(s): Bond Analysis, Spreadsheet
System(s): IBM
Special Requirements: Lotus 1-2-3
Price: $99   **AAII Discount:** 50%
Return Policy: 90 Days, Restocking Fee: None
Demo: Yes ($10)
Technical Support: Phone

Description: A collection of Lotus 1-2-3 and Symphony macros that work together to form a bond analysis system. Uses a window to display the cell values of settlement date, maturity date, coupon, price, yield, date issued, call date and call price. The window is hidden by pressing a zoom key. Does not interfere with user's spreadsheet layout. Bond data is given wherever the cursor is positioned.

Product: BOND$MART
Securities: Bond
Function(s): Bond Analysis
System(s): IBM
Special Requirements: None
Price: $395 **AAII Discount:** 30%
Return Policy: 90 Days, Restocking Fee: None
Demo: Yes ($10)
Technical Support: Phone

Description: Handles calculations for government, corporate, agency or municipal bonds and notes; interest at maturity notes and CDs; T-bills or discount securities; zero-coupon bonds; short/long odd lot first coupon bonds; Eurobonds; Japanese discount notes. Calculations include yield to maturity and/or call, before or after taxes; current yield; CD equivalent yield; Macaulay Duration and horizon duration; price volatility; reinvestment rate-to-yield; discount rate-to-price and others. Uses the Security Industry Association (SIA) Standard as a default for bond calculations, but user may set own parameters. Includes a spreadsheet interface for data transfer to a Lotus 1-2-3 spreadsheet for further analysis.

Micro Trading Software, Ltd. (203) 762-7820
Box 175
Wilton, CT 06897

Product: STOCK WATCHER
Securities: Stock, Index, Mutual Fund, Option, Futures
Function(s): Communications, Technical Analysis
System(s): Macintosh
Special Requirements: Modem for data downloading
Price: $195 **AAII Discount:** 30%
Return Policy: NA
Demo: Yes
Technical Support: Phone

Description: Analyzes stocks, commodities, mutual funds and market indexes. Features: cycle and trendline analysis; high resolution graphics; generation of graphs and summary reports; 4 graph sizes that display any of the dozens of built-in technical indicators such as stochastics, MACD, moving averages, oscillators, on-balance volume, advance/decline line, relative strength and TRIN. Automatic current day and historical quote retrieval from CompuServe and DJN/R.

Product: WALL STREET WATCHER
Securities: Stock, Index, Mutual Fund, Option, Futures
Function(s): Communications, Technical Analysis
System(s): Macintosh
Special Requirements: Modem for data downloading
Price: $495   **AAII Discount:** 20%
Return Policy: NA
Demo: Yes
Technical Support: Phone

Description: Charts over 20 indicators such as simple, weighted and exponential moving averages with percent bands of high, low or closing prices; moving averages of volume; Wilder's Relative Strength Index; stochastics; Granville's on balance volume; MACD, rate of change/momentum and moving average oscillators; Williams' %R; TRIN (Arm's Index); advance/decline lines; cumulative advance/decline lines; McClellan summation index and oscillator; moving average of new highs/new lows differential; and point and figure charting. Five technical indicators on each of 3 separate windows can be plotted at once. Price swings can be measured in terms of price, time and percent retracement. Time cycles can be marked and projected using Fibonacci and Gann time periods. Includes a macro language to automate chart preparations. Daily and historical stock and commodity quotes can be automatically retrieved from Dow Jones News/Retrieval and CompuServe.

Miller Associates   (702) 831-0429
P.O. Box 4361
Incline Village, NV 89450

Product: SOPHISTICATED INVESTOR
Securities: Stock, Index, Mutual Fund

Function(s): Portfolio Management, Security Screening, Simulations/Games
System(s): IBM
Special Requirements: Lotus 1-2-3 useful
Price: $195   **AAII Discount:** 15%
Return Policy: 30 Days (if unopened), Restocking Fee: None
Demo: Yes ($5)
Technical Support: Phone (9 a.m. - 3 p.m. PST)

Description: Optimizes stock portfolios for maximum return and minimum risk based upon a version of Markowitz's Modern Portfolio Analysis. Features full statistical correlation of a portfolio with the S&P 500, complete with alpha and beta computations, standard error of estimate and correlation coefficient determinations. Linear optimization allows users to make portfolios consistent with their stock, risk and return constraints. Allows "what if" analysis. Handles portfolios of up to 50 stocks.

MindCraft Publishing Corporation   (617) 259-0448
P.O. Box 256
Lincoln, MA 01773

Product: NIBBLE INVESTOR
Securities: Stock
Function(s): Technical Analysis
System(s): Apple II
Special Requirements: None
Price: $29.95   **AAII Discount:** None
Return Policy: 30 Days, Restocking Fee: None
Demo: No
Technical Support: BBS

Description: Produces high resolution charts for tracking weekly high, low and closing prices, volume and 13- and 52-week moving averages. Provides a variety of gain/loss, market and sales reports.

Product: NIBBLE MAC INVESTOR
Securities: Stock
Function(s): Technical Analysis
System(s): Macintosh

Special Requirements: Hypercard version available
Price: $29.95　　　　　　　　　　　　　　**AAII Discount:** None
Return Policy: 30 Days, Restocking Fee: None
Demo: No
Technical Support: BBS

Description: Produces high resolution charts for tracking weekly high, low and closing prices, volume and 13- and 52-week moving averages. Provides a variety of gain/loss, market and sales reports. Hypercard version is also available.

Money Tree Software　　　　　　　　　　　　(503) 929-2140
1753 Wooded Knolls Drive
Suite 200
Philomath, OR 97370

Product: EASY MONEY
Securities: Stock, Bond, Mutual Fund, Real Estate
Function(s): Financial Planning, Spreadsheet, Tax Planning
System(s): IBM
Special Requirements: Lotus 1-2-3
Price: $550
Return Policy: NA
Demo: Yes ($45)
Technical Support: $250/year, includes: Phone (8 a.m. - 5 p.m. PST), Annual Program Updates

Description: Addresses the changing needs of the personal financial planning market of the late 1980s. Features quick data entry, easy to understand reports, charts, graphs and diagrams. A 30-page report covers all items needed for a comprehensive plan including a new life cycle asset allocation section, retirement and insurance planning, income tax, estate tax, budget, education funding and more.

Product: ELDERLY TAX PLANNER
Securities: Stock, Bond, Mutual Fund, Real Estate
Function(s): Financial Planning, Spreadsheet, Tax Planning
System(s): IBM
Special Requirements: Lotus 1-2-3
Price: $95　　　　　　　　　　　　　　　　**AAII Discount:** None

Return Policy: NA
Demo: Yes
Technical Support: $25/year, includes: Phone (8 a.m. - 5 p.m. PST), Annual Program Updates

Description: Computes income taxes and determines the taxable portion of Social Security benefits and the effect of moving savings or investments into tax-free municipal funds or tax-deferred annuities; shows the resulting tax savings and the effect on spendable income and capital.

Product: MONEYCALC IV
Securities: Stock, Bond, Mutual Fund, Real Estate
Function(s): Financial Planning, Spreadsheet, Tax Planning
System(s): IBM
Special Requirements: Lotus 1-2-3
Price: $775   **AAII Discount:** None
Return Policy: NA
Demo: Yes
Technical Support: $400/year, includes: Phone (8 a.m. - 5 p.m. PST), Annual Program Updates

Description: A system for financial planning. The 50 programs may be used as separate report modules or interfaced with the Client Data Module for client data input. Includes all TRA '86 tax features, multiple year projections of taxes, net worth, cash flow, estate plans, retirement, survivor and disability needs, etc.

Product: RETIREMENT SOLUTIONS
Securities: Not Applicable
Function(s): Financial Planning, Spreadsheet, Tax Planning
System(s): IBM
Special Requirements: Lotus 1-2-3
Price: $195   **AAII Discount:** None
Return Policy: NA
Demo: Yes
Technical Support: $50/year, includes: Phone (8 a.m. - 5 p.m. PST), Annual Program Updates

Description: Collection of 8 programs covering retirement planning. Principle report, Lump Sum Distribution, calculates all taxes due on a qualified plan distribution (regular tax, 5- and 10-year average, IRA Rollover) and projects benefits before- and after-tax through life expectancy. Computes minimum distribution requirements, early and excess distribution tax penalties.

Money Won (800) 463-6639
Ten Tower Office Park Drive (617) 982-0285
Woburn, MA 01801 fax: (418) 622-0802

Product: MYWAY
Securities: Stock
Function(s): Communications, Portfolio Management, Technical Analysis
System(s): IBM
Special Requirements: Modem for data downloading
Price: $144   **AAII Discount:** None
Return Policy: NA
Demo: Yes ($9.95)
Technical Support: Phone

Description: A stock trading management program. User can analyze the stock market to determine, based on available resources, when and how many shares of stock to buy or sell. Capabilities are enhanced with the use of stock data from DJN/R and CompuServe. Uses dollar cost averaging to give specific trading recommendations at every market cycle. Trading Module includes current status and value of shares on hand, profit or loss, cash and cash reserve positions, most recent trade and the latest updated price record of every transaction to date. Calculates user's next probable stock transaction. Provides built-in "what if" scenarios to simulate projections and make trading decisions. Accommodates up to 999 separate portfolios, each with up to 999 individual stocks. Risk Report feature is designed to make year-end tax reporting easier. Using first-in first-out approach it accommodates most tax reporting methods including Canada's. Keeps track of all trading activity and generates reports.

Montgomery Investment Group (707) 795-5673
1455 Roman Drive fax: (707) 795-5722
Rohnert Park, CA 94928

Product: @BONDS PRO SERIES AND PREMIUM SERIES*
Securities: Bond
Function(s): Bond Analysis, Spreadsheet
System(s): IBM
Special Requirements: Lotus 1-2-3 version 2.X or 3.X
Price: Pro Series $395; Premium Series $695 **AAII Discount:** 15%
Return Policy: 30 Days, Restocking Fee: 20%
Demo: Yes
Technical Support: Phone (9 a.m. - 4 p.m. PST)

Description: A Lotus 1-2-3 add-in. Allows users to calculate yields, prices, duration, modified duration, etc. Fixed income instruments that can be evaluated are U.S. treasuries, notes, corporates, munis, zeros, etc. Custom templates can be created to employ quantitative techniques such as horizon, market timing, rolling yield curve, portfolio optimization and more. Premium series can evaluate odd first-coupon and callable bonds.

Product: @OPTIONS PRO SERIES AND PREMIUM SERIES
Securities: Option, Futures
Function(s): Options Analysis, Spreadsheet
System(s): IBM, Macintosh
Special Requirements: Lotus 1-2-3 version 2.X or 3.X
Price: Pro Series, $395; Premium Series, $695 **AAII Discount:** 15%
Return Policy: 30 Days, Restocking Fee: 20%
Demo: Yes
Technical Support: Phone (9 a.m. - 4 p.m. PST)

Description: A Lotus 1-2-3 add-in. Allows users to calculate theoretical options prices, implied volatilities and sensitivity values such as delta, gamma and theta directly within spreadsheets. A choice of 7 options pricing models is available including: Binomial (Cox-Ross-Rubinstein), Black-Scholes, Modified Black-Scholes, and Adesi-Whaley (Quadratic). Enables analysis on any underlying asset: stocks, bonds, futures, indexes, commodities, foreign exchange and more. Is not a Lotus macro or template but a collection of functions that extend the capabilities of Lotus specifically for option trading and analysis. Works as a program within a program and has real-time capabilities.

Product: BONDS XL PRO AND PREMIUM SERIES*
Securities: Bond
Function(s): Bond Analysis, Spreadsheet
System(s): IBM, Macintosh
Special Requirements: Excel 2.X or 3.X
Price: Pro Series, $395; Premium Series $695   **AAII Discount:** 15%
Return Policy: 30 Days, Restocking Fee: 20%
Demo: Yes
Technical Support: Phone (9 a.m. - 4 p.m. PST)

Description: Allows users to calculate yields, prices, duration, modified duration, etc. Fixed income instruments that can be evaluated are U.S. treasuries, notes, corporates, munis, zeros, etc. Custom templates can be created to employ quantitative techniques such as horizon, market timing, rolling yield curve, portfolio optimization and more. Premium series can evaluate odd first-coupon and callable bonds.

Product: MORTGAGE SECURITY CALCULATOR
Securities: Bond
Function(s): Security Screening
System(s): IBM
Special Requirements: None
Price: $995   **AAII Discount:** 15%
Return Policy: 30 Days, Restocking Fee: 20%
Demo: Yes
Technical Support: Phone (9 a.m. - 4 p.m. PST)

Description: Program analyzes 3 basic mortgage securities: fixed-rate, graduated-payment and rate-adjusting. Price, prepayment and yield are the 3 main factors used in analyzing mortgage securities. Given any 2 of these factors, program will determine the 3rd. Output screen provides the calculated price, duration and convexity of the 3 cash flow sets represented by the whole security (MBS), the principal only strip (PO) and the interest only strip (IO). Adjustments for servicing, remaining term, seasoning and more are incorporated. Market price movements under "shocked" interest rate scenarios may be measured (e.g., the effect of +/- 100 basis points is quickly recalculated for either the MBS, PO or IO). Allows user to evaluate the sensitivity of an entire portfolio to interest rate changes.

Product: OPTIONS XL PRO AND PREMIUM SERIES
Securities: Option, Futures
Function(s): Options Analysis, Spreadsheet
System(s): IBM
Special Requirements: None
Price: Pro Series, $395; Premium Series, $695   **AAII Discount:** 15%
Return Policy: 30 Days, Restocking Fee: 20%
Demo: Yes
Technical Support: Phone (9 a.m. - 4 p.m. PST)

Description: Utility calculates option theoretical values, volatilities and sensitivities directly within the Excel spreadsheet. Up to 7 option valuation models are available: Black-Scholes, Black, Modified Black-Scholes, Quadratic (Adesi-Whaley), Pseudo-American (Garman-Kohlhagen), and Binomial (Cox-Ross-Rubenstein). Has functions that calculate theoretical values, deltas, gammas, thetas, vegas, implied volatilities and more. Takes advantage of graphics capabilities and spreadsheet format of Excel and has real-time capabilities.

NAIC Software   (313) 543-0612
P.O. Box 220
1515 E. Eleven Mile Road
Royal Oak, MI 48068

Product: COMREP
Securities: Stock
Function(s): Fundamental Analysis, Security Screening
System(s): IBM
Special Requirements: None
Price: $50   **AAII Discount:** 20%
Return Policy: NA
Demo: No
Technical Support: Phone

Description: Uses the data files from the EvalForm program to produce a comparison report of the chosen stock's data files. Based on the NAIC's Stock Comparison Report; used to compare different companies' Stock Selection Guide data. Will provide comparisons for companies in different industries but was developed to study stocks within the same industry group.

Product: EVALFORM
Securities: Stock
Function(s): Fundamental Analysis, Security Screening
System(s): Apple II, IBM
Special Requirements: None
Price: $105 **AAII Discount:** 24%
Return Policy: NA
Demo: No
Technical Support: Phone

Description: Follows method of stock selection based on theory used by the NAIC. Included are a visual analysis chart, risk/reward ratio, value ratios and relationships, buy-hold-sell ranges, data editors, an update utility and a section that indicates if the statistics fall in prescribed ranges. Automatically recalculates figures based on "what if" situations.

Product: SSG PLUS*
Securities: Stock
Function(s): Fundamental Analysis, Security Screening
System(s): IBM
Special Requirements: Hard drive, Epson graphics or HP PCL emulation
Price: $179 **AAII Discount:** 18%
Return Policy: NA
Demo: Yes ($15)
Technical Support: Phone

Description: Provides fundamental stock analysis using the tools of NAIC. The NAIC Stock Selection Guide is featured with interactive graphics and "what if" abilities to help users arrive at buy-hold-sell prices for a stock. Once several stocks have been studied, user can compare 2 to 5 companies at once. Also included is a balance sheet and additional data report and simple data sort capabilities.

Product: TAKE STOCK*
Securities: Stock
Function(s): Fundamental Analysis, Security Screening
System(s): Macintosh
Special Requirements: 2 MB RAM and hard drive, Excel 2.2+
Price: $150 **AAII Discount:** None
Return Policy: NA
Demo: No
Technical Support: Phone

Description: For investment in common stocks. User can input all of the required data in less than 10 minutes and produce not only all of the information found in the NAIC investment tools but more information relating to the operation and financial health of the company under study. Has plain language summary of reasons to buy and items to check.

New England Software, Inc. (203) 625-0062
Greenwich Office Park #3 fax: (203) 625-0718
Greenwich, CT 06831

Product: GB-STAT
Securities: Not Applicable
Function(s): Statistical Analysis
System(s): IBM
Special Requirements: None
Price: $399.95 **AAII Discount:** None
Return Policy: 30 Days, Restocking Fee: None
Demo: No
Technical Support: Phone (9 a.m. - 5 p.m. EST)

Description: A fully integrated, statistical analysis/data management/graphics package. Menu-driven, handles missing data and has flexible data entry. High quality graphics capabilities are fully integrated. Almost 300 statistical analyses include ANOVA, standard deviations, t-tests, variance and co-variance, correlation, means, linear, non-linear and polynomial regression, nonparametric procedures, frequency distributions, multivariate statistics, time-series analysis, factor analysis, cross tabulation stepwise regression. Graphs both the data and statistical results. Import functions, with automatic conversions, perform statistical analyses of data taken from virtually all programs.

Product: GRAPH-IN-THE-BOX ANALYTIC
Securities: Not Applicable
Function(s): Technical Analysis
System(s): IBM
Special Requirements: None
Price: $199.95 **AAII Discount:** None
Return Policy: 30 Days, Restocking Fee: None
Demo: Yes
Technical Support: Phone (9 a.m. - 5 p.m. EST)

Description: Makes 16 types of graphs (useful in financial, mathematical, scientific and technical work) based on x-y, double-Y axes and linear and logarithmic scaling. Captures the data from any program running and produces trend, spline and max-min/high-low-close/error bar charts. Delivers line equations with the graphs and performs 45 data manipulation functions and calculations of captured numbers. Output on laser, plotter and postscript printers.

Product: GRAPH-IN-THE-BOX EXECUTIVE*
Securities: Not Applicable
Function(s): Technical Analysis
System(s): IBM
Special Requirements: Hard drive
Price: $299.95 **AAII Discount:** None
Return Policy: 30 Days, Restocking Fee: None
Demo: Yes
Technical Support: Phone (9 a.m. - 5 p.m. EST)

Description: Program makes business graphs. Has 15 types of charts, text charts and organization charts; 9 fonts and 3D effects, plus 57 built-in advanced data manipulation functions and procedures for mathematical and statistical analysis. Capture data and text directly from the screen of the program showing it, manipulate and enhance the data, then display it as a graph or chart. Uses a new swapping technique to save memory, yet uses only 10K when not activated.

NewTEK Industries (213) 874-6669
P.O. Box 46116
Los Angeles, CA 90046

Product: COMMISSION COMPARISONS
Securities: Stock, Bond, Option
Function(s): Financial Planning
System(s): IBM
Special Requirements: None
Price: $39.95   **AAII Discount:** None
Return Policy: NA
Demo: No
Technical Support: Phone (9 a.m. - 5 p.m. PST)

Description: Shows how 15 selected discount brokerages and 1 full-service brokerage compare in commission costs for any transaction in stocks, options or bonds. The number of shares, contracts or bonds and prices are entered, and each brokerage commission is calculated and sorted by cost. Displays the vital statistics of the brokerage of choice, including toll-free phone numbers, nationwide offices and special trading requirements, if any.

Product: COMPU/CHART EGA
Securities: Stock, Index, Mutual Fund, Option
Function(s): Communications, Technical Analysis
System(s): IBM
Special Requirements: 1200 baud modem, EGA or VGA graphics
Price: $299.95   **AAII Discount:** 20%
Return Policy: NA
Demo: Yes ($7)
Technical Support: Phone (9 a.m. - 5 p.m. PST)

Description: Program uses high-resolution color graphics for an optimal display of charts and indicators on screen or printer. Charts include the scanner, displaying 9 different markets per screen, the oscillator-scan, displaying 5 different oscillator windows per market, moving averages, which allows the juxtaposition of detailed oscillators, price-volume charting and exponential-average divergence with the moving averages chart in a choice of time frames and status report. Stochastics (with user assigned periods), moving up/down volume ratio, channel lines, back-scanner, inter-day monitor, dynamic bar indicator, immediate update report, adaptable format and use of high-resolution color to distinguish trends and patterns allow user to tailor analysis time to the market situation.

Product: RETRIEVER PLUS
Securities: Stock, Index, Mutual Fund, Option
Function(s): Communications
System(s): IBM
Special Requirements: 1200 baud modem
Price: $79.95   **AAII Discount:** None
Return Policy: NA
Demo: No
Technical Support: Phone (9 a.m. - 5 p.m. PST)

Description: A communications program automated to go on-line with Track Data. Automation removes need to repeatedly enter ID, passwords, account information and details of a download order while user is on-line and prone to make errors. Maintains a portfolio file; filenames and symbols, stocks and commodities on all the major exchanges are available as well as over 1,300 mutual funds and the most commonly used indexes. Market files may be saved in 3 Lotus formats, Track Data, Compu Trac and Compu/Chart formats.

Northfield Information Services, Inc.   (800) 262-6085
99 Summer Street   (617) 737-8360
Suite 1620
Boston, MA 02110

Product: NIS Asset Allocation System (formerly PACO)
Securities: Index, Mutual Fund
Function(s): Financial Planning, Portfolio Management, Simulations/ Games
System(s): IBM
Special Requirements: None
Price: $10,000/year   **AAII Discount:** 20%
Return Policy: NA
Demo: Yes
Technical Support: Phone (9 a.m. - 5 p.m. EST), BBS, Newsletter

Description: Deals with long-term asset allocation. Uses an exclusive optimization algorithm to find the most suitable asset mix giving appropriate consideration to user-defined constraints such as level of risk tolerance, time horizon and minimum yield. Provides a variety of output displays including detailed graphics of the efficient frontier, enabling users to see the impact of the optimization. Included are performance measurements, wealth projections and actuarial studies. Users choose from more than 2 dozen asset classes on which historical and current data is supplied on monthly data diskettes which may be overridden. Long-range forecast for the return and volatility of each asset class is published in a client newsletter. Includes database covering more than 2,000 indexes and mutual funds containing monthly data back to 1962.

Product: NIS FIXED INCOME RESEARCH ENVIRONMENT*
Securities: Bond
Function(s): Bond Analysis, Communications, Portfolio Management, Security Screening, Simulations/Games
System(s): IBM
Special Requirements: None
Price: $16,000   **AAII Discount:** 20%
Return Policy: NA
Demo: No
Technical Support: Phone (9 a.m. - 5 p.m. EST), BBS, Newsletter

Description: Provides portfolio analytic and reporting tools. Helps determine and evaluate the tactical and strategic investment decisions that will conform to the portfolio objectives, monitor, evaluate and modify fixed-income portfolios. Composed of 3 integrated elements; a "what if" capability that lets user model alternative yield environments and portfolio strategies; a specialized reporting system for fixed income portfolios that allows user to automate custom-designed portfolio reports; and a data integrator that links users accounting system, external sources of pricing data and an issue-descriptive database into a single resource.

Product: NIS MACROECONOMIC EQUITY SYSTEM
       (formerly APT Management System)
Securities: Stock, Index

Function(s): Fundamental Analysis
System(s): IBM
Special Requirements: None
Price: $12,000/year **AAII Discount:** 30%
Return Policy: NA
Demo: Yes
Technical Support: Phone (9 a.m. - 5 p.m. EST), BBS, Newsletter

Description: A combination of software and proprietary data. Assists in stock portfolio management from a macro-economic point of view. Over 3,000 stocks have been analyzed to establish relationships between changes in the economy and individual stock performance. Program provides: database showing how sensitive specific stocks are to economic events (i.e., changes in inflation, interest rates, industrial production); stock picking tool—stocks can be ranked by forecast performance in the user's own scenario of future economic conditions; an optimizer, constructing portfolios from user selected stocks to maximize the forecast return while minimizing risk; decomposes risk into factors to show the types of risk a portfolio is susceptible to. Supports multiple economic scenarios and contains its own portfolio accounting system so that calculations can be applied to actual portfolios. Can download portfolio accounting data from software such as the Advent Professional Portfolio.

Product: NIS PERFORMANCE ANALYSIS SYSTEM*
Securities: Stock, Index
Function(s): Portfolio Management
System(s): IBM
Special Requirements: None
Price: $16,000 **AAII Discount:** 20%
Return Policy: NA
Demo: No
Technical Support: Phone (9 a.m. - 5 p.m. EST), BBS, Newsletter

Description: Provides an explanation of equity portfolio performance by characterizing a portfolio and its benchmark index on beta, 11 fundamental factors and distribution among 55 industry groups. The impact on relative returns of each aspect of existing differences may be identified. Identifies the separate impact of market timing, "style" characteristics, industry selection and stock selection. Can be used to monitor and pinpoint the strengths and weaknesses of the decision process, audit compliance with policies and improve central control of a multi-manager scheme.

N-Squared Computing (503) 873-4420
5318 Forest Ridge Road fax: (214) 680-1435
Silverton, OR 97381

Product: APEX
Securities: Stock, Index, Mutual Fund, Option, Futures
Function(s): Communications, Technical Analysis
System(s): IBM
Special Requirements: Graphics Adapter
Price: Freeware; through AAII BBS **AAII Discount:** NA
 (see Appendix I)
Return Policy: NA
Demo: No
Technical Support: None

Description: Analyze financial/investment data with 5 graphics analysis programs. Create strategies using single or double moving averages, based on buying long, selling short or both. Calculate the most profitable moving average or combination of moving averages for any user data. Select up to 8 parameters to produce a fully customized strategy. Results can be sorted on gain, average gain per trade, number of trades, buy and sell drawdowns. Financial/Market Data allows complete analysis of market indexes/averages, foreign exchange rate, interest rates, industry groups and market breadth data. Warner Computer has over 330 items that can be downloaded and then updated daily. Most data goes back 10 years. Stock/Options lets user analyze any stocks or options using the high-low-close bar format with volume displayed below price. If user has option files, open interest will be stored in the file. Futures/Commodities lets user analyze futures/commodities with open-high-low-close bar charts and volume and open interest. Futures files will keep the open, high, low, close volume and open interest values for each day in the data file. Mutual Funds allows plotting/comparing up to 9 different funds. Can automatically update data through Warner Computer which tracks about 1,600 mutual funds. Point and Figure lets user do complete point and figure analysis of stocks. Stock files contain high, low, close and volume for each day.

Product: CANDLEPOWER 2*
Securities: Stock, Index, Futures
Function(s): Communications, Technical Analysis
System(s): IBM
Special Requirements: None
Price: $295   **AAII Discount:** None
Return Policy: NA
Demo: Yes ($5 applied to program purchase)
Technical Support: Phone

Description: Contains Japanese candlestick charting, Arm's equivolume charting, standard bar charting and CandlePower charting. Combines the best of Japanese candlesticks with the equivolume principles. Features include automatic candle pattern recognition, data consolidation, pop up windows and autorun. Indicators include: RSI, %K, %D, MACD, rate of change, double momentum, volume, open interest, ease of movement and price detrend oscillator. RSI, %K or %D can be used to filter the candle patterns. Includes database management and downloading capabilities for Warner Computer and DIAL/DATA. Analysis and charting reads data that is in the APEX, N-Squared, Compu Trac, CSI, MetaStock, AIQ, ASCII (PRN), TC-2000 or Technical Tools format. Data conversion is automatic.

Product: MARKET ANALYZER-XL
Securities: Stock, Index, Mutual Fund, Futures
Function(s): Communications, Security Screening, Technical Analysis
System(s): IBM
Special Requirements: Modem for data downloading
Price: $395; when purchased with Stock   **AAII Discount:** None
  and Futures Analyzer-XL, $595;
  Market Analyzer-XL, Performance
  Analyzer-XL and Stock & Future
  Analyzer-XL $695
Return Policy: NA
Demo: Yes ($15 applied to program purchase)
Technical Support: Phone

Description: Allows user to manipulate any type of numerical data and display it graphically. Any market indicator, oscillator or index can be created and then compared with one another or with a broad market average. Downloading facilities from DIAL/DATA and Warner Computer are provided along with utilities for manual updating and data maintenance. Includes a data disk containing weekly data compiled from *Barron's* Market Laboratory page.

Product: STOCK & FUTURES ANALYZER-XL
Securities: Stock, Index, Mutual Fund, Option, Futures
Function(s): Communications, Portfolio Management, Security Screening, Technical Analysis
System(s): IBM
Special Requirements: Modem for data downloading
Price: $395; when purchased with Market Analyzer-XL, $595; for Market Analyzer-XL, Performance Analyzer-XL and Stock & Futures Analyzer-XL $695   **AAII Discount:** None
Return Policy: NA
Demo: Yes ($15 applied to program purchase)
Technical Support: Phone

Description: Charting/analysis package for stocks, futures and market indexes. Data can be downloaded from DIAL/DATA and Warner Computer or manually input. Displays bar charts, line plots, histograms and point and figure charts. Create all popular indicators along with any custom indicator. On-screen construction involves moving average (arithmetic and/or exponential), trendlines, speedlines, trading bands, a full-function cursor and the ability to plot any segment of data in the database. Will also read CSI and Compu Trac data directly.

Omega Research, Inc. (305) 594-7664
3900 N.W. 79th Avenue
Suite 520
Miami, FL 33166

Product: SYSTEM WRITER PLUS*
Securities: Stock, Bond, Index, Mutual Fund, Option, Futures
Function(s): Communications, Technical Analysis
System(s): IBM, Macintosh
Special Requirements: None
Price: $1,975   **AAII Discount:** None

Return Policy: 30 Days, Restocking Fee: $45
Demo: Yes
Technical Support: Phone (8 a.m. - 7 p.m. EST), BBS, Newsletter

Description: Technical analysis program lets user historically test and optimize any trading system without programming knowledge. Users describe in plain English the buy/sell rules of any trading systems they wish to test historically. Program takes user's instructions and converts them into actual machine code. Next, it runs a historical simulation using any desired data and prepares a series of detailed reports revealing exactly how user's system performed over the last 5, 10 and 20 years. Includes charting features that enable graphic evaluation of any system's historical performance. Once a simulation has been performed, simply press one key. Within seconds a bar chart of the test data appears. Overlayed with color-coded arrows pinpointing user's system's buy and sell points. Press one more key and a graph appears in a second window at the bottom of the screen with a graph revealing the day-to-day account balance for the entire test period.

Product: TRADESTATION*
Securities: Stock, Bond, Index, Mutual Fund, Option, Futures
Function(s): Communications, Portfolio Management, Technical Analysis
System(s): IBM
Special Requirements: Windows 3.0, 80286 or better processor, 2 MB RAM, Signal or CQG datafeed
Price: $1,895   **AAII Discount:** None
Return Policy: 30 Days, Restocking Fee: None
Demo: Yes
Technical Support: $495, includes: Phone (8 a.m. - 7 p.m. EST), BBS, Newsletter

Description: Technical analysis program allows users to automate, track and back-test any trading strategy in real-time and historically on dozens of markets simultaneously without programming knowledge. Users describe, in plain English, their custom buy/sell rules which can then be applied to data charts for any desired markets. In real-time, program monitors these markets, on a tick-by-tick basis, instantly generating audio/visual alarms when buy/sell opportunities based on user's criteria occur. Exact market orders to be placed or canceled are then generated. Tracks open position profit/loss of a trade on a tick-by-tick basis and allows users to chart custom indicators and formulas historically and in real-time. Historical back-testing of systems generate detailed performance reports for the period tested. Charting features allow unlimited amounts of technical studies (built-in or custom) and tools to be overlayed and enable graphic evaluation of any system's performance. Color coded arrows overlay on charts to pinpoint every buy/sell point for a specified strategy over the tested period.

Omni Software Systems, Inc.   (219) 924-3522
146 N. Broad Street
Griffith, IN 46319

Product: INVESTMENT ANALYST
Securities: Stock, Bond, Real Estate
Function(s): Financial Planning, Fundamental Analysis
System(s): IBM
Special Requirements: None
Price: $95   **AAII Discount:** 25%
Return Policy: NA
Demo: Yes
Technical Support: None

Description: Analyzes potential investments, considering inflation or deflation, various depreciation methods, cash flow, tax rates, financing and possible future sales price. Printed statements forecast results of a present or contemplated investment, including internal rate of return, variable expense items, net gain or loss after taxes, amortization calculations, cash flow analysis and depreciation using several alternatives.

Product: PORTFOLIO MANAGEMENT SYSTEM
Securities: Stock, Mutual Fund
Function(s): Financial Planning, Portfolio Management, Tax Planning
System(s): IBM
Special Requirements: None
Price: $150   **AAII Discount:** 25%
Return Policy: NA

Demo: Yes
Technical Support: None

Description: Portfolio management system for just a few stocks. Produces reports and schedules for reporting dividends and gains or losses. Tracks dividend due dates, dividends received or reinvested dividends and additional purchases of the same stock; calculates long- and short-term gains and losses.

Product: STOCK MANAGER
Securities: Stock, Mutual Fund
Function(s): Financial Planning, Portfolio Management, Tax Planning
System(s): IBM
Special Requirements: None
Price: $200   **AAII Discount:** 25%
Return Policy: NA
Demo: No
Technical Support: None

Description: Meets recordkeeping needs of individuals requiring sophisticated accounting and reporting capabilities. Keeps portfolio data; produces over 10 separate reports from over 25 different items of information kept on each stock in the file. Long- and short-term gains and losses are automatically calculated, and the necessary forms for tax returns are prepared at the end of the year. All stocks sold during the year are deleted for the next year's portfolio. Special reports include the valuation of the portfolio at current market prices and reports for schedules B and D of the IRS 1040 form.

Ones & Zeros   (215) 248-1010
708 W. Mt. Airy Avenue   fax: (215) 248-1010
Philadelphia, PA 19119

Product: PERCENTEDGE*
Securities: Stock, Bond, Real Estate
Function(s): Financial Planning
System(s): IBM
Special Requirements: None
Price: $100   **AAII Discount:** None
Return Policy: 30 Days, Restocking Fee: None

214 / The Individual Investor's Guide to Computerized Investing

Demo: Yes
Technical Support: Phone (9 a.m. - 5 p.m. EST)

Description: Financial analysis tool. Computes return on investment (IRR) even when return is spread out among many payments, regular and irregular, at different times. Automatically merges life expectancy tables with interest calculations. User can calculate how much to accumulate and save in order to provide a given level of retirement income. Has on-screen examples and includes screens for mortgage analysis and loan amortization.

OPA Software (213) 545-3716
P.O. Box 90658
Los Angeles, CA 90009

Product: OPTION PRICING ANALYSIS*
Securities: Option
Function(s): Communications, Financial Planning, Options Analysis
System(s): IBM, Macintosh
Special Requirements: Modem for data downloading
Price: $395   **AAII Discount:** 25%
Return Policy: 30 Days, Restocking Fee: None
Demo: Yes ($25)
Technical Support: Phone (7 a.m. - 7 p.m. PST)

Description: Provides user with interpreted data screens. Features: stock prices, index, futures and options via a Modified Black-Scholes Model (MBSM); automatically selects best option and options strategy; determines CBOE margin costs; projects profits and losses for straddles, combinations and spreads; evaluates basic option strategies via an "expert system"; provides hedge ratios, deltas and omegas; determines option sensitivity to time changes; graphs option prices for changes in the issue price and time; calculates expiration dates to the year 2000; downloads market prices and volumes.

Options-80 (508) 369-1589
P.O. Box 471
Concord, MA 01742

Product: OPTIONS-80A: ADVANCED STOCK OPTION ANALYZER
Securities: Option

Function(s): Options Analysis
System(s): Apple II, IBM, Macintosh
Special Requirements: None
Price: $170   **AAII Discount:** 20%
Return Policy: 30 Days, Restocking Fee: None
Demo: Yes
Technical Support: Phone (evenings)

Description: Analyzes calls, covered writes and puts and spreads for maximizing return from stock options. Does Black-Scholes modeling and calculates market-implied volatility; plots annualized yield against the price action of the underlying stock; accounts for future payments, transaction costs and the time value of money. Will produce on-screen or printed tables and comparative charts.

OptionVue Systems International, Inc.   (800) 733-6610
175 E. Hawthorn Parkway   (708) 816-6610
Suite 180
Vernon Hills, IL 60061

Product: OPTIONS MADE EASY
Securities: Option, Futures
Function(s): Options Analysis, Simulations/Games
System(s): IBM
Special Requirements: None
Price: $29.95   **AAII Discount:** None
Return Policy: NA
Demo: No
Technical Support: Phone

Description: An options tutorial. Provides a basic introduction to the vocabulary and basic strategies for trading options.

Product: OPTIONVUE IV
Securities: Option, Futures
Function(s): Communications, Options Analysis
System(s): IBM
Special Requirements: None
Price: $895   **AAII Discount:** None
Return Policy: NA

216 / The Individual Investor's Guide to Computerized Investing

Demo: Yes ($44)
Technical Support: Phone, Newsletter

Description: For the private investor trading options on stocks, indexes, currencies, bonds and commodities. Results of investment simulation and "what if" analyses are presented. Can generate specific buy and sell recommendations based on a price forecast for the underlying security and how much money is to be invested. Fair values, implied volatility, delta, time delay and other parameters are displayed for each option as well as for the trader's existing and contemplated total position. The pricing model, a dividend-adjusted Black/Scholes formula, is also adjusted for the possibility of early exercise. Features include volatility tracking, trade commission schedules, a perpetual expiration calendar, margin requirements, function key customization and the ability to handle convertible securities and warrants. The communication module supports automatic data capture from Dow Jones News/Retrieval, Signal, ComStock, DBC Market Watch and Radio Exchange.

Orbit Software Co., Inc.　　　　　　　　　　(402) 498-5712
1330 N. 148th Plaza　　　　　　　　　　　　(402) 492-9812
Omaha, NE 68154

Product: ELECTRIC SCORECARD II*
Securities: Option, Futures
Function(s): Options Analysis, Portfolio Management
System(s): IBM
Special Requirements: Hard drive, printer
Price: $295　　　　　　　　　　　**AAII Discount:** 52.9%
Return Policy: NA
Demo: No
Technical Support: Phone (8 a.m. - 5 p.m. CST)

Description: A recordkeeping program for commodities. Shows amount of money user has gained or lost as a result of buying or selling commodities. Profit and loss on open positions and cash balance in brokerage account at all times plus margin money available for new trades. Can be used for any of 65 different futures contracts. Has feature that tells to the penny how much money will be made or lost when the price of the commodities go up or down.

Palisade Corp. (800) 432-7475
31 Decker Road (607) 277-8000
Newfield, NY 14867 fax: (607) 277-8001

Product: @RISK
Securities: Not Applicable
Function(s): Financial Planning, Fundamental Analysis, Simulations/ Games, Spreadsheet, Statistical Analysis
System(s): IBM, Macintosh
Special Requirements: Spreadsheet compatible with 1 of 4 separate versions, Lotus 1-2-3 or Excel for Windows, Excel 3.0 on the Macintosh, Lotus Symphony
Price: $395 **AAII Discount:** None
Return Policy: 30 Days, Restocking Fee: 10%
Demo: Yes
Technical Support: $150/year, includes: Phone (9 a.m. - 5 p.m. EST)

Description: Lotus 1-2-3/Symphony/Excel add-in for risk analysis using Monte Carlo simulation to analyze uncertainty. Probability distributions are added to cells in the worksheet using 30 probability distribution built-in functions including normal, log-normal, beta, uniform, triangular. Users choose Monte Carlo or Latin Hypercube sampling, select output ranges and start simulating. Output routines display results graphically and provide detailed statistics. Probability distribution functions can be used anywhere in a worksheet either alone in a cell or as part of other expressions, and their parameters can be references to other cells. Dependencies and the seed of the random number generator can be specified. Over 32,000 iterations can be run per simulation. High resolution graphics enhance manipulation of output results. Simulations can be paused and restarted.

Parsons Software (303) 669-3744
1230 W. 6th Street
Loveland, CO 80537

Product: FUNDGRAF
Securities: Stock, Index, Mutual Fund
Function(s): Technical Analysis
System(s): IBM
Special Requirements: None
Price: $100 **AAII Discount:** 10%

Return Policy: 30 Days, Restocking Fee: $15
Demo: Yes ($10)
Technical Support: Phone (10 a.m. - 6 p.m. MST)

Description: Graphs and finds the best performing mutual funds for any period up to 260 weeks. Plot price action and calculated moving averages (simple or exponential). Allows different mutual funds to be superimposed on semi-log price scales for direct comparison of performance for any period. Dividends, capital gains distributions or splits are taken into account in graphs and in calculating the percent change between time periods. Data (daily or weekly) can be entered manually and erroneous data corrected. Can download data into the files with a modem and the WCSPD program disk. Includes 4 years weekly data for 32 no-load mutual funds. Additional disks with 32 funds each are available. Calculates relative strength ratings for all funds. Buy and sell signals are generated based on either crossover or trend change.

Product: FUNDGRAF SUPPLEMENTAL PROGRAMS, DISK 1
Securities: Stock, Index, Mutual Fund
Function(s): Portfolio Management, Technical Analysis
System(s): IBM
Special Requirements: None
Price: $20   **AAII Discount:** 10%
Return Policy: NA
Demo: No
Technical Support: Phone (10 a.m. - 6 p.m. MST)

Description: Contains 4 Fundgraf programs. Make-PRN and Add-PRN move data between the Fundgraf data files and a spreadsheet program (i.e., Lotus 1-2-3, Quattro) or similar programs. Data from other sources can then be added with Add-PRN. From a Fundgraf data disk, data can be imported to a spreadsheet with Make-PRN. Checkdat checks dividends, prices and percent changes for any 2 consecutive weeks or days. It is useful for recording dividends properly. Test-SIG calculates the growth of a $1,000 initial investment made in any or all of the funds assuming that (1) the funds are sold every time the price goes below the moving average and then bought every time the price goes above the moving average, and (2) the cash is invested at a fixed interest rate while out of the market. User selects the lengths for 2 moving averages and the fixed interest rate. For comparison, it calculates the value of $1,000 at fixed interest rate, and the value of the fund if bought and held throughout the period. Results show how effective the selected moving average signal was during the period. Reports number of purchases made during the period.

Product: WCSPD FOR FUNDGRAF
Securities: Stock, Index, Mutual Fund
Function(s): Communications
System(s): IBM
Special Requirements: Modem, Warner Computer Services account
Price: $25　　　　　　　　　　　　　　　　**AAII Discount:** 10%
Return Policy: NA
Demo: No
Technical Support: Phone (10 a.m. - 6 p.m. MST)

Description: Historical data collector retrieves Warner Computer System's Price Dividend (WCSPD) data for the past 5 years. Data for mutual funds, stocks or market indexes are retrieved, then reformatted to fit the Fundgraf program data files.

P.C. Prescience　　　　　　　　　　　　　　　　(408) 773-8715
P.O. Box 60842
Sunnyvale, CA 94088

Product: MARKETMASTER*
Securities: Stock, Bond, Index, Mutual Fund, Option, Futures
Function(s): Options Analysis, Portfolio Management, Security
　　Screening, Technical Analysis
System(s): IBM
Special Requirements: None
Price: $99 and up　　　　　　　　　　　　**AAII Discount:** $50
Return Policy: 30 Days, Restocking Fee: 15%
Demo: Yes ($5)
Technical Support: Phone (9 a.m. - 5 p.m. PST), BBS

Description: System creates leading indicators to forecast both the direction and extent of price movement. The forecasts are displayed graphically on all types of monitors including color. Designed for at-a-glance decision-making. Uses up to 6 leading proprietary indicators that are automatically derived from raw data.

P-Cubed, Inc. (609) 662-3420
a division of Arminius Publications
P.O. Box 1265
Merchantville, NJ 08109-0265

Product: INVESTOR
Securities: Stock, Bond, Mutual Fund, Option, Futures
Function(s): Communications, Portfolio Management
System(s): Macintosh
Special Requirements: None
Price: $150   **AAII Discount:** 33%
Return Policy: 15 Days, Restocking Fee: Shipping/handling
Demo: Yes ($20)
Technical Support: Phone (9 a.m. - 5 p.m. EST)

Description: Menu-driven portfolio manager. Any number of portfolios may be created to track active and potential investments. Handles stocks, bonds, funds, options, margin and short sales. Separate file folders record transactions, interest earned and dividends received. Offers 8 reports: portfolio status, profit/loss, diversification, interest income, dividend income, individual security, margin account and cash account. Users can also chart portfolio performance with the graphing module. Capable of automatically contacting the Dow Jones News/Retrieval Service for quotes; provides a terminal mode for access to telecommunications services.

Performance Technologies, Inc. (800) 528-9595
4814 Old Wake Forest Road (919) 876-3555
Raleigh, NC 27609 fax: (919) 876-2187

Product: CENTERPIECE
Securities: Stock, Bond, Index, Mutual Fund, Option, Real Estate, Insurance, Limited Partnerships
Function(s): Bond Analysis, Portfolio Management
System(s): IBM
Special Requirements: None
Price: Professional system $895;   **AAII Discount:** 10%
   Signal Interface $125

Return Policy: NA
Demo: Yes ($25)
Technical Support: $150/year, includes: Upgrades, Phone (9 a.m. - 5 p.m. EST)

Description: Reports include summaries by position, performance, unrealized gains and losses by trade lot, realized gains and losses, income received and a projection of monthly income and principal redemptions. Bond analysis provides standard bond computations. Global reports include a master list of holdings, cross referenced by security and bond maturity and option expiration schedules. Performance and analytical measures include time-weighted rate of return, total return, current yield, unrealized gain or loss, yield to maturity, yield to call, duration, after-tax yield and taxable equivalent. Accounting functions include deposits, withdrawals, global income posting, automatic reinvestment lots for mutual funds, return of principal, accrued interest, splits and automatic cash, money fund and margin accounting. Sell transactions may be matched to specific buy lots. Market prices may be updated manually or via modem. Program handles stocks, bonds, mortgage-backed securities, options, mutual funds, CDs, T-bills, commercial paper and money market funds. User-defined security type is appropriate for limited partnerships and annuities. Users may optionally define subgroups or sectors for each security type. Provides asset allocation weightings by position, sector and security type. A real-time interface with Signal is available.

Product: CENTERPIECE PERFORMANCE MONITOR*
Securities: Stock, Bond, Index, Mutual Fund, Option, Real Estate, Insurance, Limited Partnerships
Function(s): Portfolio Management
System(s): IBM
Special Requirements: Centerpiece
Price: $595   **AAII Discount:** 10%
Return Policy: NA
Demo: No
Technical Support: $150/year, includes: Upgrades, Phone (9 a.m. - 5 p.m. EST)

Description: Provides performance measurement and reporting by total portfolio, asset class or individual security using BAI prescribed methods (exact method or linked internal rate of return method with monthly valuations and exact timing of capital flows). Compatible with the AIMR performance presentation guidelines. Allows comparisons with multiple market indexes and the construction of properly weighted composite returns.

Personal Computer Products   (301) 593-2571
P.O. Box 44445
Washington, DC 20026

Product: BONDCALC
Securities: Bond
Function(s): Bond Analysis
System(s): IBM
Special Requirements: None
Price: $49.95; 6-month updates $19.95   **AAII Discount:** 15%
Return Policy: NA
Demo: No
Technical Support: None

Description: Computes current redemption information for all Series E and Series EE U.S. Savings Bonds. Stores and prints information for up to 1,000 bonds per data file and enables user to organize savings bond data and to calculate accurate and up-to-date single and cumulative bond redemption information. Based on manually entered bond data, including issue year, issue month, face value, serial number and redemption month. Calculates and displays each bond's current redemption value, total interest earned and interest earned for the current year and computes the total number of bonds entered and their current cumulative face value, purchase price, redemption value, total interest earned and interest earned for the current year. Maintains a permanent record of the bond data entered and outputs the data in the form of a listing.

Personal Micro Services   (708) 513-0279
2702 Turnberry Road   fax: (708) 513-0298
St. Charles, IL 60174

Product: PORTFOLIO-PRO
Securities: Stock, Bond, Mutual Fund
Function(s): Portfolio Management

System(s): Apple II, IBM
Special Requirements: None
Price: $69.95   **AAII Discount:** 40%
Return Policy: 14 Days, Restocking Fee: None
Demo: No
Technical Support: Phone (9 a.m. - 5 p.m. CST)

Description: Tracks stocks, bonds, precious metals, IRAs and other security instruments. All functions are menu-driven, allowing the user to create portfolios, update prices, record dividends and interest and make other data entries. Program generates a current portfolio position, IRS schedule D (gains and losses), schedule B (interest and dividend income), closed-out positions (reported in sequence by sales date for 1- or multiple-year period) and an investment summary (total realized/unrealized gains/losses). Computes holding period and annualized return and months held for each security.

Piedmont Software Company   (704) 376-0935
1130 Harding Place   fax: (704) 376-5969
Charlotte, NC 28204

Product: BOND SWAP MANAGER
Securities: Bond
Function(s): Bond Analysis
System(s): IBM
Special Requirements: None
Price: $995-$4,250   **AAII Discount:** 20%
Return Policy: NA
Demo: Yes
Technical Support: None

Description: Analyzes advantages of swapping one group of fixed income securities for another. Considers all security types, callable and pre-refunded bonds, federal and local taxes, separate settlement dates, separate tax rates for income, capital gains and recovery. Has the appropriate day count method, considers accrued interest if desired. Calculates all net cash flows and income, the yield and price for each security, weighted average after-tax coupon, maturity and time remaining, adjusted duration, yield, net difference between packages, net advantage of swap by actual day count, flexible horizon date, break-even yield, internal rate of return; optimal reinvestment amount and compounding at any specified rate.

Product: MICROBOND CALCULATOR
Securities: Bond
Function(s): Bond Analysis
System(s): Apple II, IBM
Special Requirements: None
Price: $300   **AAII Discount:** 20%
Return Policy: NA
Demo: No
Technical Support: None

Description: Calculates price, yield, after-tax yield, accrued interest per hundred, extended principal and interest, yield value of 1/32, yield value of 1/4 (for municipals), bond equivalent yield, CD equivalent yield, corporate taxable yield, equivalent yield, current yield and duration. Features pricing to both maturity date and call date, use of concessions with municipals, accrued interest with odd-first-coupon periods, handles municipals pre-refunded to a premium call. Handles government and muni bonds, agency and corporate bonds, T-bills, municipal notes, short agency securities, CDs and Eurodollar deposits.

Product: MORTGAGE ISSUE YIELD ANALYZER
Securities: Bond
Function(s): Bond Analysis
System(s): IBM
Special Requirements: None
Price: $495   **AAII Discount:** 20%
Return Policy: NA
Demo: Yes
Technical Support: None

Description: Calculates various yields and cash flow printouts on monthly principal and interest payment issues. Has 3 principal paydown methods: stored FHA experience tables, flexible payment delay-days field and user-defined servicing fees. Calculates yield to maturity, figures bond equivalent yield, displays realized yield based on reinvestment rate, computes half-life and average life, prints cash flows for each year and provides a pro-forma accounting profile, amortization and accretion according to GAAP.

Pine Grove Software (800) 242-9192
67-38 108th Street (718) 575-9192
Suite D-1
Forest Hills, NY 11375

Product: AMORTIZEIT!*
Securities: Not Applicable
Function(s): Financial Planning, Real Estate Analysis, Tax Planning
System(s): IBM
Special Requirements: None
Price: $55   **AAII Discount:** 10%
Return Policy: 60 Days, Restocking Fee: None
Demo: Yes ($5)
Technical Support: $24, includes: Phone (8 a.m. - 10 p.m. EST), BBS

Description: Amortization program supports 8 payments and compounding periods, Rules of 78, U.S. rule, interest only loans, fixed principal loans, normal loans. Payments can be in advance or in arrears. Random or scheduled extra payments can be applied to reduce the principal balance. Calculates the interest saved as a result of extra payments. The interest due can be calculated for any number of days or between any 2 dates. User can set any payment amount for a loan and can calculate the remaining balance.

Product: SOLVEIT!
Securities: Stock, Bond, Mutual Fund, Real Estate
Function(s): Financial Planning, Real Estate Analysis
System(s): IBM
Special Requirements: None
Price: $99   **AAII Discount:** None
Return Policy: 60 Days, Restocking Fee: None
Demo: Yes ($5)
Technical Support: Phone (8 a.m. - 10 p.m. EST), BBS

Description: Program includes: future value of a deposit, future value of a series, present value and time to double, present value of a series, net present value, uneven cash flow, interest due, time to withdrawal funds, required payment needed for a future sum, interest rate earned, equivalent interest rate, purchasing power and inflation, loan calculator, amortization table, remaining balance of a loan after any payment, balloon payment, accelerated payments, depreciation routines, (MACRS, ACRS), gross profit margin of series, break-even point, economic order quantity, net worth statement, affordable house price, second mortgage, rental income property analysis, personal, family or business budget cash flow, weighted average and calendar math.

Portfolio Software, Inc. (617) 328-8248
14 Lincoln Avenue
Quincy, MA 02170

Product: STOCK PORTFOLIO ALLOCATOR
Securities: Stock, Bond, Mutual Fund, Option, Futures
Function(s): Portfolio Management
System(s): IBM
Special Requirements: None
Price: $39   **AAII Discount:** 14%
Return Policy: NA
Demo: No
Technical Support: Phone (9 a.m. - 6 p.m. EST)

Description: Applies Markowitz algorithm to portfolio selection. Shows how to allocate funds among securities in a portfolio to minimize risk and maximize probability of obtaining a desired portfolio rate of return. Has a built-in database editor for creating and maintaining files of security prices and dividends. Customized programs can be made available which will input desired data formats and produce desired outputs.

Precise Software Corp. Phone not given
1000 Campbell Road
Suite 208-128
Houston, TX 77055

Product: PORTFOLIO EVALUATOR
Securities: Stock, Bond, Index, Mutual Fund, Option, Futures, Real Estate
Function(s): Communications, Portfolio Management

System(s): IBM
Special Requirements: Modem for data downloading
Price: $19.95   **AAII Discount:** None
Return Policy: NA
Demo: No
Technical Support: None

Description: Allows for an unlimited number of portfolios and securities. Features include Auto Run for unattended updates and batch report printing, 3-D pie and bar charts and on-line help screens. Provides over 20 reports including portfolio appraisal, unrealized gains/losses, security cross reference, ROI, schedules B and D. Prices may be entered manually or be retrieved automatically from Dow Jones, Warner Computer, Compu Trac, MetaStock or Quote Monitor. Exports quotes and reports to Lotus 1-2-3, ASCII or DIF. Includes coupons for free time on Dow Jones News/Retrieval and Warner Computer.

Precision Investment Services Inc.   (604) 688-8823
1045 Haro Street   fax: (604) 688-8590
Suite 320
Vancouver, BC V6E 328
Canada

Product: POWER TRADER PLUS
Securities: Stock, Index, Mutual Fund, Option, Futures
Function(s): Communications, Portfolio Management, Technical Analysis
System(s): IBM
Special Requirements: Windows 3.0
Price: $1,995   **AAII Discount:** 40%
Return Policy: NA
Demo: Yes
Technical Support: None

Description: Works with all Windows 3.0 program applications. Can run simultaneously with DOS and DOS programs. Using a product called RUMBA from Wall Data, users can connect their PCs to any mainframe computer. Gives real-time quotes, technical analysis and portfolio management. Features include: most actives defined by volume, net change, percent change and value change. These can be filtered by gainers and/or losers, maximum and minimum price and a minimum volume. Quick Quote provides instant stock quotes. Features historical databases; investor defined alerts—buy, bid, ask, trade, high, low, close price and by volume; news information received when broadcast; intra-day tick charts or intervals from one day to one minute. All are updated in real-time. Multiple ticker windows and profile windows show the investor long-term analysis including annual dividends, payout dates and P/E ratios. The charts allow user to simultaneously overlay up to 4 moving averages, plus place over 15 indicators into the programmable mechanical trade systems. This will generate buy or sell indicators. Calculates commissions according to defined commission tables and unrealized and/or realized gains or losses. Displays multiple charts and indicators.

Programmed Press (516) 599-6527
599 Arnold Road
West Hempstead, NY 11552

Product: BONDS AND INTEREST RATES SOFTWARE
Securities: Stock, Bond, Index, Mutual Fund, Option, Futures, Real Estate
Function(s): Bond Analysis, Fundamental Analysis
System(s): Apple II, Commodore, IBM, TRS-80
Special Requirements: None
Price: $119.95   **AAII Discount:** 10%
Return Policy: NA
Demo: No
Technical Support: Phone

Description: Contains 16 interactive programs for forecasting and evaluating price, risk and return on fixed-income securities, such as bonds, mortgages, T-bills, present value of annuities and lump sums.

Product: COMMODITIES AND FUTURES SOFTWARE PACKAGE
Securities: Index, Option, Futures
Function(s): Options Analysis, Technical Analysis
System(s): Apple II, Commodore, CP/M, IBM, TRS-80
Special Requirements: None
Price: $119.95   **AAII Discount:** 10%
Return Policy: NA

Demo: No
Technical Support: Phone

Description: Has 13 interactive programs for forecasting price, risk and return on futures contracts. Contracts include commodities, stock index futures, soybean spreads and arbitrage using options (reverse conversion or conversion of options).

Product: FOREIGN EXCHANGE SOFTWARE PACKAGE
Securities: Index, Option, Futures
Function(s): Options Analysis, Statistical Analysis, Technical Analysis
System(s): Apple II, Commodore, CP/M, IBM, TRS-80
Special Requirements: None
Price: $119.95   **AAII Discount:** 10%
Return Policy: NA
Demo: No
Technical Support: Phone

Description: Contains 11 interactive programs for analyzing and forecasting exchange rates for foreign currencies.

**Product: INVESTMENT AND STATISTICAL SOFTWARE
           PACKAGE**
Securities: Stock, Bond, Index, Option, Futures, Real Estate
Function(s): Bond Analysis, Options Analysis, Statistical Analysis, Technical Analysis
System(s): Apple II, Commodore, CP/M, IBM, TRS-80
Special Requirements: None
Price: $119.95   **AAII Discount:** 10%
Return Policy: NA
Demo: No
Technical Support: Phone

Description: Includes 50 programs for statistical forecasting and evaluation of stocks, bonds, options, futures and foreign exchange.

Product: OPTIONS AND ARBITRAGE SOFTWARE PACKAGE
Securities: Stock, Index, Option, Futures

Function(s): Options Analysis, Technical Analysis
System(s): Apple II, Commodore, CP/M, IBM, TRS-80
Special Requirements: None
Price: $119.95　　　　　　　　　　　　**AAII Discount:** 10%
Return Policy: NA
Demo: No
Technical Support: Phone

Description: Six option valuation models: Black-Scholes, Stoll-Parkinson, empirical put and call models, stock index futures and arbitrage analysis.

Product: STATISTICAL ANALYSIS AND FORECASTING SOFTWARE PACKAGE
Securities: Stock, Bond, Index, Option, Futures
Function(s): Statistical Analysis, Technical Analysis
System(s): Apple II, Commodore, CP/M, IBM, TRS-80
Special Requirements: None
Price: $119.95　　　　　　　　　　　　**AAII Discount:** 10%
Return Policy: NA
Demo: No
Technical Support: Phone

Description: Twenty interactive programs covering the various types of averages, variation, moving averages, exponential smoothing for forecasting, seasonal variation, trends, growth rates, time series decomposition, multiple correlation and regression.

Product: STOCK MARKET SOFTWARE
Securities: Stock, Index, Mutual Fund, Option, Futures
Function(s): Fundamental Analysis, Options Analysis, Portfolio Management, Technical Analysis
System(s): Apple II, Commodore, CP/M, IBM, TRS-80
Special Requirements: 64K
Price: $119.95　　　　　　　　　　　　**AAII Discount:** 10%
Return Policy: NA
Demo: No
Technical Support: Phone

Description: Contains 17 programs for forecasting and evaluating price, risk and return on equity investments including stocks, stock market index futures and arbitrage using options. Includes 220-page Computer Assisted Investment Handbook.

Pumpkin Software (708) 416-3530
P.O. Box 4417
Chicago, IL 60680

Product: OPTION EVALUATOR
Securities: Stock, Option, Futures
Function(s): Options Analysis
System(s): IBM
Special Requirements: None
Price: $129   **AAII Discount:** None
Return Policy: NA
Demo: No
Technical Support: None

Description: Menu-driven tool for use in trading futures, stock index (OEX), and/or securities options. Program calculates fair market value (FMV), implied and historical volatility, delta, theta and vega for all futures and stock index options (FMV and implied volatility for securities options) based on user input. Produces 2 different types of delta sheets (option matrices) for use in projecting future option value over a wide series of user-chosen underlying and strike prices, for individual or multiple option strategies. Included is a special program module with a perpetual calendar and complete option expiration date and exchange information. An optional graphics module can be used to predict future implied volatility levels.

Quant IX Software (800) 247-6354
5900 N. Port Washington Road (414) 961-0669
Suite 142 fax: BBS:(414) 961-2592
Milwaukee, WI 53217

Product: QUANT IX PORTFOLIO EVALUATOR
Securities: Stock, Bond, Mutual Fund
Function(s): Communications, Fundamental Analysis, Portfolio Management

System(s): IBM
Special Requirements: DOS 3.1+, 640K RAM, hard drive
Price: $119   AAII Discount: 25%
Return Policy: NA
Demo: Yes; $10
Technical Support: Phone (8 a.m. - 4 p.m. CST), BBS

Description: Consists of 2 independent programs in 1. Portfolio manager features: single or multiple portfolio management for stocks, bonds, mutual funds, government issues, cash items, etc., total accounting, automatic pricing through either CompuServe or Warner. Reports show market values, investment income, gains and losses (realized and unrealized), commissions, transactions between 2 dates, percentage returns, percentage of asset type and portfolio totals and income tax information. Security analysis features: fundamental ratio analysis, 6 security valuation models, diversification analysis, "what if" testing and portfolio and security risk assessments. Also has built-in communications with on-line help.

Quotron Systems, Inc.   (215) 896-8780
(formerly American Financial Systems)
17 Haverford Station Road
Haverford, PA 19041

Product: BROKER'S NOTEBOOK
Securities: Stock, Bond, Index, Mutual Fund, Option, Futures, Real Estate
Function(s): Communications, Portfolio Management
System(s): IBM
Special Requirements: None
Price: $1,295—prices for Quotron service subscribers and networks vary   AAII Discount: None
Return Policy: NA
Demo: Yes
Technical Support: Phone (9 a.m. - 5 p.m. EST), Newsletter

Description: Prospecting, client and portfolio management system available in both stand-alone and network configurations. Tracks all client conversations and activity, enabling immediate access to holding, transaction and account information. Exact targeting of sales activities is possible using screens of up to 800 user-defined objective codes, with support for mass-mail campaigns with letter, label and envelope printing. Custom reports are included in addition to standard reports such as holdings, profit and loss, income summary and daily to-do. Links to popular word processors and spreadsheets. Allows for desktop-published, graphical reporting, while links to Quotron enable real-time pricing and market data access. Transaction downloads available from ADP, CRI, PaineWebber and others.

Radix Research Ltd. (604) 592-5308
2280 Woodlawn Crescent fax: (604) 370-2001
Victoria, BC V8R 1P2
Canada

Product: OVM THE OPTION VALUATION MODEL VERSION 3.0
Securities: Stock, Index, Bond, Option, Futures
Function(s): Communications, Options Analysis
System(s): IBM
Special Requirements: Modem for data downloading
Price: $495 (Canadian)　　　　　　　　　　**AAII Discount:** 5%
Return Policy: NA
Demo: Yes ($15 Canadian)
Technical Support: Phone (8 a.m. - 6 p.m. PST), Newsletter

Description: Menu-driven option analysis on almost any type of underlying asset. Includes multiple valuation models, each optimized for equities, futures, bonds, indexes and commodities. Any combination of expiration date and expiration month cycle can be selected. Once selected, all future expiration dates are automatically calculated. ScratchPad enables unlimited chaining of assumptions for "what if" scenarios. Using the Binary Step Method developed by Radix Research, it produces almost instantaneous implied volatility figures without a co-processor. Multiple volatility calculations are supported using the Parkinson Extreme Value Method. Worksheet menu includes commissions, T-bill revenue and accrued interest for bonds on both naked and covered positions. Price is $495 in Canadian dollars but is adjusted each day according to the U.S./Canadian exchange rate.

**Product: OVM THE OPTION VALUATION MODEL
　　　　　　VERSION IV***
Securities: Stock, Bond, Index, Mutual Fund, Option, Futures

Function(s): Communications, Options Analysis, Technical Analysis
System(s): IBM
Special Requirements: Modem for data downloading
Price: $899 (Canadian)   **AAII Discount:** 5%
Return Policy: NA
Demo: Yes ($100, 30 day trial)
Technical Support: Phone (8 a.m. - 6 p.m. PST), Newsletter

Description: A total option trading system. Universal worksheet evaluates any option and/or underlying asset position. User time and price change results are shown in tabular and graphical form. Automatic position ranking gives buy/sell recommendations based on user-selected parameters. Includes a database and multi-source downloader. Automatically builds implied volatility history files for any asset. User can combine graphs of implied volatility, underlying momentum, MACD, etc. Includes: instant quote recall, option and volatility statistics, advanced volatility calculations and multiple valuation models, commission, margin and dividends, and a built-in perpetual calendar.

Product: 20/20
Securities: Stock, Bond, Index, Mutual Fund, Option, Futures, Currencies
Function(s): Communications, Technical Analysis
System(s): IBM
Special Requirements: Modem for data downloading
Price: $199 (Canadian)   **AAII Discount:** 5%
Return Policy: NA
Demo: Yes ($15 Canadian)
Technical Support: Phone (8 a.m. - 6 p.m. PST), Newsletter

Description: Full-featured, graphical analysis software package using 3rd-generation computer techniques. Contains DataLink, an integrated down-loader for retrieval of historical and closing price data. Other features: pull-down menus, hot-keys, pick-lists and context sensitive on-screen help manual. Contains all popular indicators plus Smart-Cursor and big-system features such as AutoScale and Compression to graph from 1 to 12 years of data on the screen or printer. Supports most printers including lasers with custom chart capability in printouts. Comes complete with 5 years of data for the indexes. Price is $199 in Canadian dollars but is adjusted each day according to the U.S./Canadian exchange rate.

Product: 20/20 PLUS
Securities: Stock, Index, Bond, Mutual Fund, Option, Futures, Currencies
Function(s): Communications, Technical Analysis
System(s): IBM
Special Requirements: Modem for data downloading
Price: $299 (Canadian)   **AAII Discount:** 5%
Return Policy: NA
Demo: Yes ($15 Canadian)
Technical Support: Phone (8 a.m. - 6 p.m. PST)

Description: Includes all features found in 20/20 plus the McClellan Oscillator for index trading using indexes such as the OEX or S&P 500. Implements the full Sherman McClellan Oscillator and Summation Index and color coded buy and sell signals. The price is $299 in Canadian dollars but is adjusted each day according to the U.S/Canadian exchange rate.

RazorLogic Systems   (408) 778-0889
P.O. Box 335   fax: (408) 778-9976
Morgan Hill, CA 95038

Product: PERSONAL STOCK TECHNICIAN (PST)*
Securities: Stock, Index, Bond, Mutual Fund, Option, Futures, Real Estate
Function(s): Communications, Statistical Analysis, Technical Analysis
System(s): IBM
Special Requirements: Modem for data downloading
Price: $99.50   **AAII Discount:** 50%
Return Policy: 30 Days, Restocking Fee: None
Demo: Yes ($15)
Technical Support: BBS

Description: A stock market technical analysis and tracking program designed to support short- or long-term portfolio decision-making. Alerts user to buy or sell opportunities, gathers and analyzes current or past price and volume data using a wide range of common and advanced indicators; calculates and plots oscillators, moving averages, momentum rate-of-change, support-resistance, on-balance volume, relative strength indicators (RSI), stochastics and more.

RDB Computing (708) 982-1910
8910 N. Kenton Avenue
Skokie, IL 60076

Product: RDB COMPUTING CUSTOM TRADER*
Securities: Stock, Futures
Function(s): Technical Analysis
System(s): IBM
Special Requirements: None
Price: Determined individually   **AAII Discount:** None
Return Policy: NA
Demo: Yes
Technical Support: Phone (10 a.m. - 6 p.m. CST)

Description: Provides a foundation upon which to build technical analysis programs. Includes setup screens, charts, system performance statistics. Supports various data formats. It can be enhanced and modified on a custom programming basis to provide new and unique technical analysis indicators, charts and trading systems.

Real-Comp, Inc. (408) 996-1160
P.O. Box 1210
Cupertino, CA 95015

Product: REAL ANALYZER
Securities: Real Estate
Function(s): Financial Planning, Portfolio Management, Real Estate Analysis, Tax Planning
System(s): Amiga, IBM
Special Requirements: None
Price: $195   **AAII Discount:** 10%
Return Policy: 30 Days, Restocking Fee: None
Demo: Yes ($45)
Technical Support: Phone (8 a.m. - 5 p.m. PST), Newsletter

Description: Helps users decide when to buy, sell or exchange their home or income property by projecting cash flow, profitability before and after taxes and ROI. User can compare properties, evaluate alternative financing, structure loans and compare renting with owning. Includes ability to compose a title page, a partial 1st-year analysis and formatted reports.

Product: REAL PROPERTY MANAGEMENT
Securities: Real Estate
Function(s): Financial Planning, Portfolio Management, Real Estate Analysis
System(s): IBM
Special Requirements: None
Price: $395 to $595   **AAII Discount: 10%**
Return Policy: 30 Days, Restocking Fee: None
Demo: Yes ($45)
Technical Support: Phone (8 a.m. - 5 p.m. PST), Newsletter

Description: For property managers and owners. Records and budgets 12 months of income, expense, profit, cash flow and bank balance for properties such as apartments, offices, condominium associations, etc. Reports balance due by unit and lost revenue, maintains tenant files and compares "actuals" to "budget" by account, unit and month. Generates formatted reports customized for both the owner and the accountant. Checks may be printed by the Check Writer and Vendor file. Tenant invoicing, 1099 Form Writer, Disbursement Sort by Unit/Account/Vendor, Macro Reporting, Export, Metering and Cost Allocation Module are optional.

RealData, Inc.   (800) 899-6060
78 N. Main Street   (203) 838-2670
South Norwalk, CT 06854   fax: (203) 852-9083

Product: BOTTOM DOLLAR
Securities: Real Estate
Function(s): Financial Planning, Portfolio Management, Real Estate Analysis, Tax Planning
System(s): IBM
Special Requirements: None
Price: $100   **AAII Discount: 10%**
Return Policy: All sales final

Demo: Yes
Technical Support: Phone (9 a.m. - 5:30 p.m. EST), Newsletter

Description: Program creates all types of loan schedules. Users can print reports or preview them on computer screen. Users choose between a summary that shows just calendar year totals or a detailed schedule that tracks the payment-by-payment progress of the loan.

Product: COMMERCIAL/INDUSTRIAL REAL ESTATE APPLICATIONS
Securities: Real Estate
Function(s): Financial Planning, Real Estate Analysis, Spreadsheet, Project Cost Analysis
System(s): IBM, Macintosh
Special Requirements: DOS—Lotus 1-2-3, Macintosh—Excel or Works
Price: $100   **AAII Discount:** 10%
Return Policy: All sales final
Demo: Yes ($25)
Technical Support: Phone (9 a.m. - 5:30 p.m. EST), Newsletter

Description: The package contains 3 templates: Project Cost Analysis produces a budget that a lender can evaluate as part of the developer's request for financing. Gives an overview of the proposed project and summarizes the costs of land, construction, design and engineering, financing, development and leasing. Automatically derives the maximum loan a project will support and calculates the income needed to produce a required rate of return. Evaluates the income and expenses for the lease-up period and analyzes the first year of operation. It also projects the possible resale at the end of the first year. Rentroll produces an annual property operating statement. Program will calculate to scheduled and effective gross income, as well as the vacancy loss and show each expense as it costs in dollars per square foot and as a percentage of gross income. LeaseTrack is a tickler file that helps user keep track of the status of up to 32 rental units per property.

Product: FINANCIAL ANALYSIS
Securities: Real Estate

Function(s): Financial Planning, Portfolio Management, Real Estate Analysis, Spreadsheet, Tax Planning
System(s): IBM, Macintosh
Special Requirements: DOS—Lotus 1-2-3, Macintosh—Excel or Works
Price: $195 **AAII Discount:** 10%
Return Policy: All sales final
Demo: Yes ($25)
Technical Support: Phone (9 a.m. - 5:30 p.m. EST), Newsletter

Description: Includes 18 financial analysis models for use with spreadsheets. Templates analyze the financial statement of a business, calculate yield on a wraparound mortgage, calculate modified internal rate of return and modified financial management rate of return, compare true costs of alternative assets, maintain a complete, up-to-date personal financial statement and much more.

Product: ON SCHEDULE
Securities: Real Estate
Function(s): Financial Planning, Real Estate Analysis, Spreadsheet
System(s): IBM, Macintosh
Special Requirements: DOS—Lotus 1-2-3, Macintosh—Excel or Works
Price: $195 **AAII Discount:** 10%
Return Policy: All sales final
Demo: Yes
Technical Support: Phone (9 a.m. - 5:30 p.m. EST), Newsletter

Description: Helps produce a month-by-month plan for drawing, using and repaying a development loan. Predicts and manages numerous inflows and outflows of cash for homes in the final, intermediate and beginning phase of construction, each with different cash requirements. While drawing down funds, user may be writing contracts on units soon to close, collecting the proceeds of sales written several months ago and applying some of these proceeds to reduce outstanding loan balance.

Product: PROPERTY MANAGEMENT III
Securities: Real Estate
Function(s): Financial Planning, Real Estate Analysis, Tax Planning
System(s): IBM, Macintosh

Special Requirements: IBM—DOS 3.2+, Macintosh—O/S 6.04/6.07 or system 7.0
Price: $395-$1,495　　　　　　　　　　**AAII Discount:** None
Return Policy: All sales final
Demo: Yes ($45)
Technical Support: Phone (9 a.m. - 5:30 p.m. EST), Newsletter

Description: Features property, unit and lease profiles; accounts receivable; accounts payable; lease abstracts (or complete leases can be stored on disk for every tenant); automatic billing of monthly rent, 3 other user-defined recurring charges and unlimited non-recurring charges; open-item, accrual-based accounting, with transaction detail retained for past months; detailed tenant statements, with aging and automated collection letters; complete payables system with cash management and discount scheduling; automatic posting and payment of recurring monthly expenses, such as mortgage payments; cash requirements report, check printing and vendor 1099s; tenant's share of CAM charges automatically transferred posted from AP to tenant's account; integrated general ledger that updates immediately as AR and AP transactions are posted; up-to-date financial statements available to print at any time, and sample chart of accounts provided on disk. Each property can have a different chart of accounts; user can copy COA set-up from the sample or from an existing property to a new property. Each property can have a different fiscal year. Repair/work order tracking keeps tabs on repairs requested, in progress and completed. Pop-up lists find GL account number, property ID, lease number—almost anything that is stored in list form—without leaving or losing user's place on the screen.

Product: REAL ESTATE INVESTMENT ANALYSIS
Securities: Real Estate
Function(s): Financial Planning, Real Estate Analysis, Spreadsheet, Tax Planning
System(s): IBM, Macintosh
Special Requirements: DOS—Lotus 1-2-3, Macintosh—Excel or Works
Price: $295　　　　　　　　　　**AAII Discount:** 10%
Return Policy: All sales final
Demo: Yes ($25)
Technical Support: Phone (9 a.m. - 5:30 p.m. EST), Newsletter

Description: Includes 4 real estate applications for use with Lotus 1-2-3 or Excel. Templates provide 10-year sensitivity analysis for income-producing real estate, an income and expense analysis, print an amortization schedule, calculate internal rates of return and develop an annual operating statement. Lease analysis included. Has an 8-page business plan summarizing all the supporting reports about the purchase, financing, resale, taxes and operation of any income-producing property. The plan is formatted for presentation to the bank or partners. Tax-change upgrades are provided at a very nominal cost.

Product: REAL ESTATE PARTNERSHIP PLUS
Securities: Real Estate
Function(s): Financial Planning, Real Estate Analysis, Spreadsheet, Tax Planning
System(s): IBM, Macintosh
Special Requirements: DOS—Lotus 1-2-3, Macintosh—Excel or Works
Price: $295   **AAII Discount:** 10%
Return Policy: All sales final
Demo: Yes ($25)
Technical Support: Phone (9 a.m. - 5:30 p.m. EST), Newsletter

Description: Includes 4 applications. The partnership model begins as property analysis. Instead of examining the federal tax ramifications for an individual investor REPP allows user to enter a series of assumptions about how to allocate income, cash flows and sale proceeds to the limited and general partners. Allows user to specify a preferred return for the limited partners. Program then generates a detailed, summarized property analysis and produces a partnership analysis that shows how the benefits of the partnership should be allocated to each class of partner year by year and how the partner's capital accounts can be expected to progress each year. Also produces the straightforward overview report, with comparison of invested funds performance to other vehicles, such as CDs, T-bills, etc.

Reality Technologies   (800) 346-2024
3624 Market Street   (215) 387-6055
Philadelphia, PA 19104   fax: (215) 387-2179

Product: WEALTHBUILDER BY MONEY MAGAZINE
Securities: Stock, Bond, Mutual Fund

Function(s): Financial Planning, Portfolio Management, Security Screening, Tax Planning
System(s): IBM, Macintosh
Special Requirements: Hard drive
Price: $169.95   **AAII Discount:** None
Return Policy: 30 Days, Restocking Fee: None
Demo: Yes ($9.95)
Technical Support: Phone (9 a.m. - 5 p.m. EST), BBS, Newsletter

Description: Helps user take stock of current financial situation and plan financial future. User enters information about present financial position, including asset holdings, income and expenses; then outlines each financial objective such as home purchase, education or retirement. Program computes what user needs to budget on an annual basis and recommends an optimal asset allocation for each objective based on the Capital Asset Pricing Model applied to a database of up to 1,400 mutual funds, 5,000 stocks, 6,000 bonds from Standard & Poor's and current economic conditions. The program compares user's projected assets at current level of budgeting and investment to the level of assets necessary to reach goals. Will print a recommended action plan, detailing the next financial steps. Helps with tax, insurance and estate planning and allows "what if" analysis. User can change any information or assumption to see the impact on overall financial picture.

Realty Software Company   (801) 649-6149
133 Paseo de Granda   (213) 372-9419
Redondo Beach, CA 90277

Product: HOME PURCHASE
Securities: Real Estate
Function(s): Real Estate Analysis
System(s): Apple II, IBM
Special Requirements: None
Price: $75   **AAII Discount:** 10%
Return Policy: NA
Demo: No
Technical Support: Phone (8 a.m. - 5 p.m. PST)

Description: Analyzes the effects of insurance, property taxes, utility expenses, interest rates, closing costs, debt service and the buyer's tax bracket on the total cash necessary for purchase and the total monthly payment. Calculations include leverage achieved, loan-to-value ratio and return on investment.

Product: INCOME PROPERTY ANALYSIS
Securities: Real Estate
Function(s): Real Estate Analysis
System(s): Apple II, IBM
Special Requirements: None
Price: $75   **AAII Discount:** 10%
Return Policy: NA
Demo: No
Technical Support: Phone (8 a.m. - 5 p.m. PST)

Description: Supplies financial analysis of almost any income-producing property. Up to 4 loans may be entered along with rents, vacancy factor, insurance, taxes, repairs, etc.

Product: LOAN AMORTIZATION
Securities: Real Estate
Function(s): Real Estate Analysis
System(s): Apple II, IBM
Special Requirements: None
Price: $75   **AAII Discount:** 10%
Return Policy: NA
Demo: No
Technical Support: Phone (8 a.m. - 5 p.m. PST)

Description: Amortizes loan payments. Calculates automatically or on a fixed payment basis, displaying a schedule of loan payments (including dates), payment number, payment amount, principle, interest and loan balance.

Product: MANAGER'S OPTION
Securities: Real Estate
Function(s): Real Estate Analysis
System(s): IBM

Special Requirements: None
Price: $375   **AAII Discount:** 10%
Return Policy: NA
Demo: Yes ($25)
Technical Support: Phone (8 a.m. - 5 p.m. PST)

Description: Accounting functions include owner/building information, management fees, balance sheets, checks to owners, 1099 forms, tenant deposit interest, lists of owners and owner account balance.

Product: PROPERTY LISTINGS COMPARABLES
Securities: Real Estate
Function(s): Real Estate Analysis
System(s): Apple II, IBM
Special Requirements: None
Price: $300   **AAII Discount:** 10%
Return Policy: NA
Demo: Yes ($25)
Technical Support: Phone (8 a.m. - 5 p.m. PST)

Description: Maintains real estate listings and comparable sold properties. Includes a screening capability for selecting properties. Property information is entered and updated by filling in a form on the computer screen. Selections of properties on file can be made using various criteria such as minimum and maximum price, number of bedrooms and baths, heat type and city. Performance selections can be made based on a maximum gross factor, a maximum price per square foot of improvements and a minimum cash flow requirement.

Product: PROPERTY MANAGEMENT PLUS
Securities: Real Estate
Function(s): Budgeting, Real Estate Analysis
System(s): IBM
Special Requirements: None
Price: $575   **AAII Discount:** 10%
Return Policy: NA
Demo: Yes ($25)
Technical Support: Phone (8 a.m. - 5 p.m. PST)

Description: Handles both residential and commercial properties for 1 or many owners. Features include tenant information, late rent report, vacancy report, expired lease report, automatic late charge, rent statements, bank reconciliation, graph income and expenses, ledger detail, operating statements, income detail report, expense detail report, check printing, rent receipts, bank deposit slips and a word processor.

Product: REAP PLUS
Securities: Real Estate
Function(s): Financial Planning, Real Estate Analysis, Tax Planning
System(s): IBM
Special Requirements: None
Price: $150   **AAII Discount:** 10%
Return Policy: NA
Demo: No
Technical Support: Phone (8 a.m. - 5 p.m. PST)

Description: Provides instant analysis of any real estate investment including internal rate of return calculations. Features include a 5-year forecast projection of rents, vacancy factors, operating expenses, debt service, depreciation and appreciation. Shows before- and after-tax cash flows for each year. Functions as a 5-year spreadsheet for tax-sheltered real estate investments without requiring any additional software.

Relevance III, Inc.   (615) 333-2005
(formerly R. Maynard Holt & Company)   fax: (615) 297-0078
4400 Belmont Park Terrace
259 King Henry Court
Nashville, TN 37215

Product: RELEVANCE III-ADVANCED MARKET ANALYSIS
Securities: Stock, Index, Bond, Mutual Fund, Option, Futures
Function(s): Technical Analysis
System(s): IBM
Special Requirements: Hard drive, EGA or better
Price: $800   **AAII Discount:** 4%
Return Policy: NA

Demo: No
Technical Support: Phone (9:30 a.m. - 4:30 p.m. CST), Newsletter

Description: Scans 1 to 50 or more markets each night with trading methods to filter out and trade the opportunities. Select trading methods including Gann, Andrews, Elliott, Fibonacci, Wyckoff, etc. Other features include moving averages, stochastics, Wilder's RSI, directional movement, commodity channel index, MACD, Williams' %R, accumulation distribution index, ultimate oscillator, day-by-day simulation mode, risk reward analysis, candlesticks, time/price studies and 9 pages of trading plans for each market.

RESCOM (203) 783-4614
201-743 Ellice Avenue fax: (204) 783-0021
Winnepeg, MB R3G OB3
Canada

Product: INTERNATIONAL MANAGER*
Securities: Stock, Index, Bond, Mutual Fund, Option, Futures, Real Estate
Function(s): Communications, Portfolio Management
System(s): IBM
Special Requirements: None
Price: $15,000   **AAII Discount:** 5%
Return Policy: 30 Days, Restocking Fee: None
Demo: Yes ($500-refundable)
Technical Support: Cost: 15%/year, includes: Phone (8:30 a.m. - 5 p.m. CST), Newsletter

Description: A portfolio and fund management program. Features include: unlimited multi-currency cash balances; time-weighted performance measurement to industry standards; trade date and settlement date accounting; handles all securities from forward contracts to futures; variable report generation with standard database products. Can manage mutual funds as well as institutional and private client accounts. The time weighted rate of return calculations conform to BAI and FAF standards. Has fixed income features including bond duration calculations and a bond rating facility; a modified general account summary to provide "as of" reporting; amortization calculations. An "Asset Allocation" system enables user to structure a portfolio in accordance to a predefined criteria. Includes a "Custodian/Safekeeping" reference for each portfolio item. The "Linked Accounts" enables user to group accounts by either family or organization for reporting or trading purposes.

Product: MARKETMATE*
Securities: Stock, Index, Bond, Mutual Fund, Option, Futures
Function(s): Communications, Portfolio Management
System(s): IBM
Special Requirements: None
Price: $1,750   **AAII Discount:** 20%
Return Policy: 30 Days, Restocking Fee: None
Demo: Y ($250-refundable)
Technical Support: Cost: 15%/year, includes: Phone (8:30 a.m. - 5 p.m. CST), Newsletter

Description: A portfolio management and analysis program developed for the retail broker. Interfaces with the quote service and prices all portfolio positions (held by the firm or those that are delivered out or held elsewhere) on a real-time basis with 1 keystroke. Bid, ask, last and volumes are shown integrated with quantity held, percent and dollar gain/loss, yield, percent of portfolio, annual income and other information. Sets pricing objectives for each position and advises when these targets are close to being met including ones that are at another firm or are stocks a client might buy if the price drops to his target price. Downloads of trades, interest and dividends are reflected in the account through manual entry or automated download. Portfolio analysis routines provide many "what if" scenarios on a specially designed spreadsheet. Portfolio modelling shows what changes should be made to an existing portfolio to suit the present investment climate. Can access other programs without exiting including technical analysis and word processing programs.

Research Press, Inc.   (800) 800-3510
4500 W. 72nd Terrace   (913) 383-3505
Box 8137
Prairie Village, KS 66208

Product: PENROLL
Securities: Not Applicable

Function(s): Financial Planning, Spreadsheet, Tax Planning
System(s): IBM
Special Requirements: Lotus 1-2-3
Price: $95   **AAII Discount:** 30%
Return Policy: 60 Days, Restocking Fee: None
Demo: No
Technical Support: $3/minute or $300/2 hours, includes: Phone (8 a.m. - 5 p.m. CST)

Description: A Lotus 1-2-3 worksheet that compares up to 50 years of after-tax investment of a lump-sum pension distribution to the tax-deferred rollover of a lump-sum pension settlement to an IRA account. Computes the 10% penalty tax on any premature distributions and the 15% excess distribution tax. Users can specify either of the 2 methods of payout from both the lump-sum investment and the rollover investment—a fixed minimum annual amount of a specified percentage of the year-end account balance. Rollover analysis includes minimum distribution requirements for each year after age 70.5 based on life expectancy data entered by the user—for either single or joint life expectancies. A part of the program permits graphic comparisons of the annual balance in the IRA account.

Product: PENTAX
Securities: Not Applicable
Function(s): Financial Planning, Spreadsheet, Tax Planning
System(s): IBM
Special Requirements: Lotus 1-2-3
Price: $95   **AAII Discount:** 30%
Return Policy: 60 Days, Restocking Fee: None
Demo: No
Tech support: $3/minute or $300/2 hours, includes: Phone (8 a.m. - 5 p.m. CST), BBS, Newsletter

Description: An analysis of the options available to retired taxpayers relative to the tax on lump-sum distributions. A Lotus 1-2-3 worksheet that computes the lump-sum tax 5 different ways for 3 different tax years. For each year from 1989 through 1991, computes the 10-year and the 5-year averaging tax with and without the 20% capital gains tax. Computes amount of any 10% penalty tax on premature distributions in excess of 3 alternate exclusions. Produces a simulated copy of form 4972.

Product: TAX TOOLS
Securities: Not Applicable
Function(s): Financial Planning, Spreadsheet, Tax Planning
System(s): IBM
Special Requirements: Lotus 1-2-3
Price: $95   **AAII Discount:** 30%
Return Policy: 60 Days, Restocking Fee: None
Demo: No
Technical Support: $3/minute or $300/2 hours, includes: Phone (8 a.m. - 5 p.m. CST)

Description: Provides 13 investment and tax planning worksheets.

Ret-Tech Software   (708) 246-1387
(formerly David W. Rettger)
5304 Johnson Avenue
Western Springs, IL 60558

Product: CHARTPRO
Securities: Stock, Bond, Index, Mutual Fund, Option, Futures
Function(s): Communications, Technical Analysis
System(s): IBM
Special Requirements: 640K RAM, hard drive recommended, EGA or VGA graphics, modem for data downloading
Price: $54   **AAII Discount:** None
Return Policy: NA
Demo: Yes ($5)
Technical Support: Phone (9 a.m. - 5 p.m. CST), BBS

Description: Creates daily, weekly and monthly high/low/close bar charts using high resolution color graphics. Menu-driven, the master version permits the user to calculate many technical studies including: simple, exponential, displaced and volume-weighted moving averages; parabolic time/price; on-balance volume, relative strength, momentum and point and figure charts, support/resistance study, Fibonacci fans, line oscillator, directional movement indicator, commodity cycle index, Williams' %R, moving average envelope, directional movement index,

MACD, CCI, accumulation/distribution index, fast/slow stochastics, Gann fans, Fibonacci support/resistance lines, Bollinger bands, Candle charts, McClellan Oscillator and more. Also included with the master version are a program for manual data entry and programs for accessing the Dow Jones News/Retrieval for auto quote retrieval and automatic entry into the ChartPro files. Supports Prodigy, GEnie and other sources. Documentation is included for all routines.

Product: MEGATECH CHART SYSTEM*
Securities: Stock, Bond, Index, Mutual Fund, Option, Futures
Function(s): Communications, Technical Analysis
System(s): IBM
Special Requirements: Hard drive, EGA or VGA graphics; 80286, 80386 or 80486 recommended
Price: $133   **AAII Discount:** None
Return Policy: NA
Demo: No
Technical Support: Phone (9 a.m. - 5 p.m. CST), BBS

Description: Uses unlimited banks of 30 pre-programmable, 1-key recall screens with up to 16 charts per screen. Charts may include technical studies such as various moving averages, point and figure, candle charts, stochastics, ARMS Index, McClellan oscillator, trend lines, fans, angles, parallel lines, money flow, open interest, spreads, multiple-tissue overlay, MACD, CCI, relative strength, oscillators, DMI, parabolic time/price and others. Additional features include customizable screens, zoom up/down, chart scroll, "Tech on Tech", note pads for each issue and true autoprint. Support for Dow Jones, Prodigy and GEnie data retrieval is included. Others available on request.

Revenge Software   (516) 271-9556
P.O. Box 1073
Huntington, NY 11743

Product: AN OPTION VALUATOR/AN OPTION WRITER
Securities: Option
Function(s): Options Analysis
System(s): Apple II, IBM
Special Requirements: None

Price: $99.95   **AAII Discount:** 25%
Return Policy: 30 Days, Restocking Fee: $25
Demo: Yes ($10)
Technical Support: Phone (8 a.m. - 4 p.m. EST)

Description: A package for evaluating stock options. Consists of 2 interactive programs, An Option Valuator and An Option Writer, enabling the user to analyze options. An Option Valuator uses the Black-Scholes equations to predict the future fair market value of a call or put option, calculate option volatility and hedge ratios. An Option Writer evaluates covered option writing strategies, computes and displays total investment, maximum profit, maximum percent profit, total investment cost, number of days to option expiration, percent investment yield, annualized investment yield, yield if option exercised, break-even stock price and total profit. Features: graph displays, an options calendar giving the complete expiration date when only the month and year are entered and an option editor permitting the user to modify any option parameter so that the effect of the change on other parameters may be observed. Includes a manual.

RK Microsystems   (414) 786-7333
17365 Alvin Lane
Brookfield, WI 53045

Product: LOAN PRO*
Securities: Not Applicable
Function(s): Financial Planning, Real Estate Analysis
System(s): IBM
Special Requirements: None
Price: $40   **AAII Discount:** 10%
Return Policy: NA
Demo: No
Technical Support: None

Description: A loan analysis tool. Produces amortization schedules for simple interest, compound interest and Rule of 78s loans. Handles balloon payments, odd period interest and payments in advance and in arrears. Program allows for 7 different payment/compounding period types. User can choose from either a standard 360-day year or a 365-day year. Program will solve for any unknown loan parameter, calculate the APR used for comparing home loans and analyze leases. Help screens are available for each line of input. Amortization schedules can be displayed on screen and printed.

Product: OPTION TOOLS DELUXE
Securities: Option
Function(s): Options Analysis
System(s): IBM
Special Requirements: None
Price: $50   **AAII Discount:** 10%
Return Policy: NA
Demo: Yes ($5)
Technical Support: None

Description: Evaluates long- and short-positions in equity options, S&P 100 index options or writing covered calls. Calculates theoretical values including dividends, using the Black-Scholes and Cox-Ross-Rubinstein Binomial models. Calculates and shows on-screen or printout option values, expiration dates, breakeven points, dollar gains/losses, rates of return, hedge ratios and normal probabilities of stock price movements. "What if" analysis on up to 3 options can be performed with results displayed for each option individually and all options combined. Data may be saved. Calculates market implied volatility and saves value for retrieval in other parts of the program. A data file of historical volatilities is included and may be modified.

RLJ Software Applications   (517) 439-9605
306 N. Wolcott Street
Hillsdale, MI 49242

Product: STOCKCAL
Securities: Stock
Function(s): Fundamental Analysis
System(s): IBM
Special Requirements: None
Price: $39.95   **AAII Discount:** 12.5%
Return Policy: 30 Days, Restocking Fee: None
Demo: No
Technical Support: Phone (5 p.m - 9 p.m. EST)

Description: Performs a number of calculations for the Stock Selection Guide recommended for use by the National Association of Investment Clubs. Calculation results may be printed on a single sheet of computer paper; printout gives a plot of sales and earnings as well as numerical data. Included is a projection of future sales and earnings, debt and shared outstanding, historical sales and earnings growth rates calculated by a least squares regression analysis, projected buy, hold and sell ranges.

Roberts-Slade, Inc.   (800) 433-4276
750 N. 200 West   (801) 375-6850
Suite 301B   fax: (801) 373-2775
Provo, UT 84601

Product: CHARTISTALERT*
Securities: Stock, Bond, Index, Mutual Fund, Option, Futures
Function(s): Communications, Fundamental Analysis, Options Analysis, Portfolio Management, Security Screening, Technical Analysis
System(s): IBM
Special Requirements: None
Price: $195/month   **AAII Discount:** None
Return Policy: NA
Demo: No
Technical Support: Phone (7 a.m. - 5 p.m. MST), Newsletter

Description: Includes PlatformAlert features plus unlimited history on tick, intraday, daily, weekly and monthly prices. User can view up to 3,000 bars on screen. Includes hundreds of advanced technical indicators, trend line analysis, studies on tick charts, spreads and complete overlay functions.

Product: ENHANCED CHARTIST
Securities: Stock, Index, Mutual Fund, Option, Futures
Function(s): Communications, Options Analysis, Portfolio Management, Technical Analysis
System(s): Macintosh
Special Requirements: None
Price: $2,590   **AAII Discount:** 4%
Return Policy: NA

Demo: Yes
Technical Support: Phone (7 a.m. - 5 p.m. MST), Newsletter

Description: Includes many features available on Master Chartist. Tracks and charts commodities, options, stocks and indexes; has more than 50 popular technical indicators; provides options analysis and advanced trendlines. Takes advantage of multiple windows and multiple monitors. With the right hardware, can drive up to 6 live monitors. Each monitor can contain a display that may include charts, quotes, portfolio management and/or most multifinder applications. Displays 1,024 live quotes, 22 live windows and can store 2 years of daily history and 9 years of weekly history. Also charts 168 items on an intra-day and tick-by-tick basis.

Product: MASTER CHARTIST
Securities: Stock, Index, Mutual Fund, Option, Futures
Function(s): Communications, Options Analysis, Technical Analysis
System(s): IBM, Macintosh
Special Requirements: None
Price: $1,295   **AAII Discount:** 6%
Return Policy: 30 Days, Restocking Fee: $200
Demo: NA
Technical Support: $295/year, includes: Phone (7 a.m. - 5 p.m. MST), Newsletter

Description: Has multiple windows, unique point and click interface and high resolution graphics. Supports several data vendors and can track and chart commodities, options and stocks. More than 50 technical indicators are available with options analysis and advanced trendline analysis. With the Mac II, can drive up to 6 live monitors with each monitor having its own unique graphic display.

Product: PLATFORMALERT*
Securities: Stock, Bond, Index, Mutual Fund, Option, Futures
Function(s): Communications, Fundamental Analysis, Options Analysis, Portfolio Management, Security Screening, Technical Analysis
System(s): IBM
Special Requirements: None

Price: $125/month　　　　　　　　　　　　AAII Discount: None
Return Policy: NA
Demo: None
Technical Support: Phone (7 a.m. - 5 p.m. MST), Newsletter

Description: Tracks stocks, commodities and options. Includes 125 customized quote fields, baskets, news, ranking, ticker tapes, matrix pages, fixed pages, portfolio management, price, block and volume alerts.

Product: RISKALERT*
Securities: Stock, Bond, Index, Mutual Fund, Option, Futures
Function(s): Communications, Fundamental Analysis, Options Analysis, Portfolio Management, Security Screening, Technical Analysis
System(s): IBM
Special Requirements: None
Price: $390/month　　　　　　　　　　　　AAII Discount: None
Return Policy: NA
Demo: None
Technical Support: Phone (7 a.m. - 5 p.m. MST), Newsletter

Description: Includes PlatformAlert and ChartistAlert features plus 8 volatility calculations: Black, Black-Scholes, Cox-Ross-Rubinstein (Binomial), Pseudo American and Adesi-Whaley. Theoretical values and derivatives with net calculations. Unique options fields, option matrix, varying volatility chart variations and other options charting.

RTR Software, Inc.　　　　　　　　　　　　(919) 829-0789
19 W. Hargett Street　　　　　　　　　　fax: (919) 829-0891
Suite 204
Raleigh, NC 27601

Product: TECHNIFILTER PLUS
Securities: Stock, Bond, Index, Mutual Fund, Option
Function(s): Security Screening, Technical Analysis
System(s): IBM
Special Requirements: None
Price: $299　　　　　　　　　　　　　　　AAII Discount: None
Return Policy: 30 Days, Restocking Fee: $10

Demo: No
Technical Support: Phone (9 a.m. - 6 p.m. EST)

Description: Tests technical trading strategies and filters through a large number of issues for technical situations. User can test a strategy on 1 issue, or many, for up to 2,000 time units. The optimization port can fine-tune a strategy by providing parameter values that give the most profit. User can use and modify strategies provided or can design originals. Features screens such as: issues below their 200-day average, with RSI below 40 and volume 50% above the 10-day average volume. A point and figure filter identifies issues in standard patterns; an individual filter allows each issue to have a separate selection criteria. Can chart indicators and overlay trading strategies on these charts, and some versions work with data from Dow Jones Market Analyzer, Savant's Technical Investor, Equis, MetaStock, Compu Trac and Inmark's Market Maker.

SASI Software Corp.   (503) 625-5384
P.O. Box 457
Sherwood, OR 97140

Product: MARKETEDGE*
Securities: Stock, Bond, Index, Mutual Fund, Futures
Function(s): Technical Analysis
System(s): IBM
Special Requirements: None
Price: $179   **AAII Discount:** 27.9%
Return Policy: 30 Days
Demo: Yes ($10)
Technical Support: Phone (6 p.m. - 10 p.m. PST)

Description: A market timing package that focuses on timing of the overall market to identify major tops and bottoms. Market breadth data (advances, declines, volume) is integrated into a Master Breadth Index. Other indicators featured include stochastics, RSI and Bollinger Bands. Features include pop-up menus, on-screen help windows and full color graphs.

Savant Corporation   (800) 231-9900
120 Bedford Center Road   (603) 471-0400
Bedford, NH 03110

Product: ENHANCED COMMUNICATIONS
Securities: Stock, Bond, Index, Mutual Fund, Option, Futures
Function(s): Communications
System(s): IBM
Special Requirements: Modem
Price: $245   **AAII Discount:** None
Return Policy: NA
Demo: No
Technical Support: Phone (9 a.m. - 5 p.m. EST)

Description: Communications program for users of Savant's Fundamental Investor, Investor's Portfolio and Technical Investor. Retrieves prices from Signal, Warner, TrackData and Dow Jones News/Retrieval. Includes: data validation, data insertion, timed retrieval, symbol aliasing for different databases, custom log-on/log-off procedures, script files and macro procedures.

Product: FUNDAMENTAL DATABRIDGE
Securities: Stock
Function(s): Communications
System(s): IBM
Special Requirements: None
Price: $145   **AAII Discount:** None
Return Policy: NA
Demo: No
Technical Support: Phone (9 a.m. - 5 p.m. EST)

Description: Moves fundamental data into and out of the Fundamental Investor. Allows use of Savant fundamental data in other programs, such as spreadsheets, databases or word processors. Any program that can read a standard text or DIF file, such as Lotus 1-2-3, can read data files written by program. Also converts fundamental data from outside sources (if stored in compatible text or DIF files) into a format the Fundamental Investor can use.

Product: FUNDAMENTAL INVESTOR
Securities: Stock
Function(s): Communications, Fundamental Analysis, Security
   Screening

System(s): IBM
Special Requirements: Modem for data downloading
Price: $395   **AAII Discount:** None
Return Policy: NA
Demo: Yes
Technical Support: Phone (9 a.m. - 5 p.m. EST)

Description: Provides fundamental analysis, communications and fundamental screening. Allows storage of over 300 data items with data available on more than 10,000 companies. Data can be entered and edited manually or automatically by modem. User can screen all securities in the database greater than, less than or equal to each parameter; sort stocks on a single parameter (before or after screening); calculate financial ratios from basic financial information (using spreadsheet-like functions); sort stocks based on a group of user-specified parameters. Allows automatic retrieval of fundamental data from Ford Investor Services and Warner.

Product: INVESTOR'S PORTFOLIO
Securities: Stock, Bond, Mutual Fund, Option, Futures, Real Estate
Function(s): Portfolio Management
System(s): IBM
Special Requirements: None
Price: $495   **AAII Discount:** None
Return Policy: NA
Demo: Yes
Technical Support: Phone (9 a.m. - 5 p.m. EST)

Description: Program tracks stocks, bonds, stock dividends, short positions and open orders. Maintains records of commissions, fees, taxes; gives warnings when positions fall below or exceed set limits; calculates the actual compound return on investment, including commissions, dividends, margin interest and taxes; prints IRS schedules and more.

Product: TECHNICAL DATABRIDGE
Securities: Stock, Bond, Index, Mutual Fund, Option, Futures
Function(s): Communications
System(s): IBM

Special Requirements: None
Price: $145　　　　　　　　　　　　　　**AAII Discount:** None
Return Policy: NA
Demo: No
Technical Support: Phone (9 a.m. - 5 a.m. EST)

Description: Allows transfer of data between Technical Investor and spreadsheet programs. Data can be moved into a spreadsheet for complex user-defined calculations. Results of those calculations can be returned for analysis and charting to the Technical Investor. Allows transfer of data between standard text files, Savant data files and DIF files, giving users the ability to use the Technical Investor data in their own programs, convert DIF files into text files and to convert between different types of Savant data files.

Product: TECHNICAL INVESTOR
Securities: Stock, Bond, Index, Mutual Fund, Option, Futures
Function(s): Communications, Technical Analysis
System(s): IBM
Special Requirements: Modem for data downloading
Price: $395　　　　　　　　　　　　　　**AAII Discount:** None
Return Policy: NA
Demo: No
Technical Support: Phone (9 a.m. - 5 p.m. EST)

Description: Combines charting, communications and technical database programs; fully integrates with the other Savant investor products, all of which can be accessed from one screen. The database stores daily high/low with close/volume information for up to 2,500 securities, with up to 40 years daily data for a security. Charts include price and volume bars; high, low and close price lines; point and figure charts; positive/negative volume indicators; relative strength and others. Plot multiple stocks on the same window, or use the multiple-window feature to compare charts for different securities side by side. The communications package updates prices automatically from the Warner, Merlin or Dow Jones News/Retrieval, providing current quotes or up to 10 years of historical data on stocks, commodities, market indexes, etc. Most securities are handled automatically; any type of security may be entered manually.

Product: TECHNICAL SELECTOR
Securities: Stock, Bond, Index, Mutual Fund, Option, Futures
Function(s): Security Screening, Technical Analysis
System(s): IBM
Special Requirements: None
Price: $295   **AAII Discount:** None
Return Policy: NA
Demo: No
Technical Support: Phone (9 a.m. - 5 a.m. EST)

Description: Security filter program for Savant's Technical Investor. Analyzes studies to select stocks, mutual funds, options, etc., that exhibit bullish or bearish tendencies or breakouts. Includes relative strength index, stochastics, moving average crossovers, volume accumulation and moving average convergence/divergence. Filters the data on several studies, prints statistical and filter reports and creates lists of securities that pass each filter.

Scientific Consultant Services, Inc.   (516) 696-3333
20 Stagecoach Road
Selden, NY 11784

Product: NEXTURN: ADVANCED*
Securities: Stock, Index, Mutual Fund, Option, Futures
Function(s): Technical Analysis
System(s): IBM
Special Requirements: Math co-processor recommended
Price: $649   **AAII Discount:** 20%
Return Policy: NA
Demo: Yes ($49)
Technical Support: Phone (afternoon/early evening EST)

Description: Artificial intelligence system using neural networks to forecast turning points in stock indexes and stock index futures (S&P 500 and OEX). Analyzes seasonality and performs automatic candlestick pattern identification. Displays data in candlestick chart format, complete with Bollinger Bands, neural network and other signals, as well as other indicators. Forecasts market tops and bottoms months in advance using a cycle model. Menu-driven architecture. Reads data files in users formats. Text-mode and graphics reports.

Product: NEXTURN: BASIC*
Securities: Index, Mutual Fund, Option, Futures
Function(s): Communications, Technical Analysis
System(s): IBM
Special Requirements: Math co-processor recommended
Price: $499 **AAII Discount:** 20%
Return Policy: NA
Demo: Yes ($49)
Technical Support: Phone (afternoon/early evening EST)

Description: A neural network forecasting system for stock indexes and stock index futures (e.g., S&P 500 and OEX) that identifies short-term tops and bottoms, generates forecasts months in advance. Requires the daily closing prices and comes with 5 years of data. Built-in data editor for manual entry, but will download directly from Signal receiver. Text-mode and graphics reports.

Product: STOCK ANALYZER
Securities: Stock, Mutual Fund, Option
Function(s): Communications, Technical Analysis
System(s): IBM
Special Requirements: Hard drive
Price: $599 **AAII Discount:** 20%
Return Policy: NA
Demo: Yes ($49)
Technical Support: Phone (afternoon/early evening EST)

Description: Designed to help user time entry into long and short positions in individual stocks or stock options. Screens a large database to find stocks with the highest potential for winning trades. Based on the observation that earnings reports (and the resultant moves) are often followed, 1 quarter later, by similar moves. Is able to display several indicators including MACD, MFI, OBV, RSI and stochastics. Works with both small and large capitalization issues. Has built-in downloading feature, text-mode and graphics reports.

Product: TOTAL RETURN*
Securities: Index, Option, Futures
Function(s): Simulations/Games, Technical Analysis

System(s): IBM
Special Requirements: Hard drive, math co-processor
Price: $2,500; additional $995 for S&P module   **AAII Discount:** 20%
Return Policy: NA
Demo: No
Technical Support: Phone (afternoon/early evening EST)

Description: Trading system that allows the user to bring a large amount of diverse information to bear upon trades. Contains a mechanical trading model that uses a volatility break-out approach and dynamic-Gann for exiting stops. Provides money management and loss control. Can manage a trade once entered, even though the entry may have been triggered by another system. Program analyses seasonality, critical dates and prices. Computes a wide variety of indicators and prepares charts with the time access in either trading days or Julian days, in either candlestick or bar format. Will directly drive printer to its maximum resolution. Multiple text-mode report options include SystemWriter-like historical performance evaluations and a report containing trading instructions that user can fax to a broker to act on. Currently available for trading the major commodities; version under development for trading stocks.

Scientific Press, Inc.   (800) 451-5409
651 Gateway Boulevard   (415) 583-8840
Suite 1100   fax: (415) 583-6371
South San Francisco, CA 94080

Product: ASSET ALLOCATION TOOLS
Securities: Not Applicable
Function(s): Portfolio Management, Spreadsheet
System(s): IBM
Special Requirements: Lotus 1-2-3
Price: $2,500   **AAII Discount:** None
Return Policy: NA
Demo: Yes
Technical Support: Phone

Description: Menu-driven, Lotus-based program for optimizing a portfolio over different classes of assets. Calculates optimal mix of asset classes for an investor, subject to the investor's tolerance for risk.

Analysis involves these steps: user selects proxies for the asset classes over which the portfolio is to be optimized, then AAT computes historic statistics on risks, returns and correlations of these proxies, and determines the optimal portfolio for a variety of risk tolerances. User reviews the inputs (historic statistics) and the outputs (optimization results)—in graphs or in numerical form—and reprocesses as needed. User can project the optimization results out to any horizon and compare the results with targets.

Securities Software and Consulting   (800) 234-0556
Corporate Place   (203) 242-7887
705 Bloomfield Avenue   fax: (203) 286-8091
Bloomfield, CT 06002

Product: CAMRA THE COMPLETE ASSET MANAGEMENT, REPORTING AND ACCOUNTING SYSTEM*
Securities: Stock, Bond, Index, Mutual Fund, Option, Futures, MBS, CMO, and other derivatives
Function(s): Bond Analysis, Communications, Portfolio Management
System(s): IBM
Special Requirements: None
Price: Contact vendor   **AAII Discount:** None
Return Policy: NA
Demo: Yes
Technical Support: Cost varies, includes: Phone (8:30 a.m. - 5:30 p.m. EST), BBS, Newsletter

Description: Developed for financial services industry, a fully integrated, real-time, multi-user system that provides complete asset management, reporting and accounting. Processes a full complement of instruments including futures, options and mortgage-backed securities. Processing ability includes duration and convexity as well as accounting. Provides an ad hoc query feature and standard management, accounting and regulatory reports, including schedules D, DA and DB. Users can establish multiple portfolios, block and allocate trades to multiple portfolios with a single entry, manage and segment portfolios, perform calculations on securities and generate standard or ad hoc reports. Provides cash flows, weighted average returns and performance measurements on a segmented portfolio basis and calculates weighted averages by portfolio creating average amounts to maturity or worst. Users can create indexes and assign spread over the index for automatic reset. Is menu-driven and uses field sensitive pop-up help screens. Supports multi-currency processing and provides net asset valuation.

Software Advantage Consulting Corp. (800) 729-2431
38442 Gail (313) 463-4995
Mt. Clemens, MI 48043

Product: INVESTOR'S ADVANTAGE 3.0 FOR PC COMPATIBLES
Securities: Stock, Index, Mutual Fund, Option, Futures
Function(s): Communications, Financial Planning, Options Analysis, Technical Analysis
System(s): IBM
Special Requirements: Modem for data downloading
Price: $399.95 **AAII Discount:** None
Return Policy: NA
Demo: Yes ($40, 30 day trial)
Technical Support: Phone (8 a.m. - 7 p.m. EST)

Description: Analysis tool for stock selection and market timing. Charts stocks, mutual funds, market indexes, commodities and options in CGA or EGA resolution. Individual equity studies include high/low/close, Japanese candlesticks, volume, relative strength, on-balance volume, moving averages (9 variable settings for advanced, centered, simple and exponential), stochastics, MACD, Wilder's RSI and DMI, momentum, open interest and more. General market barometers include DJIA, NYSE Composite, advance/declines, put/call ratio, odd lot short ratio, overbought/oversold ratio, McClellan oscillator, summation index, traders index, 15 most active (daily), 20 most active (weekly), specialist short ratio, new highs/new lows. Zoom feature on all charts. Reports include a relative strength ranking report, moving average breakout report, overbought/oversold report (using stochastics) and the monthly percentage report. Data export for spreadsheet use as well as MetaStock/Compu Trac and Market Maker data formats. Automatic downloading of quotes from Warner Computer Systems (downloading software is included).

Product: INVESTOR'S ADVANTAGE 2.0 FOR THE AMIGA
Securities: Stock, Index, Mutual Fund, Option, Futures
Function(s): Communications, Technical Analysis

System(s): Amiga
Special Requirements: Modem for data downloading
Price: $399.95   **AAII Discount:** None
Return Policy: NA
Demo: Yes
Technical Support: Phone (8 a.m. - 7 p.m. EST)

Description: Analysis tool for stock selection and market timing. Charts stocks, mutual funds, market indexes, commodities and options in 640 by 200 resolution color. Individual equity studies include high/low/close, volume, relative strength, volume, moving averages (3 durations per issue), stochastics, Wilder's RSI, momentum, sine waves (for cycle analysis), trendlines and more. Individual charts include readout of high/low/close and volume. General market barometers include DJIA, NYSE Composite, advance/declines, put/call ratio, odd lot/short ratio, overbought/oversold ratio, new high/new lows, specialist short ratio and the 20 most active indicator. Zoom feature on all charts. Relative strength report sorts stocks strongest to weakest to help identify best performers. Time market entries and exits using market barometers. Other reports include the monthly percentage change report. Data export for spreadsheet use. Automatic downloading of quotes from Warner Computer Systems (downloading software is included).

SOFTWARE EDGE, INC.   (800) 321-5250
112 Ocean Bay Drive   (305) 451-6270
Key Largo, FL 33037

Product: RETIREMENT SURPRISE!*
Securities: Not Applicable
Function(s): Financial Planning
System(s): IBM
Special Requirements: None
Price: $49   **AAII Discount:** None
Return Policy: 30 Days, Restocking Fee: None
Demo: Yes
Technical Support: Phone (9 a.m. - 5 p.m. EST)

Description: Helps determine what is adequate retirement capital. Organizes income, expense and savings data, then displays investment earnings, shortfall and required capital (lump sum, annual and monthly amounts), listed year-by-year to age 90. All years are displayed simultaneously with recalculation for any investment return and inflation rate. Provisions are made for early Social Security, fixed or variable income, pensions with and without COLA, etc.

Sorites Group, Inc. (703) 569-1400
P.O. Box 2939 fax: (703) 569-1424
Springfield, VA 22152

Product: SORITEC
Securities: Stock, Bond, Option, Futures, Real Estate
Function(s): Fundamental Analysis
System(s): IBM
Special Requirements: None
Price: $595   **AAII Discount:** None
Return Policy: 45 Days, Restocking Fee: None
Demo: Yes ($25)
Tech support: $150/year, includes: Phone (9 a.m. - 6 p.m. EST)

Description: A problem-oriented 4th-generation language. Features: econometrics, simulation, forecasting, statistics, mathematics, data entry and manipulation. Handles time series and cross sectional analysis. Applications include economic research and policy analysis; sales forecasting and market research; stock, bond and commodity price forecasting; public utility load and rate analysis; laboratory research; production and cost function estimation and Monte Carlo simulation.

Spreadsheet Solutions Corp. (800) 634-8509
600 Old Country Road (516) 222-1429
Garden City, NY 11530 fax: (516) 222-1517

Product: FINCALC
Securities: Bond
Function(s): Financial Planning, Real Estate Analysis, Spreadsheet
System(s): IBM
Special Requirements: Lotus 1-2-3 or Symphony
Price: $99.95   **AAII Discount:** None
Return Policy: 30 Days, Restocking Fee: None
Demo: No
Technical Support: Phone (9 a.m. - 4:30 p.m. EST)

Description: Financial add-in product for Lotus 1-2-3 and Symphony. Supplies the power of a Hewlett-Packard HP-12C calculator by providing 5 new time-value-of-money functions with 2 menu-driven templates. Functions and templates generate amortization schedules and perform cash flow analysis on annuity and lump sum payments.

Product: FIXED INCOME
Securities: Bond
Function(s): Bond Analysis, Spreadsheet, Portfolio Management
System(s): IBM, Sun Sparc
Special Requirements: Lotus 1-2-3 or Symphony for DOS, WingZ, 20/20 or Lotus for Sun Sparc
Price: $795 DOS, $2,495 Sun Sparc   **AAII Discount:** None
Return Policy: 30 Days, Restocking Fee: None
Demo: Yes
Technical Support: Phone (9 a.m. - 4:30 p.m. EST)

Description: Library of 50 new @functions for fixed-income securities calculations and portfolio management. Functions adhere to the Securities Industry Association guidelines for municipal, corporate, treasury and agency issues. Functions available are price, yield, duration and convexity plus day counting, accrued interest and mortgage-backed securities functions and the ability to compute weighted averages. Simplifies fixed-income analysis by enabling the user to construct analytics inside Lotus.

SPSS, Inc.   (800) 543-6609
444 N. Michigan Avenue   (312) 329-3500
Suite 3000   fax: (312) 329-3668
Chicago, IL 60611

Product: SPSS/PC+
Securities: Not Applicable
Function(s): Statistical Analysis
System(s): IBM
Special Requirements: None
Price: $195   **AAII Discount:** Call
Return Policy: 30 Days, Restocking Fee: None

Demo: No
Technical Support: Basic service free, Phone (9 a.m. - 5 p.m. CST), BBS, Newsletter

Description: An interactive, menu-driven data management, analysis and presentation software package that features automatic error-checking, extensive on-line help and the ability to read and write ASCII files for the exchange of data with other microcomputer packages. Includes a split-screen editor as well as a communications protocol for transferring files between micro and mainframe computers. Statistical routines range from simple descriptive measures and cross-tabulation tables to regression analyses, including logistics. Data management facilities allow for selecting, sorting and weighing cases, merging multiple files, data aggregation and creating new variables. A complete report writer produces custom formatted reports with the user having control over titles, margins and the calculation of summary statistics. The system handles files of up to 500 variables and an unlimited number of cases, and it includes Graph-in-the-Box from New England Software.

Product: SPSS/PC+ TREND (formerly SPSS/PC Trends)
Securities: Not Applicable
Function(s): Statistical Analysis
System(s): IBM
Special Requirements: None
Price: $395   **AAII Discount:** Call
Return Policy: 30 Days, Restocking Fee: None
Demo: No
Technical Support: Basic service free, Phone (9 a.m. - 5 p.m. CST), BBS, Newsletter

Description: Analysis tools include 2 stage least squares and weighted least squares regression, uni- and bi-variate spectral analysis and Box-Jenkins analysis based upon ARIMA algorithms. Also contains more than a dozen smoothing models, curve-fitting and 3 autoregressive models. User can compare fits among alternative models as well as save and reuse models. Validation and forecasting periods can be changed and modified, and missing values can be correctly estimated with the latest statistical algorithms.

Strategic Planning Systems, Inc. (800) 488-5898
21021 Soledad Canyon Road (805) 254-5897
Suite 504 fax: (805) 254-2609
Santa Clarita, CA 91351

Product: QUOTEMASTER
Securities: Stock, Bond, Index, Mutual Fund, Option, Futures
Function(s): Communications, Technical Analysis
System(s): Macintosh
Special Requirements: Signal or Telemet America
Price: $395 **AAII Discount:** 10%
Return Policy: NA
Demo: Yes
Technical Support: Phone (10 a.m. - 4 p.m. PST)

Description: Monitors all major U.S. financial markets in real-time. Can access information for all major stock exchanges, commodity exchanges and for futures, options, NASDAQ securities, mutual funds and money market funds. Supports security data sent over FM airwaves by Signal and Telemet America. User is able to constantly monitor 1,250 securities at 1 time from an available choice of 40,000 securities. Securities may be grouped in individual window with no limit to the number of securities allowed per window. Program produces intra-day and inter-day charts on any security.

Product: QUOTEMASTER PROFESSIONAL*
Securities: Stock, Bond, Index, Mutual Fund, Option, Futures
Function(s): Communications, Technical Analysis
System(s): Macintosh
Special Requirements: Signal or Telement America
Price: $495 **AAII Discount:** 10%
Return Policy: NA
Demo: Yes
Technical Support: Phone (10 a.m. - 4 p.m. PST)

Description: Includes all the features of QuoteMaster plus intra-day charts can be set up from tick by tick up to 45 minutes. User can draw trendlines, zoom in or zoom out on charts to set grid lines and high/low/close intervals. User can double click mouse on any chart to track and display chart values on the bottom of the screen. Chart types include: MACD, envelopes, %R, RSI, volume accumulation, volume accumulation oscillator, linear regression, trading bands, accumulation-distribution, on-balance volume and momentum.

Superior Software, Inc. (800) 421-3264
16055 Ventura Boulevard (818) 990-1135
Suite 650
Encino, CA 91436

Product: CF: CASH FLOW ANALYSIS
Securities: Stock
Function(s): Financial Planning, Fundamental Analysis
System(s): IBM
Special Requirements: None
Price: $495 single user; limited **AAII Discount:** None
  site $695; unlimited site $995
Return Policy: 30 Days, Restocking Fee: $25
Demo: Yes
Technial Support: Phone (8:30 a.m. - 5 p.m. PST), BBS

Description: Provides complete business analysis for business plans, substantiating bank loans and efficient management; cash flow projections for up to 5 years; easy data input. Will view or print monthly or yearly reports including line of credit, net income, cash flow, working capital, sales, gross profit, G & A expense, A/R, A/P, accrued expense and data input summary. Will calculate ending balance sheet; perform ratio analyses providing liquidity, leverage, profitability, activity and growth ratios; automatically amortize debt payments and calculate taxes; an inventory formula, Gross Profit %, automatically increases or decreases inventory to maintain a fixed gross profit percentage for each subschedule or total of income. Features menu-driven formulas and depreciation, full formula traceback with one keystroke and consolidation of divisions. "What if" situations are changeable and results are viewed immediately. Reports provide complete projected financial package for bank loans.

Product: ES: THE ESTATE PLAN ANALYZER
Securities: Not Applicable
Function(s): Financial Planning
System(s): IBM

Special Requirements: None
Price: $495, single user; limited site, $845; unlimited site, $1,195
AAII Discount: None
Return Policy: 30 Days, Restocking Fee: $25
Demo: Yes
Technical Support: Phone (8:30 a.m. - 5 p.m. PST), BBS

Description: Calculates up to 14 types of estate plans in 20 minutes. Calculations determine the best possible planning so documentation may begin—enter asset values, how title to that asset is held and deductions to the estate and create different scenarios by altering assumptions. Prints single page reports for each plan. Includes new 15% excess retirement accumulations tax on pension plan or IRA distributions. Computes generation skipping transfer taxes and irrevocable life insurance trust option. Toggle on or off the state tax override to allow more accuracy in non-federal state death-tax credit states.

Survivor Software Ltd. (213) 410-9527
11222 La Cienga Boulevard fax: (213) 338-1406
Suite 450
Inglewood, CA 90304

Product: MACMONEY
Securities: Stock, Bond, Mutual Fund
Function(s): Financial Planning
System(s): Macintosh
Special Requirements: None
Price: $119.95
AAII Discount: 25%
Return Policy: 30 Days, Restocking Fee: $5
Demo: Yes ($25)
Technical Support: Phone (9 a.m. - 5 p.m. PST), Newsletter

Description: Allows user to track expenditures and income by entering bank, cash and credit-card transactions. Enter as many as 6,000 transactions each year in up to 250 categories. Reports include net worth (personal balance sheet), net income (income and expenses), cash flow, major expenses and tax categories.

Product: MARKET CHARTER*
Securities: Stock, Bond, Index, Mutual Fund

Function(s): Communications, Technical Analysis
System(s): Macintosh
Special Requirements: Hypercard 1.2
Price: $59.95   **AAII Discount:** 25%
Return Policy: NA
Demo: Yes ($5)
Technical Support: Phone (9 a.m. - 5 p.m. PST), Newsletter

Description: A hypercard stack for stock charting and technical analysis. Price/value histories of stocks, mutual funds, market indexes and/or other market information are maintained and charted on a weekly basis. A moving average for weekly closing prices is also calculated for each chart.

Tech Hackers Inc.   (212) 344-9500
50 Broad Street   fax: (212) 344-9519
New York, NY 10004

Product: @NALYST
Securities: Stock, Bond, Index, Option, Futures, Real Estate, MBS
Function(s): Spreadsheet, Bond Analysis, Financial Planning, Options Analysis, Portfolio Management
System(s): IBM, Macintosh
Special Requirements: Lotus 1-2-3 version 2.0+, Symphony or Excel 2.1+
Price: $195 to $1,495 depending on   **AAII Discount:** 10%
   configuration
Return Policy: 30 Days, Restocking Fee: Shipping charges
Demo: No
Technical Support: Phone (9 a.m. - 5 p.m. EST), Newsletter

Description: Provides 150 new add-in @functions for Lotus 1-2-3, Symphony and Microsoft Excel. Functions perform industry-standard security calculations such as yield-to-maturity of a bond, theta of an option or the implied PSA of a GNMA. Securities handled include Treasury, agency, municipal and corporate bonds, bills, CDs, options and mortgage-backed securities. Performs generalized cash flow analysis, probability and statistical calculations and data and business day arithmetic. Functions integrate into any worksheet and recalculate automatically like built-in functions.

Technical Analysis of Stocks & Commodities Magazine
3517 S.W. Alaska Street
Seattle, WA 98126

(800) 832-4642
(206) 938-0570
fax: (206) 938-1307

Product: TECHNICAL ANALYSIS CHARTS
Securities: Stock, Index, Mutual Fund, Option, Futures
Function(s): Technical Analysis
System(s): Apple II
Special Requirements: None
Price: $129.95   **AAII Discount:** None
Return Policy: NA
Demo: No
Technical Support: None

Description: Charts, displays and prints any indicator or sequence of data that fits in a standard CSI/Compu Trac or Dow Jones Market Analyzer format. Gives user ability to create stock/commodity charts with the Apple II. Pull-down menus allow access to all commands with either the keyboard or mouse and let user instantly customize the look of trading charts. Can plot raw market data or the results of technical analyses. Acts as a convenient "switcher" between DOS 3.3 and Pro-DOS operating systems. Includes one subroutine for reading market data from disk into memory and another that performs technical analysis studies.

Technicom, Inc.
736 N.E. 20th Avenue
Ft. Lauderdale, FL 33304

(305) 523-5394

Product: ACCOUNT MANAGER V*
Securities: Option, Futures
Function(s): Financial Planning, Portfolio Management, Tax Planning
System(s): IBM
Special Requirements: None
Price: $695   **AAII Discount:** 10%
Return Policy: NA
Demo: No
Technical Support: Phone (9 a.m. - 5 p.m. EST)

274 / The Individual Investor's Guide to Computerized Investing

Description: An accounting system for futures and options traders. Keeps track of open and closed positions and prints P&S statements for any selected period in accordance with CFTC and IRS requirements. Detailed equity runs may also be printed. Program monitors a mini portfolio of the contracts traded and entries for trades from portfolio which is displayed on the screen. Completed trades are automatically offset with full accounting for trading profits or losses, commissions and exchange fees. Also monitors margins and keeps track of excess funds that may be deposited to a separate interest bearing account. Will handle up to 9,999 different clients and 99 different brokers. The number of records it keeps is only limited by the capacity of the hard disk.

Product: PROGRAM WRITER II*
Securities: Option, Futures
Function(s): Technical Analysis
System(s): IBM
Special Requirements: None
Price: $995   **AAII Discount:** 10%
Return Policy: None
Demo: No
Technical Support: Phone (9 a.m. - 5 p.m. EST)

Description: A program "shell" that may be used with modules supplied or with user-created trading modules. Performs analysis and testing of virtually any trading formula and allows the use of up to 4 separately optimizable parameters. A range for each of the parameters may be entered, and program will test every combination and automatically determine the best ones for any futures contract in the file. Incorporates a separate "walk-forward" testing capability that simulates exact trading and reports profits and losses. Any amount of historical data may be analyzed at one time and the program will automatically test rolling over of individual contracts. Any number of contracts may be rolled over with all profits and losses monitored. A high resolution graphics section is included that displays exact results of trading any period of time up to 284 days. A buy/sell stop envelope is displayed along with actual price data allowing the user to see how the system performs in the actual markets. The graphics screen also displays profits and losses on a daily basis as it scans across the screen with a moveable cursor. Works with data from either CSI, Compu Trac, Technical Tools or MetaStock.

Techserve, Inc.　　　　　　　　　　　　　　(800) 826-8082
P.O. Box 70056　　　　　　　　　　　　　　(206) 747-5598
Bellevue, WA 98007

Product: CAPTOOL
Securities: Stock, Bond, Index, Mutual Fund, Option, Futures, Real Estate
Function(s): Bond Analysis, Communications, Financial Planning, Fundamental Analysis, Portfolio Management, Security Screening, Tax Planning, Technical Analysis
System(s): IBM
Special Requirements: Hard drive; modem for data downloading
Price: $99　　　　　　　　　　　　　　**AAII Discount:** 20%
Return Policy: 45 Days, Restocking Fee: 10%
Demo: Yes
Technical Support: Phone (8 a.m. - 5 p.m. PST), BBS

Description: Investment manager that combines PFROI portfolio manager with stock and bond evaluators, batch processing of multiple portfolios and client management. Tracks investment cost bases (4 tax lot methods), computes portfolio and security ROI before/after taxes, generates over 20 portfolio reports including client statement and graphics. Stock evaluation is performed by financial ratio screening and a risk-adjusted discounted internal cash flow calculation. Bond evaluation includes yield-to-call and maturity and bond swap comparison including swap NPV. Prices may be downloaded from DJN/R, CompuServe, GEnie, DIAL/DATA, Warner and others. Graphs price open/high/low/close/volume with moving average for technical evaluation. Also plots user-specified macro economic indicators. Has help screens, 280-page manual, example files.

Product: CAPTOOL GLOBAL INVESTOR*
Securities: Stock, Bond, Index, Mutual Fund, Option, Futures, Real Estate
Function(s): Bond Analysis, Communications, Financial Planning, Fundamental Analysis, Portfolio Management, Security Screening, Tax Planning, Technical Analysis

System(s): IBM
Special Requirements: Hard drive; modem for data downloading
Price: $299 **AAII Discount:** 33%
Return Policy: 45 Days, Restocking Fee: 10%
Demo: Yes
Technical Support: Phone (8 a.m. - 5 p.m. PST), BBS

Description: International, multi-currency version of CapTool investment manager. Permits securities denominated in different currencies to co-exist in a common portfolio. Currency exchange rate records hold up to 10 user-defined currencies plus a portfolio base currency. Also features a fund accounting module for management of pooled investments such as investment club, pension or trust fund. Customizable report headers and labels permit user translation into non-English reports. Supports international date and decimal formats, optional 132-column display on most VGA displays, utilizes math co-processors. Includes help screens, 325-page manual and example files.

Product: PFROI
Securities: Stock, Bond, Index, Mutual Fund, Option, Futures, Real Estate
Function(s): Communications, Financial Planning, Portfolio Management, Security Screening, Tax Planning
System(s): IBM
Special Requirements: Modem for data downloading
Price: $49 with printed manual; **AAII Discount:** 20%
$29 with on-disk manual (printed manual version only)
Return Policy: 45 Days, Restocking Fee: 10%
Demo: Yes
Technical Support: Phone (8 a.m. - 5 p.m. PST), BBS

Description: Portfolio manager. Tracks investment cost bases (4 tax lot methods) and computes portfolio and security ROI (IRR method, both time and dollar weighted variations) both before and after estimated taxes. Generates over 20 reports with output to screen, text and Lotus-compatible WKS files or to printer. Estimated taxes are computed with user-configurable tax rates. Features: valuation and allocation graphics, beta computation and price downloading from DJN/R, CompuServe, GEnie, DIAL/DATA, Warner and others. Handles most security types (stocks, bonds, mutual funds, zero coupon bonds, options, etc.) and transactions including mutual fund reinvestment, fractional shares, splits, shorts, return of capital, etc. Handles multiple portfolios with no limit on number of securities per portfolio. Has help screens, 170-page manual and example fields.

Telemet America, Inc. (800) 368-2078
325 First Street (703) 548-2042
Alexandria, VA 22314

Product: DISCOVER
Securities: Stock, Index, Mutual Fund, Option, Futures
Function(s): Communications, Financial Planning, Options Analysis, Portfolio Management, Technical Analysis
System(s): IBM
Special Requirements: Windows 3.0, mouse, Telemet subscription
Price: $599   **AAII Discount:** None
Return Policy: 25 Days, Restocking Fee: None
Demo: Yes ($25)
Technical Support: Phone (8:30 a.m. - 5:30 p.m. EST), Newsletter

Description: User can follow the market in real-time. Uses Microsoft Windows, updated continuously on-screen, to provide high resolution graphs and windows with high/low/last quotes on the screen at the same time. Supports the DDE interface in other windows programs (e.g., user can "hot link" to Excel spreadsheet).

Telescan, Inc. (800) 324-8353
10550 Richmond Avenue (713) 952-1060
Suite 250 fax: (713) 952-7138
Houston, TX 77042

Product: TELESCAN PORTFOLIO MANAGER (TPM)*
Securities: Stock, Bond, Index, Mutual Fund, Option, Real Estate
Function(s): Communications, Portfolio Management
System(s): IBM
Special Requirements: Modem for data downloading
Price: $395   **AAII Discount:** 10%
Return Policy: 30 Days, Restocking Fee: None
Demo: Yes ($10)
Technical Support: Phone (8 a.m. - 10 p.m. CST), Newsletter

Description: A portfolio management program that tracks the purchase and sale of stocks, options, mutual funds, corporate bonds, tax-free bonds, government bonds and Treasury bills. Automatically maintains a cash account and retains a permanent history of sold securities for tax accounting including dates of trades, lots, cost basis, sale price, commissions and profit or loss. Reports include: statements of account, asset allocations, values of individual portfolios, dividend and interest transactions and tax summaries formulated to match IRS requirements. Report can be prepared simultaneously for one, several or all of your portfolios. Offers: unlimited portfolios, easy corrections on prices and commissions, fraction converter, bond calculator, option builder, on-screen alerts for when goals and risk levels are met and new highs or lows are obtained and password security protection. Downloads from Telescan or Dow Jones News/Retrieval.

Tempo Investment Products, Inc. (517) 832-3148
4102 Elm Court
Midland, MI 48640

Product: MARKET ACTION TIMER
Securities: Stock, Index, Mutual Fund
Function(s): Technical Analysis, Spreadsheet
System(s): IBM
Special Requirements: Lotus 1-2-3 or Quattro Pro
Price: $99   **AAII Discount:** 15%
Return Policy: 30 Days, Restocking Fee: $15
Demo: No
Technical Support: None

Description: A menu-driven spreadsheet in which user adds 8 weekly data points: the Dow Jones Industrial Average, the S&P 500 Composite, number of advancing stocks, number of declining stocks, the NASDAQ (Over the Counter) Composite and the weekly price (net asset value) of 3 high-quality no-load stock mutual funds—20th Century Select, Nicholas, Fidelity Magellan. Program then calculates 13- and 30-week moving averages, compares current market movement to the trend and advises on the market situation. The M.A.T. Composite formula gives user a buy/sell signal.

Product: MATPORT*
Securities: Stock, Index, Mutual Fund
Function(s): Technical Analysis, Spreadsheet
System(s): IBM
Special Requirement: Lotus 1-2-3 or Quattro Pro
Price: $50   **AAII Discount:** 15%
Return Policy: 30 Days, Restocking Fee: $15
Demo: No
Technical Support: None

Description: Includes all the features of Market Action Timer plus data for 3 additional 20th century funds and IBM, Digital Equipment, Corning, Dow Chemical and Fidelity Intermediate-term Bond Fund.

Tiger Software   (619) 483-1214
P.O. Box 9491
San Diego, CA 92109

Product: PEERLESS STOCK MARKET TIMING
Securities: Stock, Index, Mutual Fund, Option, Futures
Function(s): Technical Analysis
System(s): IBM, Macintosh
Special Requirements: None
Price: $275 plus $100   **AAII Discount:** None
    for back data (1969-1991)
Return Policy: NA
Demo: Yes
Technical Support: None

Description: Predicts the general market's likely short- and intermediate-term direction and magnitude of moves. Automatic "signal-arrows" pinpoint key reversal points. Helps time the purchase and sale of mutual funds and index options/futures as well as individual stocks at critical market junctures. Users get all the daily DJIA, breadth and volume data back to 1969 to replicate the major Peerless buy and sell signals; 51 reversing signals, 1969-1990, produced an average DJIA gain of 10.8% on each trade—the average lasting 5 months. Perfect sell signals were automatically generated at the market tops of October 1987, October 1989, January 1990 and July 1990. Users employ a Help Table to learn the past reliability and significance of each of the 6 different major buy and sell signals. Users may also plot short-term volume, breadth and momentum indicators using their choice of moving averages and price bands.

Product: TIGER MULTIPLE STOCK SCREENING & TIMING SYSTEM
Securities: Stock
Function(s): Communications, Security Screening, Technical Analysis
System(s): IBM
Special Requirements: Modem for data downloading
Price: $895   **AAII Discount:** None
Return Policy: NA
Demo: No
Technical Support: None

Description: Two hundred and sixty individual stocks are updated nightly from Dow Jones New/Retrieval and ranked for relative strength, price versus volume divergences and consistent long-term accumulation as measured by proprietary Intra-Day Volume formula. A composite Power Ranking of 260 stocks is then created. Back-testing, which users may themselves replicate, has discovered that the top 10 power-ranked stocks regularly outperform the DJIA over the next 6 months, while the lowest power-ranked stocks regularly underperform the DJIA. A short-term timing scan is run against the top and bottom stocks, and final sets of printed recommendations appear as the most bullish or bearish. Graphs of these stocks, or any others, are then printed with automatic arrowed short-term buy and sell signals. Stocks with significant divergences, unusual volume, price and relative strength breakouts, stochastic buy and sell signals are flagged and graphed with highlighting buy and sell arrows. Users may plot daily and weekly charts, adjust moving averages and price bands and experiment with over 20 different indicators. Includes its own verification and optimization programs as well as back daily and weekly data on 260 high capitalization stocks, a 6-month subscription to "Peerless Forecasts" and Hot-Line.

Time Trend Software   (508) 663-3330
337 Boston Road   fax: (508) 667-1269
Billerica, MA 01821

Product: DATA RETRIEVER
Securities: Stock, Bond, Index, Mutual Fund, Option, Futures
Function(s): Communications
System(s): IBM
Special Requirements: Modem
Price: $45   **AAII Discount:** 10%
Return Policy: 45 Days, Restocking Fee: None
Demo: No
Technical Support: Phone (9 a.m. - 5 p.m. EST)

Description: Downloads current and historic data from Warner Computer Systems on mutual funds (NAV and distributions), stocks, market indexes and commodities. Designed to be used with Fund Master TC but can also write DIF and ASCII files for importing and exporting data to other programs.

Product: ENHANCED FUND MASTER OPTIMIZER
Securities: Stock, Bond, Index, Mutual Fund
Function(s): Security Screening, Simulations/Games, Technical Analysis
System(s): IBM
Special Requirements: Fund Master TC
Price: $150   **AAII Discount:** 10%
Return Policy: 45 Days, Restocking Fee: None
Demo: No
Technical Support: Phone (9 a.m. - 5 p.m. EST)

Description: A simulation module that runs in conjunction with Fund Master TC or Fund Pro. Analyzes results and gives parameters for best performance of various trading strategies. Can use moving average or exponential average crossover, double average crossover, overbought/oversold simulations and MACD.

Product: FUND MASTER TC
Securities: Stock, Bond, Index, Mutual Fund
Function(s): Portfolio Management, Technical Analysis
System(s): IBM
Special Requirements: None
Price: $289   **AAII Discount:** 10%

Return Policy: 45 Days, Restocking Fee: None
Demo: Yes
Technical Support: $90/year, Phone (9 a.m. - 5 p.m. EST)

Description: Program geared toward mutual funds but is flexible enough to handle stocks. Charting features include moving averages, exponential averages, arithmetic or logarithmic scales, trading bands, trendlines, trend channels, zoom graphics, overlay capabilities and relative strength charting. Analysis of indexes and market indicators to determine market entry and exit points. Momentum ranking and VersaRank reports determine mutual fund or stock selection according to relative strength. User-definable equations are supported in VersaRank. Can monitor up to 20 portfolios, and files can contain over 7 years of daily data. Automatic update of portfolios and year-end tax reports are available.

Product: FUND PRO
Securities: Stock, Bond, Index, Mutual Fund
Function(s): Communications, Portfolio Management, Technical Analysis
System(s): IBM
Special Requirements: Modem for data downloading
Price: $789   **AAII Discount:** 10%
Return Policy: 45 Days, Restocking Fee: None
Demo: Yes
Technical Support: $90/year, includes: Phone (9 a.m. - 5 p.m. EST)

Description: Has Fund Master TC functions but can handle up to 1,000 portfolios. Features: client billing, global purchases and sales and global adjustments for distributions. Calculate total funds and composite annualized rate of return for managed funds. Compares client and composite performance to market standards (e.g., the S&P 500).

Timeworks   (800) 323-7744
625 Academy Drive   (708) 559-1300
Northbrook, IL 60062   fax: (708) 559-1399

Product: SWIFTAX
Securities: Not Applicable
Function(s): Financial Planning, Tax Planning

System(s): Apple II, Commodore, IBM
Special Requirements: None
Price: $79.95   **AAII Discount:** None
Return Policy: 60 Days, Restocking Fee: None
Demo: No
Technical Support: Phone (8:30 a.m. - 5:00 p.m. CST), BBS

Description: Personal tax preparation program for federal and state taxes. Includes 5 kinds of on-screen help, more than 65 forms, schedules and worksheets and laser printing. Has a what if feature for comparing various tax alternatives. Program supports electronic filing. Imports Quicken, Lotus and ASCII files. The early bird version for getting a head start in taxes is available in October. The final edition contains all Congress-approved forms and is available in January 1992. Early bird purchasers receive the final edition free.

Tools for Timing   (800) 325-1344
(formerly Mike Burk)   (612) 939-0076
829 Old Settlers Trail #3
Hopkins, MN 55343

Product: ADVANCE—DECLINE LINE TUTORIAL*
Securities: Index
Function(s): Technical Analysis, Simulations/Games
System(s): IBM
Special Requirements: Hard drive, CGA or better, will not work with Hercules
Price: $75   **AAII Discount:** None
Return Policy: 60 Days, Restocking Fee: None
Demo: No
Technical Support: Phone (7:30 a.m. - 8:30 a.m. CST), Newsletter

Description: Tutorial on timing stock market with the advance-decline line and indicators derived from it exclusively. Shows indicators and demonstrates when they are most effective. Annual survey with captioned graphs shows how the indicators worked throughout each year at intervals of 5 trading days from 1978 to the present. Includes data from the 1st of 1978 to the day prior to shipping.

Product: HISTORICAL ADL*
Securities: Index
Function(s): Technical Analysis, Simulations/Games
System(s): IBM
Special Requirements: Hard drive, CGA or better, will not work with Hercules
Price: $175　　　　　　　　　　　　　**AAII Discount:** None
Return Policy: 60 Days, Restocking Fee: None
Demo: No
Technical Support: Phone (7:30 a.m. - 8:30 a.m. CST), Newsletter

Description: For the market historian. Includes daily data from October 1, 1928. User can view the DJIA and advance-decline line along with a selection of popular momentum indicators applied to either or both the advance-decline line or the DJIA. Any period from as little as 10 trading days to over 60 years can be put on screen at one time. Includes data from 10/1/1928 to the day prior to shipping.

Product: HOURLY DJIA*
Securities: Index
Function(s): Technical Analysis, Simulations/Games
System(s): IBM
Special Requirements: Hard drive, CGA or better, will not work with Hercules
Price: $50　　　　　　　　　　　　　**AAII Discount:** None
Return Policy: 60 Days, Restocking Fee: None
Demo: No
Technical Support: Phone (7:30 a.m. - 8:30 a.m. CST), Newsletter

Description: Shows the DJIA on an hourly basis along with the last hour indicator and several popular momentum indicators calculated from hourly parameters. Indicators provided: last hour indicator, trading bands, Bollinger Bands, RSI, stochastics and MACD. Includes data from 7/1/1986 to the day prior to shipping.

Product: LOG SCALE COMPARISON*
Securities: Index
Function(s): Technical Analysis, Simulations/Games
System(s): IBM

Special Requirements: Hard drive, CGA or better, will not work with Hercules
Price: $50   **AAII Discount:** None
Return Policy: 60 Days, Restocking Fee: None
Demo: No
Technical Support: Phone (7:30 a.m. - 8:30 a.m. CST), Newsletter

Description: Each index is placed on its own log scale starting at the same point on the left side of the screen. The log of any number changes by the same amount when the number is doubled, so indexes on their log scales show their relative performance. The program allows users to view any period greater than 9 trading days and to select which indexes to view. Data is included to the day prior to the shipping date. Starting dates vary with the indexes: DJIA, S&P 500, DJT, DJU, 1/1/1968; NYSE composite, 9/1/1970; AMEX and OTC composites, 1/3/1972; OEX, 4/24/1984.

Product: MORON*
Securities: Index
Function(s): Technical Analysis, Simulations/Games
System(s): IBM
Special Requirements: Hard drive, CGA or better, will not work with Hercules
Price: $150   **AAII Discount:** None
Return Policy: 60 Days, Restocking Fee: None
Demo: Yes ($25)
Technical Support: Phone (7:30 a.m. - 8:30 a.m. CST), Newsletter

Description: A mechanical trading system based on the theory that the market moves in cycles defined by peaks in the number of new lows. Uses only 2 indicators, NL and ADL. Includes data from the 1st of 1978 to the day prior to shipping.

Product: NEW HIGH NEW LOW TUTORIAL*
Securities: Index
Function(s): Technical Analysis, Simulations/Games
System(s): IBM
Special Requirements: Hard drive, CGA or better, will not work with Hercules

Price: $75   **AAII Discount:** None
Return Policy: 60 Days, Restocking Fee: None
Demo: No
Technical Support: Phone (7:30 a.m. - 8:30 a.m. CST), Newsletter

Description: Tutorial on timing the stock market with the new high and low indicators exclusively. Breaks market activity into cycles defined by peaks in the new low indicator. The 24 complete cycles from the 1st of 1978 to July 1991 average about 130 trading days. Shows each of the indicators and when they are most effective. Each cycle is isolated and shown in its entirety, its beginning and its top, along with the appropriate indicators at each stage. Annual survey with captioned graphs shows how the indicators worked throughout each year at intervals of 5 trading days from 1978 to the present. Includes data from the 1st of 1978 to the day prior to shipping.

Product: PUT/CALL*
Securities: Option
Function(s): Technical Analysis, Simulations/Games
System(s): IBM
Special Requirements: Hard drive, CGA or better, will not work with Hercules
Price: $50   **AAII Discount:** None
Return Policy: 60 Days, Restocking Fee: None
Demo: No
Technical Support: Phone (7:30 a.m - 8:30 a.m. CST), Newsletter

Description: Program graphically expresses 7 different relationships of OEX put, call, volume and open interest. Indicators provided: put/call ratio, Hines ratio, put/call volume with put/call open interest, put/call volume as a percentage of put/call open interest, put/call volume as a percentage of put/call open interest smoothed, put open interest subtracted from call open interest, DJIA and OEX. Includes data from mid-1984 to the day prior to shipping.

Product: TIMER*
Securities: Index
Function(s): Technical Analysis, Simulations/Games
System(s): IBM

Special Requirements: Hard drive, CGA or better, will not work with Hercules
Price: $250   **AAII Discount:** None
Return Policy: 60 Days, Restocking Fee: None
Demo: Yes ($25)
Technical Support: Phone (7:30 a.m. - 8:30 a.m. CST), Newsletter

Description: System breaks DJIA market activity into cycles defined by peaks in the new low indicator. There have been 24 complete cycles since the 1st of 1978 averaging about 130 trading days. The 7 primary indicators are designed to enable user to pick the tops and bottoms of these cycles. Shows indicators and demonstrates when they are most effective. Each cycle is isolated and shown in its entirety, its beginning and its top, along with the appropriate indicators at each stage. Annual survey with captioned graphs shows how the indicators worked throughout each year from 1978 to the present. Includes data from the 1st of 1978 to the day prior to shipping.

Product: TIMER PROFESSIONAL*
Securities: Index
Function(s): Technical Analysis, Simulations/Games
System(s): IBM
Special Requirements: Hard drive, CGA or better, will not work with Hercules
Price: $450   **AAII Discount:** None
Return Policy: 60 Days, Restocking Fee: None
Demo: No
Technical Support: Phone (7:30 a.m. - 8:30 a.m. CST), Newsletter

Description: Provides all the features of Timer and includes a log scale comparison of all indexes of all three U.S. markets.

Product: VOLUME INDICATOR TUTORIAL*
Securities: Index
Function(s): Technical Analysis, Simulations/Games
System(s): IBM
Special Requirements: Hard drive, CGA or better, will not work with Hercules
Price: $75   **AAII Discount:** None

Return Policy: 60 Days, Restocking Fee: None
Demo: No
Technical Support: Phone (7:30 a.m. - 8:30 a.m. CST), Newsletter

Description: Tutorial on timing the stock market with volume indicators exclusively. Shows indicators and when they are most effective. Annual survey with captioned graphs shows how indicators worked throughout each year at intervals of 5 trading days from 1978 to the present. User is placed at the beginning of the 1st of 1978 or randomly in the file. In the game the date or the index value cannot be seen. Long or short positions are taken based on users interpretation of the indicators. A transcript of trade gains and losses is generated. Includes data from the 1st of 1978 to the date prior to shipping.

Townsend Analytics Ltd.   (800) 827-0141
100 S. Wacker Drive   (312) 621-0141
Suite 1506   fax: (312) 621-0487
Chicago, IL 60606

Product: OPTION RISK MANAGEMENT
Securities: Stock, Option, Futures
Function(s): Communications, Options Analysis, Portfolio Management
System(s): IBM
Special Requirements: Windows 3.0, math co-processor, Data feed
Price: Contact vendor   **AAII Discount:** None
Return Policy: NA
Demo: No
Technical Support: Phone (9 a.m. - 6 p.m. CST), BBS, Newsletter

Description: An option portfolio analysis program implemented under Microsoft Windows. Computes measure of risk and return for option positions and option spreads; results of the analyses are presented in tables and graphs. Users control parameters for interest rates, volatilities, volatility skew, vega range and market movement range. Analyzes all types of spreads and calculates profit and loss, premium value and technical measures of risk. Premiums and futures or stock prices can be entered manually or automatically via several real-time quote services. Positions can be entered in Townsend Analytics Accounts program.

Product: REALTICK III
Securities: Stock, Bond, Index, Mutual Fund, Option, Futures
Function(s): Communications, Technical Analysis
System(s): IBM
Special Requirements: Windows 3.0, Data feed
Price: Contact vendor   **AAII Discount:** None
Return Policy: None
Demo: Yes
Technical Support: Phone (9 a.m. - 6 p.m. CST), BBS, Newsletter

Description: A real-time graphics program for stocks, futures, indexes, options and other instruments implemented under Microsoft Windows for real-time multitasking and a live link to Microsoft Excel. Database maintenance is provided by a separate data server, Townsend's TA-SRV that is included with RealTick III. Displays intra-day and daily charts, technical studies, Market Profile, tables and quote screens in separate windows on multiple programmable pages. Pages can be recalled with hot keys. Does not limit the number of windows per page, number of pages or number of symbols user can follow. Market Profile allows technical studies to be overlaid on bar charts and parameters. Technical studies include a large number of moving averages, stochastics, channels and oscillators; trendlines are available. User-defined synthetics can be created in Microsoft Excel and updated in RealTick.

Product: TA-SRV
Securities: Stock, Bond, Index, Mutual Fund, Option, Futures
Function(s): Communications, Technical Analysis
System(s): IBM
Special Requirements: Windows 3.0, Data feed
Price: Contact vendor   **AAII Discount:** 10%
Return Policy: None
Demo: Yes
Technical Support: Phone (9 a.m. - 6 p.m. CST), BBS, Newsletter

Description: A real-time data server implemented under Microsoft Windows for real-time multitasking. The server is the basis of Townsend Analytics' real-time trading station. TA-SRV is included with RealTick III and Option Risk Management but is also available as a stand-alone program. Provides live or historical quotes in any time interval including tick data to Windows applications such as Microsoft Excel through the Dynamic Data Exchange protocol. Communicates with application programs and builds a database of tick data, daily data and 15 minute bar data from live quotes for a large number of futures contracts, stocks, indexes, options and other instruments. Data archiving and aging features are available. Supports data from Signal, S&P CompStock, Reuters, PC Quote and other.

Trader's Insight, Inc. (516) 423-2413
8 Renwick Avenue
Huntington, NY 11743-3052

Product: AUTO—CANDLE
Securities: Stock, Futures
Function(s): Technical Analysis
System(s): IBM
Special Requirements: Graphics card
Price: $195   **AAII Discount:** 10%
Return Policy: NA
Demo: Yes ($10)
Technical Support: Phone (12 p.m. - 9 p.m. EST)

Description: Creates candlestick charts with automatic pattern recognition. Program outlines and labels each pattern individually, enabling beginners to learn unfamiliar patterns. A menu permits the user to choose which patterns are to be recognized. Program functions as a tutor, aid and a historical research tool. User can view futures patterns for at least 4 years.

Product: RATIONAL INDICATORS*
Securities: Stock, Futures
Function(s): Technical Analysis
System(s): IBM
Special Requirements: Graphics card
Price: $345 ($445 with optional   **AAII Discount:** 10%
    candlestick charting)
Return Policy: NA
Demo: Yes ($20)
Technical Support: Phone (12 p.m. - 9 p.m. EST)

Description: Charts prices employing the Random Walk Index described in *Technical Analysis of Stocks and Commodities*, "Of Trends and Random Walks," 2/91. Decides if stock/future is trending or moving randomly. Program shows a price chart on the top 1/2 of the screen, either in bars or candles, with indicators below. User can page back 1 screen at a time or jump to a future date. No arbitrary choices are made by the user (e.g., choosing moving average length).

Trader's Software, Inc. (405) 348-0544
P.O. Box 2690 fax: (405) 341-3361
Edmond, OK 73083

Product: TRADER'S PROFIT MOTIVE SYSTEM
Securities: Futures
Function(s): Technical Analysis
System(s): IBM
Special Requirements: None
Price: $2,995　　　　　　　　　　　AAII Discount: None
Return Policy: None
Demo: Yes
Technical Support: None

Description: A fully disclosed, computerized trading system for commodity futures. Evaluates the stability of equity growth and adjusts the trading strategy in favor of the smoothest performance. Includes historical price data for 15 commodities.

Trading Techniques, Inc. (216) 645-0077
677 W. TurkeyFoot Lake Road fax: (216) 645-1230
Akron, OH 44319

Product: ADVANCED G.E.T. 3.0*
Securities: Index, Futures
Function(s): Technical Analysis
System(s): IBM
Special Requirements: EGA graphics or better; mouse recommended
Price: $2,750　　　　　　　　　　　AAII Discount: 20%
Return Policy: NA
Demo: Yes
Technical Support: Phone (8 a.m. - 6 p.m. EST)

Description: Designed for the futures market using Gann and Elliott techniques. Works on daily data in many standard formats. The major feature is its ability to provide three degree Elliott wave counts automatically without any user assistance. Also provides Gann angles, potential change in trend dates, Fibonacci calculations, auto price projections for each market swing and many other proprietary indicators. Provides unattended printing routines and has an automatic trade suggestion routine. A built-in training mode helps the user to learn the program.

Product: E.W.O.L.*
Securities: Index, Futures
Function(s): Communications, Technical Analysis
System(s): IBM
Special Requirements: Data feed from FutureSource or CQG, mouse, EGA or better
Price: $1,800   **AAII Discount:** None
Return Policy: NA
Demo: Yes
Technical Support: Phone (8 a.m. - 6 p.m. EST)

Description: Provides real-time Gann and Elliott analysis for the futures market. Uses FutureSource or CQG data to provide the user with capabilities of displaying multiple charts on the screen. The major feature is the ability to provide 3 degree Elliott wave counts automatically without any user assistance. The wave count can be displayed on charts ranging from 1 minute to a daily chart. Also provides Gann angles for intraday charts, Fibonacci calculations, auto price projections for each market swing and many other proprietary indicators. Provides unattended printing routines and has an automatic trade suggestion routine. A built-in training mode helps the user to learn the program.

Product: STOCK MASTER*
Securities: Stock, Index, Mutual Fund
Function(s): Portfolio Management, Technical Analysis, Security Screening
System(s): IBM
Special Requirements: EGA graphics or better, mouse

Price: $1,500 **AAII Discount:** 30%
Return Policy: NA
Demo: Yes
Technical Support: Phone (8 a.m. - 6 p.m. EST)

Description: Program for stocks and mutual funds. Supports CSI, Compu Trac, Metastock and Technical Tools data formats. Major feature is the capability to provide 3 degree Elliott wave counts. Wave counts can also be cross referenced from monthly or weekly down to a daily chart. Provides numerous indicators and is capable of making weekly and monthly charts from daily data and handles splits. Also has a search routine which allows the user to search entire database and select stocks that fit certain criteria such as stocks in a wave 3 or stocks trading with high volume, stocks with RSI above 80, etc.

Trend Index Company (715) 833-1234
Box 5 fax: (715) 833-8040
Altoona, WI 54720

Product: MARKET INTELLIGENCE SWING CATCHER TRADING SYSTEM
Securities: Stock, Bond, Index, Mutual Fund, Option, Futures
Function(s): Communications, Options Analysis, Portfolio Management, Security Screening, Technical Analysis
System(s): IBM
Special Requirements: Hard drive
Price: $995 **AAII Discount:** 20%
Return Policy: NA
Demo: Yes ($20)
Technical Support: Phone (9 a.m. - 7:30 p.m.), BBS, Newsletter

Description: Full-featured trading system. Automatic analysis of over 60 indicators based on recent price relationships. Each indicator is assigned a point weighing factor based on its validity. Cumulative total of all indicators is used as a set-up for the signals. Actual buy/sell signals are generated based on the indicators' total point value combined with pattern recognition parameter and cycle techniques. Monitoring the market during the day is not required. The entire trade—including the trade entry order, specific target price and stop-loss price—can be given to a broker at one time and before the market opens. Each trade entry signal is at market on opening and can be placed as one complete order. Data files can be updated manually with the utility editor updating program, featuring semiautomatic menu-prompted entry, with a built-in calendar for automatic day and date entries.

TRENDPOINT Software (301) 949-8131
9709 Elrod Road
Kensington, MD 20895

Product: TRENDPOINT
Securities: Stock, Bond, Index, Mutual Fund, Option, Futures
Function(s): Technical Analysis
System(s): IBM
Special Requirements: None
Price: $35   **AAII Discount:** 20%
Return Policy: 30 Days, Restocking Fee: None
Demo: No
Technical Support: Phone

Description: Program helps time buy and sell decisions. Calculates simple, exponential, weighted moving averages, Wilder's relative strength, momentum and standard deviation. Adjusts for dividends and splits. Input data from ASCII files or keyboard; outputs are ASCII listings and charts which can be sent to screen, printer or disk. Includes sample disk data files of the daily NYSE Composite Index for 8 years.

Product: TRENDTEK
Securities: Stock, Index, Mutual Fund, Option, Futures
Function(s): Technical Analysis
System(s): IBM
Special Requirements: None
Price: $30   **AAII Discount:** 20%
Return Policy: 30 Days, Restocking Fee: None
Demo: No
Technical Support: Phone

Description: Complements Trendpoint; preprocesses stock market breadth and volume data to calculate overbought/oversold oscillators, advance-decline lines, TRIN (Arms) index, on-balance volume, volume force, futures premiums, new highs-lows and quotient or difference between two data series. Data input is from ASCII disk files or keyboard. Data outputs are listings and ASCII disk files in a format for input to Trendpoint or other programs for further analysis and charting. Comes with 4 years of NYSE daily market breadth data (advances, declines, issues traded, up volume and down volume).

Trend Research Ltd. (919) 698-0503
(formerly One Day at a Time) fax: (919) 698-0356
5615 McLeansville Road
McLeansville, NC 27301

Product: ONE DAY AT A TIME*
Securities: Stock, Bond, Index, Mutual Fund, Option, Futures
Function(s): Simulations/Games, Technical Analysis
System(s): IBM
Special Requirements: None
Price: $395   **AAII Discount:** None
Return Policy: NA
Demo: Yes ($10)
Technical Support: Phone (9 a.m. - 5 p.m. EST)

Description: A market analysis program. Includes: RSI, DMI, trading volatility index, commodity selection index, ADXR and ADX and the parabolic system. Technical indicators include: stochastics, MACD, Fibonacci retracement lines, Bollinger bands, moving average channels, moving average channels with displacement, commodity channel index, displaced moving averages and Japanese candlesticks. Also has 3 simple moving averages, 3 exponential moving averages, an MA oscillator, volume and open interest. Program allows user to go back into the history data provided with the program and simulate a market by advancing forward one day at a time.

Trendsetter Software (800) 825-1852
P.O. Box 6481 (714) 547-5005
Santa Ana, CA 92706 fax: (714) 547-5063

Product: ANALYST RT*
Securities: Stock, Index, Mutual Fund, Option, Futures
Function(s): Communications, Technical Analysis

System(s): Macintosh
Special Requirements: Personal Hotline or Personal Analyst, 1.5 MB free RAM, 6 MB free disk space, Signal
Price: $295 **AAII Discount:** 10%
Return Policy: 30 Days, Restocking Fee: None
Demo: Yes ($5)
Technical Support: Phone (6:30 a.m. - 4 p.m. PST)

Description: Creates a trade station for stocks, commodities, options and indexes using Signal as the data feed. User selectable alerts default to Personal Hotline's buy and sell recommendations and are displayed in their own ticker when exceeded. Bar, point and figure and candle charts on 1-, 5-, 15-, 30- and 60-minute daily time periods as well as line charts based on tick data. Technical studies are available including computer generated trend lines and are overlaid directly on charts for comparison. Charts and analysis update as the market change. The module operates in the background under Multi-finder or System 7. Auto save and auto load functions maintain data while user is at work or out of town. Tick data is stored in it's own files for later review.

Product: PERSONAL ANALYST*
Securities: Stock, Index, Mutual Fund, Option, Futures
Function(s): Communications, Technical Analysis
System(s): Macintosh
Special Requirements: 1 MB free RAM; hard disk preferred
Price: $395 **AAII Discount:** 10%
Return Policy: 30 Days, Restocking Fee: None
Demo: Yes ($5)
Technical Support: Phone (6:30 a.m. - 4 p.m. PST)

Description: Charting and analysis program which includes bar, line, point & figure and candlestick charts. Automatic downloading for DIAL/DATA or via keyboard. Daily, weekly and monthly charts are created from the same data. Full complement of technical studies including volume, volume accumulation, stochastics, RSI, MACD, DMI, rate of change, pivot points, key reversals, Gann lines, Gann angles, moving averages, linear regression, computer generated trend lines. Optional intra-day charting and analysis.

Product: PERSONAL HOTLINE
Securities: Stock, Index, Mutual Fund, Option, Futures
Function(s): Communications, Options Analysis, Portfolio Management, Technical Analysis
System(s): Macintosh
Special Requirements: 1.5 MB free RAM, hard drive
Price: $595   **AAII Discount:** 10%
Return Policy: 30 Days, Restocking Fee: None
Demo: Yes ($5)
Technical Support: Phone (6:30 a.m. - 4 p.m. PST)

Description: Market timing, technical analysis and portfolio management on all markets including stocks, futures, spreads, indexes, mutual funds and options. Expert trading model based on channel analysis and chart pattern recognition provides entry, exit and stop loss recommendations. Complete charting including bar, line, candlestick and point and figure. Automatic downloading from DIAL/DATA, DJN/R, Warner, CompuServe and Signal. Daily, weekly and monthly charts are created from the same data. Full complement of technical studies. Optional intra-day charting and analysis available.

Type III, Inc.   (800) 342-3963
1327 Nathan Hale Drive   (215) 933-8521
Phoenixville, PA 19460   fax: (215) 935-3043

Product: FINANCIAL INSIGHT
Securities: Stock, Bond, Index, Mutual Fund, Option, Futures, Real Estate
Function(s): Financial Planning, Portfolio Management, Tax Planning
System(s): IBM
Special Requirements: None
Price: $79.95   **AAII Discount:** None
Return Policy: NA
Demo: No
Technical Support: None

Description: User can: keep all financial records in one place and analyze them; measure return on investment on any subject (e.g., a stock, bond, limited partnership, house, stamp collection) or any combination of subjects (e.g., all the stock bought from broker X, investments made during a full moon); display current year's Federal

1040; prepare balance sheets and income statements to show effects of changing market values; perform weekly, monthly or yearly cash flow analyses; print checks and reconcile bank statements; accept projected transactions to explore how various actions will affect any of the performance measures and apply any of its performance measures over any time period.

UniPress Software, Inc. (800) 222-0550
2025 Lincoln Highway (201) 985-8000
Edison, NJ 08817 fax: (908) 287-4929

Product: EXCLAIM! REALTIME SPREADSHEET*
Securities: Not Applicable
Function(s): Spreadsheet
System(s): UNIX
Special Requirements: UNIX, X Windows, on-line datafeed
Price: From $1,850 **AAII Discount:** None
Return Policy: 30 Days, Restocking Fee: 20%
Demo: Yes
Technical Support: 25%, Phone (9 a.m. - 6 p.m. EST), Newsletter

Description: An X Windows spreadsheet. Offers math, statistical and logical functions, as well as support for many UNIX-based features including network application sharing monitored by a floating license manager. By clicking or dragging the mouse, users can control cursor, invoke commands, select cell regions and change column widths and row heights. The mouse is also used to paste range and function names into a cell. Pull-down menus reveal all commands available in the program while dialog boxes make it easy to input data and change parameters. Fonts and colors can be selected cell-by-cell. Has business graphics including standard pie, bar, stack bar, line, multi-line, X-Y and commodity charts. Graphed data can be compared side-by-side with data in spreadsheet format.

Product: Q-CALC REALTIME SPREADSHEET*
Securities: Not Applicable
Function(s): Spreadsheet
System(s): UNIX
Special Requirements: UNIX, on-line datafeed
Price: From $1,995 **AAII Discount:** None

Return Policy: 30 Days, Restocking Fee: 20%
Demo: Yes
Technical Support: 25%, Phone (9 a.m. - 6 p.m. EST), Newsletter

Description: Spreadsheet can be linked to financial process control and other on-line datafeeds. Posts electronic dataline information automatically and performs automatic analysis and monitoring with alert messages. Supports queries to Sybase and other SQL databases as well as data export to graphics and other programs. Features a graphics option and 100% compatibility with Lotus 1-2-3 files and macros.

V.A. Denslow & Associates (708) 246-3365
4151 Woodland Avenue
Western Springs, IL 60558

Product: COMMON STOCK DECISION AIDE
Securities: Stock, Index
Function(s): Fundamental Analysis, Portfolio Management, Spreadsheet
System(s): IBM
Special Requirements: Lotus 1-2-3 version 2.01+
Price: $49 **AAII Discount:** None
Return Policy: NA
Demo: No
Technical Support: Phone (9 a.m. - 11 p.m. CST)

Description: Calculates after-tax (0%, 15%, 28%) compounded returns of common stocks from each of up to 12 past years to the present and returns each year including dividend credits. Calculates earnings growth rates, dividend yields, price/earnings ratio ranges, projected current year high and low price/share and compounded returns on user's investment. Shows growth characteristics, volatility and yields. Comparison with returns of DJIA and S&P 500 is provided. Buy/sell/hold decisions can be based on firm data rather than elementary and subjective impressions. Printouts allow study and comparisons, and graphing can be done.

Product: FINANCIAL NEEDS FOR RETIREMENT
Securities: Not Applicable

Function(s): Financial Planning, Spreadsheet
System(s): IBM
Special Requirements: Lotus 1-2-3 version 2.01+
Price: $49   **AAII Discount:** None
Return Policy: NA
Demo: No
Technical Support: Phone (9 a.m. - 11 p.m. CST)

Description: Users can project their financial outlook over a 25-year period by entering personal information such as taxable and nontaxable earning assets, average percent return, incomes from various sources. Includes Social Security, pension, IRA, SEP, Keogh, annuity plans, tax rates, living expenses, inflation rates and personal tax exemptions. Of the 23 rows of automatic calculations, the main result to watch is when or if user's assets begin to deplete and later disappear. "What if" trials show the effects of working longer, adjusting lifestyle, improving investments, making gifts, etc. Program can cover both pre- and post-retirement years. Future lump changes in assets or medical needs can be included as well as variable post-retirement earnings.

Product: MUTUAL FUND DECISION AIDE
Securities: Index, Mutual Fund
Function(s): Security Screening, Spreadsheet
System(s): IBM
Special Requirements: Lotus 1-2-3 version 2.01+
Price: $49   **AAII Discount:** None
Return Policy: None
Demo: No
Technical Support: Phone (9 a.m. - 11 p.m. CST)

Description: Evaluates fund performance using available data. Calculates average annual compounded returns and total returns from each of up to 12 past years to the current date, after load fee and after 0%, 15% and 28% taxes. Gives total return and distribution yield for each year on same bases. Adjusts data to today's values for realistic comparisons between funds at an identical time. Growth rates, volatility, trends in performance for recent years and effects of taxes and various load fees can be observed. User can rank funds on any desired criteria and make better decisions on suitability, consistency and profit potential. Compounded annual return on individual investments can be calculated over exact days held. Comparison with returns of DJIA and S&P 500 is provided. Printouts allow study and comparison, and graphing can be done. Input data is readily available from prospectuses.

Value Line Publishing (800) 654-0508
711 Third Avenue (212) 687-3965
New York, NY 10017 fax: (212) 661-2807

Product: VALUE LINE PORTFOLIO MANAGER
Securities: Stock, Mutual Fund, Option
Function(s): Portfolio Management, Security Screening
System(s): IBM
Special Requirements: None
Price: Annual rates: quarterly updates $281/year; monthly updates by phone or by mail $396/year; weekly updates $1,500/year
AAII Discount: None
Return Policy: NA
Demo: Yes
Technical Support: Phone

Description: Handles most types of investments and includes as many positions and portfolios as user's PC can hold. Combines analytical data from Value Line with standard account transaction information. A menu-driven report generator lets user design reports for special needs, or user can employ any of the 10 ready-to-use reports included in the software. All data can be downloaded to Lotus 1-2-3, Symphony or Excel. The latest statistics from Value Line research department are distributed electronically or on disk.

Vision Research Corp. (513) 435-6409
6312 Rosa Linda Drive fax: (513) 435-9429
Dayton, OH 45459

Product: TOPVISION*
Securities: Stock, Bond, Index, Mutual Fund, Futures
Function(s): Technical Analysis
System(s): IBM

Special Requirements: MDA (except Hercules), CGA or better graphics card needed if graphical display desired
Price: Model TV-4E $355; model TV-5A $829; TV-7A $1398   **AAII Discount:** 30% off TV-4E, 40% off TV-5A, 50% off TV-7A
Return Policy: 30 Days, Restocking Fee: None
Demo: No
Technical Support: Phone (9 a.m.- 5 p.m. PST), Newsletter

Description: Designed to perform 2 functions: 1) predict the price range and its trend up to 5 sessions ahead. The time interval used can be hour, day or week. Narrow predicted price ranges with up to 90% confidence level are generated both in the text and graphically. 2) rank the most profitable markets in terms of relative percent price gains or losses. Users can identify the investment alternatives which have been or are expected to be the best performers.

Volume Dynamics, Inc.   (407) 259-5751
3536 Swallow Drive
#11
Melbourne, FL 32935

Product: DYNAMIC VOLUME ANALYSIS CHARTS
Securities: Stock, Bond, Index, Option, Futures
Function(s): Communications, Technical Analysis, Security Screening
System(s): IBM
Special Requirements: Graphics; modem for data downloading
Price: $99.50   **AAII Discount:** 50%
Return Policy: None
Demo: Yes ($5)
Technical Support: Phone

Description: Technical analysis package for use in the purchase and sale of stocks, commodities and indexes. Based on a momentum theory using cumulative volume as a measure of market supply and demand forces. Primary chart co-plots price and the cumulative volume line so that their relative movements are clear; plots 200-day and the 50-day price moving average, and "n"-day moving average and daily volume bars. Auxiliary chart plots the cumulative volume line and an up/down volume factor—used to study the market momentum to confirm oversold and overbought points and to forecast price trends. Provides rules to determine buy and sell points and (past)

Guide to Investment Software / 303

charts of stocks, indexes and commodities showing points. Analysis program summarizes all 6 technical factors and flags stock with a rise in volume on any day exceeding 2 times the average daily volume.

Wall Street Prophet (404) 497-8497
1505 Thoreau Drive
Suwanee, GA 30174

Product: WALL STREET PROPHET
Securities: Stock, Bond, Index, Mutual Fund, Option
Function(s): Communications, Technical Analysis
System(s): IBM
Special Requirements: Modem for data downloading
Price: $199　　　　　　　　　　　　　　　**AAII Discount:** 50%
Return Policy: None
Demo: Yes ($5)
Technical Support: None

Description: Provides technical analysis indicators, including high-low price analysis, support and resistance prices, price breakouts, price volatility, up and down price gaps, positive and negative volume, average and on balance volume. With spreadsheet interface, users can perform technical analysis using Lotus 1-2-3. Full-color graphics and printouts are available. Data can be retrieved from Dow Jones News/Retrieval or entered manually.

War Machine♦ (206) 283-3708
1700 Taylor N.
Suite 301
Seattle, WA 98109

Product: MACQUOTES♦
Securities: Stock, Bond, Index, Mutual Fund, Option, Futures
Function(s): Communications
System(s): Macintosh
Special Requirements: Signal
Price: $195　　　　　　　　　　　　　　　**AAII Discount:** None
Return Policy: NA
Demo: No
Technical Support: Phone

Description: Allows investors to use Lotus Signal on a Macintosh. Tracks up to 250 symbols and allows up to 150 alerts. Up to 16 windows for user-customized quote pages can be displayed at one time. Runs under Multifinder and can operate in the background.

Product: WAR MACHINE♦
Securities: Stock, Bond, Index, Mutual Fund, Option, Futures
Function(s): Communications, Security Screening, Technical Analysis
System(s): IBM, Macintosh
Special Requirements: Signal
Price: $595   **AAII Discount:** None
Return Policy: NA
Demo: No
Technical Support: Phone

Description: Combines real-time or delayed data from Signal and software into a technical analysis program. Technical studies include moving averages, standard and exponential oscillators, ratios, spreads, rate of change, stochastics, volatility filter, detrended oscillators, relative strength and dual moving average envelopes. Additional features: Gann angles, a pantograph, alarms, 2 automatic trade systems and up to 4 trendlines per window. A scanning breakout trigger searches real-time data for any market breaking out of a trading range with high volatility.

Western Database   (916) 452-9009
3104 O Street
Suite 188
Sacramento, CA 95816

Product: MARKET SIMULATOR*
Securities: Stock, Index, Mutual Fund
Function(s): Simulations/Games, Technical Analysis
System(s): IBM
Special Requirements: Hard drive, color monitor, 80286 or better processor
Price: $589   **AAII Discount:** None
Return Policy: 30 Days, Restocking Fee: None
Demo: Yes ($20)
Technical Support: Phone (8 a.m. - 5 p.m. PST)

Description: Stock market investment simulator for back-testing of equity investment strategies. Has 5 years of price, earnings and dividend history of the S&P 500 stocks, major market indexes. Built-in routines for creation of moving averages, P/E ratios; historical highs/lows, market rankings, etc. Designed for use with real-time stock data; automatic split adjustment in routines. Works with mutual fund data.

Word Tech Systems (415) 254-0900
(formerly Paper Back Software)
21 Altarinda Road
Orinda, CA 94710

Product: VP-EXPERT
Securities: Not Applicable
Function(s): Expert System
System(s): IBM
Special Requirements: None
Price: $349 **AAII Discount:** None
Return Policy: 30 days, Restocking Fee: $25
Demo: No
Technical Support: $300/year, includes: Phone (8 a.m. - 5 p.m. PST), BBS, Newsletter

Description: Program develops rule-based expert systems that combine information from spreadsheets, databases or other computer programs as well as information from end-user responses to questions on-screen. Information is analyzed and acted upon as the developer of the expert system has instructed. Uses artificial intelligence to teach, advise, diagnose or recommend. Features plain English "if-then" rules; a built-in text editor; links to database, spreadsheet and ASCII files; text and graphic rule traces; confidence factors; backward and forward chaining; hypertext facility; an inductive front end; dynamic graphics support and the ability to run external programs. User can develop system to determine real estate values, financial planning and analyze securities such as stocks and mortgage-backed securities.

Zero Base Software (514) 982-0055
3575 Boulevard St. Laurent fax: (514) 844-0874
Montreal, Quebec, H2W 2M9
Canada

Product: SCENARIO
Securities: Bond, Option, Futures
Function(s): Simulations/Games
System(s): IBM
Special Requirements: None
Price: $199   **AAII Discount:** 35%
Return Policy: None
Demo: No
Technical Support: Phone (9 a.m. - 5 a.m.)

Description: Simulation software covers the spot, futures and options markets. Covers characteristics of fixed income securities and use of futures and options in hedging in addition to outlining several portfolio management techniques. Users adopt the perspective of a portfolio managers for the equivalent of 5 weeks of time. Users can run the demonstration session, referring to the study guide, step-by-step, while replicating all examples. A separate scenario set made up of 5 sessions is also available. Users can experiment with the different variables affecting volatility of fixed income investments such as coupon and maturity. Users can understand and implement strategies used by managers in managing their portfolios.

GUIDE TO FINANCIAL INFORMATION SERVICES 5

In this Chapter we describe financial databases and financial information services. These descriptions are based on information provided by the publishers and are listed alphabetically by company name. Of the 135 information services listed, 32 are appearing for the first time and 11 have been recategorized and moved from the software chapter. These are indicated with a diamond following their name. We have edited those descriptions, but we have not reviewed these services. An information services grid appears in Chapter 7 providing a summary of information found in these databases.

Each listing includes the name of the publisher, the service name, how the service is transmitted, the type of data provided, systems required to use the service, pricing information and a brief description of the service.

The method used to provide data varies among vendors. Some send disks to subscribers while others provide on-line modem or even satellite access. The method in which the service is provided is indicated through the transmission description. Before subscribing to a service, evaluate how frequently your investment strategy changes and how often you need to update your portfolio and select a service accordingly. You may need to subscribe to more than one service if, for instance, you require inexpensive historical quotes and diverse analytical data.

Once you have decided on a service, send or call for the most recent information and compare pricing against similar services. This may be a difficult task, as different services price differently. Some charge by the minute for connect time, but not beyond that; others may have an initial fee and a charge for each report generated. Response times may also vary among systems. All of these factors will affect your ultimate cost. The cost structure for these services is divided into four possible fees

— startup, access, current quote and historical quotes. Not all services will levy all for types of fees and only those that apply are indicated. Startup fees refer to any cost associated with initiating a subscription with service. Access fees refer to any costs associated with getting the main data or services of the quotes. If the service levies an extra change for current or historical quotes, these fees are indicated in the current or historical quote fee sections.

AB-Data, Inc. (201) 423-4212
1114 Goffle Road
Hawthorne, NJ 07506

Product: AB-DATA DISKS
Provides: Financial Statement Data
Transmission: Disk
Access Fees: $50/company; 15% discount for AAII members
System(s): IBM PC

Description: Provides financial information from corporate annual and quarterly reports to be used to create financial models or to review the information with a PC. Compatible with a number of word processing and spreadsheet programs including Lotus 1-2-3 and Excel. Does not include historical price data.

AI Research Corp. (415) 852-9140
2003 St. Julien Court fax: (415) 852-9522
Suite 67
Mountain View, CA 94043

Product: VENCAP DATA QUEST*
Provides: News (Company)
Transmission: Modem, Disk
Start-Up Cost: $89.95
System(s): IBM

Description: A stand-alone interactive directory of venture capital firms active in the U.S. Available in 4 versions: Western, Eastern or combined with either 250 or 399 venture capital firms. Has 14 categories of existing data updated quarterly on each venture capital firm. Features include: window menus, cross-indexing and extra query capabilities. Users can define criteria and the program searches for the appropriate venture capital firm. Users can also identify portfolio companies financed by venture capital firms.

America Online (800) 827-6364
(formerly Quantum Computer Services) (703) 448-8700
8619 Westwood Center Drive fax: (703) 883-1509
Vienna, VA 22182

Product: AMERICA ONLINE
Provides: News (General, Business, Company, Economic News/Data), Current Quotes (Stock, Index, Bond, Option, Futures, Mutual Fund), On-Line Trading
Transmission: Modem
Access Fees: $5.95/month minimum (includes 1 free hour/month); $5/hour non-prime, $10/hour prime
System(s): Apple II, Macintosh, IBM PC; modem

Description: Provides: business and financial news by NewsGrid (from UPI, Business Wire, PR Newswire, Reuters and several international wire services); market news (updated daily after market close); NYSE, AMEX, NASDAQ, advances, declines, volume, Dow Jones indexes; price change, high, low; S&P index; options index put volume, call volume, ratio; most active issues; percentage gains and losers; news on bonds, commodities, OTC, currency. Prices updated continuously during market hours, 20-minute delayed, provided by StockLink. Automated portfolio management—portfolio is directly tied to on-line broker; all transactions automatically reflected in portfolio. Displays quantity of shares, date bought, age, basis, current price, change, present value; displays cash or margin account; portfolio summary shows long- and short-term unrealized capital gains or losses; shows asset quantity, dividend/interest, current income and estimated annual income from dividends; automatically keeps tax records for current and previous years. "Shadow" portfolio: even if not trading on-line, they can maintain their own portfolio—just indicate sales and purchases and portfolio will automatically be updated. Option and Stock Watch features, by StockLink, monitor price changes on specific stocks and options during trading hours. Track any stock or option on U.S. exchanges. Offers stock trading, investor's network (advice), investing contests and small/home business resource.

Argus Research Corporation (212) 425-7500
17 Battery Place fax: (212) 509-5408
New York, NY 10004

Product: ARGUS ON-LINE
Provides: Financial Statement Data, SEC Filings, Analyst Reports, Technical Indicators, Stock Screening (Fundamental Factors)
Transmission: Modem
Start-Up Cost: $50/annual fee

312 / The Individual Investor's Guide to Computerized Investing

Access Fees: $1/minute
System(s): Any computer, modem, communications software

Description: Provides research reports from 20 Argus economists and analysts; daily market comments prior to market open, an investment/economic review of recent political and economic events and the effect on financial markets, interest rate projections, analysis by company, individual stock analysis with buy, hold, sell recommendations and earnings estimates, security screening using 28 criteria, model portfolios, utility stock research and daily technical analysis and graph of short- and long-term factors affecting stock prices. Users may also access Vickers On-Line and Market Guide which provides statistical balance sheet and income statement data on about 6,000 companies.

Automated Investments, Inc.   (416) 489-3500
3284 Yonge   fax: (416) 489-3591
Suite 401
Toronto, Ontario, M4N 3M7
Canada

Product: PROQUOTE
Provides: News (Business), Current Quotes (Stock, Index, Bond, Option, Futures, Mutual Fund), Historical Quotes (Stock, Index, Futures), Technical Indicators
Transmission: FM & Satellite for real-time data; Disk for historical data
Access Fees: $495/month plus exchange fees
Historical Quote Fees: $695 for NYSE from 1988, $595 for NASDAQ from 1990, $475 for AMEX/VSE/MSE from 1990, $795 for TSE from 1986
System(s): IBM PC, XT, AT or compatible with 640, serial port and EGA or VGA graphics

Description: Real-time quotes, charting and technical analysis. Supports securities and news supplied by Bonneville, S&P ComStock and Signal. Features: access to over 10,000 quotes and daily/weekly charts; intra-day charting; technical analysis indicators (e.g., on-balance volume, stochastic, RSI, point and figure, simple/weighted/exponential moving average, inverse volume range); creates symbols representing spread, ratios and baskets; price and volume filters and alarms; mouse or keyboard access; and ASCII capabilities.

Bonneville Market Information   (800) 255-7374
(formerly Bonneville Telecommunications)   (801) 532-3400
19 W. South Temple   fax: (801) 532-3202
Suite 200
Salt Lake City, UT 84101-1503

Product: ENSIGN III
Provides: News (General, Business, Economic News/Data), Current Quotes (Stock, Index, Bond, Option, Futures, Mutual Fund), Charting, Technical Indicators
Transmission: Modem, Satellite, Cable-TV, FM
Start-Up Cost: $1,195 for software, $597 for hardware, $125 for user installation, $397 for BMI installation
Access Fees: Level Three $10/month
Current Quote Fees: $227/month for stocks and commodities plus exchange fees
System(s): IBM AT, PS/2 or compatible with 640K, EGA or VGA graphics card, RS-232 serial port, hard disk; graphics printer recommended

Description: Covers stocks, commodities, indexes, options, mutual funds, corporate and municipal bonds. Three versions: one monitors 320 quotes including bid/ask for commodities and bid size/ask size for stocks. Has last and net on over 12,000 symbols. Two includes level one plus charting with 5 studies—stochastics, relative strength, parabolic, moving average and oscillator. Full package, level three, includes 40-plus studies, macro keys, Japanese candlesticks and more.

Product: MARKET CENTER
Provides: News (General, Business, Economic News/Data), Current Quotes (Stock, Index, Bond, Option, Futures, Mutual Fund)
Transmission: Modem, Satellite, Cable-TV, FM
Start-Up Cost: $297 for software, $597 for hardware and $397 deposit, $100 self installment fee
Current Quote Fees: $227/month for real-time quotes plus exchange fees, $49/month for delayed futures quotes
System(s): IBM AT, PS/2 or compatible, 640K, RS-232 serial port

Description: Provides up to 6,000 real-time quotes on stocks, options, commodities, mutual funds, corporate and government bonds. Has automatic options chaining, customized quote pages, ASCII transfer, stop alerts, news and wild cards. Includes energy information (e.g., rack prices or regional reports).

Bradshaw Financial Network, The (415) 479-3815
253 Channing Way fax: (415) 479-2730
Suite 13
San Rafael, CA 94903

Product: RATEGRAM*
Provides: Current Quotes (Bond, Mutual Fund), Analyst Reports
Transmission: Modem
Access Fees: Varies depending on vendor
System(s): Any computer, modem, communications software

Description: Available through CompuServe and NewsNet. Can locate the country's highest yields on liquid money-market accounts, CDs, jumbo CDs and taxable or tax-exempt money market funds. Provides weekly updates on interest rates, annual effective yields and moving averages and lists the compounding frequency and minimum deposit required. Institution's financial position is ranked based on an index.

Business Week Mutual Fund Scoreboard♦ (800) 553-3575
P.O. Box 1597 (201) 461-7921
Fort Lee, NJ 07024 fax: (201) 461-9808

Product: BUSINESS WEEK MUTUAL FUND SCOREBOARD♦
Provides: Mutual Fund Screening
Transmission: Disk
Current Quote Fees: Equity or fixed income funds only—$299/year for monthly updates or $199/year for quarterly updates, equity and fixed income funds—$399/year for monthly updates; or $299/year for quarterly updates; 15% discount for AAII members
System(s): IBM PC, modem, communications software

Description: Self-contained screening and database tool for 1,100 equity and 950 fixed-income mutual funds. User can search and rank funds meeting investment needs and objectives using multiple search and sort criteria on over 25 information fields. Updated monthly or quarterly. Includes fund name, ticker, telephone, size, fees, objective, last 3- and 12-month and 5- and 10-year performance figures, portfolio data, average weighted maturity in years, risk level, *Business Week* rating, beta and footnotes.

Cambridge Planning & Analytics, Inc.   (800) 328-3475
55 Wheeler Street   (617) 576-6465
P.O. Box 276   fax: (617) 492-5219
Cambridge, MA 02138

Product: DATADISK INFORMATION SERVICES
Provides: News (Economic News/Data), Historical Quotes (Stock, Index, Bond, Option, Futures, Mutual Fund), Financial Statement Data, Charting, Stock Screening (Fundamental Factors)
Transmission: Disk
Start-Up Cost: $200
Access Fees: Financial $695, Economic $595, Equities $495, Production, Consumer or Retail $395; Current: Equities with monthly updates $495; $200 discount for AAII members
System(s): IBM PC or compatible, 640K, CGA, EGA or VGA graphics, hard disk, graphics printer

Description: Economic, financial and business databases with software for analysis and presentation. Six databases: general economic, financial, equities (stock prices, earnings and yields), production, consumer and retail, with thousands of series covering historical and current data. Updated monthly and contains the most recently available published information. Data can be presented in tabular form or graphically and can be directed to the screen, printer or file. Equities service includes screening capabilities across companies. Data conversion on time series include: frequency conversions, moving averages, periodic rates of change, index values and rates of return, lead and lag operations and correlation and regression analysis.

CDA, Investment Technologies, Inc.   (800) 833-1394
1355 Piccard Drive   (301) 975-9600
Rockville, MD 20850   fax: (301) 590-1350

Product: CADENCE UNIVERSE ONLINE
Provides: News (Company, Economic News/Data), Historical Quotes (Stock, Index, Bond, Option, Futures, Mutual Fund), SEC Filings, Mutual Fund Screening
Transmission: Modem

Start-Up Cost: $100
Access Fees: $53/hour (from $5 through $60/report)
System(s): Any computer, modem, communications software

Description: Provides instant on-line access to CDA's library of mutual fund, bank, insurance company and investment advisors' data for performance comparisons and analysis. User can obtain returns for and compare to over 60 market and specialized indexes. To compare fund performance, users can screen for funds that fit certain criteria, such as net asset values, loads, risk factors, rates of return and fund objectives. Bar charts comparing rates of return are available. Mutual fund hypotheticals allow users to see how a fund would perform under different conditions such as withdrawals, front-end loads and tax rates. A cash report shows investments, withdrawals, dividends, taxes, market value and annual internal rate of return.

Charles Schwab & Company, Inc.　　　　　(800) 334-4455
101 Montgomery Street　　　　　　　　　　　fax: (415) 403-5503
Department S
San Francisco, CA 94104

Product: EQUALIZER
Provides: News (Business, Company Economic News/Data), Current Quotes (Stock, Index, Bond, Option, Futures, Mutual Fund), Historical Quotes (Stock, Index, Bond, Option, Futures, Mutual Fund), Financial Statement Data, SEC Filings, Analyst Reports, Earnings Estimates, Stock Screening (Fundamental Factors), Mutual Fund Screening, On-Line Trading
Transmission: Modem
Start-Up Cost: $99
Current Quote Fees: $1.45/minute prime; $0.35/minute non-prime
System(s): IBM PC, XT, AT, PS/2 or compatible with 512K, two disk drives or one with a hard disk and Hayes modem

Description: Combines on-line trading, information access and portfolio management. Schwab account members can receive the same real-time quotes, account information and on-line trading available through the GEnie Brokerage Service. Access to other data services includes: DJN/R, Warner Computer Systems and S&P MarketScope. Software information is under the Equalizer listing in Chapter 4.

Product: GENIE BROKERAGE SERVICE
Provides: Current Quotes (Stock, Index, Bond, Option, Mutual Fund), On-Line Trading
Transmission: Modem
Access Fees: $5/month
Current Quote Fees: $1.45/minute prime; $0.35/prime
System(s): Any computer, modem, communications software

Description: Automated system accessible through GEnie information service (General Electric's Network for Information Exchange). Offers on-line order entry for stocks, options, mutual funds and listed bonds; order changes and cancels and order status viewing. Trades executed through the service receive an additional 10% commission discount off Schwab's rate. Account Summary module offers access to daily updated Schwab Account cash, margin and equity balances; detailed summaries of all positions held at Schwab including security symbols, company descriptions and quantities held long or short; electronically delivered trade confirmations. Real-Time Quotes module offers access to up-to-the-minute quotes on a wide variety of securities and includes data on last trade prices, net change, daily volume, option open interest, dividend amounts, stock split information, price/earnings ratio, yield, earnings per share and 52-week high/low figures. Major market indicators are retrievable. Schwab's Investors' RoundTable offers an electronic investment bulletin board, a real-time conference area for on-line chatting on investment topics and a software library with investment resources and programs for downloading.

CISCO (312) 922-3661
327 S. LaSalle Street
Suite 1133
Chicago, IL 60604

Product: DAILY SUMMARY
Provides: Current Quotes (Index, Bond, Futures), Technical Indicators
Transmission: Modem
Start-Up Cost: $25
Access Fees: $0.25/1,000 characters ($15/month minimum)
System(s): Any computer, modem, communications software

Description: Daily summary services on futures and their related cash instruments for users who maintain their own personal computer database files and analysis programs. RSI, stochastics and trading models are included for detailed research.

Product: HISTORICAL FUTURES CONTRACTS
Provides: Historical Quotes (Index, Futures)
Transmission: Modem
Historical Quote Fees: $4/life of contract
System(s): Any computer, modem, communications software

Description: Historical futures price and volume data that dates from 1969 to the present.

Product: MARKET PROFILE
Provides: Current Quotes (Index, Futures), Charting, Technical Indicators
Transmission: Modem
Start-Up Cost: $125
Access Fees: $35/month
System(s): Any computer, modem, communication software

Description: Market Profile charts for all U.S. futures as well as contracts traded on the LIFFE. User can access intra-day profiles, multiple-day overlays, Stiedlmayer charts, LDB reports and dial-up quotes.

Citicorp Database Services (212) 898-7200
88 Pine Street fax: (212) 742-8956
16th Floor
New York, NY 10005

Product: CITIBASE
Provides: News (General, Business, Company, Economic News/Data), Historical Quotes (Index)
Transmission: Modem
Start-Up Cost: $100
Access Fees: $65/hour connect time plus $20/hour communications charge
System(s): Any computer, modem, communications software

Description: Historical U.S. macroeconomic and financial information from various public and private releases. Macroeconomic: business cycle indicators, national income and product accounts, import/export prices for the U.S., business formation, construction, manufacturing and trade, prices, industrial production, capacity and productivity, population, energy, labor statistics, flow of funds, personal consumption expenditures, employment and earnings, consumer and producer price indexes, forecasts and projections and federal fiscal operations. Financial data: money supply, interest rates and yields from the Federal Reserve Bank, exchange rates, banking statistics, credit, stock market, commodities and futures, S&P indexes. International data: International Financial Statistics database from IMF and OECD Main Economic Indicators. Data ranges from daily to annual. Updated daily.

Commodity Systems Inc. (CSI)   (800) 327-0175
200 W. Palmetto Park Road   (407) 392-8663
Boca Raton, FL 33432   fax: (407) 392-1379

Product: CSI DATA RETRIEVAL SERVICE
Provides: News (Economic News/Data), Current Quotes (Stock, Index, Option, Futures, Mutual Fund), Historical Quotes (Stock, Index, Option, Futures, Mutual Fund), Technical Indicators
Transmission: Modem, Disk
Start-Up Cost: $39; 10% discount for AAII members
Current Quote Fees: $25/month and up
Historical Quote Fees: $0.20/month for stock data, $0.29/month for futures contract data, $0.29/month each strike price, put or call
System(s): IBM PC or compatible with 640K memory, two drives, CGA, EGA, VGA or Hercules, and Hayes modem; Apple II+/IIe/IIc with two drives and Hayes modem

Description: Daily updates and historical data on all U.S. stocks, mutual funds, futures, foreign futures, futures and stock index options and cash markets. Has: Quicktrieve/Quickmanager and Quickplot/Quickstudy to download, manage, graphically review and analyze market information. Technical indicators: average of 2 or more fields, call/put ratio, commodity channel index, CSI stop and intermarket relative movement, MACD, non-seasonal and on-balance volume, PDI, relative strength index, single field detrend, spread/ratio of 2 volatility systems, Williams' %R and Williams' accumulation/distribution.

CompuServe
5000 Arlington Center Boulevard
Columbus, OH 43220

(800) 848-8199 x195
(614) 457-8600
fax: (614) 457-0348

Product: COMPUSERVE
Provides: News (General, Business, Company, Economic News/Data), Current Quotes (Stock, Index, Bond, Option, Futures, Mutual Fund), Historical Quotes (Stock, Index, Bond, Option, Futures, Mutual Fund), Financial Statement Data, SEC Filings, Analyst Reports, Earnings Estimates, Charting, Technical Indicators, Stock Screening (Fundamental Factors, Technical Factors) Mutual Fund Screening, On-Line Trading
Transmission: Modem
Start-Up Cost: Free introductory membership and $15 usage credit for AAII members (expires 11/30/92)
Access Fees: $6/hour at 300 baud, $12.50/hour at 1200 or 2400 baud, $22.50/hour at 9600 baud
Current Quote Fees: $0.015/quote
Historical Quote Fees: $0.05/quote
System(s): Any computer, modem, communications software

Description: Has over 1,400 products and services. Quick Quote provides 20-minute delayed price and volume data on thousands of stocks, options, market indicators, closed-end funds and exchange rates. End-of-day quotes for open-end mutual funds, bonds and commodities. MicroQuote II provides over 12 years of pricing history on over 100,000 publicly traded securities plus 20 years of dividend distribution data. *Money* magazine's financial information center includes performance information and details on over 1,700 mutual funds. Detailed company reports and earnings estimates are provided by such sources as S&P, Value Line, Disclosure and Institutional Brokers Estimate System (I/B/E/S). Members can discuss opportunities in the Investors' Forum, where on-line support is provided for popular software products such as MetaStock Professional. Several databases provide details on international companies. VESTOR provides stock recommendations and 2 on-line brokers are available 24 hours a day. Interfaces are available supporting the transfer of information to microcomputer software packages. Other services: MMS International (provides daily analysis of the markets) and RateGram (reports the highest yielding federally insured CD rates).

Comtex Scientific Corp. (800) 624-5089
911 Hope Street (203) 358-0007
Stamford, CT 06907 fax: (203) 358-0236

Product: MARKET NEWSALERT
Provides: News (Business), Financial Statement Data, SEC Filings, Analyst Reports
Transmission: Modem
Start-Up Cost: Varies depending on vendor
System(s): Any computer, modem, communications software

Description: Offers coverage of the corporate arena including news, press releases and SEC filings on listed companies as well as OTC companies. News is available by company and industry as well as by the type of business activity (e.g., mergers, joint ventures, new product introductions). Distributed by Track Data.

Product: OMNINEWS
Provides: News (Business), Financial Statement Data, SEC Filings, Analyst Reports
Transmission: Modem
Start-Up Cost: Varies depending on vendor
System(s): Any computer, modem, communications software

Description: Combines real-time corporate news and SEC filing information with political, economic and market events affecting business. Compiled from 10+ major international news wires, the SEC and other specialized sources. Distributed by Bloomberg, Bridge Information Systems, Citibank, Desktop Data, Olde Discount Corp., PC Quote, Telekurs and Pont Data.

Product: OTC NEWSALERT
Provides: News (Business), Financial Statement Data, SEC Filings, Analyst Reports
Transmission: Modem
Start-Up Cost: Varies depending on vendor
System(s): Any computer, modem, communications software

Description: Has information on the OTC marketplace and news on over 10,000 large and small NASDAQ and unlisted pink sheet companies. Data includes earnings and dividend information, stock splits, joint ventures, new product introductions, key personnel changes, SEC filing notices, IPOs, more. Information is updated continuously throughout the day. Stories are headlined for quick review, and data is retained for retrieval by company name and/or ticker symbol for up to 180 days. Available on Bridge Information System, Quotron, Telerate Inc./CMQ Communications, SHARK and Telescan.

CONNECT, INC. (800) 262-2638
10101 Bubb Road (408) 973-0110
Cupertino, CA 95014 fax: (408) 973-0497

Product: CONNECT BUSINESS INFORMATION NETWORK
Provides: News (Business), Current Quotes (Stock, Index, Option, Futures, Mutual Fund)
Transmission: Modem
Start-Up Cost: $99.95
Access Fees: $10/hour prime, $5/hour non-prime
System(s): IBM PC or Macintosh, modem

Description: Provides global computer communications through an icon-driven network enhanced by transparent connecting protocol and high-speed capabilities. Includes S&P Ticker III, a 15-minute delayed feed from all North American Stock Exchanges. Ticker III access may be fully automated through proprietary software. Features include screen or tone alarms activated by price or volume levels.

Data Broadcasting Corporation (800) 367-4670
(formerly FNN-Data Broadcasting Corp.) (415) 571-1800
1900 S. Norfolk Street fax: (415) 571-8507
San Mateo, CA 94402

Product: MARKETWATCH
Provides: News (Business), Current Quotes (Stock, Index, Option, Futures)
Transmission: Satellite, Cable-TV
Start-Up Cost: $99 for software
Access Fees: $30/month for DataReceiver

Current Quote Fees: Delayed stock and option quotes $60-$90/month; real-time stock and option quotes $135-$180/month
System(s): IBM PC, serial port

Description: Use the DataReceiver to receive quotes, news and other financial information. Allows simultaneous viewing of up to 5 windows—user-selectable—to create and display personalized portfolios, monitors, tickers and quotes. Visual alarms and alerts notify of trading in monitored stocks or if price/volume limits are exceeded.

Product: MARKETWATCH PLUS
Provides: News (Business), Current Quotes (Stock, Index, Option, Futures)
Transmission: Satellite, Cable-TV
Start-Up Cost: $149 for software
Access Fees: $50/month for DataReceiver PLUS
Current Quote Fees: Delayed stock and option quotes from $60-$90/month; real time stock and option quotes $135-$180/month; commodities are additional
System(s): IBM PC, serial port

Description: Includes MarketWatch features plus DataReceiver PLUS and MarketWatch PLUS software audio alarms, the ability to receive market information when the PC is turned off and the ability to request quotes while working in another program. Also provides capabilities for transferring files into other popular software programs (such as Lotus 1-2-3) for further analysis.

Product: NEWS REAL♦
Provides: News (General, Business, Company Economic News/Data), Current Quotes (Stock, Bond, Option, Futures, Mutual Fund), Historical Quotes (Stock), Financial Statement Data, SEC Filings
Transmission: Modem
Start-Up Cost: $179
Access Fees: $11.95/month database fee plus on-line DJN/R charges
System(s): IBM PC, modem

Description: Electronic news manager that delivers customized business and financial news. Downloads from DJN/R, articles or stock market quotes in user-chosen categories. Accesses stories from Dow Jones News Service, selected stories from the *Wall Street Journal* and *Barron's* as recent as a few seconds and as far back as 90 days. Offers 15-minute delayed quotes. Accesses more than 55 Dow Jones databases including articles from the *Washington Post, Forbes, Fortune, Money, Inc., Financial World* and over 150 regional business journals since 1985. Gives access to Dun and Bradstreet Financial Records on more than 750,000 companies and more than 4,700 company profiles from Standard & Poor's. Compatible with Signal which offers real-time quotes for over 50,000 stocks, options, futures, indexes and funds.

Product: QUOTREK
Provides: Current Quotes (Stock, Index, Option, Futures, Mutual Fund)
Transmission: FM
Start-Up Cost: $495
Current Quote Fees: $70/month plus surcharges of $3-$88/exchange
System(s): No computer needed

Description: Hand-held receiver provides real-time quotes in over 30 major cities. Monitors over 50,000 issues on the major stock, options and futures exchanges plus the Dow Jones News Alert service and over 80 key indexes. A 40-character LCD display shows last sale, net change, high and low, previous day's close and total volume. A built-in battery lasts 8 hours on a single charge.

Product: SIGNAL
Provides: Current Quotes (Stock, Index, Option, Futures, Mutual Fund), Historical Quotes (Stock, Index, Mutual Fund)
Transmission: Satellite, FM for Current Quotes, Disk for Historical data
Start-Up Cost: $595 for receiver and software
Current Quote Fees: $150/month plus surcharges of $3-$88/exchange
System(s): IBM PC, XT, AT or 100% compatible with 384K and DOS 2.0 or later

Description: Combination hardware and software package that delivers real-time market quotes to a personal computer. A special FM receiver captures stock data from FM radio subchannels broadcast in major metropolitan areas or nationwide if used with a satellite. User can view information 3 ways: detail, summary and alert (set by the user). Depending on the exchange accessed, display pages contain the following information: last trade or bid, net change or net change from the previous close, today's volume, today's high and low trades and time of the last trade. Works with over 90 different analytical software packages. Data Broadcasting also makes historical data available to users. Equity, mutual funds and indexes and indicators for the NYSE, AMEX, NASDAQ, U.S. regional, Toronto and Montreal exchanges. Historical data goes back to 1978 in daily, weekly or monthly time periods and is available on 360K or 1.2 M diskettes in ASCII, Lotus 1-2-3 or MetaStock file formats. Also available are open interest, exchange listed, exchange traded and Dow Jones News Alerts.

Data Transmission Network Corp.   (800) 779-5000
9110 W. Dodge Road   (402) 390-2328
Suite 200   fax: (402) 390-7188
Omaha, NE 68114

Product: DTN WALL STREET
Provides: News (Business, Company, Economic News/Data), Current Quotes (Stock, Index, Bond, Option, Futures, Mutual Fund), Analyst Reports, Technical Indicators
Transmission: Satellite, Cable-TV
Start-Up Cost: $295
Current Quote Fees: $34.95/month
System(s): Terminal comes with service, including serial port for IBM compatible computer hook-up

Description: Electronic video service provides 15-minute delayed quotes for stocks, bonds and mutual funds and 10-30-minute delayed quotes for futures plus financial news and information. Information is transmitted by KU-band and C-band satellite signals or cable TV in selected areas. All equipment is provided including programmable receiver, video monitor, KU-band satellite dish or cable splitter and serial port for connecting a personal computer. Supports many analytical and portfolio management software programs.

Delphi   (800) 695-4005
1030 Massachusetts Avenue   (617) 491-3393
Cambridge, MA 02138   fax: (617) 491-6642

Product: DELPHI*
Provides: News (General, Business, Company, Economic News/Data), Current Quotes (Stock, Index, Bond, Option, Futures, Mutual Fund), Analyst Reports
Transmission: Modem
Access Fees: Basic plan—$5.95/month includes first hour, $6/hour thereafter; 20/20 plan—$20/month includes 20 hours, $1.20/hour thereafter
System(s): Any computer, modem, communications software

Description: Offers a range of services including quotes and market analysis, CD rates, futures information, portfolio, stock and market analysis, press release wires (Business Wire and PR Newswire) and software shopping. Translation service is available, as is UPI news.

Dial/Data   (718) 522-6886
Division of Track Data Corp.   fax: (718) 522-6847
61 Broadway
New York, NY 10006

Product: DIAL/DATA
Provides: Current Quotes (Stock, Index, Option, Futures), Historical Quotes (Stock, Index, Bond, Option, Futures, Mutual Fund), Technical Indicators
Transmission: Modem
Start-Up Cost: $25
Current Quote Fees: $0.01 to $0.035/issue per day
Historical Quote Fees: $0.01 to $0.035/issue per day
System(s): Any computer, modem, communications software

Description: Supplies daily or historical price data for indexes, stocks, futures, options, mutual funds, bonds, government issues, money markets and stock dividends. Covers all U.S., Canadian and European exchanges. Users can select daily, weekly or monthly frequencies for retrieval. Data for stocks include open high, low, close and volume. Data for futures include open, high, low, close, volume and open interest. Technical data is available from 1970 for all original S&P issuers. Stock splits and dividends are reported the evening they occur. Service through ADP or via modem over Telenet network.

Product: TRACK/ON LINE
Provides: News (General, Business, Company, Economic News/Data), Current Quotes (Stock, Index, Option, Futures), Historical Quotes (Stock, Index, Bond, Option, Futures, Mutual Fund), Financial Statement Data, SEC Filings, Analyst Reports, Earnings Estimates, Technical Indicators, Mutual Fund Screening, On-Line Trading
Transmission: Modem
Current Quote Fees: $0.36/minute
Historical Quote Fees: $0.36/minute
System(s): Any computer, modem, communications software

Description: Business and financial information. Has delayed quotes from all major exchanges, including Canadian and London exchanges, on stock, options and futures. Historical quotes from 1970 for stocks and futures. News database has current and historical news from Comtex Scientific Corp.'s ExecuGrid and Business Wire's full text corporate news releases. Includes: mutual fund information and performance results from Investment Company Data, insider trading data from Invest/Net Group, risk arbitrage from Merrin Financial, institutional holdings and 144 filings from Vickers Stock Research Corp., earnings estimates from Zacks Investment Research, equity analysis, technical indicators, economic and monetary projections, bond data and more from S&P MarketScope. Has analysis on put/call option series, volatility analysis, market pulse and option scanning.

Dialog Information Services, Inc. (800) 334-2564
3460 Hillview Avenue (415) 858-3785
Palo Alto, CA 94304 fax: (415) 858-7069

Product: BOND BUYER FULL TEXT*
Provides: News (Business)
Transmission: Modem
Start-Up Cost: $45 for access to entire Dialog service
Access Fees: $2.50/minute
System(s): Any computer, modem, communications software

Description: Corresponds to the publications, *The Bond Buyer* and *Credit Markets*, that specialize in the fixed-income investment market. Provides daily coverage of government and Treasury securities, financial futures, corporate bonds and mortgage securities. Covers U.S. Congressional actions, worldwide monetary and fiscal policies and regulatory changes relating to the bond industry. Lists planned bond issues, bond calls and redemptions and results of bond sales.

Product: BUSINESS DATELINE*
Provides: News (Business, Company)
Transmission: Modem
Start-Up Cost: $45 for access to entire Dialog service
Access Fees: $2.10/minute
System(s): Any computer, modem, communications software

Description: Contains full text of articles from regional business publications from the U.S. and Canada, including Crain News Service publications, 9 daily newspapers and BusinessWire. Articles cover regional business activities and trends and information about small companies, new start-ups, family-owned and closely-held firms, their products or services and the executives who run these companies.

Product: DIALOG BUSINESS CONNECTION
Provides: News (Business), Historical Quotes (Stock, Index), Financial Statement Data, SEC Filings, Analyst Reports, Technical Indicators, Stock Screening (Fundamental Factors), Mutual Fund Screening, On-Line Trading
Transmission: Modem
Start-Up Cost: $45 for access to entire Dialog service
Access Fees: Varies
System(s): Any computer, modem, communications software

Description: Menu-driven, applications-oriented service that offers on-line access to data on over 2 million public and private companies. Users select the type of information they seek from menus and the service automatically selects the applicable database and retrieves the data. Databases on the service include Dun and Bradstreet, Standard & Poor's, Moody's and Disclosure. Five applications sections are available: corporate intelligence provides detailed information on companies; financial screening enables users to identify companies based on their financial characteristics; products and markets provides detailed information about a specific product or industry; sales prospecting aides users in locating new clients or customers; travel planning allows users to plan and book trips.

Product: DIALOG/MONEYCENTER*
Provides: News (General, Business, Company, Economic News/Data), Current Quotes (Stock, Index, Bond, Option, Futures), Historical Quotes (Stock, Index, Bond, Option, Futures)
Transmission: Modem
Start-Up Cost: $45 for access to entire Dialog service
Access Fees: $2.00/minute
System(s): Any computer, modem, communications software

Description: Includes financial information of three kinds: news, quotes and fixed pages. News provides coverage of broad domestic and international events that influence markets gathered from worldwide news bureaus. Quotes are real-time and slightly delayed bids and offers on government securities. Covers a wide assortment of other money-market instruments, fixed income and mortgage-backed securities and foreign exchange. Fixed pages are single screens of information on a variety of topics including credit markets, mortgage-backed securities, economic indicators, foreign exchange, energy prices and more. Information can be searched via a menu or using standard program commands.

Product: DIALOG QUOTES AND TRADING
Provides: Current Quotes (Stock, Option), On-Line Trading
Transmission: Modem
Start-Up Cost: $45 for access to entire Dialog service
Access Fees: $0.60/minute
System(s): Any computer, modem, communications software

Description: Provides 20-minute delayed stock and options quotes from the NYSE, AMEX, NASDAQ and the 4 major options exchanges. Order entry allows the purchase or sale of any stock or option listed in the *Wall Street Journal*. Up to 75 portfolios can be set up with the value of the portfolios' securities updated to reflect current market prices. Service can also track portfolio gains and losses and project dividend income. Tax records maintained on the service can include securities, stocks, options, mutual funds and bonds and can reflect all stocks and options transactions. Quantitative tools to evaluate stock option transactions are also available.

Product: FIRST RELEASE
Provides: News (Business), Current Quotes (Stock, Index, Bond, Option, Futures, Mutual Fund), Historical Quotes (Stock, Index, Bond, Option, Futures, Mutual Fund), Analyst Reports
Transmission: Modem
Start-Up Cost: $45 for access to entire Dialog service
Access Fees: $1.60/minute
System(s): Any computer, modem, communications software

Description: Provides access to the latest news from 4 major news wire databases updated within 15 minutes of transmission over the wire. Business wire delivers timely news stories that are simultaneously distributed to over 700 news media and more than 100 institutions and firms in the investment community. Knight-Ridder financial news provides the complete text of news stories on worldwide financial and commodity markets and the events that move them. Financial coverage centers on credit markets, foreign exchange, mortgage-backed securities and financial futures, as well as banking, economic news and corporate earnings. Commodity coverage includes both cash and futures market analysis. Weather information is available from Global Weather services, Knight-Ridder's weather forecasting center. Reports on the expected impact that government policy will have on the financial and commodity markets are available. PR newswire contains the complete text of business/financial news releases. Reuters contains the full text of news releases from the Reuter Business Report which provides breaking news and market commentaries as well as fast follow-up analysis. Reuter Library Service is the source of world news.

Product: SEC ONLINE*
Provides: SEC Filings
Transmission: Modem
Start-Up Cost: $45 for access to entire Dialog service
Access Fees: $1.40/minute
System(s): Any computer, modem, communications software

Description: Full text database of reports filed by public companies with the SEC. Includes all companies on the New York and American Stock Exchanges, plus over 2,000 NASDAQ National Market companies. Contains the actual, unedited text of these companies' 10-Ks, 10-Qs, 20-Fs, annual reports and proxy statements including any amendments to them. Provides the following documents as filed with the SEC: Annual Report (not required to be filed with the SEC), Form 20-F (official annual report filed by non-U.S. registrants 6 months after the fiscal year-end), Form 10-K (official annual report filed by U.S. public companies 90 days after fiscal year-end), Form 10-Q (official quarterly report filed 45 days after the close of each quarter) and Proxy Statement (official report/notification to shareholders of shareholder meetings and issues to be voted upon.)

Disclosure Inc. (301) 951-1300
5161 River Road fax: (301) 657-1962
Bethesda, MD 20816

Product: COMPACT D/'33
Provides: SEC Filings, Analyst Reports
Transmission: CD-ROM
Access Fees: Commercial—$9,500/year, Non-profit—$7,600/year
System(s): IBM PC

Description: Has access to 1933 Act Registrations and Prospectuses data; issue-by-issue securities information for SEC reporting companies which consists of extracts from Registration Statements and prospectuses filed with the SEC. Coverage of transactions includes those reported in '33 Act Registration Statements filed on Forms S-1, S-2, S-3, S-4, S-8, S-18, F-1, F-2, F-3, F-4, pre- and post-effective amendments, final prospectus and supplements. Each disk has: key-word searchable full text sections plus are templated for controlled-vocabulary searching; over 12 preformatted display options; capability to customize display and report formats and to generate mailing labels and lists of registrant companies, agents and legal counsel.

Product: COMPACT D/CANADA
Provides: Financial Statement Data, Analyst Reports, Stock Screening (Fundamental Factors)
Transmission: CD-ROM
Access Fees: Commercial—$4,000/year, Non-profit—$3,475/year
System(s): IBM PC

Description: Offers unlimited access to facts and figures on more than 6,000 public, private and crown companies in all 10 Canadian provinces. Uses Easy Menu Mode or Dialog commands for data searching and display. Retrieved data can be displayed, printed and transferred to disk or downloaded to spreadsheets and other software packages. Organized into 3 main sections: Resume includes company name, address, CUSIP, business rankings, corporate status (e.g., public or private), holding company information, legal counsel and date of latest annual financial information; the Financial Section, containing annual financials for up to 5 years, includes income statements, balance sheets (assets/liabilities), and key ratios; Summary Quarterly Financials are included for sales, income, dividends, outstanding shares and earnings-per-share. Text Section includes a filings list, president's letter, ownership information, company officers, merger and acquisition data. Over 100 search variables are available.

Product: COMPACT D/SEC
Provides: Financial Statement Data, SEC Filings, Analyst Reports, Earnings Estimates, Stock Screening (Fundamental Factors)
Transmission: CD-ROM
Access Fees: Commercial—$6,000/year, Non-profit rate—$4,700/year, Spectrum ownership data—$2,000/year
System(s): IBM PC

Description: Offers corporate information on public companies whose securities are traded on the NYSE, AMEX, NASDAQ and OTC. Abstracted from the documents filed with the SEC. Has over 250 database search variables. Disk contains the Zacks Investment Database of Wall Street Estimates with research and analysis covering more that 4,000 companies. Disclosure/Spectrum Ownership profiles are an option with detailed stockholder information for over 5,500 companies. Each disk contains: profiles of 11,000 public companies; annual (5-year comparative) balance sheets and income statements; annual cash flow statements (up to 3 years); quarterly financial reports (up to 6 years); 5-year summary and 5-year growth rates for net income, sales and EPS; officer/director names, titles, ages and salaries (for top 6); president's letter, management discussion and footnotes to financials; ratios and price/earnings data; corporate earnings estimates; all subsidiaries; abstracts of extraordinary events; a listing of documents filed with the SEC; listing of exhibits filed with 10-Ks, 10-Qs, 8-Ks; Registrations Statements and ownership profiles.

Product: DISCLOSURE DATABASE
Provides: Financial Statement Data, SEC Filings, Analyst Reports, Earnings Estimates
Transmission: Modem
Access Fees: Varies depending on vendor
System(s): Any computer, modem, communications software

Description: Contains financial and textual data from documents filed with the SEC on 12,000 companies. Has over 250 variables including company name, address, phone number, ticker symbol, SIC codes, description of business, quarterly and annual income statements and balance sheets, annual funds flow data, 32 annual financial ratios, officers and directors listing, weekly pricing information, subsidiaries listing, *Fortune, Forbes,* CUSIP and DUNS numbers, stock ownership data, management discussion and president's letter. Available through Dialog Information, Mead Data Central, DJN/R, BRS Information Technologies, ADP Network, CompuServe, I.P. Sharp Associates, Warner Computer, VU/Text and Quotron.

Product: DISCLOSURE/SPECTRUM OWNERSHIP DATABASE
Provides: SEC Filings, Analyst Reports
Transmission: CD-ROM
Access Fees: Varies depending on vendor
System(s): Any computer, modem, communications software

Description: Contains stock ownership information for companies from documents filed with the SEC by corporate insiders, 5 percent owners and institutional owners. Includes: company name, exchange, ticker symbol, SIC codes, outstanding shares, stockholder names, number of most recent shares traded, total number of shares held and date of latest filing. Available through Dialog Information Services, DJN/R, BRS Information Technologies and CompuServe.

Product: DISCLOSURE/WORLDSCOPE EUROPE
    (formerly Compact D/Europe)
Provides: Historical Quotes (Stock), Financial Statement Data
Transmission: CD-ROM
Access Fees: Commercial—$3,000/year, Non-profit—$2,625
System(s): IBM PC

Description: Offers information on 2,000 European companies from 14 countries. Updated quarterly. Includes: general corporate information (name/address/telephone number, SIC codes, description of business, number of employees, current outstanding shares, auditor, etc.); financial information contains over 500 data items including 5-year summary of sales/net income/EPS, balance sheet, income statement, key financial items, funds flow statement, per share data and investment ratios; explanatory footnotes; country and industry averages; financials presented in local currency (selected key data presented in U.S. dollars); over 100 directly comparable financial ratios/growth rates; company-specific accounting practices; 3-years of stock prices. Use a menu system or command entry mode for data searching and display. Data can be displayed, printed and transferred to disk or downloaded to spreadsheets and other software packages.

Product: DISCLOSURE/WORLDSCOPE GLOBAL*
Provides: Historical Quotes (Stock), Financial Statement Data
Transmission: CD-ROM
Access Fees: Commercial—$6,000/year, Non-profit—$4,700
System(s): IBM PC

Description: Offers access to information on 7,000 companies from 25 countries around the world. Updated quarterly. Includes: general corporate information (name/address/telephone number, SIC codes, description of business, number of employees, current outstanding shares, auditor, etc.); detailed financial information comprising over 500 data items including 5-year summary of sales/net income/EPS, balance sheet, income statement, key financial items, funds flow statement, per share data and investment ratios; explanatory footnotes; country and industry averages; financials presented in local currency (selected key data presented in U.S. dollars); over 100 directly comparable financial ratios/growth rates; company-specific accounting practices identified; and 3-years of stock prices. Operates with either a menu system or command entry mode for data searching and display. Retrieved data can be displayed, printed and transferred to disk or downloaded to spreadsheets and other software packages.

Product: DISCLOSURE/WORLDSCOPE PACIFIC RIM*
Provides: Historical Quotes (Stock), Financial Statement Data

Transmission: CD-ROM
Access Fees: Commercial—$3,000/year, Non-profit—$2,625
System(s): IBM PC

Description: Offers access to information on 1,500 companies in 7 Pacific Rim countries. Updated quarterly. Includes: general corporate information (name/address/telephone number, SIC codes, description of business, number of employees, current outstanding shares, auditor, etc.); detailed financial information comprising over 500 data items including 5-year summary of sales/net income/EPS, balance sheet, income statement, key financial items, funds flow statement, per share data and investment ratios; explanatory footnotes; country and industry averages; financials presented in local currency (key data presented in U.S. dollars); over 100 directly comparable financial ratios/growth rates; company-specific accounting practices identified; and 3-years of stock prices. Operates with either a menu system or command entry mode for data searching and display. Retrieved data can be displayed, printed and transferred to disk or downloaded to spreadsheets and other software packages.

Dow Jones News/Retrieval (800) 522-3567 x2251
P.O. Box 300 (609) 520-4641
Princeton, NJ 08540 fax: (609) 520-4660

Product: DOW JONES NEWS/RETRIEVAL
Provides: News (General, Business, Company, Economic News/Data), Current Quotes (Stock, Index, Bond, Option, Futures, Mutual Fund), Historical Quotes (Stock, Index, Bond, Option, Futures, Mutual Fund), Financial Statement Data, SEC Filings, Analyst Reports, Earnings Estimates, Technical Indicators, Stock Screening (Fundamental Factors, Technical Factors), Mutual Fund Screening, On-Line Trading
Transmission: Modem
Start-Up Cost: $29.95 (includes 3 free hours during first 30 days)
Access Fees: 300 baud: prime—$0.72-$0.90/minute plus $0.60/information unit, non-prime—$0.12-$0.60/minute plus $0.18/information unit; 1200 baud: prime—$0.72-$2.04/minute plus $0.60/information unit, non-prime—$0.21-$1.50/minute plus $0.18/information unit; 2400 baud: prime—$0.72-$2.85/minute plus $0.60/information unit, non-prime— $0.30-$1.80/minute plus $0.18/information unit. Also has non-prime $25/month flat access plan for Dow Jones News,

current and historical quotes, Dow Jones Averages, symbols directory and futures quotes.
System(s): Any computer, modem, communications software

Description: Contains a broad selection of business and financial information composed of more than 60 on-line services. Users can receive real-time or delayed quotes from all major exchanges. Historical quotes dating back to 1979 are available for stocks, indexes, mutual funds and futures. Historical quotes on options date back 1 year. Includes more than 550 international, national and regional publications including exclusive access to the text of the Dow Jones Newswires, the *Wall Street Journal* and *Barron's*. Financial and investment services include excerpts from SEC records on more than 10,000 companies, financial information and company profiles from S&P, research reports from Business Research Corp., consensus earnings forecasts from Zacks, fundamental corporate financial and market performance data from Media General and Money Market Service's weekly economic and foreign exchange survey. Stocks may also be traded via Fidelity Brokerage Services, Inc.

Dunn & Hargitt Investment Management   (317) 423-2624
22 N. Second Street   fax: (317) 423-4495
Lafayette, IN 47902

Product: COMMODITY DATABANK
Provides: Historical Quotes (Futures), Technical Indicators
Transmission: Disk
Historical Quote Fees: Varies with quantity, minimum order of $50
System(s): Any computer, modem, communications software

Description: Historical database covering futures, commodities, currencies and debt instruments. Information dates back to 1959.

Estima (formerly Doan Associates)   (800) 822-8038
1800 Sherman Avenue   (708) 864-8772
Suite 612   fax: (708) 864-6221
Evanston, IL 60201

Product: OECD MAIN ECONOMIC INDICATORS
Provides: News (Economic News/Data), Historical Quotes (Futures)
Transmission: Disk

Access Fees: $600-$2,100/year depending on update schedule
System(s): IBM PC, XT, AT and PS/2 or compatible; Macintosh

Description: A compilation of macroeconomic data on the principal Western economies. Includes GNP and its principal components, industrial production, money, stock, exchange rate versus the dollar, principal interest rates, unemployment, price indexes and more. Most data series are monthly, with some quarterly. In most cases, data go back to 1960. User can obtain either the full set (data on 25 countries) or a reduced set including data from the U.S., Japan, U.K., Germany, France, Italy and Canada.

Fidelity Investments (800) 225-5531
82 Devonshire Street
Boston, MA 02190

Product: FIDELITY INVESTORS EXPRESS
Provides: News (Business), Current Quotes (Stock, Index, Option, Mutual Fund), Analyst Reports, On-Line Trading
Transmission: Modem
Access Fees: $12/month
System(s): Any computer, modem, communications software

Description: Accessed through Dow Jones News/Retrieval, allows investors to buy and sell stocks, options and mutual funds. Provides stock quotes, portfolio and account management and a review of Fidelity's products and services.

Ford Investor Services (619) 755-1327
11722 Sorrento Valley Road fax: (619) 455-6316
San Diego, CA 92121

Product: FORD DATA BASE
Provides: Historical Quotes (Stock), Stock Screening (Fundamental Factors)
Transmission: Modem, Disk
Access Fees: Monthly updates $300/month; Twice monthly updates $400/month; Weekly updates $600/month; or $96/hour on-line access
System(s): IBM PC or compatible

Description: Screening service and database. Covers 2,000 companies with 77 fundamental data items on each company. Provides standard financial information including normal earnings, quality ratings and independently derived earnings and dividend growth rates. Two proprietary indicators—price/value ratio and an earnings trend parameter provided to help identify undervalued common stocks.

FutureSource (800) 621-2628
955 Parkview Boulevard (312) 977-9067
Lombard, IL 60148 fax: (708) 620-4315

Product: FUTURESOURCE ANALYST
Provides: News (Business), Current Quotes (Index, Bond, Option, Futures), Historical Quotes (Index, Bond, Futures), Charting, Technical Indicators
Transmission: Satellite
Access Fees: $250/month plus exchange fees and transmission costs
System(s): IBM AT or compatible with 640K, (1 MB, EMS, recommended) EGA or VGA color card and monitor, 20 MB hard drive and one floppy drive

Description: Combines real-time futures and options quotes with some technical analysis. Features: Futures World News, charting intra-day and daily price data. Flexible pages allow for mixing of charts, technical studies, prices or news. Add-on features: Market Profile and OptionSource, a theoretical option calculator and strategy simulator.

Product: FUTURESOURCE TECHNICAL
Provides: News (Business, Economic News/Data), Current Quotes (Index, Bond, Option, Futures), Historical Quotes (Index, Bond, Futures), Charting, Technical Indicators
Transmission: Satellite
Access Fees: $370/month plus exchange fees
System(s): IBM AT or compatible with 640K (1 MB EMS recommended), CGA, VGA, EGA, 20 MB hard drive and one floppy drive

Description: Combines real-time futures and options quotes with technical analysis. Features: Futures World News and charting of tick, intra-day, daily, weekly or monthly price data. Can mix charts, technical studies, spreads, prices or news. Add-ons: Market Profile and OptionSource, a theoretical option calculator and strategy simulator.

GE Information Services   (800) 638-9636
401 N. Washington Street   (301) 340-4000
Rockville, MD 20850

Product: GENIE*
Provides: News (General, Business, Company, Economic News/Data), Current Quotes (Stock, Index, Bond, Option, Futures, Mutual Fund), Historical Quotes (Stock, Index, Bond, Option, Futures, Mutual Fund), Analyst Reports, Stock Screening (Fundamental Factors), On-Line Trading
Transmission: Modem
Access Fees: Flat fee access of $4.95/month for basic service; other service options: non-prime $6/hour, prime $18/hour
System(s): Any computer, modem, communications software

Description: Provides access to broad range of topics through a three-tiered pricing structure. For a flat rate of $4.95/month users have access to over 100 GE*Basic services such as roundtables where ideas can be exchanged with other members, closing stock and mutual fund prices, news, weather and sports, Grolier's Encyclopedia, electronic mail, shopping, and games and entertainment. For an hourly rate of $6, users have access to GEnie Value services such as libraries of files, real-time conferences, a broader range of security quotes with a portfolio tracking feature, newswire services and additional on-line games. GEnie$Professional service provides access to additional fee services such as historical quotes, analytical reports, stock screening and selection, market and stock analysis through VESTOR, on-line brokerage through Charles Schwab and access to DJN/R.

Genesis Financial Data Services   (800) 642-8860
P.O. Box 49578   (719) 260-6111
Colorado Springs, CO 80949   fax: (719) 260-6113

Product: DATA CONNECTIONS (formerly Data Express)
Provides: Current Quotes (Stock, Index, Option, Futures, Mutual Fund), Historical Quotes (Stock, Index, Option, Futures, Mutual Fund)
Transmission: Modem, Disk

Start-Up Cost: $85 (software and data)
Current Quote Fees: $60/month for unlimited access to stocks, commodities and indexes
Historical Quote Fees: $1.50/year for stock history, $2.25/contract for commodities
System(s): IBM or Macintosh

Description: Provides historical and daily price data on stocks, futures, mutual funds and options. Stock information dates back to 1983; futures information to 1968. Index, option and mutual fund data date back to 1990. Information can be downloaded via modem or is available on disk. Start-up package includes: Navigator communication and data management software, 7 months of updating and 5 years of continuous contracts for 21 commodities or 5 years of stock history for the Dow Jones Industrial Average stocks.

Glance Market Data Services   (800) 663-8936
171 West Esplanade   (604) 984-6222
Suite 200   fax: (604) 984-8171
North Vancouver, BC V7M 3J9
Canada

Product: FUTURE ACCESS*
Provides: Current Quotes (Stock, Index, Bond, Option, Futures, Mutual Fund), Historical Quotes (Stock, Index, Bond, Option, Futures, Mutual Fund), Charting, Technical Indicators
Transmission: Modem, Disk
Start-Up Cost: $99
Access Fees: $25/year
Current Quote Fees: $35-$99/month
Historical Quote Fees: Depends on length of data and ranges from $30 to $75 U.S.
System(s): IBM PC, 640K, hard disk

Description: Provides access to end of day data for major commodity markets in North America and London through global and local telephone networks. File transfer involves data compression which leads to reduced file size, transfer time, communication expenses and disk space. Supports ASCII, Compu Trac, CSI, Technical Tools and MetaStock file formats and automatically updates files daily. Menu-driven system provides data management, electronic mail, printing and graphics printing for over 200 dot matrix, inkjet and laser printers. Bar and candlestick charts are plotted along with moving averages, relative strength, spreads and stochastics. Options and features include six data packages holding as few as 27 commodities of 150 contracts or 97 commodities with more than 450 contracts. A personal portfolio can be arranged with only those items the user wants to follow.

Heizer Software   (800) 888-7667
1941 Oak Park Boulevard   (510) 943-7667
Suite 30   fax: (510) 943-6882
Pleasant Hill, CA 94523

Product: DOW INDUSTRIALS
Provides: Historical Quotes (Index)
Transmission: Disk
Start-Up Cost: $12
System(s): IBM or Macintosh, Excel or Works software

Description: Provides monthly price averages for the Dow Jones Industrials. Provides monthly averages from 1951 through 1990.

Product: DOW MONTH-BY-MONTH SET
Provides: Historical Quotes (Index)
Transmission: Disk
Start-Up Cost: $25
System(s): IBM or Macintosh, Excel or Works software

Description: Provides monthly averages of Dow Jones industrials, transportation, utility and composite for the last 35 years.

Product: S&P DAILY 1980-1990 (formerly S&P Daily 1980's)
Provides: Historical Quotes (Index)
Transmission: Disk
Start-Up Cost: $39
System(s): IBM PC or Macintosh, Excel or Works software

Description: Provides daily closing prices for the S&P composite. Includes prices for every trading day from 1/1/80 to 12/31/90. Includes monthly S&P dividend yields and monthly T-bill rates.

Product: S&P DAILY 1953-1991
Provides: Historical Quotes (Index)
Transmission: Disk
Start-Up Cost: $99
System(s): IBM or Macintosh, Excel or Works software

Description: Provides daily prices for the S&P 500 stock price index going back to 1953.

Product: S&P 1957-1991 MONTHLY
Provides: Historical Quotes (Index)
Transmission: Disk
Start-Up Cost: $12
System(s): IBM or Macintosh, Excel or Works software

Description: Provides monthly averages of the S&P Stock Price Index going back to 1957.

Information Edge, Inc. (800) 334-3669
96 Lake Drive W. (201) 305-8440
Wayne, NJ 07470

Product: FUND/SEARCH FOR FUNDS*
Provides: News (Business, Company, Economic News/Data), Current Quotes (Stock, Index, Bond, Option, Futures, Mutual Fund), Historical Quotes (Stock, Mutual Fund), Financial Statement Data, SEC Filings, Earnings Estimates, Mutual Fund Screening
Transmission: Modem
Start-Up Cost: $95 Demo; $295 for current database
Access Fees: Mutual fund data—$295/year
Current Quote Fees: $0.36/minute online quotes and analysis plus news
System(s): PC-AT 640K RAM; 20 MB Hard Drive

Description: Program allows users to view and analyze—screen, sort, graph—historical mutual fund information. Features include: graphic analysis of 7 historical performance measures including annual/total return, yield, NAV, etc.; comparative graphics allowing users to display as many as 5 different mutual funds simultaneously; hypothetical portfolio allows users to create multiple portfolios of funds, diversify the portfolios to minimize risk (using modern portfolio theory algorithms), and to graphically compare their performance. Screens and sorts on more than 30 user-defined criteria such as risk and beta; annual yield; and annual or total return for 1 month, 3 months, 1-, 5- and 10-year periods. Hypothetical illustrations on investment return, varying the amount and period of investment, reinvestment and load assumptions, may be developed. Results may be saved to a file or printed.

Product: FUND/SEARCH FOR FUNDS II*
Provides: News (Business, Company, Economic News/Data), Current Quotes (Stock, Index, Bond, Option, Futures, Mutual Fund), Historical Quotes (Stock, Mutual Fund), Financial Statement Data, SEC Filings, Earnings Estimates, Mutual Fund Screening
Transmission: Modem
Start-Up Cost: $95 Demo; $295 for current database
Access Fees: Mutual fund data—$295 per year
Current Quote Fees: $0.36/minute online quotes and analysis plus news
System(s): PC-AT 640K RAM; 20 MB hard drive

Description: Users can view and analyze—screen, sort, graph—historical mutual fund information. Features: graphic analysis of 7 historical performance measures, including annual/total return, yield, NAV, etc.; comparative graphics allows users to display as many as 5 different mutual funds simultaneously; hypothetical portfolio allows users to create multiple portfolios of funds, diversify the portfolios to minimize risk (using modern portfolio theory algorithms) and to graphically compare their performance. Screens and sorts on more than 30 user-defined criteria such as risk and beta; annual yield; and annual or total return for 1 month, 3 months, 1-, 5- and 10-year periods. Hypothetical illustrations on investment return, varying the amount and period of investment, reinvestment and load assumptions may be developed. Results may be saved to a file or printed.

Intex Solutions, Inc. (617) 449-6222
35 Highland Circle fax: (617) 444-2318
Needham, MA 02194

Product: INTEX CMO/REMIC MODELING SERVICE*
Provides: News (Business, Company)
Transmission: Disk

Start-Up Cost: Varies
System(s): IBM

Description: Program "reverse engineers" agency CMOs or REMICs using a proven CMO Macro Modeling Language. Supplied by the 10th of each month, each new agency CMO prospectus is translated into descriptive files. These files can be integrated into existing analytic systems or fed directly into the Intex OAS Model for CMOs or the Intex CMO/REMIC Modeling Toolkit. Systems provide a full range of option-adjusted spread analytics and static measures.

Invest/Net (305) 384-1500
3265 Meridian Parkway
Suite 130
Ft. Lauderdale, FL 33331

Product: INSIDER TRADING MONITOR
Provides: News (Business), SEC Filings, Stock Screening (Fundamental Factors)
Transmission: Modem, Disk
Access Fees: $1/per minute ($35/month minimum)
System(s): Any computer, modem, communications software

Description: A database of all securities transactions by officers, directors and major shareholders of all publicly held corporations required to file under the Securities Act of 1934. Tracks securities by watch list and provides summary and ranking reports by list or portfolio. Over 9,600 U.S. securities are tracked including those on the pink sheets, and over 30,000 transactions, updated within 24 hours of release by the SEC, are added monthly. Includes the Toronto Stock Exchange listed companies. The service tracks all Form 144 filings (intention to sell) daily. Also available through DJN/R.

Investability Corporation (312) 822-0237
P.O. Box 11162
Chicago, IL 60611

Product: INVESTABILITY MUTUAL FUND DATABASE*
Provides: Mutual Fund Screening
Transmission: Disk

Access Fees: $29.95/quarter, $99.95/year (4 shipments)
System(s): IBM PC or compatible, 640K, hard disk, internal clock

Description: Information on over 2,700 mutual funds. Includes total assets, year started, address/phone, investment objective; minimum/maximum loads; most-recently reported expense ratio; minimum purchase requirements; latest quarter, 1-, 3-, 5- and 10-year returns on a before- and after-load basis. Has statistical measures—beta, alpha, R-square and standard deviation. Funds can be sorted and ranked by return as a whole or by objective. After-load rankings show how a $1,000 investment would have grown over the selected time period. Fund family sort tables list the funds distributed by more than 300 companies. User can find individual funds or distribution companies. Help is through on-line screens and disk-resident documentation.

Investment Company Data, Inc. (800) 735-4234
2600 72nd Street (515) 270-8600
Suite A fax: (515) 270-9022
Des Moines, IA 50317

Product: ICDI MUTUAL FUND DATABASE*
Provides: Current Quotes (Mutual Fund), Historical Quotes (Mutual Fund), Charting, Technical Indicators, Stock Screening (Technical Factors), Mutual Fund Screening
Transmission: Modem, Disk
Start-Up Cost: $50
Current Quote Fees: Non-prime: fund profiles—$0.35/fund; NAV (daily and monthly)—$0.01/NAV; distribution—$0.12/distribution; monthly total return—$0.20
System(s): Any computer, modem, communications software

Description: Mutual fund database and analysis software. Database includes total returns, total net assets, net asset values, distributions, asset compositions, cash flow analysis, loads and more for over 2,800 mutual funds and indices. The monthly database begins in 1962 or the fund's inception date; daily database begins in 1971 for 200 funds and as early as 1985 for the remainder. Software packages for subscribers include a monthly data spreadsheet, Hypothetical, Asset Allocation and Online Systems. Hypothetical System provides performance reports and graphs of users' hypothetical investments in a fund or portfolio. Asset Allocation System determines how to allocate assets to receive the optimal return. Online System provides a direct link to the daily database of performance, statistical and fund profile information which can be calculated between any two dates.

Investment Technologies, Inc.   (908) 494-1200
510 Thornall Street   fax: (908) 906-0209
Suite 190
Edison, NJ 08837

Product: VESTOR
Provides: News (Economic News/Data), Current Quotes (Stock, Index, Option, Futures), Historical Quotes (Stock, Index, Option, Futures), Financial Statement Data, Analyst Reports, Charting, Technical Indicators, Stock Screening (Fundamental Factors, Technical Factors)
Transmission: Modem
Start-Up Cost: $49.99 for direct dial in service (includes $50 usage credit)
Access Fees: CompuServe—$15/hour surcharge; GEnie—$2-$4/report; Direct Dial-in $2-$4/report
System(s): Any computer, modem, communications software

Description: On-line equity analysis system. Offers buy/sell recommendations on 6,000 stocks, options, futures and market indexes. Uses technical and fundamental analysis to evaluate equities. Includes screening, portfolio management and analysis, options, futures and averages. Access through Quotron, GEnie, Delphi and DIAL/DATA.

Iverson Financial Systems, Inc.   (415) 349-4767
1020 Foster City Boulevard   fax: (415) 349-4954
Suite 290
Foster City, CA 94404

Product: SHD (SECURITIES HISTORY DATA)
Provides: Historical Quotes (Stock, Index, Mutual Fund), Technical Indicators, Stock Screening (Technical Factors)
Transmission: Modem, Disk, Tape, Cartridge
Historical Quote Fees: Daily: $0.0025/data point, Weekly: $0.01/data point, Monthly: $0.03/data point, special packages available at discounted prices
System(s): Any computer, modem, communications software

Description: Covers end-of-day data for equity issues and indicators for the NYSE, AMEX, NASDAQ, Toronto and Montreal exchanges from 1980 to present (some issues date back to 1972). End of day data for mutual funds and money market information available back to 1986. Data includes: open, high, low, close and volume; dividends and splits; earnings; shares outstanding; rating; corporate actions. Data may be received in ASCII, Lotus 1-2-3, MetaStock or Compu Trac file format; transmitted at up to 9600 baud; or 9 track, 1,600 bpi, standard 1/2 inch magnetic tape or UNIX compatible tape cartridge.

J & J Financial Company◆ (800) 748-0805
9311 San Pedro Avenue (512) 349-2181
Suite 510 fax: (512) 349-8967
San Antonio, TX 78216

Product: MUTUAL FUND ANALYZER◆
Provides: Current Quotes (Mutual Fund), Mutual Fund Screening
Transmission: Disk
Start-Up Cost: $265
Access Fees: $85
System(s): IBM

Description: Menu-driven program includes historical simulation. Investment results which would have been achieved over some select past time period for any combination of asset classes and relative weightings can be created. Initial dollar values, cash flows in and out of the funds and all loads can be inserted. Results are shown in tabular and graphical forms. Return histograms are provided. Performance Measurement consists of 2 facilities. First, the performance summary presents the 1 month, quarter, most recent year, most recent 3 years and most recent 5 years of return on either an annualized basis or a cumulative basis; second, the regression system provides the ability to run least squares regression analysis of 1 time series as the independent variable and up to 8 dependent variables. Ranking ranks, for any selected time frame, all asset classes with a sector on 1 of 3 different criteria: rate of return (descending order), standard deviation of return (ascending order) or rate of return/ standard deviation (descending order). Output display includes the ranked asset classes with percentile ranks within sector, annualized rate of return, standard deviation and return/standard deviation. Data Management has 3 functions. It copies the monthly update of the data files from floppy disk to the hard disk subdirectory, reassigns the sector assessment of a particular asset class and exports an asset class return time series to an external ASCII file.

Product: MUTUAL FUND AND PORTFOLIO MANAGERS DIRECTORY◆
Provides: News (Business, Company), Mutual Fund Screening
Transmission: Disk
Start-Up Cost: $195
Access Fees: $55
System(s): IBM

Description: Menu-driven database of over 2,600 mutual funds that contains specific information about each fund: management company, portfolio manager, address, phone numbers, fees, investment objectives, asset class distributions, etc. Current month returns and percentile rankings of returns are provided for 10 different time intervals. Allows sorting and retrieving across all functions (returns, rankings of return, fees, etc.) and inserting returns into the system and ranking of returns against a mutual fund database, specific types of funds (equity, fixed income, municipal and money market) and specific investment objectives (aggressive growth, special funds, high quality corporate bonds, etc.).

Keystone Investment Systems (317) 259-6303
4720 Kingsway Drive fax: (317) 251-0418
Suite 100
Indianapolis, IN 45205

Product: HOFFMAN BOND UPDATE*
Provides: Analyst Reports, Technical Indicators, Stock Screening (Technical Factors)
Transmission: Modem
Access Fees: All calls: $1.50 for first minute; $0.75/additional minute
System(s): Any computer, modem, communications software

Description: A Treasury bond report that forecasts trading ranges for the cash 30-year Treasury bond, cash 10-year Treasury bond and bond futures contracts trading on the CBOT, every hour on the hour during the trading day. A caller-paid investment information service accessed via touch-tone telephone. Every hour the system predicts the next hour's high and low ranges for T-bonds and futures, predicts whether the next hour's pattern will be bullish or bearish; makes buy and sell recommendations and price level recommendations for each market and projects daily high and low ranges for each market. At the end of the day, the update carries a T-bond recap and predictions for the next day's highs and lows. The model utilizes principles of quantum mechanics and chaos theory to predict market turning points and market price ranges.

Knight-Ridder Financial Publishing (800) 621-5271
(formerly Commodity Perspective) (312) 454-1801
30 S. Wacker Drive fax: (312) 454-0239
Suite 1820
Chicago, IL 60606

Product: CP HISTORICAL DATA
Provides: Historical Quotes (Option, Futures)
Transmission: Disk
Historical Quote Fees: 1-3,000 quotes/order—$0.03/quote; over 3,000 quotes/order—$0.015/quote
System(s): IBM PC or compatible

Description: Historical price information on over 300 futures, options and cash markets. Daily prices go back 50 years in some markets.

Lotus Development Corp. (800) 343-5414
55 Cambridge Parkway (617) 577-8500
Cambridge, MA 02142 fax: (617) 225-7058

Product: LOTUS ONE SOURCE
Provides: Historical Quotes (Stock, Index, Bond, Option, Futures, Mutual Fund), Financial Statement Data, SEC Filings, Analyst Reports
Transmission: CD-ROM
Access Fees: $7,000 to $20,000/year subscription
System(s): IBM PC, XT, AT PS/2 or compatible with 640K

Description: System of business and financial information products. These integrated systems enable user to organize, analyze and disseminate information. The CD/Investment product line (U.S.

Equities, U.S. Research, International Equities) provides U.S. and international financial information on companies, stocks and financial issues. Full integration with Lotus 1-2-3. Includes: Standard & Poor's Compustat, Muller, Ford, Lynch, Jones & Ryan, Interactive Data, Media General and Value Line. The CD/Corporate product line (U.S. Public Companies, U.S. Private+, U.S. Mergers and Acquisitions, U.K. Public Companies, U.K. Private Companies, European M&A) contains a range of U.S. and international company financial, textual and M&A information. Data providers include: UMI/Data Courier, Disclosure, Thomson, Media General, Market Guide, MacMillan, Predicasts, ICC, Extel and IDD. The CD/Banking product line (commercial banks, bank holding companies, savings banks, savings and loans) contains U.S. bank data for users specializing in correspondent banking, bank acquisition and credit analysis. Transfers data to 1-2-3.

Lowry's Reports, Inc. (407) 842-3514
631 U.S. Highway One fax: (407) 842-1523
Suite 305
North Palm Beach, FL 33408

Product: LOWRY'S MARKET TREND ANALYSIS DATABASE ON DISKETTE
Provides: Current Quotes (Index), Historical Quotes (Index), Technical Indicators
Transmission: Disk
Access Fees: $25/year plus $2.50/month for periods less than one year; 15% discount for AAII members
System(s): IBM PC or compatible

Description: Daily information provided from 1/1/40 for DJIA high, low and close; Lowry's Buying Power Index, Selling Pressure Index and Short-Term Index; NYSE advances, declines, unchanged issues; NYSE upside volume, downside volume, unchanged volume; NYSE points gained and points lost; NYSE new highs and lows (from 1962+); and Lowry's average power rating (weekly from 1950+). Points, volume and issues measure internal strength of the market. Calculates 6-, 12-, 30-, 60-, 90-, 120- and 200-day moving averages. Can use trend and relationship of the 30-day figures to confirm the buying power and selling pressure indexes. Points, issues and volume can be displayed as cumulative indexes or as a difference of values plotted as an oscillator. Cumulative index of net points is an unweighted index of the broad market derived from the net gains and losses of all issues traded daily on the NYSE. Disk is in ASCII, MetaStock or Compu Trac format.

Lynch, Jones & Ryan   (212) 243-3137
345 Hudson Street
New York, NY 10014

Product: INSTITUTIONAL BROKERS' ESTIMATE SYSTEM (I/B/E/S)
Provides: News (Business), Earnings Estimates, Financial Statement Data
Transmission: Modem
Current Quote Fees: Expanded report $2.00/company; Brief report $0.50/company
System(s): Any computer, modem, communications software, Compu-Serve account

Description: Provides consensus earnings estimates on over 3,400 publicly traded corporations. Estimates are compiled from earnings forecasts made by over 2,500 professional securities analysts at 145 brokerage and research firms. Takes individual earnings estimates and groups them by company and by fiscal period. Average earnings estimates for the current and next fiscal year and the 5-year projected growth rate are then produced. Available through Compu Serve.

Market Momentum Services   (800) 873-5682
111 Pavonia Avenue   (201) 420-3878
Jersey City, NJ 07310   fax: (201) 963-4817

Product: MARKET MOMENTUM SERVICES*
Provides: News (Business, Company), Historical Quotes (Stock, Index, Bond, Futures), Technical Indicators, Stock Screening (Fundamental Factors, Technical Factors)
Transmission: Modem
Access Fees: $250/month, $2,500 annually
System(s): IBM PC compatible, 2400 baud modem

Description: Uses a proprietary system to measure macro and micro momentum within the general market. Uses over 14 pieces of market information—over 3 time periods—to measure trader's (10-30 day) and investor's (30-90 days) momentum within the general marketplace and over 5,000 individual equities. Market commentary (including specific trading strategies) covering the general market, S&P spot futures contract, 30-year bond spot futures, spot gold and spot-soft crude is updated daily at midnight. A mid-day update reflects any changes in opinion or late breaking developments during the trading day. Also available daily are Gabriel's early buy and early sell candidates.

MarketView Software, Inc. (312) 786-0110
2020 Dean Street fax: (708) 377-7940
Suite D1
St. Charles, IL 60174

Product: MARKETVIEW
Provides: News (Business), Current Quotes (Index, Option, Futures, Mutual Fund), Historical Quotes (Index, Futures), Charting, Technical Indicators
Transmission: Satellite
Current Quote Fees: $595/month plus exchange fees
System(s): IBM AT, PS/2 and compatible with 640K, EGA or VGA graphics and 40 MB hard disk

Description: Combines real-time data and software to produce a graphic presentation of market price information. Features: high resolution color graphics; U.S. and foreign options and futures data; multi-window display screens; options valuation and analysis; major world cash market prices; portfolio valuation; intra- and inter-day history; technical analysis; volatility charts; news story alerts and more.

Mead Data Central, Inc. (800) 227-9597
9443 Springboro Pike (513) 865-6800
P.O. Box 933 fax: (513) 865-6909
Dayton, OH 45401-9964

Product: LEXIS FINANCIAL INFORMATION SERVICE
Provides: News (General, Business, Company, Economic News/Data), Current Quotes (Stock, Index, Bond, Mutual Fund), Historical Quotes (Stock, Index, Bond, Mutual Fund), Financial Statement Data, SEC Filings, Analyst Reports, Earnings Estimates
Transmission: Modem
Start-Up Cost: $50

Access Fees: $50/month
Current Quote Fees: $1.00/quote plus connect time
Historical Quote Fees: $0.15/price observation, $0.25/dividend observation plus connect time
System(s): MDC Session Manager required

Description: In addition to stock quotes, contains international news and country analysis reports by country, region and topic. It also offers the ALERT library, which carries news updated every 3 hours. International files can be searched all at once, by country or by region. Part of the NEXIS service of Mead Data Central, which is a computer-assisted electronic information service offering full-text articles from hundreds of the world's leading news and business sources, including the *New York Times*.

Media General Financial Services   (800) 446-7922
301 E. Grace Street   (804) 649-6587
Richmond, VA 23219   fax: (804) 649-6097

Product: MEDIA GENERAL DATABASE SERVICE
Provides: Historical Quotes (Stock, Index, Mutual Fund), Financial Statement Data, Technical Indicators, Stock Screening (Fundamental Factors, Technical Factors), Mutual Fund Screening
Transmission: Modem, Disk, CD-ROM
Start-Up Cost: Varies with service
Current Quote Fees: Varies with service
Historical Quote Fees: Varies with service
System(s): IBM for disk updates; any computer, modem, communications software for on-line access

Description: Provides statistical information on all NYSE and AMEX listed common stocks and NASDAQ National Market issues. Includes income statement and balance sheet data, historical price and volume statistics and calculated fundamental and technical ratios. Maintains large databases which track mutual funds, industries and the financial markets. All or selected parts of data is available on-line through Dialog, Dow Jones News/Retrieval, Telescan, Thomson Financial Networks and Warner. Lotus One Source provides the common stock database on CD-ROM. Customized IBM PC diskettes, hard copy reports and magnetic tapes are available from Media General.

MFD, Inc. (415) 664-7777
1 San Marcos Avenue
San Francisco, CA 94116

Product: MUTUAL FUND ONLINE DATABASE
Provides: Current Quotes (Index, Mutual Fund), Technical Indicators, Stock Screening (Technical Factors), Mutual Fund Screening
Transmission: Modem, Disk
Start-Up Cost: $175; 20% discount for AAII members
Access Fees: $20/month
System(s): IBM PC

Description: A software and on-line database. Compares mutual funds and analyzes the optimal time to buy and sell. Data is acquired automatically via modem within 24 hours after the close of the market each week. (A weekly data disk is available via mail.) Database contains 275 funds. Data, adjusted for dividends and distributions, includes current market price, exponential moving averages (EMA), percent change in NAV, modified momentum, load-adjusted percent and beta-adjusted percent gain(loss) calculated on 4-, 13-, 26-, 39- and 52-week basis. Menu-driven sorting system allows relative performance of any fund to be viewed with any desired parameters. Graphs allow the choice of the NAV plus any 2 EMAs or a market index or a second fund for viewing comparative performance. Investment guidelines for using the data are offered for consideration and use.

Micro Code Technologies (212) 983-9839
501 5th Avenue fax: (212) 697-9395
22nd Floor
New York, NY 10017

Product: FREE FINANCIAL NETWORK (FFN)
    (formerly Financial Software Exchange)
Provides: News (Business), Historical Quotes (Stock, Index, Bond, Option, Futures, Mutual Fund), Analyst Reports, Charting, Technical Indicators
Transmission: Modem
Start-Up Cost: Free to end-users
Access Fees: Free to end-users
System(s): IBM compatible modem, communications software

Description: A 64-line BBS for financial computing. Includes: closing stock quotes, financial magazines, professional associations, investment newsletters, recommendations, investment and financial computing roundtables and forums. Sections can be rented for distribution to financial customers. Up to 9600 baud capability on-line 24 hours a day. Set up free account by typing NEW when asked for user ID.

MJK Associates (408) 456-5000
1885 Lundy Avenue fax: (408) 456-0302
#207B
San Jose, CA 95131-1835

Product: MJK
Provides: Current Quotes (Stock, Index, Futures), Historical Quotes (Stock, Index, Futures)
Transmission: Modem, Disk
Start-Up Cost: $35-$50
Historical Quote Fees: Varies with type and amount of data
System(s): Any computer, modem, communications software

Description: A time-sharing commodity data information service with daily futures and cash data for all major commodities and about 700 stock issues. Available 24 hours a day, 7 days a week with local phone access in most U.S. cities and world capitals. Features include simulation, evaluation, optimization and data downloading service.

MP Software, Inc.♦ (800) 735-0700
P.O. Box 37 (617) 449-8460
Needham Heights, MA 02194 fax: (617) 449-3978

Product: MARKET BASE♦
Provides: Historical Quotes (Stock), Financial Statement Data, Charting, Stock Screening (Fundamental Factors)
Transmission: Disk
Access Fees: Varies; intro package with complete database, $59
System(s): IBM PC, hard disk

Description: An advanced fundamental analysis system and data-on-disk subscription service for over 4,500 common stocks on the NYSE, AMEX and NASDAQ National Market System. Data Includes companies' 5-year and interim quarterly financial histories from the income statement, balance sheet and cash flow report combined with last closing price, numerous ratios and relationships, institutional and closely held positions, etc. Includes closing price trend graphs for the last 60 months and 52 weeks. Capabilities include screening on over 100 data fields, sorting by any field, report generator, creation of new relationships and weighted scores and changeable display formats. Choose weekly, monthly or quarterly updates.

National Computer Network   (800) 942-6262
1929 N. Harlem Avenue   (312) 622-6666
Chicago, IL 60635   fax: (312) 622-6889

Product: ACCURON
Provides: Current Quotes (Stock, Index, Option, Futures), Historical Quotes (Stock, Index, Bond, Option, Futures, Mutual Fund)
Transmission: Modem
Start-Up Cost: $129.95
Current Quote Fees: Historical data $0.03/issue per day; Daily data $0.04/issue per day
System(s): IBM PC with modem

Description: Combined software and database system providing access to over 195,000 securities including stock, corporate and government bonds, mutual funds, indexes, financial and commodity futures and all U.S.-listed stock, index and futures options. Requests are entered off-line; the program then automatically accesses the database, retrieves the data and formats for use in analytical software. Data formats supported include Compu Trac, Swing Trader, Meta-Stock, Orion/CSI, Investor's Tool Kit, Quick Plot, Memory Systems Inc., Micro Vest, Lotus and Dow Jones Market Analyzer.

Product: LIVE-LINE*
Provides: Current Quotes (Stock, Index, Option, Futures)
Transmission: Modem
Current Quote Fees: $6-$10/hour, $25 monthly minimum charge
System(s): IBM PC with modem

Description: Menu-driven, real-time quote display system that monitors all U.S. equities, options, indices, futures and options of futures. Monitors up to 66 issues constantly, while affording access to any issue's real-time data. Provides theoretical values for stock, index and future options.

Product: NITE-LINE
Provides: Historical Quotes (Stock, Index, Bond, Option, Futures, Mutual Fund)
Transmission: Modem, Disk
Start-Up Cost: $30
Current Quote Fees: $9-$34
System(s): Any computer, modem, communications software

Description: Financial database provides closing market data and up to 12 years of historical data from all U.S. and some Canadian exchanges on commodity futures, futures options, stocks, indices, stock options, bonds and mutual funds. Data includes high, low, close, open interest, volume, bid, ask, settle and more. An off-line data service has most of the data going back to 1972 with some data extending back to 1929. Data formats include 9 or 10 character, right or left justified, decimal, fractional, RTR and spreadsheet.

NewsNet (800) 345-1301
945 Haverford Road (215) 527-8030
Bryn Mawr, PA 19010

Product: NEWSNET*
Provides: News (Business), SEC Filings, Analyst Reports, Technical Indicators
Transmission: Modem
Access Fees: $120/year or $15/month; $1/minute at 1200 baud, $1.50/minute at 2400 baud
System(s): Any computer, modem, communications software

Description: Specializes in the quick delivery of news and time-critical information. Offers full text retrieval of more than 350 business and industry newsletters, noted for high-value information content and timeliness. Finance-related newsletters cover areas such as security and industry analysis, SEC filings, federally insured instrument yields, technical market studies, insider stock trades, real asset investment and mutual fund investing. Electronic mail, indexed back issue search, constant updating and NewsFlash are some features. PR Newswire has over 7,000 news sources with detailed, timely information. Releases have names and telephone numbers for further contact. NewsFlash allows users to search for specific information at no extra cost.

Northfield Information Services, Inc.   (800) 262-6085
99 Summer Street   (617) 737-8360
Suite 1620
Boston, MA 02110

Product: NIS EQUITY RESEARCH SERVICE
Provides: Historical Quotes (Stock), Financial Statement Data, Earnings Estimates, Technical Indicators, Stock Screening (Fundamental Factors, Technical Factors)
Transmission: Disk
Access Fees: $16,500/year; 20% discount for AAII members
System(s): IBM PC or compatible

Description: A stock market database. More than 4,500 companies are analyzed each month by a series of 24 quantitative models. The models output over 70 numerical indicators which describe some value, risk or performance aspect of the stock. A consensus return forecast is also provided. Database updates are delivered monthly by mail for use in a supplied PC-based database management software package. Common tasks such as sorting or screening the data can be automated with keyboard macros, while report generation can range from simple tables to presentation quality complete with graphics. Data exchange with other software packages is supported.

Ohio Farm Bureau Federation   (614) 249-2427
Two Nationwide Plaza   fax: (614) 249-2200
6th Floor
Columbus, OH 43215

Product: AGRIQUOTE
Provides: News (Business, Economic News/Data), Current Quotes (Options, Futures), Historical Quotes (Futures), Charting, Technical Indicators
Transmission: Modem
Start-Up Cost: $149 plus $50
Access Fees: $239/year—includes all delayed quotes and basic news

Current Quote Fees: AgriVisor $250/year, Doanes $180/year, Pro Farmer $180/year, $347/year delayed, Real Time $99/month plus exchange fees
System(s): Any computer or printer with serial or parallel port

Description: Real-time market information service for commodity futures and options markets. Uses FM sidebands to deliver quotes in OH, MI and IL, and C-band home satellite (own the equipment) and KU-band satellite (equipment available for lease) in areas not covered by the FM sideband signal. Includes standard delayed quotes for all major exchanges, tick-by-tick quotations, options, USDA reports of U.S. agricultural weather, Midwest cash livestock and grain prices, specialty crop information and financial market information. AgriVisor and Doanes, for grain and livestock marketing advice, are available. Also includes electronic mail and BBS offering agricultural and market analysis programs and spreadsheets.

Oz Software, Inc.♦ (800) 359-9359
1400 Post Oak Boulevard (713) 877-1206
Suite 800 fax: (713) 877-1650
Houston, TX 77056

Product: INVESTMENT WIZARD♦
Provides: News (General, Business, Company, Economic News/Data), Analyst Reports
Transmission: Disk
Access Fees: $245/year for monthly updates; $390/year for biweekly updates
System(s): IBM

Description: A digest of investment and economic opinion and analysis from Wall Street analysts, economists and experts. Articles and reports from leading periodicals, magazines, newsletters and research reports are summarized and cross-referenced by analyst, investment subject, industry group, individual stock or mutual fund. All opinions are listed in both reverse chronological order and by the bias of the opinion—bullish or bearish. Analysts' or experts' previous opinions can be checked for accuracy using historical charts. Published twice monthly and is current to within 3 days of original publication. Information is stored on PC— no on-line charges.

Paradigm Trading Systems
330 Townsend Street
Suite 204
San Francisco, CA 94107

(415) 896-5433
fax: (415) 896-0488

Product: PARADIGM OPTIONS DATABASE*
Provides: Current Quotes (Stock, Index, Option, Futures), Historical Quotes (Stock, Index, Option, Futures)
Transmission: Modem
Start-Up Cost: $100
Access Fees: $100/month
System(s): Any computer, modem, communications software

Description: Provides delayed and historical data for stocks, indexes, options and futures. Historical data dates back 10 years. Data may be accessed by any computer or Paradigm produced programs which access and analyze the data.

PC Quote, Inc.
401 S. LaSalle Street
Suite 1600
Chicago, IL 60605

(800) 225-5657
(312) 786-5400
fax: (312) 427-8607

Product: PC QUOTE
Provides: News (Business), Current Quotes (Stock, Index, Bond, Option, Futures, Mutual Fund), Technical Indicators
Transmission: Satellite
Access Fees: $395/month plus exchange fees
System(s): IBM PS/2 models 50, 60, 70, 80 or approved compatible

Description: Delivers last-sale, bid/ask, open, high, low and volume quotations from U.S. stock, option and commodity exchanges and Canadian stock exchanges. Delivers dividends, P/E ratios, yields, 52-week high/low and mutual fund data. Features include limit minders and alerts, financial news, block (basket) tickers, option page, top 10-page and option theoretical values.

Prodigy Services Company
445 Hamilton Avenue
White Plains, NY 10601

(800) 822-6922
(914) 993-8000

Product: PRODIGY
Provides: News (General, Business, Company, Economic News/Data), Current Quotes (Stock, Index, Bond, Mutual Fund), Financial Statement Data, Analyst Reports, Stock Screening (Fundamental Factors), Mutual Fund Screening, On-Line Trading
Transmission: Modem
Start-Up Cost: $49.95
Access Fees: Basic service: $8.33-$12.95/month; Strategic Investor: $14.95/month
System(s): IBM PC with 512K, one disk drive, CGA, EGA, MCGA or Hercules graphics and 1200 or 2400 baud Hayes modem; Macintosh Plus or higher with Hayes 1200 or 2400 baud modum.

Description: General purpose on-line videotext service, a joint venture between IBM and Sears, that provides national and international news, weather, travel information, entertainment, features, BBS, games, computer news and shopping. Finance-related services include economic, market, industry and company news; stock, bond and mutual fund quotes; financial columns, on-line brokerage and banking; and finance-related BBSs. Strategic Investor, an optional service, provides data and screening on more than 4,500 stocks and 2,500 mutual funds. This data can be viewed on-line, printed or downloaded for use in other programs such as spreadsheets. Reports include investment strategies, economic, industry and company analyses and news.

Public Brand Software (800) 426-3475
P.O. Box 51315 (317) 856-7571
Indianapolis, IN 46251

Product: BUSINESS CONDITIONS DIGEST HISTORICAL DATA
Provides: News (Economic News/Data), Historical Quotes (Index)
Transmission: Disk
Start-Up Cost: $10
System(s): IBM PC or compatible

Description: Provides the same information as the Business Cycle Indicators; covers 41 years—1945 to 1986.

Product: BUSINESS CYCLE INDICATORS
Provides: News (Economic News/Data), Historical Quotes (Index)
Transmission: Disk

Access Fees: $100/year
System(s): IBM PC or compatible

Description: Official data on 250 economic indicators, indexes and composite indexes from the Department of Commerce, Bureau of Economic Analysis. Contains the last 4 years of data, by month, in a flat ASCII format that can be used in spreadsheets with some data manipulation through a provided program. Data includes GNP, personal consumption, M1, M2, Fed rate, average prime rate, CPI, PPI, production, vendor performance, business inventories, unemployment, overtime, payrolls, salaries, new orders, rentals, new incorporations, profits, S&P 500, housing starts, home loan rates, mortgage debt, delinquent loans, personal savings, retail sales, imports, exports, government purchases, defense department obligations and leading, lagging and coincidental indicators. Foreign economic, industrial and securities market data is provided for the U.K., Canada, West Germany, France, Italy, Japan and the OEC.

Quick & Reilly, Inc. (800) 634-6214
460 California Avenue (415) 324-4554
Suite 302
Palo Alto, CA 94306

Product: QUICKWAY
Provides: News (General, Business, Company, Economic News/Data), Current Quotes (Stock, Index, Option, Futures, Mutual Fund), Historical Quotes (Stock, Index, Option, Futures, Mutual Fund), Financial Statement Data, Analyst Reports, On-Line Trading
Transmission: Modem, Cable-TV
Access Fees: Prime time: $0.44/minute; non-prime: $0.27/minute
Historical Quote Fees: $0.04/quote
System(s): Any computer, modem, communications software

Description: Service to buy and sell securities 24 hours a day, receive real-time, delayed or historical security prices, automatically maintain tax records and manage a portfolio on-line. Users can specify price ranges and system flags price breakouts. Users can establish as many accounts as needed to handle a variety of securities. Can handle individual or joint accounts, IRA, Keogh, pension, profit sharing, custodial, trust, estate, corporate, partnership and investment club.

Quotron Systems, Inc.　　　　　　　　　　(800) 366-5050
5454 Beethoven Street　　　　　　　　　　　(212) 898-7148
Los Angeles, CA 90066　　　　　　　　fax: (212) 747-8752

Product: QUOTDIAL
Provides: News (Business), Current Quotes (Stock, Index, Bond, Option, Futures, Mutual Fund), Financial Statement Data, Technical Indicators,
Transmission: Modem
Start-Up Cost: $50
Access Fees: Plan A: monthly minimum $10; prime time $30/hour; non-prime $10/hour, plus exchange fees; Plan B: monthly minimum $175; high density location $10/hour; medium density $12/hour; low density $17/hour
System(s): Any computer, modem, communications software

Description: A dial-in service that accesses Quotron's price and market database. Provides real-time, 15-minute delay and after-market data on stocks, bonds, mutual funds, options, commodities and market indexes. Also offers intra-day graphs, market statistics, dividends and earnings information and earnings forecasts.

Rugg & Steele, Inc.♦　　　　　　　　　　(800) 237-8400
6433 Topanga Canyon Boulevard　　　　　　(818) 340-0179
Suite 108　　　　　　　　　　　　　　fax: (818) 702-8851
Canoga Park, CA 91303

Product: MUTUAL FUND SELECTOR♦
Provides: Historical Quotes (Mutual Fund), Mutual Fund Screening
Transmission: Disk
Access Fees: Monthly updates: equities or fixed income—$299/year, equities and fixed income—$499; Quarterly updates: equities or fixed income—$199/year, equities and fixed income—$299
System(s): IBM PC, hard disk or high density disk drive

Description: Provides 51 pieces of information on 1,230 equity funds and/or 1,030 bond funds. Data on 31 market indexes is also provided for comparison. Screening/filtering process allows users to create and display a temporary database consisting of only those mutual funds that meet the specified conditions. All reports can be applied to filtered groups of funds or the whole universe. Reports consist of:

Current Fund Ranking showing the absolute and decile rank for a single fund within most fields of the database; Averages showing the average value for all meaningful fields; Short-Term Performance containing the Rugg Consistency index along with the 1-, 3-, 6-, 9- and 12-month and year-to-date performance numbers; Long-Term Performance containing annual performance data for the last 3-, 5- and 10-year periods; Risk and Statistics containing various risk and statistical performance measures; Screening including data on loads, expenses, asset size, cash position, turnover rate, ticker, minimum initial and subsequent purchases, and the availability of telephone switching; Directory of Information Report containing information necessary to contact the funds; and Long-Term Market Index Report reporting on the 31 market indexes followed by the service.

S&P ComStock (formerly ComStock) (800) 431-5019
600 Mamaroneck Avenue (914) 381-7000
Harrison, NY 10528 fax: (914) 381-7021

Product: S&P COMSTOCK (formerly ComStock)
Provides: News (General, Business, Company), Current Quotes (Stock, Index, Option, Futures, Mutual Fund), Financial Statement Data, Analyst Reports, Technical Indicators,
Transmission: Modem, Satellite
Access Fees: $345/month and higher
System(s): Any computer, modem, communications software

Description: Provides real-time information from over 50 markets and exchanges—both domestic and international. Includes equities, options, futures, commodities, foreign exchange, currency analysis and news. Provides instantaneous retrieval on any issue from exchanges; system may be programmed for 10 user-defined pages holding 22 through 66 symbols. Offers Dow Jones Broadtape News, Dow Jones Corporate Report, Platt's Global Alert, MMS International's Currency Market Analysis and S&P MarketScope Alert for extra fees. Provides direct interface with many analytical software programs. Real-time software is available for charting and analysis, options evaluation, portfolio management and spreadsheet interface capabilities. Information is provided via satellite or dedicated phone line. Uses a receiver with its own memory and processor allowing PC to be turned off or applied to other uses while quotes are being continuously updated.

Savant Corporation♦ (800) 231-9900
120 Bedford Center Road
Bedford, NH 03110

Product: DISCLOSURE DATA FOR THE FUNDAMENTAL INVESTOR♦
Provides: Financial Statement Data
Transmission: Disk
Access Fees: Contact vendor
System(s): IBM PC

Description: A database of over 10,000 companies. Covers all major companies traded on the national exchanges and OTC markets as well as several thousand smaller companies. Service is available through 6 different subscription series. Information includes income statement and balance sheet items (e.g., assets and earnings); sales, net income and earnings per share growth rates; dividend yield; price/earnings and price/sales ratios; price as percent of book value; percent institutional and insider ownership.

Product: S&P'S DATA FOR THE FUNDAMENTAL INVESTOR♦
Provides: Financial Statement Data
Transmission: Disk
Access Fees: Contact vendor
System(s): IBM PC

Description: A database of over 4,000 companies. Covers all major companies traded on the national exchanges and OTC markets. Available through 4 different subscription series. Information includes income statement and balance sheet items (e.g., assets and earnings); sales, net income and earnings per share growth rates; dividend yield; price/earnings and price/sales ratios; price as percent of book value.

SEC Online, Inc. (516) 434-9000
400 Oser Avenue
Suite 2W
Hauppauge, NY 11788

Product: SEC ONLINE*
Provides: SEC Filings

Transmission: Modem
Access Fees: Varies depending on vendor
System(s): Any computer, modem, communications software

Description: Provides unedited reports filed by public corporations with the SEC. Files for each company trading on the NYSE, AMEX, and NASDAQ contain full-text copies of 10Ks, 10Qs, annual reports, proxy statements and 20Fs. A "resume" of basic corporate facts and information is located within each company file. Reports are indexed enabling users to scan any document easily. Users can download reports or instruct SEC Online to print a copy for shipment overnight. The system is currently available on Mead Data Central's Lexis Financial Information Network, Thompson Financial Network and Westlaw.

SilverPlatter Information, Inc. (800) 343-0064
100 River Ridge Drive (617) 769-2599
River Ridge Office Park fax: (617) 769-8763
Norwood, MA 02062

Product: PREDICASTS F&S INDEX PLUS TEST*
Provides: News (General, Business, Company, Economic News/Data), Analyst Reports
Transmission: CD-ROM
Access Fees: $2,500/year for U.S.; $3,500/year for international
System(s): IBM

Description: A digest of over 1,000 worldwide trade and business journals, periodicals, the business press and government publications. Includes full text and abstracts from the PROMT database in over 80% of the records. Includes: market share; merger and acquisition information; government regulations, expenditures and revenues; joint ventures; financial reporting.

Product: SEC ONLINE ON SILVERPLATTER*
Provides: News (Company), Financial Statement Data, SEC Filings
Transmission: CD-ROM
Access Fees: $1,600/year for quarterly updates
System(s): IBM PC, 640K, hard disk

Description: Full-text database containing 10Ks for all NYSE, AMEX and selected NMS/NASDAQ companies. The 10Ks appear as they are filed with the SEC including all footnotes, selected exhibits, business segment statement, financial, mergers and acquisitions, research and development, distribution, corporate strategy, subsidiaries, legal proceedings, accounting principles, new products/technology and competition. User can search for any word or phrase in the document.

Stock Data Corp. (301) 280-5533
905 Bywater Road fax: (301) 280-6664
Annapolis, MD 21401

Product: STOCK MARKET DATA
(formerly Stock Market Data on Diskette)
Provides: Historical Quotes (Stock, Index), Stock Screening (Technical Factors), Mutual Fund Screening, On-Line Trading
Transmission: Modem, Disk
Current Quote Fees: $1.50/day for 9000 issues; $450/year for weekly updates
System(s): IBM XT, AT or PS-2

Description: Provides stock market information for the NYSE, AMEX and NASDAQ markets collected daily and mailed weekly on diskette or downloaded via modem. Historical data is available from April 1987 and is stored in all of the most common formats. Some customization can be done free of charge, and "C" source code for direct data access can be provided. Several utility programs are included with any purchase: Lookup routine to view any issue instantly; Stock Screening to screen the entire market or any portion of the market for issues that meet specifications; Daily Volume Analysis to test for accumulation or distribution of an issue; Stock Symbol-Company Name to look up over 7,000 company names.

Street Software Technology, Inc. (212) 922-0500
230 Park Avenue fax: (212) 922-0588
Suite 857
New York, NY 10169

Product: DAILY PRICING SERVICE
Provides: Historical Quotes (Bond, Option, Futures)
Transmission: Modem, Disk
Access Fees: $450/month
System(s): Any computer

Description: Provides closing bid and asked quotes for a list of U.S. Treasury notes, bonds, bills, agencies, strips, mortgage-backed securities and interest rate futures/options. Includes CUSIP numbers for integration with user's system. Pricing files available by 5:00 p.m. EST. Local dial-up (domestic or international) at 1200/2400 baud available via the Telenet network.

Product: FIXED-INCOME PRICING SERVICES*
Provides: Current Quotes (Bond, Option, Futures), Historical Quotes
   (Bond, Option, Futures)
Transmission: Modem, Disk
Start-Up Cost: $300
Access Fees: Varies
System(s): Any computer

Description: Provides prices for Treasury notes, bonds and bills; Treasury strips; Mortgage-backed securities; U.S. agencies; REFCO strips; interest rate futures and options. Provides intra-day Treasury, agency and mortgage-backed security pricing and weekly CMO/REMIC pricing. Prices are obtained from the trading floor of a major primary dealer.

Product: TRADER'S SPREAD SYSTEM (TSS)
Provides: Current Quotes (Bond, Option, Futures), Historical Quotes
   (Bond, Option, Futures)
Transmission: Modem, Disk
Access Fees: $600/month
System(s): Any computer

Description: Menu-driven package. Accesses the manufacturer's 6-month database of prices and yields for U.S. Treasury and agency securities, financial futures and options and money market instruments. Has 10 different quote sheets that are updated by 5:00 EST. U.S. Treasury note/bond quote sheet includes weekend yield calculations.

Product: TREASURY HISTORICAL DATA
Provides: Historical Quotes (Bonds)
Transmission: Disk
Access Fees: Varies
System(s): Any computer

Description: Each data file contains an entire month of prices or yields; historical data from 1975. The source of data is the trading floor of a primary dealer. Contains Treasury notes, bonds, bills, agencies, strips, money market, mortgage-backed and fixed maturity treasuries/agencies. Individual categories also available.

Technical Tools (415) 948-6124
334 State Street fax: (415) 948-5697
Suite 201
Los Altos, CA 94022

Product: QUOTELINE DATA SERVICE
Provides: Historical Quotes (Stock, Index, Futures)
Transmission: Modem, Disk
Start-Up Cost: $50—software only; $150—software plus 6 months historical commodities data; $250—software plus 6 months historical equity data
Access Fees: $1/month maintenance fee
Current Quote Fees: $27-$132/month for stock, $35-$55/month for commodities
Historical Quote Fees: Package prices range from $100 and up
System(s): IBM PC

Description: Provides historical futures and index data in daily and tick form and historic data on 5,000 U.S. equities. Histories available individually or in packages. Market histories include every trading day for every contract traded, some dating back to 1968. Includes cash prices for most futures markets. Utility program allows user to translate data into any chosen format and over any interval. With additional software, user can create continuous contracts, update data daily and diagnose and correct problems in files. Monthly update-by-mail subscriptions are available. Starter kit includes 6 months of history for 35 commodities or stocks, $20 system credit and software.

Technova Research Inc.   (800) 228-2933
4747 Troost   (816) 931-5652
Kansas City, MO 64110

Product: TECHNOVA*
Provides: News (General, Business, Economic News/Data), Current Quotes (Stock, Index, Bond, Option, Futures, Mutual Fund), Historical Quotes (Index, Futures), Charting, Technical Indicators
Transmission: Modem, Satellite
Current Quote Fees: $575/month
System(s): IBM 386 PC, 1 MB RAM, 30 MB hard disk

Description: On-line trading system for futures and options on futures. Contains technical analysis studies and permits use of pre-programmed or self-designed technical indicators. Includes quote retrieval that can be displayed on customized screen and news retrieval (up to 24 hours old) via Knight-Ridder Commodity News Services. Supports up to 3,500 futures and futures options. Options analytic and real-time calculation of implied volatility are displayed for all options markets. Permits calculation of any type of option position or strategy (e.g., spreads, straddles).

Telemet America, Inc.   (800) 368-2078
325 First Street   (703) 548-2042
Alexandria, VA 22314

Product: POCKET QUOTE PRO
Provides: News (Business, Company), Current Quotes (Stock, Index, Bond, Option, Futures, Mutual Fund), SEC Filings, Technical Indicators
Transmission: FM
Start-Up Cost: $395
Current Quote Fees: $27.50/month
System(s): None if used portably; IBM PC, 192K, serial port, two disk drives, graphics card

Description: A hand-held, calculator-size quote monitor. Gives direct access to real-time stock, option, index and futures prices within about 50 miles of almost 2 dozen major metropolitan areas in the U.S. User can key in ticker symbols of any issue and stay in touch with all the markets. Features include the monitoring of 160 issues; programmable limit alerts will notify user when specific price or volume points are reached; flexible services (real-time and delayed quotes can be mixed); business headlines from DJN/R; computer interface capabilities.

Product: RADIO EXCHANGE
Provides: News (Business, Company), Current Quotes (Stock, Index, Bond, Option, Futures, Mutual Fund), SEC Filings, Technical Indicators
Transmission: Satellite, FM
Start-Up Cost: $394
Current Quote Fees: $33/month
System(s): IBM PC with 192K, one serial port, two disk drives, graphics card

Description: Digital radio interface that offers up-to-the-second market prices. Screen shows real-time stock, option, index and futures prices. Tracks up to 328 issues and charts intra-day and/or end-of-day prices. Price and volume limits on any issue can be programmed for immediate notice when limits are reached. Can export prices on up to 300 issues to other PC applications through a file utility. Other features include flexible services (real-time and delayed quotes on all exchanges in the U.S. can be selected and mixed); business news from Dow Jones News/Retrieval; integrated charting capability.

Product: TELEMET ENCORE
Provides: News (Business, Company), Current Quotes (Stock, Index, Bond, Option, Futures, Mutual Fund), SEC Filings, Technical Indicators
Transmission: FM
Access Fees: $139/month
Current Quote Fees: $27.50/month
System(s): IBM PC with 512K, one serial port, two disk drives, graphics card

Description: Offers up-to-the-second market prices and tracks almost 10,000 issues. File Export utility can export to other PC applications. Real-time stock, option, index and futures prices are available within 50 miles of almost 2 dozen metro areas by FM. Quotes, charts and news system using the Microsoft Windows environment offers multiple views of the markets. Program price and volume limits on any issues for alert when limits are reached. Features include flexible service options (real-time or delayed quotes can be selected and mixed); business news from Dow Jones News/Retrieval; integrated real-time 2-minute and/or end-of-day price charting; link to the Microsoft Excel spreadsheet in real-time for analysis and specialized computations; programmable price and volume points trigger alerts.

Product: TELEMET ORION SYSTEM
Provides: News (Business, Company), Current Quotes (Stock, Index, bond, Option, Futures, Mutual Fund), SEC Filings, Technical Indicators
Transmission: Satellite
Access Fees: $294/month
Current Quote Fees: $27.50/month
System(s): IBM PC with 640K, one serial port, two disk drives, graphics card

Description: Satellite delivered market quotation and news system that gives instant stock, option, index and futures quotes, real-time and historical charts and business news using Microsoft Windows. Features include: flexible service options (real-time and delayed services can be mixed); a hypertext interface to financial stories from Dow Jones News/Retrieval (headlines and in-depth stories); a link to the Microsoft Excel spreadsheet in real-time for analysis; programmable price and volume points that trigger alerts; ability to export quotes on 20,000 issues to other PC applications with a file export utility.

Telescan, Inc. (800) 324-8353
10550 Richmond Avenue (713) 952-1060
Suite 250 fax: (713) 952-7138
Houston, TX 77042

Product: TELESCAN ANALYZER
Provides: News (General, Business, Company), Current Quotes (Stock, Index, Mutual Fund, Option), Historical Quotes (Stock, Index,

Mutual Fund), Financial Statement Data, SEC Filings, Earnings Estimates, Charting, Technical Indicators, Stock Screening (Fundamental Factors, Technical Factors), Mutual Fund Screening

Transmission: Modem

Start-Up Cost: $99.95 (10% discount for AAII members); $25/year maintenance

Access Fees: Flat rate option—$45/month for unlimited non-prime; Standard database charges—$0.60/minute prime time, $0.30/minute non-prime time, 25% surcharge for 2400 baud access

System(s): IBM PC or 100% compatible with 384K; Hayes 1200 or 2400 baud modem. IBM color graphics or enhanced graphics adapter or Hercules adapter board; MS-DOS 2.1 or higher

Description: Combination of charting software and on-line data provides technical and fundamental indicators to analyze a database of more than 11,000 stocks (all NYSE, AMEX and NASDAQ), 2,000 mutual funds, 560 industry groups with 6 group indicators and market indexes. Updated approximately every 20 minutes. Information goes back 18 years. Graphs can be retrieved in 4 to 8 seconds and contain technical studies such as moving averages, MACD, stochastics and Welles Wilder RSI. Other data elements and features available include insider trading analysis, inflation adjustment, earnings estimates, on-line investment newsletters and news retrieval.

Product: TELESCAN EDGE

Provides: News (General, Business, Company), Current Quotes (Stock, Index, Option, Mutual Fund), Historical Quotes (Stock, Index, Mutual Fund), Financial Statement Data, SEC Filings, Earnings Estimates, Charting, Technical Indicators, Stock Screening (Fundamental Factors, Technical Factors)

Transmission: Modem

Start-Up Cost: $249; 10% discount for AAII members

Access Fees: $2/search prime time, $1/search non-prime or $15/month unlimited non-prime time searches; additional on-line access fees of $0.60/minute prime time (25% surcharge for 2400 baud), $0.30/minute non-prime (25% surcharge for 2400 baud)

System(s): IBM PC or compatible with 384K, two disk drives or hard disk, CGA, EGA, VGA or Hercules Graphics, Hayes 1200 or 2400 baud modem and Telescan Analyzer

Description: A security search program that works with the Telescan Analyzer. Searches more than 11,000 stocks listed in the NYSE, AMEX and NASDAQ using up to 15 criteria out of 50 fundamental and technical factors taking less than 15 seconds to find stocks or industry groups that fit the user's goals. Features: daily updates, scoring of every stock on each of 50 technical and fundamental indicators, weighing to emphasize more important criteria while still considering less important criteria, ability to specify which industry groups to include or exclude, scrolling lists and on-screen help menus, off-line compilation of search requests and integration with Telescan Analyzer.

Product: TELESCAN MUTUAL FUND EDGE*
Provides: News (General, Business, Company), Current Quotes (Stock, Index, Option, Mutual Fund), Historical Quotes (Stock, Index, Mutual Fund), Earnings Estimates, Charting, Technical Indicators, Mutual Fund Screening
Transmission: Modem
Start-Up Cost: $100; 10% discount for AAII members
Access Fees: $2/search prime time, $1/search non-prime or $15/month unlimited non-prime time searches; additional on-line access of $0.60/minute prime time (25% surcharge for 2400 baud), $0.30/minute non-prime (25% surcharge for 2400 baud)
System(s): IBM PC or compatible with 384K, two disk drives or hard disk, CGA, EGA, VGA or Hercules Graphics, Hayes 1200 or 2400 baud modem and Telescan Analyzer

Description: A mutual fund search program that works with the Telescan Analyzer. Sorts through more than 2,000 mutual funds divided into 24 categories. Users may search all funds or restrict the search to one or more categories; 20 of 80 different criteria may be used to screen funds. Features: scoring of every fund on each of the 80 factors, weighing to emphasize more important criteria while still considering less important criteria, scrolling lists and on-screen help menus, off-line compilation of search requests and integration with Telescan Analyzer.

Product: TELESCAN PROSEARCH*
Provides: News (General, Business, Company), Current Quotes (Stock, Index, Option, Mutual Fund), Historical Quotes (Stock, Index,

Mutual Fund), Financial Statement Data, SEC Filings, Earnings Estimates, Charting, Technical Indicators, Stock Screening (Funda-mental Factors, Technical Factors)

Transmission: Modem

Start-Up Cost: $395 plus $100 for optional forecasting module; 10% discount for AAII members

Access Fees: $2/search prime time, $1/search non-prime or $15/month unlimited non-prime time searches; additional on-line access of $0.60/minute prime time (25% surcharge for 2400 baud), $0.30/minute non-prime (25% surcharge for 2400 baud)

System(s): IBM PC or compatible with 384K, two disk drives or hard disk, CGA, EGA, VGA or Hercules Graphics, Hayes 1200 or 2400 baud modem and Telescan Analyzer

Description: An expanded security search program (versus Telescan Edge) that works with the Telescan Analyzer. Searches more than 11,000 stocks listed on NYSE, AMEX and NASDAQ. Uses up to 30 criteria out of 100 funda-mental and technical factors to return up to 200 securities in less than 15 seconds. Features: daily updates, scoring of every stock for 100 technical and fundamental indicators, weighing to emphasize more important criteria while still considering less important criteria, ability to specify which industry groups to include or exclude, scrolling lists and on-screen help menus, off-line compilation of search requests. Ranks stocks in order of how well they fit search criteria. Lets user back-test search strategies to find ones that worked in the past and integrate with Telescan Analyzer.

Thomson Financial Networks (800) 662-7878
(formerly InvesText, Div. of Thomson Financial) (617) 345-2000
11 Farnsworth Street fax: (617) 330-1986
Boston, MA 02210

Product: INVESTEXT/PLUS

Provides: News (Company, Economic News/Data), Historical Quotes (Stock), Financial Statement Data, Analyst Reports, On-Line Trading

Transmission: Modem

Start-Up Cost: $75 (includes $50 credit)

Access Fees: Online connect charge: $15.00/hour, plus online print/read charge: $5.50, offline print charge: $5.95

System(s): Any computer, modem, communications software

Description: On-line retrieval system for searching full-text databases of international company and industry reports from over 150 investment bands, consulting and research firms. System includes more than 200,000 reports covering 14,000 companies and 53 industries. Provides data and analysis on industry trends, market share, business strategies, emerging technologies and more. Access is also available to data from other services including CORIS, Data-Star, DIALOG, Dow Jones News/Retrieval, Ferntree Information, Kokusai Information Service, NewsNet and Lexis/Nexis. Reports are also available directly in presentation-quality laser-printed format.

Tick Data Inc. (800) 822-8425
720 Kipling Street (303) 232-3701
Suite 115 fax: (303) 232-0329
Lakewood, CO 80215

Product: TICK-BY-TICK HISTORICAL PRICE DATA (formerly Historical Tick-By-Tick Futures and Options Data)
Provides: Historical Quotes (Stock, Index, Option, Futures), Technical Indicators
Transmission: Modem, Disk
Start-Up Cost: $49
Historical Quote Fees: $10/month/commodity; $2/1,000 characters via modem
System(s): IBM PC, Macintosh

Description: Supplies historical time and sales data on futures and options contracts. Software converts data to Compu Trac, CSI, Lotus 1-2-3, MetaStock or ASCII formats; connects to Tick Data for dial-up service and displays and prints graphs. Diskette data from 1977; on-line data stores information for the last 45 trading days.

Trade*Plus (800) 972-9900
480 California Avenue (415) 324-4554
Suite 301
Palo Alto, CA 94306

Product: TRADE*PLUS*
Provides: News (General, Business, Company), Current Quotes (Stock, Index, Option, Futures), Historical Quotes (Stock, Index, Option, Futures), Analyst Reports, On-Line Trading

Transmission: Modem
Access Fees: $15/month minimum which includes 1st hour of connect time; access charges: $0.44/minute prime, $0.10/minute non-prime
System(s): Any computer, modem, communications software

Description: Real-time market quotation system. Displays last sale market prices and allows the purchase and sale of securities. Every stock and option listed in the *Wall Street Journal* can be traded with this service. Simple commands allow user to obtain quotes, place orders, and review portfolio and tax records. Price data can be transferred into spreadsheet programs. Users can receive information such as: high, low, close, volume, dividend, yield and current price. Additional services include instant comment service and historical data which is accessible through this system from other sources. Users place their orders through a number of brokers; call for the list. Orders that are ordinarily handled by a broker, such as stop-loss, good-till-canceled, buy, sell, and limit orders, margin purchases and short sales can be executed. Same brokerage fees as phone orders.

TRENDPOINT Software♦ (301) 949-8131
9709 Elrod Road
Kensington, MD 20895

Product: TRENDPOINT DATA LIBRARY♦
Provides: Historical Quotes (Index, Option, Futures, Mutual Fund), Technical Indicators
Transmission: Disk
Historical Quote Fees: $2.50-$3.50/data file (minimum order $25)
System(s): IBM PC

Description: Historical ASCII or MetaStock format data files. Use with Trendpoint, Trendtek, Lotus 1-2-3 and other analysis programs. Data includes over 200 stock market data files for all major stock averages, NYSE and NASDAQ breadth data, TRIN (Arms) index, new high/lows, trading volume, interest rates, short sales, most active stocks, futures premiums, OEX option volume and open interest and some mutual funds. Most daily data go back to 1972; some weekly data go back to 1928.

TriStar Market Data, Inc.　　　　　　　　　　(415) 627-2345
600 Montgomery Street
17th Floor
San Francisco, CA 94111

Product: MARKETMAX*
Provides: News (General, Business, Company, Economic News/Data), Current Quotes (Stock, Index, Bond, Option, Futures), Historical Quotes (Stock, Index, Bond, Option, Futures), Financial Statement Data, SEC Filings, Analyst Reports, Earnings Estimates, Charting, Technical Indicators
Transmission: Modem
Start-Up Cost: $2,250/office, $250/workstation
Access Fees: $750/month (exchange fees extra)
System(s): Macintosh, 68030, 2 MB RAM, 20 MB Hard disk

Description: Real-time financial market data information system utilizing the Macintosh point and click user interface to navigate customized windows. Can link with Wingz, a graphic spreadsheet from Informix Software, so a user-defined template can change with the flow of data. Graphs real-time of historical data tracing back 10 years. Simultaneously calculates implied volatility, delta and gamma on an options class using the most current data. Market diaries contain comprehensive active issues and top gainers and losers. Audible or visual notification upon triggering of pre-defined limits. Multi-source integrated news is accessible.

Unified Information　　　　　　　　　　(800) 862-7283
429 N. Pennsylvania　　　　　　　　　　　(317) 634-3300
Indianapolis, IN 46204　　　　　　　　fax: (317) 632-7805

Product: UNIFIED BROKERAGE SYSTEM*
Provides: Current Quotes (Stock, Index, Bond, Option, Futures, Mutual Fund), Historical Quotes (Stock, Index, Bond, Option, Futures, Mutual Fund), On-Line Trading
Transmission: Modem
Current Quote Fees: Prime time—$8/month, non-prime—$16/month
System(s): IBM, Macintosh, Atari, modem, communications software

Description: Provides on-line brokerage through the CompuServe network. Allows users to view account, enter brokerage orders, make purchases and redemptions of mutual funds and to have checks listed by expense category. Users can download account information. Requires an open brokerage account with Unified. There is no charge from CompuServe for the service.

Value Line Publishing♦ (800) 654-0508
711 Third Avenue (212) 687-3965
New York, NY 10017 fax: (212) 661-2807

Product: VALUE/SCREEN II♦
Provides: Financial Statement Data, Earnings Estimates, Stock Screening (Fundamental Factors)
Transmission: Modem, Disk
Access Fees: Quarterly update: $281/year; monthly updates: $396/year; weekly updates: $1,500/year
System(s): IBM, Macintosh

Description: Stock screening program based on information from Value Line. Supplies 50 critical fundamental data items on approximately 1,600 stocks. The user can simultaneously conduct stock screens based on up to 25 different criteria. All data can be downloaded to a spreadsheet program such as Lotus 1-2-3, Symphony or Excel. Includes a user guide.

Vickers Stock Research (800) 645-5043
226 New York Avenue (516) 423-7710
Huntington, NY 11743 fax: (516) 423-7715

Product: VICKERS ON-LINE
Provides: News (Business), Current Quotes (Stock, Bond, Mutual Fund), SEC Filings
Transmission: Modem
Access Fees: $50/year; $1/minute
System(s): Any computer, modem, communications software

Description: Provides access to the continuously updated institutional holdings and trading activity of stocks and corporate and convertible bonds. Includes insider trading activity such as Form 4s, 144s and 13Ds. Subscribers are given a personal access code and a user's manual. New subscribers receive up to 30 minutes of time free within their first month.

VU/TEXT Information Services, Inc. (800) 323-2940
325 Chestnut Street (215) 574-4400
Suite 1300 fax: (215) 627-0194
Philadelphia, PA 19106

Product: VU/TEXT INFORMATION SERVICES
Provides: News (General, Business, Company, Economic News/Data), Current Quotes (Stock, Index, Futures)
Transmission: Modem
Start-Up Cost: $50
Access Fees: $15/month plus $2.40/minute for newspaper, magazine, wire services
Current Quote Fees: $1.40/minute for stock and commodities quotes
System(s): Any computer, modem, communications software

Description: Provides up-to-date access to national and regional publications and market quotes. Includes the full text of over 60 newspapers and 160 regional business journals such as *Crain's New York Business*, *Business Atlanta* and *The Houston Business Journal*. Provides 15-minute delayed stock quotes (NYSE, AMEX and NASDAQ), commodity quotes, market summaries and real-time DJIA with its VU/QUOTE database. The Knight-Ridder Financial News database on VU/TEXT offers daily updated financial market information (part of Knight Ridder's MoneyCenter) including banking, economic issues, commodities, credit markets, the Federal Reserve, foreign exchange and indexes, energy and textiles. Other business information includes the full text of *Fortune* and *Money*, *The Journal of Commerce* with its transportation coverage and international trade and business news, Business Wire and PR Newswire's press releases from more than 10,000 companies, and *The Wall Street Transcript's* interviews and industry roundtables.

Warner Computer Systems, Inc. (800) 336-5376
17-01 Pollitt Drive (201) 797-4633
Fair Lawn, NJ 07410 fax: (201) 791-8717

Product: EXCHANGE MASTER (formerly Financial Access)
Provides: Current Quotes (Stock, Index, Bond, Option, Futures, Mutual Fund), Historical Quotes (Stock, Index, Bond, Option, Futures, Mutual Fund), Financial Statement Data, Analyst Reports
Transmission: Modem, Disk
Start-Up Cost: $60
Access Fees: Day rate $1.70/minute, night rate $0.60, or per quote: day $0.0495 first "100" and $0.0195 over "100"; night $0.0295 first "50" and $0.0075 over "50"
System(s): Any computer, modem, communications software

Description: Provides usage-based access to proprietary financial databases. Includes: stocks—end of day and historical pricing, dividend and earnings information on over 20,000 issues. Historical data are fully adjusted and date back 10 years. Futures—complete historical data on all U.S. exchanges and the Winnipeg exchange. Mutual funds—over 2,000 mutual funds with up to 10 years history on a daily or weekly basis; this includes same-day distribution and ex-date information, as well as NAVs. Stock and index options —contains data on all options including price (high, low, close), tickers, exchange and more. Data is kept for the life of the option plus 1 month after the expiration of the option. Corporate, government and municipal bonds—contains data on over 9,000 corporate bonds as well as Treasury and agency issues. Municipal bonds are added by request only. Bonds are priced weekly and monthly using a matrix system. Items include price, maturity date and coupon rate. Over 350 market indexes and indicators. With up to 10 years of history is available.

Western DataBase (916) 452-9009
3104 "O" Street
Suite 188
Sacramento, CA 95816

Product: 5-BY-500 DATABASE
Provides: Historical Quotes (Stock)
Transmission: Disk
Start-Up Cost: $289
Access Fees: $129/year for quarterly updates
System(s): IBM

Description: Database for simulation modeling and testing trading strategies. Contains the most recent 5 years of weekly trading history on the S&P 500 stocks with name, exchange, symbol, high, low, close, volume, trading days, dividend history, split adjustment factors, EPS, shares outstanding, industry code, S&P classification and betas. Also includes 5-year history of the S&P and Dow Jones composite indexes.

Worden Brothers (919) 490-5250
111 Cloister Court
Suite 104
Chapel Hill, NC 27514

Product: TELECHART 2000*
Provides: Current Quotes (Stock, Index), Historical Quotes (Stock, Index), Charting, Technical Indicators
Transmission: Modem, Disk
Start-Up Cost: $19; $5 discount for AAII members
Current Quote Fees: $0.0125/quote for first 50 quotes, $0.005/quote thereafter
Historical Quote Fees: $0.005/quote
System(s): IBM PC, hard disk, modem

Description: Includes software program and a dial-up database. Software downloads data, provides bar charts and popular and proprietary technical indicators and allows for exporting of data in ASCII format. A quote is one day's high, low, and close prices and volume.

X*Press Information Services Ltd. (800) 772-6397
4643 S. Ulster Street (303) 721-1062
Suite 340 fax: (303) 779-1228
Denver, CO 80237

Product: X*PRESS EXECUTIVE
Provides: News (General, Business, Company, Economic News/Data), Current Quotes (Stock, Index, Bond, Option, Futures, Mutual Fund), Financial Statement Data, SEC Filings, Earnings Estimates
Transmission: Cable-TV, Satellite
Start-Up Cost: $100-$180
Current Quote Fees: $20.95-$26.95/month
System(s): Amiga, Atari, IBM, Macintosh

Description: Delivers a steady flow of market quotes on over 30,000 stocks, indexes, funds, rights and warrants, commodities, futures and options from the major North American exchanges on a 15-minute delayed basis. Also contains interest and money rates, exchange rates, precious metals reports, market statistics, mergers and acquisitions filings, S&P MarketMovers, Business Wire and PR Newswire. Carries business and financial news from Knight-Ridder and up-to-the-minute national and international news from major news wires around the world provided by TASS (Soviet Union), Kyodo (Japan), Xinjua (China), Deutsche Presse-Agentur (Germany), Central News Agency (Taiwan), Agence France Presse (France) and more. Contains consumer news, sports scores/reports, weather information from 50 states, personal computer news, movie/book reviews and special interest topics.

Zacks Investment Research   (800) 767-3771
155 N. Wacker   (312) 630-9880
Chicago, IL 60606

Product: ZACKS ON-LINE*
Provides: Earnings Estimates
Transmission: Modem, Disk
Start-Up Cost: Unlimited access directly from Zacks, $7,500; individual company reports also available through DJN/R and Telescan at varying prices
System(s): IBM

Description: Provides history of analysts' ratings (expectations) for a given analyst on a given company. Includes EPS estimates and stock recommendations and analysts revisions; monitors the number of analysts following a given company during the current quarter;

surprise reports; histograms on earnings; earnings report and dates expected. Available directly from Zacks and individual company reports also available through DJN/R and Telescan.

INVESTMENT SOFTWARE GRID

6

The Software Grid is designed to help narrow the wide selection of software products to those that may meet your needs. It focuses on the systems required to operate the software, its cost, the types of assets the program can manipulate, the program's ability to receive data from financial information services and share data with other programs and the types of functions performed by the program.

The grid contains page references to the full product descriptions in Chapter 4 and a number of abbreviations which are categorized by table headings and explained below:

Systems

A	= Apple II	K	= Kaypro-CP/M
Am	= Amiga	Mac	= Macintosh
At	= Atari	Sun	= Sun Sparc Station
C	= Commodore 64/128	T	= TRS-80
IBM	= IBM PC and compatible		

Import/Export and Communications Script Headings

1-2-3	Lotus 1-2-3	D/D	DIAL/DATA
AIQ	AIQ Systems	DIF	Data Interchange Format
Bon	Bonneville	DJN/R	Dow Jones News/Retrieval
CGM	Computer Graphics Metafile	DTN	Data Transmission Network
CIS	CompuServe Information Service	Excel	Microsoft Excel
		Ford	Ford Investor Services
CQG	CQG System One	FS	Future Source
CSI	Commodity Systems, Inc.	Fund'l Investor	Fundamental Investor
CSV	Comma Separated Values		
CT	Compu Trac	GE	GEnie Information Service
D+S	Dollar's & Sense	ICD	Investment Company Data

Continued

IDC	Interactive Data Corp.	Quo	Quotron
IPS	I.P. Sharp	Reut	Reuters
KR	Knight-Ridder	S&P	Standard & Poor's ComStock
MSP	MetaStock Professional		
MW	MarketWatch	SD	Stock Data
MYM	Managing Your Money	Sig	Signal
N2	N-Squared	SW	Systems Writer Plus
NCN	National Computer Network	SYLK	Symbolic Link
PCM	PC Market	TA	Telemet America
PCQ	PC Quote	TC	TeleChart 2000
PCX	PC Paintbrush	TD	Track Data
PIC	Lotus 1-2-3 Graphics File	TT	Technical Tools
PRN	Lotus 1-2-3 ASCII File	WCS	Warner Computer Service
Pro	Prodigy	X*P	X*Press

Chart Types

B	= Bar	C	= Candlestick
L	= Line	S	= Semi-log Scale
P	= Point & Figure	H	= Histogram
E	= Equivolume		

Software Products	Page	Systems	Price ($)	AAII Discount (%)	Stock	Bond	Index	Mutual Fund	Option	Futures	Real Estate	Import/Export Abilities
Account Manager V*	274	IBM	695	10					♦	♦		Imp CSI
Acquisition & Disposition Anal.	72	IBM	195	10							♦	
Advanced Channel Entry**	138	IBM	995-1,995							♦		
Advance--Decline Line Tutorial*	284	IBM	75				♦					
Advanced G.E.T. 3.0*	292	IBM	2,750	20			♦			♦		Imp TT, FS, CSI, MSP
AIS Market Analyst	60	IBM	1,395	35						♦		
American Investor	75	IBM	150		♦							
Amortizelt!*	226	IBM	55	10								
Amortizer Plus*	149	IBM	100	10								Exp ASCII, 1-2-3
Analyst RT*	296	Mac	295	10	♦		♦	♦	♦	♦		
Andrew Tobias' Checkwrite Plus	185	IBM	50									
Andrew Tobias' Fin. Calculator	185	IBM	45									
Andrew Tobias' Managing the Mkt.	186	IBM	150		♦	♦		♦	♦			Exp ASCII, MYM
Andrew Tobias' Mng. Your Money	186	IBM, Mac, A	150-220		♦	♦	♦	♦	♦	♦	♦	
Andrew Tobias' Tax Cut	187	IBM	90		♦	♦		♦	♦	♦	♦	
An Option Valuator/Writer	251	IBM, A	100	25					♦			

Communication Scripts For Information Services	Financial Planning/ Portfolio Mgmt.					Fundamental Analysis				Technical Analysis						Specialized Analysis					
	Check Book	Budgeting	Financial Planning	Tax Planning	Portfolio Management	Portfolio/Security Return	Economic Forecasting	Fin. Statement Analysis	Fundamental Screening	Stock Valuation	Chart Types	Built-in Buy/Sell Signals	Backtesting	User-Defined Indicators	Available Indicators	Technical Screening	Bond Analysis	Options Analysis	Real Estate Analysis	Simulations/Games	Spreadsheet	Statistical Analysis
	♦		♦	♦	♦																	
																			♦			
											NA	♦	♦		NA							
											H				5							
											B	♦	♦	♦								
Tech Tools											B	♦	♦									
																				♦		
			♦	♦															♦			
			♦	♦																		
Sig											B, C, P											
	♦	♦		♦																		
			♦																			
DJN/R																						
	♦	♦		♦	♦														♦			
				♦																		
																			♦			

Investment Software Grid / 389

Software Products	Page	Systems	Price ($)	AAII Discount (%)	Stock	Bond	Index	Mutual Fund	Option	Futures	Real Estate	Import/Export Abilities
A-Pack: Analytical Package for Bus.	191	IBM	199	35	◆	◆			◆	◆	◆	
APEX	209	IBM	freeware		◆		◆	◆	◆	◆		
Asset Allocation Tools	263	IBM	2,500									
Asset Mix Optimizer	87	IBM	700/yr		◆	◆		◆			◆	
@Bonds Pro Series & Premium*	199	IBM	395-695	15		◆						
@nalyst	273	IBM, Mac	195-1,495	10	◆	◆	◆		◆	◆	◆	
@Options Pro Series & Premium	199	IBM, Mac	395-695	15					◆	◆		
@Risk	218	IBM, Mac	395									
Auto--Candle*	291	IBM	195	10	◆					◆		Imp CT, CSI, MSP
Autoprice	180	IBM	79	10						◆		Imp ASCII; Exp ASCII, CSI, PCM
Basic Cycle Analysis*	144	IBM	350-450	20	◆	◆	◆	◆	◆	◆	◆	Imp ASCII, CT, CSI; Exp ASCII
Best Bid	183	IBM	500	15		◆						
BMW	192	IBM	99	50	◆							
BNA Estate Tax Spreadsheet	77	IBM	1,295									
BNA Fixed Asset Mgmt. System	78	IBM	995			◆						
BNA Income Tax Spreadsheet	78	IBM	495-890									

Communication Scripts For Information Services	Check Book	Budgeting	Financial Planning	Tax Planning	Portfolio Management	Portfolio/Security Return	Economic Forecasting	Fin. Statement Analysis	Fundamental Screening	Stock Valuation	Chart Types	Built-in Buy/Sell Signals	Backtesting	User-Defined Indicators	Available Indicators	Technical Screening	Bond Analysis	Options Analysis	Real Estate Analysis	Simulations/Games	Spreadsheet	Statistical Analysis
			♦							♦												♦
WCS											B, L, P		♦									
					♦	♦																
																	♦				♦	
		♦			♦	♦											♦	♦			♦	♦
																		♦			♦	
			♦				♦	♦		♦	B, L									♦	♦	
											B, C											
ACRES, DTN, AgriQuote																						
											B, L, S		♦									♦
																	♦				♦	
																	♦				♦	
			♦	♦																	♦	
			♦	♦													♦					
			♦	♦																		

Software Products	Page	Systems	Price ($)	AAII Discount (%)	Stock	Bond	Index	Mutual Fund	Option	Futures	Real Estate	Import/Export Abilities
BNA Real Estate Investment Spread	79	IBM	595								♦	
Bollinger Bands*	172	IBM	185	10	♦		♦					
Bondcalc	223	IBM	50	15		♦						
Bond Manager	66	IBM	80			♦						
Bond Portfolio	156	IBM, Mac	25			♦						
Bond Portfolio Manager	173	IBM, Mac, A	89	20		♦						
Bond Pricing	157	IBM, Mac	8			♦						
Bonds & Interest Rates Software	229	IBM, A, C64, T	120	10	♦	♦	♦	♦	♦	♦	♦	
Bondseye	137	IBM	65			♦						
BOND$MART	193	IBM	395	30		♦						
Bond Swap Manager	224	IBM	995-4,250	20		♦						
Bonds XL Pro & Premium Series*	200	IBM, Mac	395-695	15		♦						
Bottom Dollar	238	IBM	100	10							♦	
BrainMaker Neural Net. Sim.	85	IBM, Mac	195		♦	♦	♦	♦	♦	♦	♦	Imp 1-2-3, dBase, Excel
Broker's Notebook	233	IBM	1,295		♦	♦	♦	♦	♦	♦	♦	Imp ASCII; Exp ASCII, 1-2-3
Buysel	115	IBM, K	100	20	♦				♦	♦		

Communication Scripts For Information Services	Check Book	Budgeting	Financial Planning	Tax Planning	Portfolio Management	Portfolio/Security Return	Economic Forecasting	Fin. Statement Analysis	Fundamental Screening	Stock Valuation	Chart Types	Built-in Buy/Sell Signals	Backtesting	User-Defined Indicators	Available Indicators	Technical Screening	Bond Analysis	Options Analysis	Real Estate Analysis	Simulations/Games	Spreadsheet	Statistical Analysis
			♦	♦															♦			
											L				2							
																	♦					
					♦	♦											♦					
					♦												♦				♦	
					♦	♦											♦				♦	
					♦												♦				♦	
									♦								♦					
					♦												♦					
																	♦					
																	♦					
																	♦				♦	
			♦	♦	♦														♦			
														♦						♦	
ADP, CRI, Quo, Sig					♦	♦																
												♦						♦				

Investment Software Grid / 393

Software Products	Page	Systems	Price ($)	AAII Discount (%)	Stock	Bond	Index	Mutual Fund	Option	Futures	Real Estate	Import/Export Abilities
Calcugram Stock Options System	116	IBM, K, T	170	20					♦	♦		
Call/Put Options	156	IBM, A	199						♦			Exp ASCII
CAMRA*	264	IBM	varies		♦	♦	♦	♦	♦	♦		Imp/Exp ASCII
CandlePower 2*	210	IBM	295		♦		♦			♦		Imp AIQ, ASCII, CT, CSI, MSP, TT
CapTool	276	IBM	99	20	♦	♦	♦	♦	♦	♦	♦	Imp ASCII; Exp ASCII, 1-2-3
CapTool Global Investor*	276	IBM	299	33	♦	♦	♦	♦	♦	♦	♦	Imp ASCII; Exp ASCII, 1-2-3
Centerpiece	221	IBM	895	10	♦	♦	♦	♦	♦		♦	Imp/Exp ASCII
Centerpiece Perform. Monitor*	222	IBM	595	10	♦	♦	♦	♦	♦		♦	Imp/Exp ASCII
CF: Cash Flow Analysis	271	IBM	495+									Exp ASCII
ChartistAlert*	254	IBM	195 per mo.		♦	♦	♦	♦	♦	♦		
ChartPro	250	IBM	54		♦	♦	♦	♦	♦	♦		Imp most formats; Exp ASCII
COMEX Comcalc	94	IBM	50						♦	♦		
COMEX, The Game	95	IBM	70	30					♦	♦		
Commercial Finance	72	IBM	95	10							♦	
Commercial/Ind. Real Estate App's	239	IBM, Mac	100	10							♦	
Commission Comparisons	205	IBM	40		♦	♦			♦			

394 / The Individual Investor's Guide to Computerized Investing

Communication Scripts For Information Services	Check Book	Budgeting	Financial Planning	Tax Planning	Portfolio Management	Portfolio/Security Return	Economic Forecasting	Fin. Statement Analysis	Fundamental Screening	Stock Valuation	Chart Types	Built-in Buy/Sell Signals	Backtesting	User-Defined Indicators	Available Indicators	Technical Screening	Bond Analysis	Options Analysis	Real Estate Analysis	Simulations/Games	Spreadsheet	Statistical Analysis
																		◆				
																		◆				
					◆	◆											◆					
D/D, WCS											B, C, E	◆			10							
DJN/R, CIS, D/D, GE, WCS			◆	◆	◆	◆	◆		◆	◆	B, L				1		◆					
DJN/R, CIS, D/D, GE, WCS			◆	◆	◆	◆	◆		◆	◆	B, L				1		◆					
DJN/R, Sig, WCS					◆	◆											◆					
					◆	◆																
Bon, KR, Reut, Sig					◆			◆	◆	◆	B, C, E, P	◆				◆						◆
DJN/R, GE, Prodigy					◆						B, C, P											
																		◆				
																				◆		
																			◆			
			◆																◆		◆	
			◆																			

Investment Software Grid / 395

Software Products	Page	Systems	Price ($)	AAII Discount (%)	Stock	Bond	Index	Mutual Fund	Option	Futures	Real Estate	Import/Export Abilities
Commodities and Futures Software	229	IBM, A, C64, K, T	120	10			♦		♦	♦		
Common Stock Decision Aide	300	IBM	49		♦		♦					
Complete Bond Analyzer	173	IBM, Mac, A	89	20		♦						
Compu/CHART EGA	205	IBM	300	20	♦		♦	♦	♦			
Compusec Portfolio Manager	116	A	80	20	♦			♦	♦	♦		
Compu Trac	101	IBM, Mac	695-1,900		♦	♦	♦	♦	♦	♦		Imp/Exp ASCII, DIF
ComRep	201	IBM	50	20	♦							
Convertible Bond Analyst	66	IBM	100			♦						
Covered Options	117	IBM	100	20					♦	♦		
Credit Rating Booster	117	IBM, T	30	20								
Crystal Ball*	107	Mac	395									
Dantes' Retirement Plan'r	103	IBM	30	17								
Data Retriever	282	IBM	45	10	♦	♦	♦	♦	♦	♦		Imp/Exp ASCII, DIF
DBC/Link1	99	IBM	149	20					♦			Imp ASCII; Exp OptionVue IV
DBC/Link2	99	IBM	98	20	♦		♦	♦	♦			Imp ASCII; Exp CT, 1-2-3, MSP, N2
DBC/Link6	100	IBM	69-98	20		♦				♦		Imp ASCII; Exp CT, 1-2-3, MSP

Communication Scripts For Information Services	Check Book	Budgeting	Financial Planning	Tax Planning	Portfolio Management	Portfolio/Security Return	Economic Forecasting	Fin. Statement Analysis	Fundamental Screening	Stock Valuation	Chart Types	Built-in Buy/Sell Signals	Backtesting	User-Defined Indicators	Available Indicators	Technical Screening	Bond Analysis	Options Analysis	Real Estate Analysis	Simulations/Games	Spreadsheet	Statistical Analysis
																♦		♦				
					♦	♦				♦											♦	
				♦		♦																
Track Data											B, P	♦			13+							
DJN/R					♦	♦																
											B,C,E,L,P,S		♦	♦	50	♦		♦			♦	♦
								♦	♦	♦												
																	♦					
																		♦				
			♦																			
			♦																	♦		♦
			♦																			
WCS																						
MW																						
MW																						
MW																						

Software Products	Page	Systems	Price ($)	AAII Discount (%)	Stock	Bond	Index	Mutual Fund	Option	Futures	Real Estate	Import/Export Abilities
Discover	278	IBM	599		♦		♦	♦	♦	♦		Imp/Exp ASCII, DIF
Discovery	102	IBM	350	15	♦		♦		♦	♦		
DollarLink	111	IBM	1,300	10	♦		♦	♦	♦	♦		Imp ASCII; Exp ASCII, CT, MSP, SW
DownLoader	134	IBM	69-195		♦		♦	♦	♦	♦		Imp MSP; Exp ASCII, DIF, 1-2-3
DTN Quote Catcher	105	IBM	50		♦	♦	♦	♦		♦		
Dynamic Volume Analysis Charts	303	IBM	100	50	♦	♦	♦		♦	♦		
Easy Money	196	IBM	550		♦	♦		♦			♦	
Economic Investor	130	IBM	399		♦		♦					
Elderly Tax Planner	196	IBM	95		♦	♦		♦			♦	
ELECTRIC SCORECARD II*	217	IBM	295	53					♦	♦		
Encore! Plus	140	IBM	895	10								Imp/Exp ASCII, CSV, 1-2-3
Enhanced Chartist	254	Mac	2,590	4	♦		♦	♦	♦	♦		
Enhanced Communications	258	IBM	245		♦	♦	♦	♦	♦	♦		Exp Fund'l Investor
Enhanced Fund Master Optimizer	282	IBM	150	10	♦	♦	♦	♦				Imp Time Trend
Entry/Exit/Equity (E*E*E) System	171	IBM	95-695	10	♦		♦			♦		Imp ASCII, CT, CSI; Exp ASCII
Epoch Pro	189	IBM	995		♦	♦	♦			♦		Imp ASCII, CT, CSI, FS, TT

Communication Scripts For Information Services	Financial Planning/Portfolio Mgmt.					Fundamental Analysis				Technical Analysis						Specialized Analysis					
	Check Book	Budgeting	Financial Planning	Tax Planning	Portfolio Management	Portfolio/Security Return	Economic Forecasting	Fin. Statement Analysis	Fundamental Screening	Stock Valuation	Chart Types	Built-in Buy/Sell Signals	Backtesting	User-Defined Indicators	Available Indicators	Technical Screening	Bond Analysis	Options Analysis	Real Estate Analysis	Simulations/Games	Spreadsheet	Statistical Analysis
TA			♦		♦						B, L, S							♦				
											B, P				50+							
Bon, PCQ, Sig					♦						B, L			♦	60+			♦				
CIS, D/D, MS DJN/R, Sig																						
DTN																						
D/D											B			♦		♦						
			♦	♦																	♦	
					♦		♦		♦	♦												
			♦	♦																	♦	
					♦													♦				
		♦	♦								B, L, P, S								♦	♦	♦	♦
BMI, CQI, Sig					♦						B, C, P				7			♦				
DJN/R, Sig, TD, WCS																						
															4	♦				♦		
					♦	♦					B, L	♦	♦	♦	187							
											B, L	♦	♦	♦	1							

Investment Software Grid / 399

Software Products	Page	Systems	Price ($)	AAII Discount (%)	Stock	Bond	Index	Mutual Fund	Option	Futures	Real Estate	Import/Export Abilities
Equalizer	90	IBM	99		♦	♦		♦	♦			
Equivolume Charting Software	68	IBM	365-565		♦	♦	♦	♦	♦	♦		
ES: The Estate Plan Analyzer	271	IBM	495+									
Eurotrader*	138	IBM	995							♦		
EvalForm	202	IBM, A	105	24	♦							
E.W.O.L.*	293	IBM	1,800				♦			♦		
Excalibur	145	Mac	2,900		♦		♦			♦		Imp/Exp ASCII
eXclaim! Real-Time Spreadsheet*	299	UNIX	1,850+									Imp/Exp ASCII, 1-2-3
Exec-Amort Loan Amortizer Plus	132	IBM	150	10							♦	Exp ASCII
Family Budget	118	IBM, A	35	20								
Fibnodes	91	IBM	795	20	♦			♦	♦	♦		
Final Judgement	150	IBM	600	33	♦			♦				Imp/Exp ASCII
Financial Analysis	239	IBM, Mac	195	10							♦	
Financial & Interest Calculator	174	IBM, Mac, A	89	20	♦	♦	♦	♦	♦	♦	♦	
Financial Insight	298	IBM	80		♦	♦	♦	♦	♦	♦	♦	
Financial Mgmt. System	118	IBM, K	150	20	♦	♦	♦	♦	♦	♦	♦	

Communication Scripts For Information Services	Financial Planning/ Portfolio Mgmt.					Fundamental Analysis				Technical Analysis						Specialized Analysis						
	Check Book	Budgeting	Financial Planning	Tax Planning	Portfolio Management	Portfolio/Security Return	Economic Forecasting	Fin. Statement Analysis	Fundamental Screening	Stock Valuation	Chart Types	Built-in Buy/Sell Signals	Backtesting	User-Defined Indicators	Available Indicators	Technical Screening	Bond Analysis	Options Analysis	Real Estate Analysis	Simulations/Games	Spreadsheet	Statistical Analysis
					♦																	
											E				NA							
														♦	♦							
								♦	♦	♦												
FutureSource, CQG															4+							
											B, C, P, S	♦	♦	♦	NA							♦
																					♦	
				♦															♦			
		♦	♦	♦																		
														♦	2			♦				
				♦	♦		♦	♦		♦												
		♦	♦	♦	♦														♦		♦	
			♦		♦	♦																
	♦		♦	♦	♦	♦																
								♦		♦												

Investment Software Grid / 401

Software Products	Page	Systems	Price ($)	AAII Discount (%)	Stock	Bond	Index	Mutual Fund	Option	Futures	Real Estate	Import/Export Abilities
Financial Navigator	141	IBM	495	10	◆	◆		◆	◆		◆	Exp ASCII, DIF, PRN
Financial Needs for Retirement	300	IBM	49									
Financial Pak	146	IBM	150	20				◆				
Financial Planning Organizer	110	IBM	35									
Financial Toolkit*	164	IBM	200									
FINCalc	267	IBM	100			◆						
FISTS	80	IBM	1,250	10		◆			◆	◆		Exp 1-2-3
Fixed Income	268	IBM, Sun	795-2,495			◆						
Fixed Income Data Obtainer*	165	IBM	95			◆						
Forecast Pro	81	IBM	495									Exp ASCII, 1-2-3
Foreign Exchange Software	230	IBM, A, C64, K, T	120	10			◆		◆	◆		
Fundamental Databridge	258	IBM	145		◆							Imp/Exp ASCII, DIF
Fundamental Investor	258	IBM	395		◆							
Fundgraf	218	IBM	100+	10	◆		◆	◆				
Fundgraf Supplemental Programs	219	IBM	20	10	◆		◆	◆				
Fund Master TC	282	IBM	289	10	◆	◆	◆	◆				Imp/Exp ASCII, DIF

Communication Scripts For Information Services	Financial Planning/ Portfolio Mgmt.					Fundamental Analysis				Technical Analysis						Specialized Analysis				
	Check Book	Budgeting	Financial Planning	Tax Planning	Portfolio Management	Portfolio/Security Return	Economic Forecasting	Fin. Statement Analysis	Fundamental Screening	Stock Valuation	Chart Types	Built-in Buy/Sell Signals	Backtesting	User-Defined Indicators	Available Indicators	Technical Screening	Bond Analysis	Options Analysis	Real Estate Analysis	Simulations/Games	Spreadsheet	Statistical Analysis
	◆	◆			◆													◆	◆			
			◆																		◆	
				◆	◆																	
			◆																			
			◆		◆																◆	
			◆			◆														◆	◆	
					◆	◆											◆	◆				
					◆	◆											◆		◆			◆
Interactive Data Corp			◆		◆												◆				◆	
																					◆	◆
																◆		◆				◆
Ford, WCS							◆															
											L	◆			2+							
					◆										2+							
DJN/R					◆						L,S		◆	◆	NA							

Investment Software Grid / 403

Software Products	Page	Systems	Price ($)	AAII Discount (%)	Stock	Bond	Index	Mutual Fund	Option	Futures	Real Estate	Import/Export Abilities
Fund Pro	283	IBM	789	10	♦	♦	♦	♦				Imp/Exp ASCII, DIF
Fund Profit	151	IBM	295	15		♦	♦	♦				Imp/Exp DIF
Fundwatch	119	IBM	40	20	♦	♦		♦				
Futures Markets Analyzer	170	IBM	995							♦		Imp TT, CSI, Genesis
GannTrader 2	146	IBM	1,295	10	♦	♦	♦	♦	♦	♦		Imp CT, CSI, MSP, Quicktrieve
GB-Stat	203	IBM	400									Imp ASCII, DIF; Exp ASCII, CGM
Global Trader	57	IBM	150	10	♦							
GrafMaker	82	IBM	195		♦	♦	♦		♦	♦		Imp/Exp ASCII, dBase, 1-2-3
GRAND MASTER*	133	IBM	3,000	5						♦		
Graph-in-the-Box Analytic	204	IBM	200									Imp ASCII, DIF; Exp ASCII, CGM
Graph-in-the-Box Executive*	204	IBM	300									Imp ASCII, DIF; Exp ASCII, CGM, PCX, PI
Hedgemaster	95	IBM	100						♦	♦		
Historical ADL*	284	IBM	175				♦					
Home Appraiser	119	IBM, K	40	20							♦	
Home Purchase	243	IBM, A	75	10							♦	
Hourly DJIA*	285	IBM	50				♦					

Communication Scripts For Information Services	Check Book	Budgeting	Financial Planning	Tax Planning	Portfolio Management	Portfolio/Security Return	Economic Forecasting	Fin. Statement Analysis	Fundamental Screening	Stock Valuation	Chart Types	Built-in Buy/Sell Signals	Backtesting	User-Defined Indicators	Available Indicators	Technical Screening	Bond Analysis	Options Analysis	Real Estate Analysis	Simulations/Games	Spreadsheet	Statistical Analysis
DJN/R					♦						L,S		♦	♦	NA							
											L	♦										
					♦											♦						
							♦															
											B											
											B, L, S											♦
																♦						
											B, L, S											
												♦	♦									♦
											B, L											♦
											B, L											♦
																				♦		
											H, L				6					♦		
																			♦			
																			♦			
											H, L				6					♦		

Investment Software Grid / 405

Software Products	Page	Systems	Price ($)	AAII Discount (%)	Stock	Bond	Index	Mutual Fund	Option	Futures	Real Estate	Import/Export Abilities
HRA Sell/Buy Educator	152	IBM	80+ 20/mo.	30	♦							
Income Property Analysis	244	IBM, A	75	10							♦	
IndexExpert	62	IBM	1,588				♦		♦			Imp/Exp ASCII, DIF
INSIGHT	80	IBM	2,500	10	♦		♦	♦	♦	♦		Imp/Exp ASCII, CT
International Manager*	247	IBM	15,000	5	♦	♦	♦	♦	♦	♦		Imp/Exp ASCII
Intex Bond Amortization*	165	IBM	295			♦						
Intex Bond Calculations	165	IBM	395+			♦						
Intex CMO/REMIC Modeling Toolkit*	166	IBM	varies			♦						
Intex Fixed-Income Sub.*	166	IBM	varies		♦	♦			♦	♦		
Intex Mortgage-Backed Calculat'n	167	IBM	395+			♦						
Intex Option-Adjusted Models*	167	IBM	varies			♦						
Intex Option Price Calculations	168	IBM	395+						♦			
Investability MoneyMap*	168	IBM	20	10								
INVESTigator +	170	IBM	99		♦		♦	♦	♦	♦		Imp/Exp ASCII
Investing Advisor	120	IBM, T	40	20	♦		♦	♦			♦	
Investment Analysis	73	IBM	295	10							♦	

Communication Scripts For Information Services	Financial Planning/ Portfolio Mgmt.					Fundamental Analysis				Technical Analysis						Specialized Analysis				
	Check Book	Budgeting	Financial Planning	Tax Planning	Portfolio Management	Portfolio/Security Return	Economic Forecasting	Fin. Statement Analysis	Fundamental Screening	Stock Valuation	Chart Types	Built-in Buy/Sell Signals	Backtesting	User-Defined Indicators	Available Indicators	Technical Screening	Bond Analysis	Options Analysis	Real Estate Analysis	Simulations/Games	Spreadsheet	Statistical Analysis
								◆		◆												
																			◆			
D/D, Sig, PCQ					◆						B, L	◆	◆	◆	6+	◆		◆		◆		
Sig, S&P					◆						B, C, L, P	◆		◆	8	◆		◆				
ADP, S&P, PCQ, TA					◆	◆																
					◆												◆				◆	
			◆		◆	◆											◆				◆	
					◆												◆					
			◆		◆	◆											◆				◆	
			◆		◆	◆											◆				◆	
					◆	◆												◆			◆	
			◆		◆	◆												◆			◆	
			◆																			
WCS					◆						B, C, L, P				25							
												◆		◆	NA							
																			◆			

Investment Software Grid / 407

Software Products	Page	Systems	Price ($)	AAII Discount (%)	Stock	Bond	Index	Mutual Fund	Option	Futures	Real Estate	Import/Export Abilities
Investment Analyst	213	IBM	95	25	♦	♦					♦	
Investment and Statistical Software	230	IBM, A, C64, K, T	120	10	♦	♦	♦		♦	♦	♦	
Investment IRR Analysis	174	IBM, Mac, A	89	20	♦	♦					♦	
Investment Master	147	IBM	50	20				♦				
Investment Performance Chart	157	IBM, Mac	15		♦	♦		♦				
InvestNow!-Personal	132	IBM	79	10	♦		♦	♦	♦			
InvestNow!-Professional	133	IBM	129	10	♦			♦	♦	♦		
Investor	221	Mac	150	33	♦	♦		♦	♦	♦		
INVESTOR'S ACCOUNTANT*	153	IBM	395	25	♦	♦	♦	♦	♦	♦	♦	Imp/Exp ASCII
Investor's Advantage for PC Comp.	265	IBM	400		♦		♦	♦	♦	♦		Imp CT, MSP; Exp ASCII
Investor's Advantage for the Amiga	265	Am	400		♦		♦	♦	♦	♦		
Investor's Portfolio	259	IBM	495		♦	♦		♦	♦	♦	♦	
IRMA	120	IBM, At	50	20	♦	♦	♦	♦	♦		♦	
It's Alive*	83	IBM	195	10	♦	♦	♦	♦	♦	♦		Imp ASCII, CT, MSP
Land & Lease Analysis	73	IBM	195	10							♦	
LINK/Utility*	100	IBM	49	20	♦	♦	♦	♦	♦	♦		Imp/Exp ASCII, CT, MSP

Communication Scripts For Information Services	Check Book	Budgeting	Financial Planning	Tax Planning	Portfolio Management	Portfolio/Security Return	Economic Forecasting	Fin. Statement Analysis	Fundamental Screening	Stock Valuation	Chart Types	Built-in Buy/Sell Signals	Backtesting	User-Defined Indicators	Available Indicators	Technical Screening	Bond Analysis	Options Analysis	Real Estate Analysis	Simulations/Games	Spreadsheet	Statistical Analysis
				♦			♦			♦												
																♦	♦	♦				♦
					♦	♦	♦			♦								♦			♦	
					♦																	
						♦															♦	
																	♦					
							♦											♦				
DJN/R					♦																	
any				♦	♦	♦					B, L, S	♦	♦		4							
WCS											B, C											
WCS											B											
					♦	♦																
			♦	♦	♦	♦																
Sig															NA	♦						
																		♦				

Investment Software Grid / 409

Software Products	Page	Systems	Price ($)	AAII Discount (%)	Stock	Bond	Index	Mutual Fund	Option	Futures	Real Estate	Import/Export Abilities
LiveWire Personal Investor	84	IBM	345	call	♦	♦	♦	♦	♦	♦		Imp/Exp ASCII, DIF, MSP
LiveWire Professional*	85	IBM	695	call	♦	♦	♦	♦	♦	♦		Imp/Exp ASCII, DIF
Loan Amortization	244	IBM, A	75	10							♦	
Loan Arranger	120	IBM, At	30	20								
Loan Master	147	IBM	50	20		♦						
Loan Pro*	252	IBM	40	10								
Log Scale Comparison*	285	IBM	50				♦					
Lotus Improv 1.0*	176	NeXT	695									Imp ASCII, 1-2-3
Lotus 1-2-3 for OS/2	177	IBM	695									Imp/Exp ASCII, DIF, dBase
Lotus 1-2-3 Release 3.1	178	IBM	495-695									Imp/Exp ASCII, DIF, dBase
Lotus 1-2-3 Release 2.3	177	IBM	495-595									Imp/Exp ASCII, DIF, dBase
Lotus Spread for Deskmate	178	IBM	220									Imp/Exp ASCII, DIF, dBase
LotusWorks	179	IBM	149									Imp/Exp ASCII, DIF, dBase
MacInTax 1040 1991 Personal Ed.	90	Mac	100									
MacMoney	272	Mac	120	25	♦	♦		♦				Imp CheckFree, D&S, Quicken; Exp ASCII
MacQuotes**	304	Mac	195		♦	♦	♦	♦	♦	♦		

Communication Scripts For Information Services	Check Book	Budgeting	Financial Planning	Tax Planning	Portfolio Management	Portfolio/Security Return	Economic Forecasting	Fin. Statement Analysis	Fundamental Screening	Stock Valuation	Chart Types	Built-in Buy/Sell Signals	Backtesting	User-Defined Indicators	Available Indicators	Technical Screening	Bond Analysis	Options Analysis	Real Estate Analysis	Simulations/Games	Spreadsheet	Statistical Analysis
WCS, DJN/R, Cablesoft				♦	♦	♦					B		♦		7							
WCS, DJN/R, Cablesoft				♦	♦	♦					B		♦		25+						♦	
																			♦			
			♦	♦																		
				♦																		
			♦																♦			
											L, S									♦		
											L,S										♦	
											L,S										♦	
											L,S										♦	
											L,S										♦	
											L,S										♦	
											L,S										♦	
				♦																		
	♦	♦																				
Sig																						

Investment Software Grid / 411

Software Products	Page	Systems	Price ($)	AAII Discount (%)	Stock	Bond	Index	Mutual Fund	Option	Futures	Real Estate	Import/Export Abilities
Macro*World Investor	74	IBM	900	22	◆	◆	◆	◆		◆		Imp/Exp ASCII
Manager's Option	244	IBM	375	10							◆	
Managing for Success	76	IBM	50									
Market Action Timer	279	IBM	99	15	◆		◆	◆				
Market Analyzer	113	IBM	349	30	◆	◆	◆	◆	◆			Exp ASCII
Market Analyzer Plus	114	IBM, Mac	499	30	◆	◆	◆	◆	◆	◆		Imp/Exp ASCII, DIF, SYLK
Market Analyzer-XL	210	IBM	395-695		◆		◆	◆		◆		Imp CT, CSI, DIF; Exp DIF
Market Charter*	272	Mac	60	25	◆	◆	◆	◆				Imp/Exp ASCII
MarketEdge*	257	IBM	179	28	◆	◆	◆	◆		◆		Imp/Exp ASCII, DIF, 1-2-3
MarketExpert	62	IBM	488				◆	◆	◆	◆		Imp/Exp ASCII, DIF
Market Forecaster	121	IBM, Mac, A	270-300	20	◆			◆				
Mrkt. Intelligence Swing Catcer	294	IBM	995	20	◆	◆	◆	◆	◆	◆		Imp CSI, TT, CT, MSP
Market Maker for Windows	162	IBM	295	25	◆	◆	◆	◆	◆	◆		Imp CT, MSP; Exp Excel, 1-2-3
Market Manager Plus	114	IBM, Mac	299	30	◆	◆		◆	◆	◆	◆	Exp SYLK
Market Manager PLUS Professional	115	IBM	499	30	◆	◆		◆	◆			Exp ASCII, DIF
MarketMaster*	220	IBM	99+	50	◆	◆	◆	◆	◆	◆		Imp CSI, CT, MSP

412 / The Individual Investor's Guide to Computerized Investing

Communication Scripts For Information Services	Check Book	Budgeting	Financial Planning	Tax Planning	Portfolio Management	Portfolio/Security Return	Economic Forecasting	Fin. Statement Analysis	Fundamental Screening	Stock Valuation	Chart Types	Built-in Buy/Sell Signals	Backtesting	User-Defined Indicators	Available Indicators	Technical Screening	Bond Analysis	Options Analysis	Real Estate Analysis	Simulations/Games	Spreadsheet	Statistical Analysis
					♦		♦	♦	♦	♦		♦	♦			♦				♦		♦
																			♦			
																				♦		
											L	♦			2						♦	
DJN/R											B, L	♦			4							
DJN/R					♦	♦					B, C, L, P	♦		♦	10+							
D/D, WCS											L, S			♦		♦						
GE, CIS											P				4							
													♦									
D/D, WCS, Sig, PCQ											B		♦		24	♦						
												♦	♦	♦								
CSI, DTN, TT					♦						B	♦	♦		60+	♦		♦				
TD, WCS											B, C, E, L, P	♦	♦	♦	12							
DJN/R					♦																	
DJN/R					♦	♦																
					♦							♦	♦			♦		♦				

Investment Software Grid / 413

Software Products	Page	Systems	Price ($)	AAII Discount (%)	Stock	Bond	Index	Mutual Fund	Option	Futures	Real Estate	Import/Export Abilities
MarketMate*	248	IBM	1,750	20	♦	♦	♦	♦	♦	♦		Imp/Exp ASCII
Market Simulator*	305	IBM	589		♦		♦	♦				Imp/Exp ASCII, dBase
Market Timer	121	IBM	120	20					♦			
MARKETWATCH*	154	IBM	59		♦	♦	♦	♦	♦	♦		Imp/Exp ASCII
Market Window	139	IBM	595-1,695						♦	♦		Imp CSI, DTN, Ford, Exp Quick
Markex	183	IBM	90	10				♦				
Master Brain Bond Port. Mgmt.*	107	IBM, Mac	379	10		♦						
Master Brain Pop-Up Bond Calc*	108	IBM, Mac, A	149	20		♦						
Master Chartist	255	IBM, Mac	1,295	6	♦		♦	♦	♦	♦		Imp/Exp ASCII
MATPORT*	280	IBM	50	15	♦		♦	♦				
McClellan Oscillator Prog.*	144	IBM	350-450	20	♦							Exp ASCII
MegaTech Chart System*	251	IBM	133		♦	♦	♦	♦	♦	♦		Imp most formats; Exp ASCII,
MESA	190	IBM	350		♦	♦	♦			♦		Imp ASCII, CT, CSI, FS, N2, TT
MetaStock--Professional	135	IBM	349	10	♦	♦	♦	♦	♦	♦		Imp ASCII, 1-2-3; Exp ASCII, DIF, PCX
MicroBond Calculator	225	IBM, A	300	20		♦						
Microcalc Fin. Calculator Library*	191	IBM, Mac	189	53							♦	

Communication Scripts For Information Services	Check Book	Budgeting	Financial Planning	Tax Planning	Portfolio Management	Portfolio/Security Return	Economic Forecasting	Fin. Statement Analysis	Fundamental Screening	Stock Valuation	Chart Types	Built-in Buy/Sell Signals	Backtesting	User-Defined Indicators	Available Indicators	Technical Screening	Bond Analysis	Options Analysis	Real Estate Analysis	Simulations/Games	Spreadsheet	Statistical Analysis
ADP, S&P, PCQ, TA					◆	◆																
													◆	◆						◆		
												◆	◆									
any											B, L, S	◆	◆		4							
DTN					◆						B, P			◆	20							
																◆						
					◆												◆				◆	
																	◆					
Bon, CQG, Reut, Sig															50+			◆				
											L	◆			2					◆		
											B, L				2							
DJN/R, GE, Prodigy											B, C, P											
											B, L	◆	◆		5							
											B, C, L, P, S		◆	◆	60+			◆				◆
																		◆				
		◆	◆					◆		◆										◆		

Software Products	Page	Systems	Price ($)	AAII Discount (%)	Stock	Bond	Index	Mutual Fund	Option	Futures	Real Estate	Import/Export Abilities
Microcomputer Bond Program	122	IBM, Mac, A, At, C64, K, T	60	20		♦						
Microcomputer Chart Program	122	IBM, K, T	60	20	♦		♦	♦				
Microcomputer Stock Program	123	IBM, Mac, A, At, C64, K, T	60	20	♦							
MicroSoft Excel	192	IBM, Mac	495									Imp/Exp ASCII, DIF, dBase, 1-2-3
Microstat-II	131	IBM	395	25								Imp/Exp ASCII, DIF, TC
Millionaire	76	Mac, C64	30-50		♦							
Millionaire II	77	IBM, Mac, A	40-50		♦							
Money	123	IBM, K	40	20							♦	
MoneyCalc IV	197	IBM	775		♦	♦		♦			♦	
Money Decisions	123	IBM	150	20	♦	♦	♦	♦			♦	
MORON*	286	IBM	150				♦					
Mortgage Issue Yield Analyzer	225	IBM	495	20		♦						
Mortgage Loans-- Refinance or Not	175	IBM, Mac, A	89	20							♦	
Mortgage Security Calculator	200	IBM	995	15		♦						
Multivariable Box-Jenkins	67	IBM	250	15	♦	♦	♦	♦	♦	♦	♦	Imp/Exp ASCII
Mutual Fund Decision Aide	301	IBM	49				♦	♦				

Communication Scripts For Information Services	Financial Planning/ Portfolio Mgmt.					Fundamental Analysis				Technical Analysis						Specialized Analysis				
	Check Book	Budgeting	Financial Planning	Tax Planning	Portfolio Management	Portfolio/Security Return	Economic Forecasting	Fin. Statement Analysis	Fundamental Screening	Stock Valuation	Chart Types	Built-in Buy/Sell Signals	Backtesting	User-Defined Indicators	Available Indicators	Technical Screening	Bond Analysis	Options Analysis	Real Estate Analysis	Simulations/Games	Spreadsheet	Statistical Analysis
																	♦					
											B, L				2							
												♦										
											B, L, S			♦								♦	♦
																						♦
																				♦		
																				♦		
			♦	♦															♦			
		♦	♦	♦																	♦	
				♦		♦										♦	♦		♦			♦
															2					♦		
																♦						
																			♦		♦	
																♦						
			♦																			♦
					♦	♦															♦	

Investment Software Grid / 417

Software Products	Page	Systems	Price ($)	AAII Discount (%)	Stock	Bond	Index	Mutual Fund	Option	Futures	Real Estate	Import/Export Abilities
Mutual Fund Hypotheticals	87	IBM	600/yr.					♦				
Mutual Fund Investor	64	IBM	70		♦	♦	♦	♦			♦	Imp/Exp ASCII
Mutual Fund Manager	109	IBM	35-49					♦				
Mutual Fund Reinvestment	158	IBM, Mac	15					♦				
MyWay	198	IBM	144		♦							
NAIC Stock Selection Guide	158	IBM, Mac	30		♦							
Navigator	148	IBM, Mac	150	50	♦		♦	♦	♦	♦		Imp/Exp ASCII, CT, CSI, MSP
Navigator Access	141	IBM	99		♦	♦	♦		♦	♦		Imp/Exp 1-2-3
Neuralyst for Excel*	134	IBM, Mac	165	10	♦	♦	♦	♦	♦	♦	♦	Imp/Exp ASCII, DIF, Excel, 1-2-3
New High New Low Tutorial*	286	IBM	75				♦					
NexTurn: Advanced*	261	IBM	649	20	♦		♦	♦	♦	♦		Imp ASCII, CT, CSI, MSP, TT; Exp ASCII
NexTurn: Basic*	262	IBM	499	20			♦	♦	♦	♦		Imp ASCII
Nibble Investor	195	A	30		♦							
Nibble Mac Investor	195	Mac	30		♦							
NIS Asset Allocation System	206	IBM	10,000 per yr.	20			♦	♦				
NIS Fixed Income Research Env.*	207	IBM	16,000	20		♦						

Communication Scripts For Information Services	Check Book	Budgeting	Financial Planning	Tax Planning	Portfolio Management	Portfolio/Security Return	Economic Forecasting	Fin. Statement Analysis	Fundamental Screening	Stock Valuation	Chart Types	Built-in Buy/Sell Signals	Backtesting	User-Defined Indicators	Available Indicators	Technical Screening	Bond Analysis	Options Analysis	Real Estate Analysis	Simulations/Games	Spreadsheet	Statistical Analysis
					♦																	
CIS, ICD				♦	♦	♦			♦		L, S	♦			5+	♦						
											B, L											
					♦																♦	
					♦										NA	♦						
									♦	♦											♦	
Genesis database																♦						
WCS																						
													♦		5+						♦	
															2					♦		
											C	♦	♦		8							♦
											C	♦	♦		5							♦
															2							
															2							
			♦		♦																♦	♦
					♦	♦												♦			♦	♦

Investment Software Grid / 419

Software Products	Page	Systems	Price ($)	AAII Discount (%)	Stock	Bond	Index	Mutual Fund	Option	Futures	Real Estate	Import/Export Abilities
NIS Macroecon. Equity Sys.	207	IBM	12,000 per yr.	30	♦		♦					
NIS Performance Analysis Sys.*	208	IBM	16,000	20	♦		♦					
One Day at a Time*	296	IBM	395		♦	♦	♦	♦	♦	♦		Imp CT, CSI
On Schedule	240	IBM, Mac	195	10							♦	
OPENING BELL*	70	IBM	400		♦	♦	♦	♦	♦	♦		
Options-80A: Adv. Stock Option Anal.	215	IBM, Mac, A	170	20					♦			
Option Evaluator	232	IBM	129		♦				♦	♦		
OptionExpert	63	IBM	1,588		♦				♦			Imp/Exp ASCII, CSV, DIF
OptionExpert-The Strategist	163	IBM	125	20					♦			
Option Master	163	IBM, Mac, A	89	20					♦			
Option Pricing Analysis*	215	IBM, Mac	395	25					♦			
Option Risk Management	289	IBM	varies		♦				♦	♦		
Options Analysis	124	IBM, Mac, A, K, T	100	20					♦	♦		
Options and Arbitrage Software	230	IBM, A, C64, K, T	120	10	♦		♦		♦	♦		
Options Made Easy	216	IBM	30						♦	♦		
Options XL Pro & Premium Series	201	IBM	395-695	15					♦	♦		

Communication Scripts For Information Services	Check Book	Budgeting	Financial Planning	Tax Planning	Portfolio Management	Portfolio/Security Return	Economic Forecasting	Fin. Statement Analysis	Fundamental Screening	Stock Valuation	Chart Types	Built-in Buy/Sell Signals	Backtesting	User-Defined Indicators	Available Indicators	Technical Screening	Bond Analysis	Options Analysis	Real Estate Analysis	Simulations/Games	Spreadsheet	Statistical Analysis
							♦			♦												♦
					♦																	♦
											B, C		♦	♦	20					♦		
		♦	♦															♦		♦	
			♦		♦						C, S			♦	4			♦		♦	
																		♦			
																		♦			
D/D, WCS, DJN/R					♦							♦	♦		25	♦		♦	♦		
																		♦			
																		♦			
DJN/R, Sig			♦															♦				
Sig, S&P, Reut, PCQ					♦	♦												♦				
																		♦			
																♦	♦				♦
																		♦			
																		♦		♦	

Software Products	Page	Systems	Price ($)	AAII Discount (%)	Stock	Bond	Index	Mutual Fund	Option	Futures	Real Estate	Import/Export Abilities
Option Tools Deluxe	253	IBM	50	10					◆			Imp/Exp ASCII
Option–Warrant Combo	158	IBM, Mac	49						◆	◆		
OptionVue IV	216	IBM	895						◆	◆		
OPTMASTER	181	IBM	89	10					◆	◆		Imp ASCII, CSV, PCMARKET
OVM the Option Valuation Mod. 3.0	234	IBM	459	5	◆	◆	◆		◆	◆		Imp MSP; Exp ASCII
OVM the Option Valuation Mod. IV*	234	IBM	899	5	◆	◆	◆	◆	◆	◆		Imp/Exp ASCII
PC Chart Plus	152	IBM	160	10	◆	◆	◆	◆	◆	◆		Imp CSI, MSP; Exp MSP
PCMARKET	181	IBM	189	10						◆		Imp CSV
Peerless Stock Market Timing	280	IBM, Mac	275-375		◆		◆	◆	◆	◆		
Penroll	248	IBM	95	30								
Pentax	249	IBM	95	30								
PercentEdge*	214	IBM	100		◆	◆					◆	
Personal Analyst*	297	Mac	395	10	◆		◆	◆	◆	◆		Imp/Exp ASCII
Personal Balance Sheet	124	IBM, K	30	20								
PC Automatic Invest. Mgmt.	124	IBM	150	20	◆							
Personal Finance Manager	125	IBM, Mac, A, K	50	20								

Communication Scripts For Information Services	Check Book	Budgeting	Financial Planning	Tax Planning	Portfolio Management	Portfolio/Security Return	Economic Forecasting	Fin. Statement Analysis	Fundamental Screening	Stock Valuation	Chart Types	Built-in Buy/Sell Signals	Backtesting	User-Defined Indicators	Available Indicators	Technical Screening	Bond Analysis	Options Analysis	Real Estate Analysis	Simulations/Games	Spreadsheet	Statistical Analysis
																		◆				
																		◆			◆	
DJN/R, Sig, S&P, MW, TA																		◆				
																		◆				
																		◆				
											B, L, S				5			◆				
All-Quotes, D/D, GE											B, C, L, P	◆										
											B	◆	◆		10							
											B	◆	◆	◆								
				◆																		
				◆																		
		◆	◆																			
D/D											B, C, E, P											
		◆																				
					◆	◆										◆						
◆		◆																				

Investment Software Grid / 423

Software Products	Page	Systems	Price ($)	AAII Discount (%)	Stock	Bond	Index	Mutual Fund	Option	Futures	Real Estate	Import/Export Abilities
Personal Finance Planner	125	IBM, A	30	20	♦	♦		♦			♦	
Personal Finance System	126	IBM, Mac, A, At, C, K, T	40	20								
Personal Hotline	298	Mac	595	10	♦		♦	♦	♦	♦		Imp/Exp ASCII
Personal Market Analysis (PMA)	169	IBM	149	10	♦		♦	♦		♦		
Personal Portfolio Analyzer	88	IBM	40		♦	♦		♦	♦	♦		Imp ASCII
Personal Portfolio Manager	57	IBM	150		♦	♦	♦	♦	♦	♦		
Personal Stock Technician (PST)*	236	IBM	100	50	♦	♦	♦	♦	♦	♦	♦	Imp/Exp ASCII
PFROI	277	IBM	29-49	20	♦	♦	♦	♦	♦	♦	♦	Imp ASCII; Exp ASCII, 1-2-3
Plan Ahead	59	IBM	30-60	15								
PlanEASe	65	IBM	595-995								♦	Exp ASCII
PlanEASe Partnership Mod.	65	IBM	495								♦	
PlatformAlert*	255	IBM	125/mo.		♦	♦	♦	♦	♦	♦		
POOL*	69	IBM	150/mo.			♦						Imp ASCII
Porteval Portfolio Evaluator	160	IBM	99-159	20	♦	♦	♦	♦	♦	♦	♦	
PORTFOLIO ANALYZER*	154	IBM	99		♦	♦	♦	♦	♦	♦	♦	Imp/Exp ASCII
Portfolio Decisions	126	IBM	150	20	♦	♦	♦	♦	♦	♦	♦	

Communication Scripts For Information Services	Financial Planning/ Portfolio Mgmt.					Fundamental Analysis				Technical Analysis						Specialized Analysis				
	Check Book	Budgeting	Financial Planning	Tax Planning	Portfolio Management	Portfolio/Security Return	Economic Forecasting	Fin. Statement Analysis	Fundamental Screening	Stock Valuation	Chart Types	Built-in Buy/Sell Signals	Backtesting	User-Defined Indicators	Available Indicators	Technical Screening	Bond Analysis	Options Analysis	Real Estate Analysis	Simulations/Games	Spreadsheet	Statistical Analysis
		◆	◆																			
◆			◆																			
D/D, DJN/R, CIS, Sig, WCS					◆	◆					B, C, E, P	◆			NA			◆				
												◆			5+							
					◆	◆																
					◆																	
DJN/R											B, L, S	◆		◆	9							◆
DJN/R, CIS, D/D, GE, WCS			◆	◆	◆				◆						1							
			◆																			
																			◆			
																			◆			
Bon, KR, Sig, Reut, S&P					◆			◆	◆	◆	B, C, E, P	◆				◆						◆
any		◆			◆		◆	◆	◆	◆						◆	◆					
					◆																	
any				◆	◆													◆				
					◆																	

Investment Software Grid / 425

Software Products	Page	Systems	Price ($)	AAII Discount (%)	Stock	Bond	Index	Mutual Fund	Option	Futures	Real Estate	Import/Export Abilities
Portfolio Evaluator	227	IBM	20		♦	♦	♦	♦	♦	♦	♦	Imp CT, MSP; Exp ASCII, 1-2-3
Portfolio Management Sys.	213	IBM	150	25	♦			♦				
Portfolio Manager Plus	111	IBM	50	10	♦		♦	♦	♦			Imp/Exp ASCII
Portfolio-Pro	223	IBM, A	70	40	♦	♦		♦				
Portfolio Spreadsheets 3	112	IBM	195		♦	♦		♦				
Portfolio Status	127	IBM	30	20	♦	♦	♦	♦	♦	♦		
Portview 2020	127	IBM	80	20	♦	♦	♦	♦	♦	♦	♦	
Power Trader Plus	228	IBM	1,995	40	♦		♦	♦	♦	♦		
Professional Breakout System*	83	IBM	385-595	10	♦	♦	♦	♦	♦	♦		Imp ASCII, CSI, CT, MSP
Professional Portfolio	61	IBM	2,700+		♦	♦	♦	♦	♦	♦	♦	Imp/Exp ASCII, Harvard Graphics
ProfitTaker 2000	188	IBM	495-1,995	15		♦	♦			♦		Imp CSI
Program Writer II*	275	IBM	995	10					♦	♦		Imp CSI, MSP, TT
Property Income Analysis	73	IBM	195	10							♦	
Property Listings Comparables	245	IBM, A	300	10							♦	
Property Mgmt. PLUS	245	IBM	575	10							♦	
Property Management III	240	IBM, Mac	395-1,495								♦	Exp Excel, Foxbase

426 / The Individual Investor's Guide to Computerized Investing

Communication Scripts For Information Services	Check Book	Budgeting	Financial Planning	Tax Planning	Portfolio Management	Portfolio/Security Return	Economic Forecasting	Fin. Statement Analysis	Fundamental Screening	Stock Valuation	Chart Types	Built-in Buy/Sell Signals	Backtesting	User-Defined Indicators	Available Indicators	Technical Screening	Bond Analysis	Options Analysis	Real Estate Analysis	Simulations/Games	Spreadsheet	Statistical Analysis
DJN/R, WCS					♦	♦																
			♦	♦	♦	♦																
CIS, DTN, DJN/R, Pro		♦			♦	♦																
				♦	♦	♦																
Sig, DJN/R					♦	♦														♦	♦	
			♦		♦																	
				♦	♦	♦													♦			
					♦											♦						
CSI, D/D, TT, WCS											B, L	♦	♦		5+				♦			
IDC, PCQ, Sig					♦	♦																
												♦	♦									
											B		♦	♦								
																			♦			
																			♦			
																			♦			
	♦	♦	♦	♦															♦			

Software Products	Page	Systems	Price ($)	AAII Discount (%)	Stock	Bond	Index	Mutual Fund	Option	Futures	Real Estate	Import/Export Abilities
Prosper-II Plus	58	IBM	395	20	◆	◆	◆	◆	◆	◆		Imp/Exp ASCII, MSP
Prosper-II PowerOnline	59	IBM	495	20	◆	◆	◆	◆	◆	◆		Imp/Exp ASCII
Pulse Portfolio Mgmt. System	136	IBM	349	10	◆	◆		◆	◆	◆	◆	Imp/Exp ASCII, MSP
Put/Call*	287	IBM	50						◆			
Q-Calc RealTime Spreadsheet*	299	UNIX	1,995+									Imp/Exp ASCII, 1-2-3
QTRADER*	86	IBM	269	20	◆		◆	◆		◆		Imp CSI, CT, MSP, TT
Quant IX Portfolio Evaluator	232	IBM	119	25	◆	◆		◆				Exp DAT, DIF, 1-2-3, SDF, SYLK
Quickplot/ Quickstudy	96	IBM, A	60-99		◆		◆			◆		
Quicktrieve/ Quickmanager	96	IBM, A	39	10	◆		◆	◆	◆	◆		
Quote Commander*	103	IBM	100		◆	◆						Exp ASCII, MSP
Quote Exporter	143	IBM	99		◆		◆	◆	◆	◆		
QuoteMaster	270	Mac	395	10	◆	◆	◆	◆	◆			Imp/Exp ASCII
QuoteMaster Professional*	270	Mac	495	10	◆	◆	◆	◆	◆			Imp/Exp ASCII
Quote Monitor	143	IBM	295		◆		◆	◆	◆	◆		
RAMCAP-- Intelligent Asset Alloct.	60	IBM	595	17	◆	◆	◆	◆		◆	◆	Imp/Exp ASCII
Rapid	151	IBM	277	15	◆		◆	◆	◆	◆		Imp ASCII, CSI, TT, TA; Exp ASCII

Communication Scripts For Information Services	Check Book	Budgeting	Financial Planning	Tax Planning	Portfolio Management	Portfolio/Security Return	Economic Forecasting	Fin. Statement Analysis	Fundamental Screening	Stock Valuation	Chart Types	Built-in Buy/Sell Signals	Backtesting	User-Defined Indicators	Available Indicators	Technical Screening	Bond Analysis	Options Analysis	Real Estate Analysis	Simulations/Games	Spreadsheet	Statistical Analysis
DJN.R, MW, TA, Sig, X*P					♦						B, C, E, L	♦	♦		10+	♦						
TA, Sig											B, E	♦	♦		5+							
CIS, D/D, DJN/R, Sig					♦	♦														♦		
											H				2							
																					♦	
											B, C	♦	♦		20+							
CIS, WCS					♦				♦													
CSI															10+							
CSI											B				4							
					♦																	
Sig, TA											B, C											
Sig, TA											B, C											
			♦		♦																	
											B, C, L, P	♦	♦		3							

Investment Software Grid / 429

Software Products	Page	Systems	Price ($)	AAII Discount (%)	Stock	Bond	Index	Mutual Fund	Option	Futures	Real Estate	Import/Export Abilities
Rational Indicators*	291	IBM	345-445	10	♦						♦	Imp CT, CSI, MSP
Ratios	128	IBM	30	20	♦							
RDB Computing Custom Trader*	237	IBM	varies		♦						♦	Imp ASCII, CT, CSI, MSP
Real Analyzer	237	IBM, Am	195	10							♦	
Real Estate Analyzer*	160	IBM, A	350-395								♦	
Real Estate Investment Anal.	241	IBM, Mac	295	10							♦	
Real Estate Partnership Plus	242	IBM, Mac	295	10							♦	
Real Estate Resident Expert	128	IBM	100	20							♦	
Real Property Management	238	IBM	395-595	10							♦	Exp ASCII
RealTick III	290	IBM	varies		♦	♦	♦	♦	♦	♦		Imp/Exp Excel
REAP PLUS	246	IBM	150	10							♦	
Recurrence: Real-Time Cur. Trader*	71	IBM	3,000			♦	♦			♦		
Relevance III-Advanced Mrkt. Anal.	246	IBM	800	4	♦	♦	♦	♦	♦	♦		Imp CT, CSI, MSP
REMS Investor 3000	149	IBM	595	10							♦	Imp 1-2-3; Exp ASCII, 1-2-3
Residential Finance	74	IBM	95	10							♦	
Retirement Solutions	197	IBM	195									

Communication Scripts For Information Services	Check Book	Budgeting	Financial Planning	Tax Planning	Portfolio Management	Portfolio/Security Return	Economic Forecasting	Fin. Statement Analysis	Fundamental Screening	Stock Valuation	Chart Types	Built-in Buy/Sell Signals	Backtesting	User-Defined Indicators	Available Indicators	Technical Screening	Bond Analysis	Options Analysis	Real Estate Analysis	Simulations/Games	Spreadsheet	Statistical Analysis
											B, C				1							
								♦		♦												
											B, L	♦	♦		1							
			♦	♦	♦	♦													♦			
			♦																♦			
			♦	♦															♦		♦	
				♦															♦		♦	
																			♦			
	♦	♦	♦		♦														♦			
Sig, S&P, Reut, PCQ											B, C			♦								
																			♦			
											B		♦	♦								
											B, C	♦			2+							
																			♦			
																			♦			
			♦	♦																	♦	

Software Products	Page	Systems	Price ($)	AAII Discount (%)	Stock	Bond	Index	Mutual Fund	Option	Futures	Real Estate	Import/Export Abilities
RETIREMENT SURPRISE!*	266	IBM	49									
Retriever Plus	206	IBM	80		♦		♦	♦	♦			Exp 1-2-3, TD, CompuChart
RiskAlert*	256	IBM	390 per mo.		♦	♦	♦	♦	♦	♦		
Risk Analysis System*	106	IBM	2,000 per mo.		♦	♦	♦		♦	♦		
Rory Tycoon Options Trader	93	IBM	50						♦	♦		
Rory Tycoon Portfolio Analyst	93	IBM	150		♦	♦		♦	♦	♦		
Rory Tycoon Portfolio Manager	94	IBM	50-100		♦	♦		♦	♦	♦		
Scenario	307	IBM	199	35		♦			♦	♦		
Sibyl/Runner Interactive Forecst.	68	IBM	495	15	♦	♦	♦	♦	♦	♦	♦	
SolveIt!	226	IBM	99		♦	♦		♦			♦	
Sophisticated Investor	194	IBM	195	15	♦		♦	♦				Imp/Exp ASCII
SORITEC	267	IBM	595		♦	♦			♦	♦	♦	
Splot!	104	IBM	135	20	♦	♦	♦	♦	♦	♦		Imp ASCII, SD; Exp ASCII
SPSS/PC+	268	IBM	195	call								Imp/Exp ASCII, dBase, 1-2-3
SPSS/PC+ Trends	269	IBM	395	call								Imp/Exp ASCII, dBase, 1-2-3
SSG PLUS*	202	IBM	179	18	♦							

Communication Scripts For Information Services	Check Book	Budgeting	Financial Planning	Tax Planning	Portfolio Management	Portfolio/Security Return	Economic Forecasting	Fin. Statement Analysis	Fundamental Screening	Stock Valuation	Chart Types	Built-in Buy/Sell Signals	Backtesting	User-Defined Indicators	Available Indicators	Technical Screening	Bond Analysis	Options Analysis	Real Estate Analysis	Simulations/Games	Spreadsheet	Statistical Analysis
			♦																			
Track Data																						
Bon, KR, Sig Reut, WCS					♦			♦	♦	♦	B, C, E, P	♦				♦						♦
S&P, NCN					♦													♦		♦		
DJN/R, CIS Sig																		♦			♦	
					♦										4						♦	
Sig					♦	♦															♦	
																				♦		
			♦																			♦
		♦	♦	♦															♦			
			♦		♦	♦									4	♦				♦		♦
										♦												
DJN/R, Sig, X*P			♦	♦	♦	♦					B, L, P											
																						♦
								♦	♦	♦												

Investment Software Grid / 433

Software Products	Page	Systems	Price ($)	AAII Discount (%)	Stock	Bond	Index	Mutual Fund	Option	Futures	Real Estate	Import/Export Abilities
Statistical Anal. & Forecasting Soft.	231	IBM, A, C64, K, T	120	10	◆	◆	◆		◆	◆		
Stockaid 4.0	129	IBM	70	20	◆							
Stock Analyzer	262	IBM	599	20	◆			◆	◆			Imp ASCII, MSP; Exp ASCII
Stock & Futures Analyzer-XL	211	IBM	395-695		◆		◆	◆	◆	◆		Imp CT, CSI, DIF; Exp DIF
STOCKCAL	253	IBM	40	13	◆							
Stock Charting	110	IBM	70	20	◆							
Stock Charting System	89	IBM	50		◆	◆	◆	◆	◆	◆		Imp ASCII
StockExpert	63	IBM	988		◆							Imp/Exp ASCII, DIF
Stock Manager	67	IBM	80		◆				◆			
Stock Manager	214	IBM	200	25	◆			◆				
Stock Market Bargains	129	IBM	70	20	◆							
Stock Market Securities Program	98	IBM	260	10	◆	◆	◆	◆	◆			
Stock Market Software	231	IBM, A, C64, K, T	120	10	◆		◆	◆	◆	◆		
Stock Master	147	IBM	50	20	◆			◆				
Stock Master*	293	IBM	1,500	30	◆		◆	◆				Imp TT, FS, CSI, MSP
Stock Option Analysis Program	155	IBM	150	10					◆			

Communication Scripts For Information Services	Check Book	Budgeting	Financial Planning	Tax Planning	Portfolio Management	Portfolio/Security Return	Economic Forecasting	Fin. Statement Analysis	Fundamental Screening	Stock Valuation	Chart Types	Built-in Buy/Sell Signals	Backtesting	User-Defined Indicators	Available Indicators	Technical Screening	Bond Analysis	Options Analysis	Real Estate Analysis	Simulations/Games	Spreadsheet	Statistical Analysis
																◆						◆
											P		◆		4							
CIS, WCS											B	◆	◆		6+							
D/D, WCS					◆				◆		B, L, P, S			◆		◆						
WCS											B, L			◆	6							
					◆	◆					B, L, S				3+							
D/D, DJN/R, Sig, WCS, PCQ					◆						B	◆	◆		7+	◆			◆			
					◆	◆				◆												
				◆	◆	◆																
								◆		◆												
CIS, DJN/R												◆	◆	◆	4							
				◆	◆	◆			◆			◆						◆				
					◆											◆						
					◆						B, C	◆	◆	◆	10	◆						
DJN/R, Sig, WCS																		◆				

Investment Software Grid / 435

Software Products	Page	Systems	Price ($)	AAII Discount (%)	Stock	Bond	Index	Mutual Fund	Option	Futures	Real Estate	Import/Export Abilities
Stock Option Calc. and Strategies	101	IBM	40	10				♦	♦			
Stock Option Scanner	155	IBM	150	10					♦			
Stock Portfolio	159	IBM, Mac	15		♦							
Stock Portfolio Allocator	227	IBM	39	14	♦	♦		♦	♦	♦		
Stock Portfolio Evaluator	142	IBM	155	10	♦		♦	♦				
Stock Valuation	159	IBM, Mac	25		♦							
Stock Watcher	193	Mac	195	30	♦		♦	♦	♦	♦		Imp ASCII; Exp ASCII, PCX
Swiftax	283	IBM, A, C64	80									Imp ASCII, 1-2-3, Quicken
Symphony	180	IBM	695									
System Writer Plus	211	IBM, Mac	1,975		♦	♦	♦	♦	♦	♦		Imp ASCII, CT, CSI, MSP, Tick; Exp ASCII
Take Stock*	203	Mac	150		♦							
TA-SRV	290	IBM	varies	10	♦	♦	♦	♦	♦	♦		Exp Excel
Tax Preparer	161	IBM, A	250-295									
Tax Preparer: Partnership Edition	162	IBM	395									
Tax Tools	250	IBM	95	30								
Technical Analysis Charts	274	A	130		♦		♦	♦	♦	♦		

Communication Scripts For Information Services	Financial Planning/ Portfolio Mgmt.					Fundamental Analysis				Technical Analysis							Specialized Analysis				
	Check Book	Budgeting	Financial Planning	Tax Planning	Portfolio Management	Portfolio/Security Return	Economic Forecasting	Fin. Statement Analysis	Fundamental Screening	Stock Valuation	Chart Types	Built-in Buy/Sell Signals	Backtesting	User-Defined Indicators	Available Indicators	Technical Screening	Bond Analysis	Options Analysis	Real Estate Analysis	Simulations/Games	Spreadsheet	Statistical Analysis
																		♦				
DJN/R, Sig, WCS										♦								♦				
					♦																♦	
					♦																	
					♦	♦																
					♦					♦											♦	
CIS, DJN/R											B, L											
			♦	♦																		
																					♦	
Sig											B, C	♦	♦	♦	65+							
								♦	♦	♦												
Sig, S&P, Reut, PCQ																♦						
				♦																		
				♦																		
				♦																		
											B, H, L				1							

Investment Software Grid / 437

Software Products	Page	Systems	Price ($)	AAII Discount (%)	Stock	Bond	Index	Mutual Fund	Option	Futures	Real Estate	Import/Export Abilities
Technical Databridge	259	IBM	145		♦	♦	♦	♦	♦	♦	♦	Imp/Exp Savant, DIF
Technical Investor	260	IBM	395		♦	♦	♦	♦	♦	♦		
Technical Selector	261	IBM	295		♦	♦	♦	♦	♦			
Technical Trader	187	IBM, A	450-675	10	♦		♦		♦	♦		Imp CT
Technician	136	IBM	395+ 120/yr.	15			♦					Imp/Exp ASCII
TechniFilter Plus	256	IBM	299		♦	♦	♦	♦	♦			
TekCalc	82	IBM	150		♦	♦	♦	♦	♦	♦		Imp/Exp ASCII
Telescan Portfolio Manager (TPM)*	278	IBM	395	10	♦	♦	♦	♦	♦		♦	
3D*	190	IBM	199		♦	♦	♦			♦		Imp ASCII, CT, CSI, FS, N2, TT
Tiger Mult. Stock Screen. & Timing	281	IBM	895		♦							
Timer*	287	IBM	250				♦					
Timer Professional*	288	IBM	450				♦					
TopVision*	302	IBM	355-1,398	30-50	♦	♦	♦	♦		♦		
Total Return*	262	IBM	2,500-3,495	20			♦		♦	♦		Imp ASCII, CT, CSI, MSP, TT; Exp ASCII
Trader's Profit Motive System	292	IBM	2,995							♦		
TRADE$K*	97	IBM	299+	10	♦		♦			♦		Imp CSI

Communication Scripts For Information Services	Financial Planning/ Portfolio Mgmt.					Fundamental Analysis				Technical Analysis						Specialized Analysis						
	Check Book	Budgeting	Financial Planning	Tax Planning	Portfolio Management	Portfolio/Security Return	Economic Forecasting	Fin. Statement Analysis	Fundamental Screening	Stock Valuation	Chart Types	Built-in Buy/Sell Signals	Backtesting	User-Defined Indicators	Available Indicators	Technical Screening	Bond Analysis	Options Analysis	Real Estate Analysis	Simulations/Games	Spreadsheet	Statistical Analysis
DJN/R, WCS, Merlin											B, P											
													♦			♦						
CSI											B	♦	♦		8+							
EQUIS											B, L		♦	♦	100+							♦
												♦	♦	♦	6	♦						
																						♦
Telescan, DJN/R					♦	♦																
											B	♦	♦	♦	6							
DJN/R											B	♦	♦	♦		♦						
											H, L				9					♦		
											H, L, S				10							
																♦						
												♦	♦		6+					♦		
												♦	♦									
CSI					♦	♦																

Investment Software Grid / 439

Software Products	Page	Systems	Price ($)	AAII Discount (%)	Stock	Bond	Index	Mutual Fund	Option	Futures	Real Estate	Import/Export Abilities
TradeStation*	212	IBM	1,895		♦	♦	♦	♦	♦	♦		Imp ASCII, CSI, CT, MSP, Tick; Exp ASCII
Tradex 21**	139	IBM	3,000							♦		
Trading Package	92	IBM	495	20	♦	♦	♦	♦	♦	♦		Imp CT, CIS, CSI
Trading System Performance Eval.*	98	IBM	199	20	♦	♦	♦	♦	♦	♦		Imp ASCII
TRENDPOINT	295	IBM	35	20	♦	♦	♦	♦	♦	♦		Imp/Exp ASCII
TRENDTEK	295	IBM	30	20	♦		♦	♦	♦	♦		Imp/Exp ASCII
Truerate%	184	IBM	500	15	♦	♦	♦	♦	♦	♦	♦	
TurboTax Personal 1040	91	IBM	75									
20/20	235	IBM	299	5	♦	♦	♦	♦	♦	♦		Imp/Exp ASCII
20/20 Plus	236	IBM	199	5	♦	♦	♦	♦	♦	♦		Imp/Exp ASCII
Valuation Research Station	70	IBM	12,000	15	♦		♦					
Value Line Portfolio Manager	302	IBM	281–1,500		♦			♦	♦			Exp 1-2-3
VantagePoint*	188	IBM	1,950	15	♦	♦	♦			♦		Imp CSI
Viking	108	IBM	500	10	♦	♦	♦	♦	♦	♦		Imp ASCII, CSI, MSP Exp ASCII, 1-2-3
Volume Indicator Tutorial*	288	IBM	75				♦					
VP-Expert	306	IBM	349									

Communication Scripts For Information Services	Financial Planning/Portfolio Mgmt.						Fundamental Analysis				Technical Analysis							Specialized Analysis					
	Check Book	Budgeting	Financial Planning	Tax Planning	Portfolio Management	Portfolio/Security Return	Economic Forecasting	Fin. Statement Analysis	Fundamental Screening	Stock Valuation	Chart Types	Built-in Buy/Sell Signals	Backtesting	User-Defined Indicators	Available Indicators	Technical Screening	Bond Analysis	Options Analysis	Real Estate Analysis	Simulations/Games	Spreadsheet	Statistical Analysis
CQG, Sig					♦						B, L	♦	♦	♦								
											NA	♦	♦		NA							
CIS, CSI											B			♦	7+			♦				
			♦																	♦		
											L				6							
															6							
					♦	♦															♦	
			♦																			
D/D, MSP											B, H, L				8							
D/D, MSP											B, L, S	♦			6							
							♦	♦	♦	♦	B, L		♦	♦	7	♦					♦	♦
					♦			♦														
												♦	♦									
glance, IPS, TA Sig, WCS, X*P					♦		♦	♦	♦	♦	B, E, L, P, S	♦	♦	♦	40	♦		♦				♦
															2					♦		

Investment Software Grid / 441

Software Products	Page	Systems	Price ($)	AAII Discount (%)	Stock	Bond	Index	Mutual Fund	Option	Futures	Real Estate	Import/Export Abilities
Wall Street Portfolio Manager	105	IBM	50		♦	♦		♦				
Wall Street Prophet	304	IBM	199	50	♦	♦	♦	♦	♦			
Wall Street Trainer	129	IBM	30	20	♦				♦	♦		
Wall Street Watcher	194	Mac	495	20	♦		♦	♦	♦	♦		Imp ASCII; Exp ASCII, PCX
War Machine**	305	Mac	595		♦	♦	♦	♦	♦	♦		
Wave Wise Spreadsheet	171	IBM	495	20	♦	♦	♦	♦		♦		Imp CT, CSI, Sym; Exp ASCII
WCSPD for Fundgraf	220	IBM	25	10	♦		♦	♦				Imp ASCII
WealthBuilder by Money Magazine	242	IBM, Mac	170		♦	♦		♦				
What'sBest!	175	IBM, Mac	149-4,995									
Whole Market Monitor	182	IBM	295	10	♦				♦	♦		Imp TA; Exp ASCII, DIF, MSP
Zenterprise Real Estate Investor	130	IBM	70	20							♦	
ZMath	184	IBM	500	15							♦	

442 / The Individual Investor's Guide to Computerized Investing

Communication Scripts For Information Services	Check Book	Budgeting	Financial Planning	Tax Planning	Portfolio Management	Portfolio/Security Return	Economic Forecasting	Fin. Statement Analysis	Fundamental Screening	Stock Valuation	Chart Types	Built-in Buy/Sell Signals	Backtesting	User-Defined Indicators	Available Indicators	Technical Screening	Bond Analysis	Options Analysis	Real Estate Analysis	Simulations/Games	Spreadsheet	Statistical Analysis
DTN				♦	♦																	
															7							
																				♦		
CIS, DJN/R											B, L				NA							
Sig											B	♦		♦	10	♦						
											B, L	♦	♦	♦	NA						♦	♦
WCS																						
		♦	♦	♦	♦				♦													
																					♦	♦
TA																						
																			♦			
																			♦			

FINANCIAL INFORMATION SERVICES GRID 7

The Financial Information Services Grid is designed to help you select the service that best meets your needs. The services are presented alphabetically and include the page reference to the full description and price schedule in Chapter 5.

The grid provides the methods by which the data is transferred and information regarding the breadth of coverage through the Number of Securities Followed column. The Quotes information is divided into security types and indicates if the data is provided on a real-time (RT), delayed (D) or historical (H) basis. If the service provides historical data, the time period for which the data are available is indicated. The grid also indicates the main types of financial data and services provided by each database.

Financial Information Services	Page	Modem	Disk	CD-ROM	FM Radio	Satellite	Cable TV	Number of Securities Followed	Stock Quotes (Periods)	Bond Quotes (Periods)	Index Quotes (Periods)
AB-Data Disks	311		◆					NA			
Accuron	357	◆						195,000	RT, H (1971+)	H (1971+)	RT, H (1971+)
AgriQuote	359	◆						NA			
America Online	312	◆						NA	D	D	D
Argus On-Line	312	◆						400			
Bond Buyer Full Text*	328	◆						NA			
Business Conditions Digest Historical Data	362		◆					NA			H (41 yrs.)
Business Cycle Indicators	362		◆					NA			H (4 yrs.)
Business DateLine*	329	◆						NA			
Business Week Mutual Fund Scoreboard	315		◆					2,000			
Cadence Universe Online	316	◆						3,000	H (10 yrs.)	H (10 yrs.)	H (1925+)
Citibase	319	◆						NA			H (1983+)
Commodity DataBank	337		◆					NA			
Compact D/Canada	332			◆				6,000			
Compact D/SEC	333			◆				11,000			
Compact D/'33	332			◆				NA			

446 / The Individual Investor's Guide to Computerized Investing

Mutual Fund Quotes (Periods)	Closed-End Mutual Funds (Periods)	Option Quotes (Period)	Futures Quotes (Periods)	General News	Business News	Economic News/Data	Company News	Financial Statement Data	SEC Filings	Analyst Reports	Earnings Estimates	Charting	Technical Studies	Screening--Technical	Screening--Fundamental	Screening--Mutual Funds	On-Line Trading
								◆									
H (1971+)		RT, H (1971+)	RT, H (1971+)														
		RT, D	RT, D, H (5 days)		◆	◆						◆	◆				
D		D	D	◆	◆	◆	◆										◆
								◆	◆	◆			◆		◆		
					◆												
						◆											
						◆											
					◆		◆										
																◆	
H (10 yrs.)		NA	NA			◆	◆		◆							◆	
				◆	◆	◆	◆										
			H (1959+)										◆				
								◆		◆					◆		
								◆	◆	◆	◆				◆		
										◆	◆						

Financial Information Services Grid / 447

| Financial Information Services | Page | Transmission ||||| Number of Securities Followed | Stock Quotes (Periods) | Bond Quotes (Periods) | Index Quotes (Periods) |
		Modem	Disk	CD-ROM	FM Radio	Satellite	Cable TV				
CompuServe	321	◆						90,000	D, H (12 yrs.)	D, H (12 yrs.)	D, H (12 yrs.)
Connect Business Information Network	323	◆						300	D		D
CP Historical Data	350		◆					75			
CSI Data Retrieval Service	320	◆	◆					5,000	D, H (1962+)		D, H (1928+)
Daily Pricing Service	369	◆	◆					1,000		H (1975+)	
Daily Summary	318	◆						NA		D	D
Data Connections	340	◆	◆					5,000	D, H (1983+)		D, H (1970+)
Datadisk Information Services	316		◆					1,000	H (10 yrs.)	NA	H (20 yrs.)
Delphi*	327	◆						NA	D	D	D
DIAL/DATA	327	◆						20,000	D, H (17 yrs.)	H (2.5 yrs.)	D, H (17 yrs.)
Dialog Business Connection	329	◆						2M	H (1 yr.)		H (1 yr.)
Dialog/MoneyCenter*	330	◆						NA	D, H (3 days)	RT, D, H (3 days)	D, H (3 days)
Dialog Quotes and Trading	330	◆						NA	D		
Disclosure Database	334	◆						12,000			
Disclosure Data for the Fundamental Investor	366		◆					10,000			
Disclosure/Spectrum Ownership Database	334	◆						11,000			

448 / The Individual Investor's Guide to Computerized Investing

Mutual Fund Quotes (Periods)	Closed-End Mutual Funds (Periods)	Option Quotes (Period)	Futures Quotes (Periods)	General News	Business News	Economic News/Data	Company News	Financial Statement Data	SEC Filings	Analyst Reports	Earnings Estimates	Charting	Technical Studies	Screening–Technical	Screening–Fundamental	Screening–Mutual Funds	On-Line Trading
D, H (12 yrs.)	D, H (12 yrs.)	D, H (3-9 mos.)	D, H (1979+)	♦	♦	♦	♦	♦	♦	♦	♦	♦	♦	♦	♦	♦	♦
D		D	D		♦												
		H	H (25 yrs.)														
D, H (1986+)		D, H (1982+)	D, H (1949+)			♦							♦				
		D	D														
			D										♦				
D, H (1990+)		D, H (1990+)	D, H (1968+)														
NA		NA	NA			♦		♦				♦			♦		
D	D	D	D	♦	♦	♦	♦			♦							
H (2.5 yrs.)	H (2.5 yrs.)	D, H (2 yrs.)	D, H (20 yrs.)										♦				
					♦			♦	♦	♦			♦		♦	♦	♦
		D, H (3 days)	D, H (3 days)	♦	♦	♦	♦										
		D															♦
								♦	♦	♦	♦						
								♦									
										♦	♦						

Financial Information Services Grid / 449

Financial Information Services	Page	Modem	Disk	CD-ROM	FM Radio	Satellite	Cable TV	Number of Securities Followed	Stock Quotes (Periods)	Bond Quotes (Periods)	Index Quotes (Periods)
Disclosure/Worldscope Europe	334			♦				2,000	H (3 yrs.)		
Disclosure/Worldscope Global*	335	♦		♦				7,000	H (3 yrs.)		
Disclosure/Worldscope Pacific Rim*	335	♦		♦				1,500	H (3 yrs.)		
Dow Industrials	342		♦					1			H (35 yrs.)
Dow Jones News/Retrieval	336	♦						150,000	RT, D, H (1979+)	RT, D, H (1979+)	RT, D, H (1979+)
Dow Month-by-Month Set	342		♦					4			H (35 yrs.)
DTN Wall Street	326					♦	♦	20,000	D	D	RT
Ensign III	314	♦			♦	♦	♦	12,000	RT, D	RT, D	RT, D
Equalizer	317	♦						NA	RT, D, H (17 yrs.)	RT, D, H (16 yrs.)	RT, D, H (16 yrs.)
Exchange Master	382	♦	♦					NA	D, H (10 yrs.)	D, H (10 yrs.)	D, H (10 yrs.)
Fidelity Investors Express	338	♦						5,000	D		D
First Release	331	♦						NA	NA	NA	NA
5-by-500 Database	383		♦					500	H (5 yrs.)		
Fixed-Income Pricing Services*	369	♦	♦					NA		RT, D, H (1975+)	
Ford Data Base	338	♦	♦					2,000	H (1970+)		
Free Financial Network (FFN)	355	♦						NA	H (1 day)	H (1 day)	H (1 day)

Mutual Fund Quotes (Periods)	Closed-End Mutual Funds (Periods)	Option Quotes (Period)	Futures Quotes (Periods)	General News	Business News	Economic News/Data	Company News	Financial Statement Data	SEC Filings	Analyst Reports	Earnings Estimates	Charting	Technical Studies	Screening–Technical	Screening–Fundamental	Screening–Mutual Funds	On-Line Trading
								♦									
								♦									
								♦									
D, H (1979+)	RT, D, H (1979+)	RT, D, H (1 yr.)	RT, D, H (1979+)	♦	♦	♦	♦	♦	♦	♦	♦		♦	♦	♦	♦	♦
D		D	D		♦	♦	♦			♦			♦				
RT, D	RT, D	RT, D	RT, D	♦	♦	♦						♦	♦				
RT, D, H (15 yrs.)		RT, D, H (3 mo.)	D, H (14 yrs.)		♦	♦	♦	♦	♦	♦	♦				♦	♦	♦
D, H (10 yrs.)		D, H (1 mo.)	D, H (10 yrs.)					♦		♦							
D		D		♦						♦							♦
NA		NA	NA	♦						♦							
		D, H	D, H														
															♦		
H (1 day)		H (1 day)	H (1 day)	♦					♦		♦	♦					

Financial Information Services Grid / 451

Financial Information Services	Page	Modem	Disk	CD-ROM	FM Radio	Satellite	Cable TV	Number of Securities Followed	Stock Quotes (Periods)	Bond Quotes (Periods)	Index Quotes (Periods)
Fund/Search for Funds*	343	◆						1,500	D, H (1 yr.)	D	RT, D
Fund/Search for Funds II*	344	◆						1,500	D, H (1 yr.)	D	RT, D
Future Access*	341	◆	◆					15,000	D, H (1980+)	D, H (1977+)	D, H (1971+)
FutureSource Analyst	339						◆	NA		RT, H (1 yr.)	RT, H (1 yr.)
FutureSource Technical	339						◆	NA		RT, H (1-10 yrs.)	RT, H (1-10 yrs.)
GEnie*	340	◆						67,000	RT, D, H	RT, D, H	RT, D, H
GEnie Brokerage Service	318	◆						NA	RT	RT	RT
Historical Futures Contracts	319	◆						NA			H (1978+)
Hoffman Bond Update*	349	◆						NA			
ICDI Mutual Fund Database*	346	◆	◆					2,800			
Insider Trading Monitor	345	◆	◆					9,600			
Institutional Brokers' Estimate System	352	◆						3,400			
Intex CMO/REMIC Modeling Service	344		◆					NA			
Investability Mutual Fund Database*	345		◆					2,700			
Investext/Plus	376	◆						14,000	H (1982+)		
Investment Wizard	360		◆					NA			

452 / The Individual Investor's Guide to Computerized Investing

Mutual Fund Quotes (Periods)	Closed-End Mutual Funds (Periods)	Option Quotes (Period)	Futures Quotes (Periods)	General News	Business News	Economic News/Data	Company News	Financial Statement Data	SEC Filings	Analyst Reports	Earnings Estimates	Charting	Technical Studies	Screening--Technical	Screening--Fundamental	Screening--Mutual Funds	On-Line Trading
D, H (10 yrs.)		D	D		♦	♦	♦	♦	♦		♦					♦	
D, H (10 yrs.)		D	D		♦	♦	♦	♦	♦		♦					♦	
D, H (1981+)	D, H (1981+)	D, H (1989+)	D, H (1968+)									♦	♦				
		RT	RT, H (1 yr.)		♦							♦	♦				
		RT	RT, H (1-10 yrs.)		♦	♦						♦	♦				
RT, D, H	RT, D, H	RT, D, H	RT, D, H	♦	♦	♦	♦			♦					♦		♦
RT		RT															♦
			H (1969+)														
										♦			♦	♦			
D, H (1962+)												♦	♦	♦		♦	
					♦			♦							♦		
					♦		♦										
					♦		♦										
																♦	
						♦	♦	♦		♦							♦
				♦	♦	♦	♦			♦							

Financial Information Services Grid / 453

Financial Information Services	Page	Modem	Disk	CD-ROM	FM Radio	Satellite	Cable TV	Number of Securities Followed	Stock Quotes (Periods)	Bond Quotes (Periods)	Index Quotes (Periods)
Lexis Financial Information Service	353	♦						7,000	RT, H (15 yrs.)	RT, H (15 yrs.)	RT, H (15 yrs.)
Live-Line*	357	♦						NA	RT		RT
Lotus One Source	350			♦				NA	H	H	H
Lowry's Market Trend Analysis Database	351		♦					NA			D, H (1940-89)
Market Base	356		♦					4,500	H		
Market Center	314	♦			♦	♦	♦	6,000	RT, D	RT, D	RT, D
MarketMax*	379	♦						5,000	RT, H (10 yrs.)	RT, H (10 yrs.)	RT, H (10 yrs.)
Market Momentum Services*	352	♦						5,200	H (2 yrs.)	H (2 yrs.)	H (2 yrs.)
Market NewsAlert	322	♦						10,000			
Market Profile	319	♦						NA			D
MarketView	353					♦		3,000			RT, H (10 yrs.)
MarketWatch	323					♦	♦	50,000	RT, D		RT
MarketWatch PLUS	324					♦	♦	50,000	RT, D		RT
Media General Database Service	354	♦	♦	♦				6,300	H (18 yrs.)		H (18 yrs.)
MJK	356	♦	♦					790	D, H (1988+)		D, H (1988+)
Mutual Fund Analyzer	348		♦					2,600			

454 / The Individual Investor's Guide to Computerized Investing

Mutual Fund Quotes (Periods)	Closed-End Mutual Funds (Periods)	Option Quotes (Period)	Futures Quotes (Periods)	General News	Business News	Economic News/Data	Company News	Financial Statement Data	SEC Filings	Analyst Reports	Earnings Estimates	Charting	Technical Studies	Screening–Technical	Screening–Fundamental	Screening–Mutual Funds	On-Line Trading
RT, H (15 yrs.)	RT, H (15 yrs.)			♦	♦	♦	♦	♦	♦	♦	♦						
		RT	RT														
H		H	H					♦	♦	♦							
													♦				
								♦				♦				♦	
RT, D	RT, D	RT, D	RT, D	♦	♦	♦											
		RT, H (10 yrs.)	RT, H (10 yrs.)	♦	♦	♦	♦	♦	♦	♦	♦	♦	♦				
			H (2 yrs.)		♦		♦						♦	♦	♦		
					♦			♦	♦	♦							
			D									♦	♦				
D		RT	RT, H (10 yrs.)		♦							♦	♦				
		RT, D	RT, D		♦												
		RT, D	RT, D		♦												
H (5 yrs.)	H (5 yrs.)							♦					♦	♦	♦	♦	
			D, H (1969+)														
D																♦	

Financial Information Services Grid / 455

Financial Information Services	Page	Modem	Disk	CD-ROM	FM Radio	Satellite	Cable TV	Number of Securities Followed	Stock Quotes (Periods)	Bond Quotes (Periods)	Index Quotes (Periods)
Mutual Fund & Port. Managers Directory	349		◆					2,600			
Mutual Fund OnLine Database	355	◆	◆					275			D
Mutual Fund Selector	364		◆					2,200			
NewsNet	358	◆						350			
News Real	324	◆						NA	D, H (1979+)	D	
NIS Equity Research Service	359		◆					4,500	H (1 mo.)		
Nite-Line	358	◆	◆					90,000	H (1971+)	H (1971+)	H (1971+)
OECD Main Economic Indicators	337		◆					NA			
OmniNews	322	◆						10,000			
OTC NewsAlert	322	◆						10,000			
Paradigm Options Database*	361	◆						500	D, H (10 yrs.)		D, H (10 yrs.)
PC Quote	361					◆		NA	RT	RT	RT
Pocket Quote Pro	371				◆			45,000	RT, D	RT, D	RT, D
Predicasts F&S Index Plus Text	367			◆				NA			
Prodigy	362	◆						NA	D	D	D
ProQuote	313		◆		◆	◆		10,000	RT, H (1986+)	RT	RT, H (1988+)

456 / The Individual Investor's Guide to Computerized Investing

Mutual Fund Quotes (Periods)	Closed-End Mutual Funds (Periods)	Option Quotes (Period)	Futures Quotes (Periods)	General News	Business News	Economic News/Data	Company News	Financial Statement Data	SEC Filings	Analyst Reports	Earnings Estimates	Charting	Technical Studies	Screening--Technical	Screening--Fundamental	Screening--Mutual Funds	On-Line Trading
					♦		♦									♦	
D													♦	♦		♦	
H																♦	
					♦				♦	♦			♦				
D	D	D	D	♦	♦	♦	♦	♦	♦								
								♦			♦		♦	♦	♦		
H (1971+)		H (1971+)	H (1971+)														
			H (1960+)		♦												
					♦			♦	♦	♦							
					♦			♦	♦	♦							
		D, H (10 yrs.)	D, H (10 yrs.)														
RT		RT	RT	♦									♦				
D	D	RT	RT, D	♦		♦		♦					♦				
				♦	♦	♦	♦			♦							
D	D			♦	♦	♦	♦	♦		♦					♦	♦	♦
D	RT	RT	RT, H (1986+)	♦									♦				

Financial Information Services	Page	Transmission						Number of Securities Followed	Stock Quotes (Periods)	Bond Quotes (Periods)	Index Quotes (Periods)
		Modem	Disk	CD-ROM	FM Radio	Satellite	Cable TV				
QuickWay	363	◆					◆	11,000	RT, D, H (1972+)		RT, D, H (1972+)
Quotdial	364	◆						NA	RT, D	RT, D	RT, D
QuoteLine Data Service	370	◆	◆					5,066	H (1982+)		H (1982+)
QuoTrek	325				◆			50,000	RT		RT
Radio Exchange	372				◆	◆		45,000	RT, D	RT, D	RT, D
Rategram*	315	◆						15,000		RT	
S&P ComStock	365	◆					◆	65,000	RT		RT
S&P Daily 1980-1990	342		◆					NA			H (1980-90)
S&P Daily 1953-1991	343		◆					1			H (1953+)
S&P 1957-1991 Monthly	343		◆					1			H (1957+)
S&P's Data for the Fundamental Investor	366		◆					10,000			
SEC Online*	331	◆						3,000			
SEC Online*	366	◆						3,000			
SEC Online on SilverPlatter*	367			◆				4,500			
SHD (Securities History Data)	347	◆	◆					15,000	H (1972+)		H (1970+)
Signal	325		◆		◆	◆		50,000	RT, H (1978+)		RT, H (1978+)

458 / The Individual Investor's Guide to Computerized Investing

Mutual Fund Quotes (Periods)	Closed-End Mutual Funds (Periods)	Option Quotes (Period)	Futures Quotes (Periods)	General News	Business News	Economic News/Data	Company News	Financial Statement Data	SEC Filings	Analyst Reports	Earnings Estimates	Charting	Technical Studies	Screening–Technical	Screening–Fundamental	Screening–Mutual Funds	On-Line Trading
RT, D, H (1972+)		RT, D, H (1972+)	RT, D, H (1972+)	◆	◆	◆	◆	◆		◆							◆
D		RT, D	RT, D		◆			◆					◆				
			H (1968+)														
RT	RT	RT	RT														
D	D	RT	RT, D		◆		◆		◆				◆				
RT										◆							
D		RT	RT	◆	◆		◆	◆		◆			◆				
								◆									
									◆								
									◆								
							◆	◆	◆								
H (1986+)													◆	◆			
RT, H (1978+)	RT	RT	RT														

Financial Information Services Grid / 459

| Financial Information Services | Page | Transmission |||||| Number of Securities Followed | Stock Quotes (Periods) | Bond Quotes (Periods) | Index Quotes (Periods) |
		Modem	Disk	CD-ROM	FM Radio	Satellite	Cable TV			
Stock Market Data	368	◆	◆					9,000	H (1987+)		H (1987+)
Technova*	371	◆				◆		2,500	RT	RT	RT, H (10 yrs.)
Telechart 2000*	383	◆						10,000	D, H (3 yrs.)		D, H (3 yrs.)
Telemet Encore	372				◆			45,000	RT, D	RT, D	RT, D
Telemet Orion System	373					◆		45,000	RT, D	RT, D	RT, D
Telescan Analyzer	373	◆						10,000	D, H (18 yrs.)		D, H (18 yrs.)
Telescan Edge	374	◆						11,000	D, H (18 yrs.)		D, H (18 yrs.)
Telescan Mutual Fund Edge*	375	◆						11,000	D, H (18 yrs.)		D, H (18 yrs.)
Telescan ProSearch*	375	◆						11,000	D, H (18 yrs.)		D, H (18 yrs.)
Tick-By-Tick Historical Price Data	377	◆	◆					105	H (1989+)		H (1982+)
Track/On Line	328	◆						20,000	D, H (17 yrs.)	H (2.5 yrs.)	D, H (17 yrs.)
Trade*Plus*	377	◆						NA	RT, D, H		RT, D, H
Trader's Spread System (TSS)	369	◆	◆					NA		D, H (6 mo.)	
Treasury Historical Data	370	◆	◆					NA		H (1975+)	
TRENDPOINT Data Library	378		◆					5,000			H (1928+)
Unified Brokerage System*	379	◆						200	NA	NA	NA

Mutual Fund Quotes (Periods)	Closed-End Mutual Funds (Periods)	Option Quotes (Period)	Futures Quotes (Periods)	General News	Business News	Economic News/Data	Company News	Financial Statement Data	SEC Filings	Analyst Reports	Earnings Estimates	Charting	Technical Studies	Screening–Technical	Screening–Fundamental	Screening–Mutual Funds	On-Line Trading
																♦	♦
		RT	RT, H (20 yrs.)	♦	♦	♦						♦	♦				
												♦	♦				
D	D	RT	RT, D		♦		♦		♦				♦				
D	D	RT	RT, D		♦		♦		♦				♦				
D, H (18 yrs.)	D, H (18 yrs.)	D		♦	♦		♦	♦	♦		♦	♦	♦	♦	♦		
D, H (18 yrs.)	D, H (18 yrs.)	D		♦	♦		♦	♦	♦		♦	♦	♦	♦			
D, H (18 yrs.)	D, H (18 yrs.)	D		♦	♦		♦	♦	♦		♦	♦	♦	♦	♦		
D, H (18 yrs.)	D, H (18 yrs.)	D		♦	♦		♦	♦	♦		♦	♦	♦	♦			
		H (1984+)	H (1977+)										♦				
H (2.5 yrs.)	H (2.5 yrs.)	D, H (2 yrs.)	D, H (20 yrs.)	♦	♦	♦	♦	♦	♦	♦	♦		♦			♦	♦
		RT, D, H	NA	♦	♦		♦		♦								♦
		D, H (6 mo.)	D, H (6 mo.)														
H (1972+)		H (1972+)	H (1972+)										♦				
NA		NA	NA														♦

Financial Information Services Grid / 461

Financial Information Services	Page	Modem	Disk	CD-ROM	FM Radio	Satellite	Cable TV	Number of Securities Followed	Stock Quotes (Periods)	Bond Quotes (Periods)	Index Quotes (Periods)
Value/Screen II	380	♦	♦					1,600			
Vencap Data Quest	311	♦	♦					NA			
VESTOR	347	♦						6,000	D, H (125 wks.)		D, H (125 wks.)
Vickers On-Line	380	♦						12,000	RT	RT	
VU/Text Information Services	381	♦						NA	D		D
X*Press Executive	384					♦	♦	30,000	D	D	D
Zack's On-line	385	♦	♦					7,500			

Mutual Fund Quotes (Periods)	Closed-End Mutual Funds (Periods)	Option Quotes (Period)	Futures Quotes (Periods)	General News	Business News	Economic News/Data	Company News	Financial Statement Data	SEC Filings	Analyst Reports	Earnings Estimates	Charting	Technical Studies	Screening–Technical	Screening–Fundamental	Screening–Mutual Funds	On-Line Trading
								♦			♦				♦		
		D, H (125 wks.)	D, H (125 wks.)			♦		♦		♦		♦	♦	♦	♦		
RT					♦				♦								
			D	♦	♦	♦	♦										
D	D	D	D	♦	♦	♦	♦	♦	♦		♦						
											♦						

Financial Information Services Grid / 463

THE *COMPUTERIZED INVESTING* BBS

One of AAII's services is the *Computerized Investing* bulletin board. *CI*'s bulletin board system (BBS) serves two main purposes: to promote the exchange of news and messages with your fellow investors and to facilitate the distribution of program files.

CI's bulletin board system is open to all. It doesn't matter what kind of computer you have; the BBS supports all systems. You don't even have to live in Chicago — people call from virtually every state and even a few foreign countries. The periods of peak usage are weekday evenings and throughout the day on weekends, when long distance rates are the lowest. The easiest times to get through are weekdays before 5:00 p.m. and any day between midnight and 6:00 a.m. (Eastern Standard Time), although even in the wee morning hours the system is often busy.

WHAT YOU WILL NEED

If you want to access *CI*'s BBS, you will need, in addition to your computer, a modem and telecommunications software.

A modem is a device that allows your computer to communicate with another computer over ordinary telephone lines. Modems are discussed at length in the communication hardware section in Chapter 2.

Some of the more popular commercial communications (or terminal) programs for the IBM PC are Crosstalk, Procomm Plus and Smartcom. For the Macintosh, there are Microphone, Smartcom and White Knight. These cost from $75 to $300. There are also some excellent "shareware" terminal programs available for downloading from other general interest bulletin boards, such as PC-Talk and Procomm for the PC and Zterm and Terminal for the Mac. Whatever terminal program you decide upon, it should have the ability to transfer both text and non-text (program and spreadsheet) files.

HOW TO USE THE BBS

Before you attempt to access CI's bulletin board, you should make sure that your modem and software are properly configured. At 300 baud, the line settings should be 7 data bits, even parity, and 1 stop bit. At 1200 and 2400 baud, they should be 8 data bits, no parity, and 1 stop bit. Check, too, that you are set to operate in full duplex mode. The telephone numbers for our BBS are (312) 280-8565 and (312) 280-8764.

When you sign on for the first time, the system asks you several preliminary questions, among them: "What is your name and your city and state?" The system also asks you to specify several technical parameters. These are all explained in the opening message.

The only question that causes significant confusion is: "What is your password?" The password system prevents anyone else from logging on under your name and reading your personal mail. So what is your password? Whatever you want — as long as it is one word. After you give the password, the system will ask you to enter it a second time as a double check. Be sure to remember your password for future use. (On your second and all subsequent calls, the system skips the preliminary message and just asks for your name and password.)

At this point, we advise the first-time caller to put his or her terminal software in "session-capture" mode. If you do this, your software will record to disk everything that happens while you are on-line. You will then have a record of your session activity for study and review after you go off-line. Refer to your software documentation to learn how to put your software in session-capture mode.

After all the preliminaries, the system presents you with the main/message menu (Figure I-1).

FIGURE I-1
Computerized Investing BBS — Main Menu

–MAIL–	–SYSTEM–	–UTILITIES–	–ELSEWHERE–
[E]nter Messages	[A]nswer Questions	[H]elp(or?)	[F]iles
[K]ill Messages	[B]ulletins	[X]pert on/off	[G]oodbye
[P]ersonal Mail	[C]omment to Sysop		[U]tilities
[R]ead Messages	[I]nitial Welcome		[Q]uit
[S]can Messages	[O]perator Page		
[T]opic of Msgs	[W]ho's on		

We will describe the main system options in a moment. For now, suppose you wanted to end your session and go off-line. You can do this here (and elsewhere in the system) by entering "G" for "G)oodbye." Don't ever just disconnect on your end without signaling "Goodbye" first, since this will tie up the bulletin board for some time, preventing others from using it.

The system is divided into three main sections — the main/message area, file area and utilities area. You see the main/message section first when you log on to our BBS. This section is where you can communicate with other BBS users through the use of electronic mail. The file area is where you can download and upload files. The utilities section permits you to change the parameters that you specified when you first logged on to the system and registered, such as the graphics displayed on your screen and your default file protocol (Figure I-2). To switch between sections you can enter "Q" (quit to other subsystems) and specify the section you wish to go to. The main/message menu also gives you the option of directly switching to a section by entering a command from the elsewhere menu prompt.

Since the system is fairly straightforward, all the menu options will not be described here in great detail. If you ever get stuck, just select the ubiquitous "?" or "H" options for more detailed help. We will, however, describe two of the system's

FIGURE I-2
Computerized Investing BBS — Utilities Menu

-DISPLAY-	-INFORMATION-	-SYSTEM-	-ELSEWHERE-
[E]cho pref	[H]elp (or ?)	[C]lock Time-Date	[Q]uit
[G]raphics	[R]ead Profile	[F]ile Protocol	
[L]ines/Page	[S]tatistics	[P]assword Change	
[M]essage Margin	[U]ser Log	[T]oggles	

most important features — entering and receiving messages and transferring files.

ENTERING AND RECEIVING MESSAGES

Before entering a message, you must be in the main/message system. To enter a message, select "E" for "E)nter Message." The system asks you to whom you want to send the message, the subject of the message and what level of security you want to give it (i.e., whether you want the message to be private or not, and who has the right to "kill" it).

You then enter your message, line by line, with up to 25 lines maximum. Once you enter a carriage return to signal the end of a line, you cannot return to that line except through a special edit mode.

You break out of enter mode by pressing the carriage return key twice in succession. At that point, you can: A)bort (abort the message), C)ontinue (resume entering the message), D)elete (delete a line), E)dit (edit individual lines), I)nsert (insert one or more lines), L)ist (list the entire message), M)argin (set a new right margin), S)ave (send the message) or ask for more information.

To read messages, select "R" at the main menu. The system will ask you to supply the numbers of the messages you want to read. You can input numbers one at a time, or you can "stack" them: For example, if you enter 10;14;32+ you will receive messages 10, 14, and 32, plus all messages after 32. Selecting "C)ont" will cause the messages to scroll rapidly without pausing so they can be saved in a session-capture log file and read later, off line. "S)ince" lists messages forward from the point where you read last, and "T)hread" will list messages only with the same subject, enabling you to read other user's comments on a mutually interesting topic. You can also conduct a fast survey of the message list using either the "T)opic of Msgs" or "S)can Messages" options.

DOWNLOADING FILES

Downloading refers to moving files from the BBS to your computer. (Uploading is just the opposite, moving files from your computer to the BBS.) On this system, the file transfer can be accomplished using the ASCII, IModem, Kermit, Windowed XModem, YModem, YModemG, XModem, XModem/CRC, 1K XModem or ZModem protocols. One word of warning, when selecting XModem be sure to enter X for X)modem and not W for W)xmodem.

To download a file, you first have to enter the file's subsystem, which is shown in Figure I-3.

FIGURE I-3
Computerized Investing BBS — File Menu

–TRANSFER–	–INFORMATION–	–UTILITIES–	–ELSEWHERE–
[D]ownload file	[L]ist files	[H]elp (or ?)	[G]oodbye
[P]ersonal dwnld	[N]ew files	[X]pert on/off	Q]uit
[U]pload file	[S]earch files		

You can L)ist on-screen the names of the files that are available for downloading. To list filenames in a specific directory, use "L;X" where X is the directory suffix. For example, entering L;Apple will list all Apple II files. Note that the listing of spreadsheet files contains both IBM and Macintosh files. A list of directories available at the time of this writing follows:

IBM–files for the IBM PC and compatibles
APPLE–files for the Apple II family

MAC–files for Macintosh computers
COM64–files for Commodore 64/128 computers
CPM–files for Kaypro computers
SPREAD–spreadsheets and related files for IBM and Macintosh
NEW–new uploads from callers
TEXT–text files in ASCII format
CIDISKS–compressed disk files (e.g., IBM disk 9, Mac disk 5, etc.)

To begin the download process, enter "D" for "D)ownload." When the system asks which file you want to download, input the filename exactly as it appears in the files listing. To download one of the TEXT files, for example, you would enter: CORPDATA.EXE. Be sure to include a period between the filename and extension and don't add any other extraneous punctuation. (The period after EXE is merely for the end of the sentence!)

If you did not specify a default file transfer protocol when you first registered, the system asks you to specify one at this time. If your terminal software supports XModem/CRC you should select it. Whereas ASCII only enables you to transfer text files (including BASIC program files converted to text form), with all the other protocols you can transfer all types of files (including .EXE and .COM files). XModem (and other advanced protocols) checks the accuracy of the data transmission. If an error is detected in the transmission, XModem will order the system to retransmit the affected data block until it is sent correctly.

Mac users should remember to use MacBinary when downloading files. Selecting this option on your communications program helps to ensure that header information required by the Mac system to launch a file is transferred.

After you have selected the transfer protocol, the system will signal that it is ready to begin sending the file. At this point many people become confused. Nothing will happen until you instruct your software to receive the file. For several popular programs, you start the ball rolling by:

Smartcom II Version 2: Press F1, then 4, then enter 1 for XModem or 2 for ASCII.

PC-Talk: Press Alt and R.

Procomm: Press the PgDn key and select the protocol from the choices provided.

If your terminal program is not on this list, refer to your software documentation for putting your terminal program in file-receive mode.

For an ASCII transfer, after setting up to receive the file on your end, you press the carriage return key once as the signal to start. The file is then sent, a line at a time, from beginning to end. You will see the lines of ASCII code (readable text and numbers) on your screen as they flow to your system. When the file transfer is finished, the BBS will send an End Of File marker followed by five beeps. You should close your capture file as soon as you hear the beeps or you will get some extra "garbage" lines at the end of the file. (These can be deleted later using a text editor.)

Downloading with XModem is even simpler: You just put your software in receive mode and the BBS does the rest. (If a problem develops, you can abort the transfer midway by sending the cancel code, Ctrl-X.) When the file transfer is finished, XModem automatically closes the capture file for you. To use XModem, your terminal must be set to 8 data bits, no parity, and 1 stop bit (the standard 1200 and 2400 baud settings).

If you experience problems, you should:

- Ask for H)elp! (see Figure I-3). Use your communication program's session-capture feature to record all the detailed information in this help file.
- Reread and study your communication software documentation.
- Get a knowledgeable friend to assist you.

- Switch to an easier-to-use communication program.

WHAT YOU ARE PROBABLY AFTER

Our bulletin board has about 500 files for the IBM PC and compatibles, about 200 for the Macintosh and about 100 each for the Apple II, Kaypro (CP/M) and Commodore 64/128. Our public domain disk library contains some of these files, but a good number can be had only by downloading. Shareware programs, unlike free public domain programs, are copyrighted. You may download files without cost and examine shareware products for a brief trial period, but if you continue to use a program, you must register with the author. Demo programs, too, are a case where the author or company distributes a free version of a program that demonstrates a few features of the final version, but the complete package isn't supplied until a registration fee is remitted. Of course, downloading is not really free. You still have to pay the telephone charges. On the other hand, with downloading you are assured of getting the very latest program versions and new software as we receive them.

Many of the IBM files have been archived. Archiving files compresses the information contained in a file to reduce space, and it also allows many files that accompany one program to be stored together as one file. The files on our system are stored in self-extracting format, which means that you do not have to run a utility program to expand the files when you want to use them. Rather, the files automatically extract themselves from their compressed state. Once you download files from the BBS, you expand them for use simply by typing the file name at the DOS command prompt. You do need to make sure that you have enough disk space available to store the expanded file. For Macintosh users, we store spreadsheet files in an uncompressed format so they can be downloaded and translated for use with Mac-based spreadsheet programs.

STOCK MARKET AND BUSINESS RELATED BBSs

The following BBSs are either devoted exclusively to investment topics or maintain stock market, general business or real estate sections along with non-investment areas of interest. Some of the systems require a registration or subscription fee before access is granted to all features of the BBS.

Please contact our free Computerized Investing BBS in Chicago, (312) 280-8565, -8764, to update this listing.

Name	Number
Stocks & Such	(201) 377-2526
Data Base	(201) 943-5419
Computer Connections	(202) 547-2008
Investors On-Line	(206) 285-5359
Manhattan South	(212) 432-7288
PC Magazine Information	(212) 696-0360
Free Financial Network (FFN)	(212) 697-7171
The Exchange	(214) 517-8553
Business and Financial	(215) 643-7711
The Market	(301) 299-8667
Real Estate Board	(301) 384-9302
DC Metro	(301) 855-0339
Denver Computer Investors (DCIBBS)	(303) 499-8852
Executive Region	(312) 267-4749
Computerized Investing	(312) 280-8565
Computerized Investing	(312) 280-8764
Pisces Financial	(312) 281-6046
Chicago Megaphile	(312) 283-4035
PBS-BBS	(317) 856-2087
FABulous	(407) 277-3449

Continued

Name	Number
Lynn-Western Newswires	(408) 778-5994
Lynn-Western Newswires	(408) 778-9656
McAffee	(408) 998-4004
PK Ware	(414) 354-8670
Exec-PC	(414) 789-4210
Quant IX Software	(414) 961-2592
Telestock One	(512) 338-4591
WalStreet	(515) 223-1113
The List (PDSLO)	(516) 938-6722
E. KY College (Prof. BBS)	(606) 269-1565
Dollars & Bytes	(619) 483-5477
Data Bit Network	(703) 719-9648
Ret-tech	(708) 246-1385
Profit Margin	(708) 356-7895
IBM PC Info Exchange (IBBS)	(708) 882-4227
Bits & Bytes	(708) 953-0396
Keith's Little SW Shop	(713) 277-5465
Zeitgeist	(713) 530-1166
Ed Hopper's BBS	(713) 782-5454
RAD Software	(805) 962-8206
Executive Network	(914) 667-4567

BULLETIN BOARDS SPONSORED BY THE U.S. GOVERNMENT

Name	Number
Economic BBS	(202) 377-3870
Export-Import Bank	(202) 566-4699
Census Bureau	(301) 763-4576
Federal Bank of Minneapolis	(612) 340-2489

COMPUTER SPECIAL INTEREST GROUPS (SIGs) III

The following is a listing of the currently active AAII and other computer subgroups throughout the country, along with the name and phone number of the person to contact if you are interested in becoming a member of the group. Computer-user groups offer a way of exchanging ideas and knowledge of investment theory and computer programs with other people in your area. Meetings often feature hands-on demonstrations of investment software and microcomputer systems. AAII computer subgroups are composed of subscribers to *Computerized Investing*, a bimonthly newsletter published by the American Association of Individual Investors. Subscription rate is $60.00 per year, or $30.00 per year to members of AAII.

AAII COMPUTER SPECIAL INTEREST GROUPS

Atlanta
Henry R. Dunlap
1141 Oxford Crescent
Atlanta, GA 30319
(404) 255-1141

Austin
Larry Saunders
5908 Paseo Del Toro
Austin, TX 78731
(512) 327-8710

Baton Rouge
Dale Biggs
15903 Malvern Hill Avenue
Baton Rouge, LA 70817
(504) 752-6717

Boca Raton
Robert Lewison
23265 Boca Club
Colony Circle
Boca Raton, FL 33433
(407) 750-9529

Boston
Jim Yoshizawa
100 Federal Street
26th Floor
Boston, MA 02101
(617) 261-2634

Cincinnati
Dr. Richard Allnutt
112 Wallace Avenue
Covington, KY 41014
(606) 581-7719

Cleveland
Bob Watson
822 Stuart
South Euclid, OH 44121
(216) 382-1481

Columbus
Robert Bee
2064 Tuckaway Court
Columbus, OH 43228
(614) 272-5289

Connecticut
James Darkey
43 Arnold Drive
Tolland, CT 06084
(203) 875-1295

Denver
Hugh Casey
700 Mohawk
#208
Boulder, CO 80303
(303) 499-8852

Detroit
Tom Kerley
21325 Stahelin Street
Southfield, MI 48075
(313) 356-5504

Hampton Roads
Edward Schwab Jr.
2813 North Kings Road
Virginia Beach, VA 23452
(804) 486-6347

Hawaii
Keith Nakata
7 Waterfront Plaza
500 Ala Moana Boulevard
Suite 400
Honolulu, HI 96813
(808) 538-6699

Indianapolis
Terry E. Plank
4880 Winters Road
Plainfield, IN 46168
(317) 271-7909

Kansas City
Harlan Laner
121 W. 48th Street
Kansas City, MO 64112
(816) 753-2252

Long Island
Albert Golly, Jr.
P.O. Box 381
Medford NY 11763
(212) 541-3955

Los Angeles
George Kuby
P.O. Box 34545
Los Angeles, CA 90034
(213) 551-9454

Milwaukee
Robert Chernow
c/o Smith Barney
111 E. Wisconsin Avenue
Milwaukee, WI 53202

Minneapolis
Chris MacLennan
621 N. Lilac Drive
Minneapolis, MN 55422
(612) 690-1412
(612) 545-2100 Ext. 287

Nashville
Dirk Calvin
Mabry-Calvin Associates
7003 Chadwick Drive
Suite 240
Brentwood, TN 37027

Nebraska/Iowa
Len Lowder
835 S. 129th
Omaha, NE 68154-2984
(402) 333-0933

New Orleans
Cal Smith
641 Meursault Drive
Kenner, LA 70065
(504) 466-8591

New York City
Christopher G. Henry
289 Convent Avenue, Suite 6
New York, NY 10031
(212) 493-2472

Orlando
Robert E. Hilton Jr.
3801 Appleton Way
Orlando, FL 32806
(407) 356-7087

Palm Beach
Drew Mayer
50 Coconut Row
Suite 200
Palm Beach, FL 33480
(407) 622-2991

Philadelphia
Donald Lee
2033 Parkview Avenue
Abington, PA 19001
(215) 659-5594

Phoenix
Marvin Weinstein
3232 E. Stanford Drive
Paradise Valley, AZ 85253
(602) 955-0164

Pittsburgh
R. Buck Gray
R.B. Gray Co.
203 Hibiscus Drive
Pittsburgh, PA 15235
(412) 241-5634

Portland
William Hammond
619 S.E. Division Place
Portland, OR 97202
(503) 223-9346 evenings

Sacramento
Seth Hall
412 Lagomarsino Way
Sacramento, CA 95819
(916) 448-2252

St. Louis
W.R. Stephens
13002 Hunter Creek Road
Des Pares, MO 63131
(314) 821-6115

San Antonio
G. Norman Black
9002 Swinburne Court
San Antonio, TX 78240
(512) 681-0491

San Diego
Dennis Costarakis
c/o Prudential-Bache
701 "B" Street
Suite 1200
San Diego, CA 92101
(619) 531-1820

San Francisco
Dr. Arturo Maimoni
134 Crestview Drive
Orinda, CA 94563
(415) 254-1708

Seattle
Barry Griffiths
11312 83 Place N.E.
Kirkland, WA 98034
(206) 823-8459

Silicon Valley
Charles Pack
25303 La Loma Drive
Los Altos Hills, CA 94022
(415) 949-0887

OTHER COMPUTERIZED INVESTING SIGs

BAUG/NYPC Investment
George Mueden
310 W. 106th Street
#15D
New York, NY 10025
(212) 222-8751

Boston Computer Society
Investment SIG
Jim Halkett
1 Kendall Square
Cambridge, MA 02139
(508) 653-0220

Club 3000
2435 E. North Street
#117
Greenville, SC 29615

Connecticut PC Wall Street
Dick Orenstein
P.O. Box 512
Westport, CT 06881
(203) 226-5251

Houston
Frank Harvey
Box 19039
Houston, TX 77224

Market Technicians Association
71 Broadway
2nd Floor
New York, NY 10006
(212) 344-1266

478 / The Individual Investor's Guide to Computerized Investing

Microcomputer Investors Association
Jack Williams
902 Anderson Drive
Fredericksburg, VA 22405
(703) 371-5474

National Association of Investors Corporation (NAIC)
1515 E. Eleven Mile Road
Royal Oak, MI 48067
(313) 543-0612

NJ, NY, PA, CT, DE Commodity Club
Len Kuker
33 Stella Drive
Bridgewater, NJ 08807
(800) 347-5018

Westchester PC Users Group Investment SIG
Rick Bullen
26 Pinecrest Drive
Hastings-on-Hudson, NY 10706
(914) 478-5824

GLOSSARY OF COMPUTER AND INVESTMENT TERMS   IV

Add-On Board: A circuit board which plugs into a master board or bus to perform additional functions for the mother board, e.g., communications with the outside world (a modem), with the printer, or to get additional memory.

Automated Access: The process of obtaining data from an information service whereby software initiates the process, connects to the information service and obtains the requested data with little or no user intervention.

Automatic Data Retrieval: See Automated Access.

Automatic Updating: See Automated Access.

Bar Chart: A technical chart in which the opening, high, low and closing prices of a security are recorded at specified time periods — every 15 minutes, hourly or daily — and displayed as vertical bars.

BASIC: One of the most fundamental programming languages available. Considered a universal language for personal computer users.

Baud: The speed at which a modem transmits data or the number of signal elements sent over a communications line in one second. Expressed as 1200 baud, 2400 baud, etc.

Bit: Created from the words Binary digIT, the smallest unit of information.

Black-Scholes Method: Developed by Fischer Black and Myron Scholes, this model gauges whether options contracts are valued fairly. The method incorporates factors such as the volatility of a security's return, the level of interest rates, the relationship of the underlying stock's price to the option's strike price and the time remaining until the option expires.

Buffer: A section of a computer's memory used as a temporary storage area. Users may add a buffer because it allows work on more than one job at a time. For example, with a print buffer, the system will be able to print a report at the same time as the user works on a separate document.

Bulletin Board System (BBS): Remote computers that allow PC users with modems and communications software to exchange messages, news and files.

Bus: A set of electrical conductors that carries electronic signals to the various components of a computer.

Byte: Equal to eight bits.

CD-ROM: A data transfer and storage mechanism that comes in the format of an optical read-only disk identical to those used for music on compact disk players. These disks store up to 550 megabytes of data.

Cell: The intersection of a row and column in a spreadsheet.

Central Processing Unit (CPU): The part of the computer that processes information.

Circuit: An electrical pathway.

Clock: A timer within the CPU that sends out high-frequency "ticks" by which all internal events in the computer system are coordinated.

Clock Speed: The speed at which the computer's processor deals with instructions. Clock speed is measured in megahertz (MHz) or millions of cycles per second. For example a 4-MHz clock in a microcomputer emits four million "ticks" per second.

Clone Computer: A computer that replicates exactly the functions of another computer.

Communications (or Terminal) Software: A program that tells the computer how to interpret incoming data and format outgoing data. Allows user to utilize modem, connect with a wide array of on-line financial databases and exchange information with other investors and computer users. Also, usually provides a number of options to make communications easier. For example, it may enable the user to automatically dial an on-line database.

Daisy Wheel: A type of print mechanism using a wheel with character images. When the character to be printed is in the proper position, a hammer drives the wheel against the paper. A daisy wheel produces typewriter-quality copy.

Database: A file containing information on a particular subject or subjects. For example, in a database system there are many such files, each one devoted to a particular kind of data element, so that one database may hold all the employee names, another all their addresses, another all their dates of birth, etc.

Default Value: A value automatically assigned or an action automatically taken unless another is specified. In a communications system, for example, data might be automatically divided into blocks of 80 characters each unless the user tells the system to use a different block length. Therefore, 80 characters is the default block size.

DIF (Data Interchange Format) File: A standard method developed by the U.S. Navy to exchange data between different programs and computers without losing necessary formatting.

Discount Brokerage: Brokerage house that executes orders to buy and sell securities at commission rates sharply lower than those charged by a full service broker. Discount brokerages typically provide only a transaction service.

Disk Operating System (DOS): See Operating System.

DJN/R: Dow Jones New/Retrieval. See On-Line Database.

Dot Matrix Printer: A printer that operates by striking a series of pins, usually a series of nine or twenty-four dots, to print a pattern creating the impression of a character or a graphic image.

Download: The ability to transfer information from another computer to one's own computer. For example, historical quotations of particular stocks could be downloaded to a personal computer or diskette from a commercial database for later analysis.

Dump: A printout of the contents of memory used by programmers to diagnose the cause of a software failure.

Enhanced Industry Standard Architecture (EISA): A standard, proposed by a group of IBM competitors, for handling internal data transfer. The EISA is compatible with the older

AT bus but offers enhanced performance in 80386 and 80486 machines.

Export: The ability to remove data from one program for use in another program.

File Translation: A program which translates a data format used in one program to match that of another program. For example, user can transfer data files from one spreadsheet to charting program that uses a different data format.

Financial Information Services: Services providing historical, financial, market and economic information, and current stock market prices and financial news. Information is obtained through a diskette or an on-line database with a modem.

Floppy Disk: A sealed, portable and flexible circle of magnetic material for data storage and transportation. Currently popular in sizes of either 3.5" or 5.25".

Floppy Disk Drive: A computer drive (slot) that reads and writes a floppy disk.

Format (or Initialize): To set up a disk in the pattern your computer expects to find data. A disk must be formatted for a computer to read and write data.

Freeware: Programs that the authors have provided free for others to use.

Fundamental Analysis: The process of gathering basic financial, accounting and economic data on a company or industry and determining whether that company is fairly priced by market standards.

Graphical Chart: The graphing of market variables, particularly stock prices, volume and market averages. Used by technicians in an attempt to determine trends and project future values.

Graphics Hardware: The equipment used for the production of lines, angles, curves and other non-alphanumeric information by a computer such as a video display, a printer or a plotter.

Graphics Printer: A printer, including laser and dot matrix printers, with the capability to create graphics output.

Hard Disk: A small, high-capacity disk storage device. Originally developed by IBM for use with mainframes.

Histogram: A horizontal bar chart. Histograms are often used to graph statistical information.

Home Banking Service: Offered by some on-line services and larger commercial banks. This service allows the individual to pay bills (those from firms with an agreement with the bank), transfer funds, get account information and perform other banking services. These services may include on-line securities trading and access to financial information.

Individual Filter: An input-checking routine that catches "bad data" (those values unacceptable to the program) and prevents them from causing a program failure or incorrect analysis.

Institutional Investor: An organization such as a mutual fund, bank, insurance company or pension fund, operating on behalf of a broad client base that trades large blocks of securities.

Interface: The point where two distinct data-processing elements meet. An interface may exist between pieces of hardware, between two software systems, between hardware and software or between the computer and a user.

Internal Rate of Return (IRR): A time- and value-weighted measure of portfolio return. It is the rate of return, when earned each period, that makes the starting value of a portfolio equal to its ending value, accounting for cash withdrawals and deposits.

Japanese Candlestick Charts: A variant of a bar chart, showing a security's open, high, low and close. Looks like a candlestick with wicks at both ends. The body of the candlestick shows the opening and closing price for the period. The wicks show the entire trading range. If the body is filled in, the close is lower than the open; otherwise the close is higher than the open.

Keyboard Macros: A macro is a single instruction that "saves" and automatically executes a series of keystrokes needed to achieve a task.

Kilobyte: Equal to 1,024 bytes.

Laser Printer: An electrostatic printer. Paper passes a laser that forms character images in dot matrix patterns as dots of static electricity. Powder adheres to the static dots, and then heat melts the powder, fusing it on the paper to form inked printing. Resolution is typically 300 dots per inch.

Least Squares Regression Analysis: A technique for estimating the statistically best linear relationship between a dependent variable (the one you are interested in or trying to predict) and one or more independent variables. If there is only one independent variable, the results can be displayed graphically as a straight line.

Line Chart: A chart displaying successive variable stock values over time, closing prices connected by a line.

Line Plots: A horizontal line on a price chart indicating a period during which a security's supply and demand are relatively equal. Technical analysts generally look for the price to break away from the line, at which time they are likely to take a position in the direction of the movement.

Magnetic Read And Write Head: A unit on or very near to a magnetic recording surface that moves past the surface. The head senses ("reads") and/or records ("writes") tiny magnetic fields representing bits.

Markowitz Algorithm: Harry M. Markowitz's solution to the problem of finding combinations of securities that minimize risk for a given level of return or maximize return for a given level of risk.

Megabyte: Equal to 1,000 kilobytes.

Megahertz (MHz): The measurement which indicates the speed (millions of cycles per second) in which a computer's processor deals with information.

Memory Chip: A semiconductor chip that stores information in a computer.

Menu-Driven: A program that operates by providing the user with a set of choices to control the way the program proceeds.

Micro Channel Architecture (MCA): A design developed by IBM which determines how to internally transfer information. MCA works with only 16-bit or 32-bit processors — the Intel 80286, 80386, 80486.

Microprocessor: A small central processing unit contained entirely on one semiconductor chip.

Model: A mathematical representation of a real-life decision making situation. It can be entered into a computer, using the computer's power and speed to perform mathematical calculations to estimate results under various situations.

Modem: Abbreviated term for Modulator-Demodulator, a device that transforms computer information from binary form to analog form so it can be transmitted and received over telephone lines. Modems can be installed internally in most computers or can be connected externally through a serial port.

Monitor: The viewing screen of a video display device.

Mouse: A hand-held device used to move the cursor around the screen faster than is possible using the keyboard.

Moving Average: Average of security or commodity prices over a period of time — as short as a few days or as long as several years — showing trends for the latest interval. Each day (or year) it picks up figures for the latest day and drops those for the earliest day.

MS-DOS (Microsoft Disk Operating System): Disk operating system developed by Microsoft, functionally equivalent to the operating system (PC-DOS) for original IBM PCs. MS-DOS is used with compatible, non-IBM computers.

NYSE's DOT (Designated Order Turnaround) System: A computer system that facilitates order execution. The DOT system allows institutions' small buy and sell orders to be directly transmitted to the specialist on the exchange floor. The system speeds the execution of orders and boosts volume on the floor by bypassing commission brokers.

On-Line Database: A service, such as Dow Jones News/Retrieval or CompuServe, providing historical, financial, market and economic information or current stock market prices and financial news obtained via modem.

On-Line Downloading: See Download.

Operating System: (Also known as Disk Operating System.) The software that directs the computer to respond to different commands and to handle basic manipulations such as copying files and giving them names. The operating system depends not only on the CPU but also on the computer vendor. Different CPUs have different operating systems, and there may be more than one operating system for a single processor.

Password: In a data security system, a code used to gain access to protected information.

PC-DOS (Personal Computer Disk Operating System): Disk Operating System for IBM computers. Developed by Microsoft and IBM. Sold as MS-DOS for non-IBM computers.

Pie Chart: A circular chart cut by radii into segments illustrating relative magnitudes. Used to express data as parts or percentages of a whole.

Plotting: Drawing pictures, graphs and other such pictorial representations with computer control.

Point and Figure Chart: Technique used in technical analysis to follow the up or down momentum in the price moves of a security. Point and figure charting is used solely to record changes in price: Each time a price moves up by a specified amount, an X is put on the graph above the previous point; each time the price moves down, an O is placed one square down. The next column is used when price direction changes. The resulting lines of Xs and Os indicate whether the security being charted has been maintaining an up or a down momentum.

Portfolio Management: The process of updating portfolio values, keeping track of the tax consequences of portfolio decisions, analyzing performance over time and comparing that performance with some standard.

Price and Volume Charts: Price and volume displayed on the same axis in normalized form showing, for a particular stock within a given time frame, the exact relationship between volume and price.

Prompt: A program screen message asking the user to do something in order to move ahead. Prompts, like menus, are features that label a program as user-friendly.

Quantitative Analysis Software: Software that involves analysis dealing with measurable factors. In securities analysis, quantitative considerations include the value of assets; the cost of capital; the historical and projected patterns of sales, costs, profitability and a wide range of considerations in economics.

Random-Access Memory (RAM): One type of memory in the CPU of the computer. RAM is also called user-programmable memory, because its contents can be quickly and easily changed. It is volatile, that is, requires continuous power.

Read Only Memory (ROM): Memory storage device which can be written to only once but can be accessed thereafter to read its contents.

Real-Time Quote: The quote appearing on a computer screen simultaneously with the actual security trade. Both discount and full service brokerage firms offer real-time securities markets quotations.

Regression Analysis: See Least Squares Regression Analysis.

Resolution: The focus and clarity of a video display, usually measured in number of horizontal by vertical lines of dots.

Serial Port: A plug that connects the computer to a modem or other external device. Sometimes referred to as an RS-232 port, it is connected to a card that converts the computer's internal parallel communications, which takes place eight bits at a time, to serial communications, one bit at a time.

Shareware: Programs the authors have provided for others to use on a trial basis. If "adopted," users are requested to register and pay a fee. This usually includes technical support. Information about these programs may be obtained from a bulletin board system such as AAII's Computerized Investing BBS.

Spreadsheet Program: A screen-oriented, interactive program which enables the user to organize financial or other data in a row and column matrix on the screen.

Spreadsheet Template: See Template.

Technical Analysis: Directed at the interaction of supply and demand in the market for securities. Technical analysts are interested in the patterns of stock prices, volume movements and other items that reflect the interplay of market participants.

Template: Prepared instructions that can be loaded into a spreadsheet the same way a program is loaded. Templates provide the spreadsheet with the formulas needed to accomplish a particular task.

Time Horizon: The length of time an investment is held.

Time Series: A series of values of some variable over time; for example, stock prices or the consumer price index.

Uploading: Moving a file from one's computer up to another computer using data communications.

User Interface: The portion of an interactive computer program that issues messages to and receives commands from a user.

Videotext System: A broadly based information service which might include real estate listings, local retail store offerings, home shopping and other useful information.

Volatile Memory: Memory depending on continued power, which is temporarily lost whenever the computer is turned off or the system restarted. See Random Access Memory (RAM).

Yield Analysis: Analysis of the rate of return on a bond, taking into account the total of annual interest payments, the purchase price, the redemption value and the amount of time remaining until maturity.

INDEX

Abacus Software, 57
AB-Data Disks, 311, 446
AB-Data, Inc., 311, 446
Account Manager V, 274, 388
Accuron, 357
Acquisition & Disposition Analysis, 72, 388
ADS Associates, Inc., 57
Advanced Analysis, Inc., 58
Advanced Channel Entry (ACE), 138, 388
Advance—Decline Line Tutorial, 284, 388
Advanced Financial Planning, 59
Advanced G.E.T. 3.0, 292, 388
Advanced Investment Software, 60
Advanced Investment Systems, 60
Advent Software, Inc., 61
AgriQuote, 359, 446
AIQ Systems, Inc., 62
AI Research Corp., 311
AIS Market Analyst, 60, 388
American Investor, 75, 388
American River Software, 64
America Online, 311, 312, 446
AmortizeIt!, 226, 388
Amortizer Plus, 149, 388
Analyst RT, 296, 388
Analytical Service Associates, 66
Analytic Associates, 65
Andrew Tobias' Checkwrite Plus, 185, 388
Andrew Tobias' Financial Calculator, 185, 388
Andrew Tobias' Managing the Market, 186, 388
Andrew Tobias' Managing Your Money, 186, 388

Andrew Tobias' Tax Cut, 187, 388
An Option Valuator/An Option Writer, 251, 388
A-Pack: An Analytic Package for Business, 191, 390
APEX, 209, 390
Applied Decision Systems, 67
Argus On-Line, 312, 446
Argus Research Corporation, 312
Arms Equivolume Corp., 68
Asset Allocation Tools, 263, 390
Asset Backed Securities Group, 69
Asset Mix Optimizer, 87, 390
@Bonds Pro Series and Premium Series, 199, 390
A-T Financial Information, Inc., 69
Atlantic Systems Inc., 70
@nalyst, 273, 390
@Options Pro Series and Premium Series, 199, 390
@Risk, 218, 390
Auto—Candle, 291, 390
Automated Investments, Inc., 313
Autoprice, 180, 390
AVCO Financial Corp., 71

Basic Cycle Analysis, 144, 390
Berge Software, 72
Best Bid, 183, 390
Black River Systems Corp., 74
Blue Chip Software, 75
BMW, 192, 390
BNA Estate Tax Spreadsheet, 77, 390
BNA Fixed Asset Management System, 78, 390
BNA Income Tax Spreadsheet with Fifty State Planner, 78, 390
BNA Real Estate Investment Spreadsheet, 79, 392

Index / 491

BNA Software, 77
Bollinger Bands, 172, 392
Bond Buyer Full Text, 328, 446
Bondcalc, 223, 392
Bond Manager, 66, 392
Bond Portfolio, 156, 392
Bond Portfolio Manager, 173, 392
Bond Pricing, 157, 392
Bonds and Interest Rates Software, 229, 392
Bondseye, 137, 392
BOND$MART, 193, 392
Bond Swap Manager, 224, 392
Bonds XL Pro and Premium Series, 200, 392
Bond-Tech, Inc., 80
Bonneville Market Information, 314
Bottom Dollar, 238, 392
Bradshaw Financial Network, 315
BrainMaker Neural Network Simulator, 85, 392
Bristol Financial Services, Inc., 80
Broker's Notebook, 233, 392
Business Conditions Digest Historical Data, 362, 446
Business Cycle Indicators, 362, 446
Business DateLine, 329, 446
Business Forecast Systems, 81
Business Week Mutual Fund Scoreboard, 315, 446
Buysel, 115, 392
BV Engineering, 81
Byte Research & Trading, 83

CableSoft, Inc., 84
Cadence Universe Online, 316, 446
Calcugram Stock Options System, 116, 394
California Scientific Software, 85
Call/Put Options, 156, 394
Cambridge Planning & Analytics, Inc., 316
CAMRA The Complete Asset Management, Reporting and Accounting System, 264, 394

CandlePower 2, 210, 394
CapTool, 276, 394
CapTool Global Investor, 276, 394
Caribou Codeworks, 86
CDA, Investment Technologies, Inc., 87, 316
Centerpiece, 221, 394
Centerpiece Performance Monitor, 222, 394
CF: Cash Flow Analysis, 271, 394
Charles L. Pack, 88
Charles Schwab & Company, Inc., 90, 317
ChartistAlert, 254, 394
ChartPro, 250, 394
ChipSoft, Inc., 90
CISCO, 318
Citibase, 319, 446
Citicorp Database Services, 319
Coast Investment Software, 91
Coherent Software Systems, 93
Comex Comcalc, 94, 394
COMEX, The Game, 95, 394
Commercial Finance, 72, 394
Commercial/Industrial Real Estate Applications, 239, 394
Commission Comparisons, 205, 394
Commodities and Futures Software Package, 229, 396
Commodity DataBank, 337, 446
Commodity Exchange, Inc., 94
Commodity Systems Inc. (CSI), 96, 320
Common Stock Decision Aide, 300, 396
Compact D/Canada, 332, 446
Compact D/SEC, 333, 446
Compact D/'33, 332, 446
Complete Bond Analyzer, 173, 396
Compu-Cast Corporation, 98
Compu/CHART EGA, 205, 396
Compusec Portfolio Manager, 116, 396
CompuServe, 321, 448
Computer Investing Consultants, 99

Compu Trac, 101, 396
Compu Trac Software, Inc., 101
Compu-Vest Software, 101
ComRep, 201, 396
Comtex Scientific Corp., 322
Connect Business Information Network, 323, 448
CONNECT INC., 323
Convertible Bond Analyst, 66, 396
Covered Options, 117, 396
CP Historical Data, 350, 448
Credit Rating Booster, 117, 396
Crytal Ball, 107, 396
CSI Data Retrieval Service, 320, 448
Cyber-Scan, Inc., 102

Daily Pricing Service, 369, 448
Daily Summary, 318, 448
Dantes' Financial, Inc., 103
Dantes' Retirement Planner, 103, 396
Data Base Associates, 104
Data Broadcasting Corporation, 323
Data Connections, 340, 448
Datadisk Information Services, 316, 448
Data Retriever, 282, 396
Data Transmission Network Corp., 105, 326
David Bruce & Co., 106
DBC/Link1, 99, 396
DBC/Link6, 100, 396
DBC/Link2, 99, 396
Decisioneering, Inc., 106
Decision Programming Corp., 107
Delphi, 326, 327, 448
Delphi Economics, Inc., 108
Denver Data, Inc., 109
Dial/Data, 327
DIAL/DATA, 327, 448
Dialog Business Connection, 329, 448
Dialog Information Services, Inc., 328
Dialog/MoneyCenter, 330, 448
Dialog Quotes and Trading, 330, 448
Diamond Head Software, 110
Disclosure Database, 334, 448

Disclosure Data for the Fundamental Investor, 366, 448
Disclosure Inc., 332
Disclosure/Spectrum Ownership Database, 334, 448
DISCLOSURE/WORLDSCOPE EUROPE, 334, 450
DISCLOSURE/WORLDSCOPE GLOBAL, 335, 450
DISCLOSURE/WORLDSCOPE PACIFIC RIM, 335, 450
Discover, 278, 398
Discovery, 102, 398
Disk-Count Software, 110
DollarLink, 111, 398
DollarLink Software, 111
Donald H. Kraft & Associates, 112
Dow Industrials, 342, 450
Dow Jones & Company, Inc., 113
Dow Jones News/Retrieval, 336, 450
Dow Month-by-Month Set, 342, 450
DownLoader, 134, 398
DTN Quote Catcher, 105, 398
DTN Wall Street, 326, 450
DTN Wall Street Portfolio Manager, 105
Dunn & Hargitt Investment Management, 337
Dynacomp, Inc., 115
Dynamic Volume Analysis Charts, 303, 398

Easy Money, 196, 398
ECON, 130
Economic Investor, 130, 398
Ecosoft, Inc., 131
Elderly Tax Planner, 196, 398
ELECTRIC SCORECARD II, 217, 398
Electrosonics, Inc., 132
Emerging Market Technologies, Inc., 132
Encore! Plus, 140, 398
Energetex Engineering, 133
Enhanced Chartist, 254, 398
Enhanced Communications, 258, 398

Index / 493

Enhanced Fund Master Optimizer, 282, 398
Ensign III, 314, 450
Entry/Exit/Equity (E*E*E) System, 171, 398
EPIC Systems Group, 134
Epoch Pro, 189, 398
Equalizer, 90, 317, 400, 450
EQUIS International, 134
Equivolume Charting Software, 68, 400
Ergo, Inc., 137
ES: The Estate Plan Analyzer, 271, 400
Essex Trading Company Ltd., 138
Estima, 337
Eurotrader, 138, 400
EvalForm, 202, 400
E.W.O.L., 293, 400
Excalibur, 145, 400
Exchange Master, 382, 450
eXclaim! RealTime Spreadsheet, 299, 400
Exec-Amort Loan Amortizer Plus, 132, 400

Family Budget, 118, 400
FBS Systems, Inc., 139
Ferox Microsystems, 140
Fibnodes, 91, 400
Fidelity Investments, 338
Fidelity Investors Express, 338, 450
Final Judgement, 150, 400
Financial Analysis, 239, 400
Financial & Interest Calculator, 174, 400
Financial Insight, 298, 400
Financial Management System, 118, 400
Financial Navigator, 141, 402
Financial Navigator International, 141
Financial Needs for Retirement, 300, 402
Financial Pak, 146, 402

Financial Planning Organizer, 110, 402
Financial Toolkit, 164, 402
FINCalc, 267, 402
Finger Tip Systems Corp., 142
First Release, 331, 450
FISTS, 80, 402
5-by-500 Database, 383, 450
Fixed Income, 268, 402
Fixed Income Data Obtainer (FIDO), 165, 402
Fixed-Income Pricing Services, 369, 450
Ford Data Base, 338, 450
Ford Investor Services, 338
Forecast Pro, 81, 402
Foreign Exchange Software Package, 230, 402
Fossware, 143
Foundation for the Study of Cycles, 144
Free Financial Network (FFN), 355, 450
Fundamental Databridge, 258, 402
Fundamental Investor, 258, 402
Fundgraf, 218, 402
Fundgraf Supplemental Programs, Disk 1, 219, 402
Fund Master TC, 282, 402
Fund Pro, 283, 404
Fund Profit, 151, 404
Fund/Search for Funds, 343, 452
Fund/Search for Funds II, 344, 452
Fundwatch, 119, 404
Future Access, 341, 452
Futures Markets Analyzer, 170, 404
FutureSource, 339
FutureSource Analyst, 339, 452
FutureSource Technical, 339, 452
Futures Truth, Co., 145

Gannsoft Publishing Co., 145
GannTrader 2, 146, 404
GB-Stat, 203, 404
G.C.P.I., 146

GE Information Services, 340
Genesis Financial Data Services, 148, 340
GEnie, 340, 452
GEnie Brokerage Service, 318, 452
Glance Market Data Services, 341
Global Trader, 57, 404
Good Software Corp., 148
GrafMaker, 82, 404
GRAND MASTER, 133, 404
Granite Mountain Systems, 150
Graph-in-the-Box Analytic, 204, 404
Graph-in-the-Box Executive, 204, 404
Greenstone Software, 150
Guard Band Investment Software, Inc., 151
Guru Systems Ltd., 152

Halvorson Research Associates, 152
Hamilton Software, Inc., 153
H & H Scientific, 155
Harloff, Inc., 156
Hedgemaster, 95, 404
Heizer Software, 156, 342
Hinson Products, 160
Historical ADL, 284, 404
Historical Futures Contracts, 319, 452
Hoffman Bond Update, 349, 452
Home Appraiser, 119, 404
Home Purchase, 243, 404
Hourly DJIA, 285, 404
HowardSoft, 160
HRA Sell/Buy Educator, 152, 406

ICDI Mutual Fund Database, 346, 452
Income Property Analysis, 244, 406
IndexExpert, 62, 406
Information Edge, Inc., 343
Inmark Development Corporation, 162
Insider Trading Monitor, 345, 452
INSIGHT, 80, 406
Institute for Options Research, Inc., 163
Institutional Brokers' Estimate System (I/B/E/S), 352, 452

International Advanced Models, Inc., 163
International Manager, 247, 406
Intex Bond Amortization, 165, 406
Intex Bond Calculations, 165, 406
Intex CMO/REMIC Modeling Service, 344, 452
Intex CMO/REMIC Modeling Toolkit, 166, 406
Intex Fixed-Income Subroutines, 166, 406
Intex Mortgage-Backed Calculations, 167, 406
Intex Option-Adjusted Spread Models, 167, 406
Intex Option Price Calculations, 168, 406
Intex Solutions, 164, 344
Invest/Net, 345
Investability Corporation, 168, 345
Investability MoneyMap, 168, 406
Investability Mutual Fund Database, 345, 452
Investext/Plus, 376, 452
INVESTigator+, 170, 452
Investing Advisor, 120, 406
Investment Analysis, 73, 406
Investment Analyst, 213, 408
Investment and Statistical Software Package, 230, 408
Investment Company Data, Inc., 346
Investment IRR Analysis for Stocks, Bonds & Real Estate, 174, 408
Investment Master, 147, 408
Investment Performance Chart, 157, 408
Investment Software, 169
Investment Technologies, Inc., 347
INVESTment TECHnology, 170
Investment Tools, 170
Investment Wizard, 360, 452
InvestNow!—Personal, 132, 408
InvestNow!—Professional, 133, 408
Investor, 221, 408
Investor's Accountant, 153, 408

Index / 495

Investor's Advantage 3.0 for PC Compatibles, 265, 408
Investor's Advantage 2.0 for the Amiga, 265, 408
Investor's Portfolio, 259, 408
IRMA, 120, 408
It's Alive, 83, 408
Iverson Financial Systems, Inc., 347

J&J Financial, 348
Jerome Technology, Inc., 171
John Pluth's Systems and Solutions, Inc., 171

Keystone Investment Systems, 349
Knight-Ridder Financial Publishing, 350
Koltys, Inc., 172

Land & Lease Analysis, 73, 408
Larry Rosen Co., 172
Lexis Financial Information Service, 353, 454
LINDO Systems, Inc., 175
LINK/Utility, 100, 408
Live-Line, 357, 454
LiveWire Personal Investor, 84, 410
LiveWire Professional, 85, 410
Loan Amortization, 244, 410
Loan Arranger, 120, 410
Loan Master, 147, 410
Loan Pro, 252, 410
Log Scale Comparison, 285, 410
Lotus Development Corporation, 176, 350
Lotus Improv 1.0, 176, 410
Lotus One Source, 350, 454
Lotus 1-2-3 for OS/2, 177, 410
Lotus 1-2-3 Release 3.1, 178, 410
Lotus 1-2-3 Release, 2.3, 177, 410
Lotus Spreadsheet for Deskmate, 178, 410
LotusWorks, 179, 410
Lowry's Market Trend Analysis Database on Diskette, 351, 454

Lowry's Reports, Inc., 351
Lynch, Jones & Ryan, 352

MacInTax 1040 1991 Personal Edition, 90, 410
MacMoney, 272, 410
MacQuotes, 304, 410
Macro*World Investor, 74, 412
Manager's Option, 244, 412
Managing for Success, 76, 412
Market Action Timer, 279, 412
Market Analyzer, 113, 412
Market Analyzer Plus, 114, 412
Market Analyzer-XL, 210, 412
Market Base, 356, 454
Market Center, 314, 454
Market Charter, 272, 412
MarketEdge, 257, 412
MarketExpert, 62, 412
Market Forecaster, 121, 412
Market Intelligence Swing Catcher Trading System, 294, 412
Market Maker for Windows, 162, 412
Market Manager Plus, 114, 412
Market Manager PLUS Professional Version, 115, 412
MarketMaster, 180
Market Master (by P.C. Prescience), 220, 412
MarketMate, 248, 414
MarketMax, 379, 454
Market Momentum Services, 352, 454
Market NewsAlert, 322, 454
Market Profile, 319, 454
Market Simulator, 305, 414
Market Software, 182
Market Timer, 121, 414
MarketView, 353, 454
MarketView Software, Inc., 353
MarketWatch (Hamilton Software, Inc.), 154, 414
MARKETWATCH (Data Broadcasting Coporation), 323, 454
MarketWatch PLUS, 324, 454
Market Window, 139, 414

Markex, 182, 424
MASTER BRAIN Bond Portfolio Management, 107, 414
MASTER BRAIN Pop-Up Bond Calculator, 108, 414
Master Chartist, 255, 414
Math Corp., 183
MATPORT, 280, 414
McClellan Oscillator Program, 144, 414
Mead Data Central, Inc., 353
MECA Software, Inc., 185
Media General Database Service, 354, 454
Media General Financial Services, 354
MegaTech Chart System, 251, 414
Memory Systems, Inc., 187
Mendelsohn Enterprises, Inc., 188
MESA, 189, 414
MetaStock—Professional, 135, 414
MicroApplications, Inc., 191
MicroBond Calculator, 225, 414
Microcalc, 191
Microcalc Financial Calculator Library, 191, 414
Micro Code Technologies, 355
Microcomputer Bond Program, 122, 416
Microcomputer Chart Program, 122, 416
Microcomputer Stock Program, 123, 416
Microsoft Corp., 191
MicroSoft Excel, 192, 416
Microstat-II, 131, 416
MicroTempo, Inc., 192
Micro Trading Software, Ltd., 193
Miller Associates, 194
Millionaire, 76, 416
Millionaire II, 77, 416
MindCraft Publishing Corporation, 195
MJK, 356, 454
MJK Associates, 356
Money, 123, 416

MoneyCalc IV, 197, 416
Money Decisions, 123, 416
Money Tree Software, 196
Money Won, 198
Montgomery Investment Group, 198
MORON, 286, 416
Mortgage Issue Yield Analyzer, 225, 416
Mortgage Loans—To Refinance or Not, 175, 416
Mortgage Security Calculator, 200, 416
MP Software, Inc., 356
MULTBJ Multivariable Box-Jenkins, 67, 416
Mutual Fund & Portfolio Managers Directory, 349, 456
Mutual Fund Analyzer, 348, 454
Mutual Fund Decision Aide, 301, 416
Mutual Fund Hypotheticals, 87, 418
Mutual Fund Investor, 64, 418
Mutual Fund Manager, 109, 418
Mutual Fund OnLine Database, 355, 456
Mutual Fund Reinvestment, 158, 456
Mutual Fund Selector, 364, 456
MyWay, 198, 418

NAIC Software, 201
NAIC Stock Selection Guide, 158, 418
National Computer Network, 357
Navigator, 148, 418
Navigator Access, 141, 418
Neuralyst for Excel, 134, 418
New England Software, 203
New High New Low Tutorial, 286, 418
NewsNet, 358, 456
News Real, 324, 456
NewTEK Industries, 205
NexTurn: Advanced, 261, 418
NexTurn: Basic, 262, 418
Nibble Investor, 195, 418
Nibble Mac Investor, 195, 418
NIS Asset Allocation System, 206, 418

NIS Equity Research Service, 359, 456
NIS Fixed Income Research Environment, 207, 418
NIS Macroeconomic Equity System, 207, 420
NIS Performance Analysis System, 208, 420
Nite-Line, 358, 456
Northfield Information Services, Inc., 206, 359
N-Squared Computing, 209

OECD MAIN ECONOMIC INDICATORS, 337, 456
Ohio Farm Bureau Federation, 359
Omega Research, Inc., 211
OmniNews, 322, 456
Omni Software Systems, Inc., 213
One Day at a Time, 296, 420
Ones & Zeros, 214
On Schedule, 240, 420
OPA Software, 215
OPENING BELL, 70, 420
Option Evaluator, 232, 420
OptionExpert, 63, 420
OptionExpert—The Strategist, 163, 420
Option Master, 163, 420
Option Pricing Analysis, 215, 420
Option Risk Management, 289, 420
Options Analysis, 124, 420
Options and Arbitrage Software Package, 230, 420
Options-80, 215
Options-80A: Advanced Stock Option Analyzer, 215, 420
Options Made Easy, 216, 420
Options XL Pro and Premium Series, 201, 420
Option Tools Deluxe, 253, 422
OptionVue IV, 216, 422
OptionVue Systems International, Inc., 216
Option—Warrant Combo, 158, 422
OPTMASTER, 181, 422
Orbit Software Co., Inc., 217

OTC NewsAlert, 322, 456
OVM the Option Valuation Model Version IV, 234, 422
OVM the Option Valuation Model Version 3.0, 234, 422
OZ Software, 360

Palisade Corp., 218
Paradigm Options Database, 361, 456
Paradigm Trading Systems, 361
Parsons Software, 218
PC Chart Plus, 152, 422
PCMARKET, 181, 422
P.C. Prescience, 220
P-Cubed, Inc., 221
PC Quote, 361, 456
PC Quote, Inc., 361
Peerless Stock Market Timing, 280, 422
Penroll, 248, 422
Pentax, 249, 422
PercentEdge, 214, 422
Performance Technologies, Inc., 221
Personal Analyst, 297, 422
Personal Balance Sheet, 124, 422
Personal Computer—Automatic Investment Management, 124, 422
Personal Computer Products, 223
Personal Finance Manager, 125, 422
Personal Finance Planner, 125, 424
Personal Finance System, 126, 424
Personal Hotline, 298, 424
Personal Market Analysis (PMA), 169, 424
Personal Micro Services, 223
Personal Portfolio Analyzer, 88, 424
Personal Portfolio Manager, 57, 424
Personal Stock Technician (PST), 236, 424
PFROI, 277, 424
Piedmont Software Company, 224
Pine Grove Software, 226
Plan Ahead, 59, 424
PlanEASe, 65, 424
PlanEASe Partnership Models, 65, 424
PlatformAlert, 255, 424

Pocket Quote Pro, 371, 456
POOL, 69, 424
Porteval Portfolio Evaluator, 160, 424
PORTFOLIO ANALYZER, 154, 424
Portfolio Decisions, 126, 424
Portfolio Evaluator, 227, 426
Portfolio Management System, 213, 426
Portfolio Manager Plus, 111, 426
Portfolio—Pro, 223, 426
Portfolio Software, Inc., 227
Portfolio Spreadsheets 3, 112, 426
Portfolio Status, 127, 426
Portview 2020, 127, 426
Power Trader Plus, 228, 426
Precise Software Corp., 227
Precision Investment Services Inc., 228
Predicasts F&S Index Plus Text, 367, 456
Prodigy, 362, 456
Prodigy Services Company, 361
Professional Breakout System, 83, 426
Professional Portfolio, 61, 426
ProfitTaker 2000, 188, 426
Programmed Press, 229
Program Writer II, 275, 426
Property Income Analysis, 73, 426
Property Listings Comparables, 245, 426
Property Management PLUS, 245, 426
Property Management III, 240, 426
ProQuote, 313, 456
Prosper-II Plus, 58, 428
Prosper-II PowerOnline, 59, 428
Public Brand Software, 362
Pulse Portfolio Management System, 136, 428
Pumpkin Software, 232
Put/Call, 287, 428

Q-Calc RealTime Spreadsheet, 299, 428
QTRADER, 86, 428
Quant IX Portfolio Evaluator, 232, 428
Quant IX Software, 232

Quick & Reilly, Inc., 363
Quickplot/Quickstudy, 96, 428
Quicktrieve/Quickmanager, 96, 428
QuickWay, 363, 458
Quotdial, 364, 458
Quote Commander, 103, 428
Quote Exporter, 143, 428
QuoteLine Data Service, 370, 458
QuoteMaster, 270, 428
QuoteMaster Professional, 270, 428
Quote Monitor, 143, 428
QuoTrek, 325, 458
Quotron Systems, Inc., 233, 364

Radio Exchange, 372, 458
Radix Research Ltd., 234
RAMCAP—The Intelligent Asset Allocator, 60, 428
Rapid, 151, 428
Rategram, 315, 458
Rational Indicators, 291, 430
Ratios, 128, 430
RazorLogic Systems, 236
RDB Computing, 237, 430
RDB Computing Custom Trader, 237
Real Analyzer, 237, 430
Real-Comp, Inc., 237
RealData, Inc., 238
Real Estate Analyzer, 160, 430
Real Estate Investment Analysis, 241, 430
Real Estate Partnership Plus, 242, 430
Real Estate Resident Expert, 128, 430
Reality Technologies, 242
Real Property Management, 238
RealTick III, 290, 430
Realty Software Company, 243
REAP PLUS, 246, 430
Recurrence: Real-Time Currency Trader, 71, 430
Relevance III-Advanced Market Analysis, 246, 430
Relevance III, Inc., 246
REMS Investor 3000, 149, 430
RESCOM, 247
Research Press, Inc., 248

Residential Finance, 74, 430
Retirement Solutions, 197, 430
RETIREMENT SURPRISE!, 266, 432
Retriever Plus, 206, 432
Ret-Tech Software, 250
Revenge Software, 251
RiskAlert, 256, 432
Risk Analysis System, 106, 432
RK Microsystems, 252
RLJ Software Applications, 253
Roberts-Slade, Inc., 254
Rory Tycoon Options Trader, 93, 432
Rory Tycoon Portfolio Analyst, 93, 432
Rory Tycoon Portfolio Manager, 94, 432
RTR Software, Inc., 256
Rugg & Steele, Inc., 364

S&P ComStock, 365, 458
S&P Daily 1980-1990, 342, 458
S&P Daily 1953-1991, 343, 458
S&P 1957-1991 Monthly, 343, 458
S&P's Data for the Fundamental Investor, 366, 458
SASI Software Corp., 257
Savant Corporation, 257, 366
Scenario, 307, 432
Scientific Consultant Services, Inc., 261
Scientific Press, Inc., 263
SEC Online (Dialog Information Services, Inc.), 331, 458
SEC Online (SEC Online, Inc.), 366, 458
SEC Online, Inc., 366
SEC Online on SilverPlatter, 367, 458
Securities Software and Consulting, 264
SHD (Securities History Data), 347, 458
SIBYL/RUNNER Interactive Forecasting, 68, 432
Signal, 325, 458
SilverPlatter Information, Inc., 367

Software Advantage Consulting Corp., 265
SOFTWARE EDGE, INC., 266
SolveIt!, 226, 432
Sophisticated Investor, 194, 432
SORITEC, 267, 432
Sorites Group, Inc., 267
Splot!, 104, 432
Spreadsheet Solutions Corp., 267
SPSS, Inc., 268
SPSS/PC+, 268, 432
SPSS/PC+ Trends, 269, 432
SSG PLUS, 202, 432
Statistical Analysis and Forecasting Software Package, 231, 434
Stockaid 4.0, 129, 434
Stock & Futures Analyzer-XL, 211, 434
Stock Analyzer, 262, 434
STOCKCAL, 253, 434
Stock Charting, 110, 434
Stock Charting System, 89, 434
Stock Data Corp., 368
StockExpert, 63, 434
Stock Manager, 67, 434
Stock Manager, 214, 434
Stock Market Bargains, 129, 434
Stock Market Data, 368, 460
Stock Market Securities Program, 98, 434
Stock Market Software, 231, 434
Stock Master (G.C.P.I.), 147, 434
Stock Master (Trading Technologies, Inc.), 293, 434
Stock Option Analysis Program, 155, 434
Stock Option Calculations and Strategies, 101, 436
Stock Option Scanner, 155, 436
Stock Portfolio, 159, 436
Stock Portfolio Allocator, 227, 436
Stock Portfolio Evaluator, 142, 436
Stock Valuation, 159, 436
Stock Watcher, 193, 436
Strategic Planning Systems, Inc., 270

Street Software Technology, Inc., 368
Superior Software, Inc., 271
Survivor Software Ltd., 272
Swiftax, 283, 436
Symphony, 180, 436
System Writer Plus, 211, 436

Take Stock, 203, 436
TA-SRV, 290, 436
Tax Preparer, 161, 436
Tax Preparer: Partnership Edition, 162, 436
Tax Tools, 250, 436
Tech Hackers Inc., 273
Technical Analysis Charts, 274, 436
Technical Analysis of Stocks & Commodities Magazine, 274
Technical Databridge, 259, 438
Technical Investor, 260, 438
Technical Selector, 261, 438
Technical Tools, 370
Technical Trader, 187, 438
Technician, 136, 438
Technicom, Inc., 274
TechniFilter Plus, 256, 438
Technova, 371, 460
Technova Research Inc., 371
Techserve, Inc., 276
TekCalc, 82, 438
Telechart 2000, 383, 460
Telemet America, Inc., 278, 371
Telemet Encore, 372, 460
Telemet Orion System, 373, 460
Telescan Analyzer, 373, 460
Telescan Edge, 374, 460
Telescan, Inc., 278, 373
Telescan Mutual Fund Edge, 375, 460
Telescan Portfolio Manager (TPM), 278, 438
Telescan ProSearch, 375, 460
Tempo Investment Products, Inc., 279
Thomson Financial Networks, 376
3D, 190, 438
Tick Data Inc., 377

Tick-By-Tick Historical Price Data, 377, 460
Tiger Multiple Stock Screening & Timing System, 281, 438
Tiger Software, 280
Time Trend Software, 281
Timer, 287, 438
Timer Professional, 288, 438
Timeworks, 283
Tools for Timing, 284
TopVision, 302, 438
Total Return, 262, 438
Townsend Analytics Ltd., 289
Track/On Line, 328, 460
Trade*Plus, 377, 460
Trader's Insight, Inc., 291
Trader's Profit Motive System, 292, 438
Trader's Software, Inc., 292
Trader's Spread System (TSS), 369, 460
TRADE$K, 97, 438
TradeStation, 212, 440
Tradex 21, 139, 440
Trading Package, 92, 440
Trading System Performance Evaluator (T.S.P.E), 98, 440
Trading Techniques, Inc., 292
Treasury Historical Data, 370, 460
Trend Index Company, 294
Trend Research Ltd., 296
TRENDPOINT (Program), 295, 440
TRENDPOINT Data Library, 378, 460
TRENDPOINT Software, 295, 378
Trendsetter Software, 296
TRENDTEK, 295, 440
TriStar Market Data, Inc., 379
Truerate%, 184, 440
20/20, 235, 440
20/20 Plus, 236, 440
TurboTax Personal 1040, 91, 440
Type III, Inc., 298

Unified Brokerage System, 379, 460
Unified Information, 379
UniPress Software, Inc., 299

V.A. Denslow & Associates, 300
Valuation Research Station, 70, 440
Value Line Portfolio Manager, 302, 440
Value Line Publishing, 302, 380
Value/Screen II, 380, 462
VantagePoint, 188, 440
Vencap Data Quest, 311, 462
VESTOR, 347, 462
Vickers On-Line, 381, 462
Vickers Stock Research, 380
Viking, 108, 440
Vision Research Corp., 302
Volume Dynamics, Inc., 303
Volume Indicator Tutorial, 288, 440
VP-Expert, 306, 440
VU/Text Information Services, 381, 462

Wall Street Portfolio Manager, 105, 442
Wall Street Prophet, 304, 442
Wall Street Trainer, 129, 442
Wall Street Watcher, 194, 442
War Machine, 304, 305, 442
Warner Computer Systems Inc., 382
Wave Wise Spreadsheet, 171, 442
WCSPD for Fundgraf, 220, 442
WealthBuilder by Money Magazine, 242, 442
Western DataBase, 305, 382
What'sBest!, 175, 442
Whole Market Monitor, 182, 442
Worden Brothers, 383
WordTech Systems, 306

X*Press Executive, 384, 462
X*Press Information Services Ltd., 383

Zacks Investment Research, 384
Zack's On-line, 384, 462
Zenterprise Real Estate Investor, 130, 442
Zero Base Software, 306
ZMath, 184, 442

COMPUTERIZED INVESTING

Computerized Investing (CI) is a bimonthly publication of the American Association of Individual Investors — an independent, non-profit educational organization.

CI covers investment software and information services of interest to individual investors. Each issue of *CI* includes how-to articles, detailed comparisons of software and databases, in-depth program evaluations and announcements of new and updated products. New developments in computer hardware are noted and analyzed with the individual investor in mind.

In many metropolitan areas local chapters support computer-user groups which meet regularly to exchange ideas and share knowledge.

CI operates an electronic bulletin board system. Every issue lists additions to the BBS of interest to individual investors. In addition, at low cost, a variety of public domain and shareware software are available for different computer systems.

Every November, *CI* subscribers receive, as part of their subscription, *The Individual Investor's Guide to Computerized Investing*.

For subscription information, without cost or obligation, write or phone:

American Association of Individual Investors
625 N. Michigan Avenue, Suite 1900
Chicago, IL 60611
(312) 280-0170

Educational Programs
from the

American Association of Individual Investors

The American Association of Individual Investors, a non-profit education association, offers a variety of products and programs to assist individual investors to better manage their assets.

Ongoing investment education is provided through the *AAII Journal*, home study materials, educational videos, special publications, seminars, national meetings and local chapters. Many of these benefits are provided free with membership or at reduced prices.

For further information on AAII's membership and other educational programs and services, write or phone:

American Association of Individual Investors
625 North Michigan Avenue, Suite 1900
Chicago, IL 60611
(312) 280-0170
